FROM DAY TO DAY

FROM DAY TO DAY

OR

Helpful Words for the Christian Life

DAILY READINGS FOR A YEAR

BY

ROBERT MACDONALD

THE BANNER OF TRUTH TRUST

THE BANNER OF TRUTH TRUST

Head Office
3 Murrayfield Road
Edinburgh, EH12 6EL
UK

North America Office
610 Alexander Spring Road
Carlisle, PA 17015
USA

banneroftruth.org

First published by Thomas Nelson and Sons, London, 1880

This edition © The Banner of Truth Trust, 2023

*

ISBN
Print: 978 1 80040 392 5
Epub: 978 1 80040 393 2

*

Typeset in 11/14 Adobe Garamond Pro
at The Banner of Truth Trust, Edinburgh

Printed in the USA by
Versa Press, Inc.,
East Peoria, IL

THIS volume is entirely practical in its nature. Though deeply conscious of its many imperfections, I venture to cherish the hope that the Spirit of the living God may be graciously pleased to use it for the spiritual ends designed; and in a measure, at least, make its words and recorded Christian experience helpful and cheering to his children on their homeward way.

R. M.
NORTH LEITH, EDINBURGH

ROBERT MACDONALD:
An Introductory Sketch

ROBERT MACDONALD was born in Perth, Scotland, on May 18, 1813. His mother was a native of Moulin, a little to the north, and had been deeply impacted as a child by the revival there in 1798 under the ministry of Alexander Stewart. Robert himself was converted in his mid-teens whilst a student at the University of St Andrews. A key factor, as in the case of his close friend Robert Murray M'Cheyne, was the death of a godly brother.

With conversion came a change in career direction. He had toyed at first with the idea of becoming a doctor but now his all-consuming desire was to preach Christ. It meant a move from St Andrews to Edinburgh and several years of preparation for gospel ministry under Thomas Chalmers and David Welsh. Chalmers would later describe him as one of the ablest of his students.

Logiealmond and Leith

Robert Macdonald's name is particularly associated with Blairgowrie in Perthshire, but it wasn't in Blairgowrie that his ministry either began or ended. Most of his first year, from 1836 to 1837, was spent in the Perthshire village of Logiealmond, a place familiar to him from his student days. His uncle had a house in the district and Macdonald often stayed there during his long summer breaks, teaching Sunday school and conducting Sunday evening services. It is said of the year of settled ministry that followed that it was 'not without a first-fruits of that harvest which was afterwards to crown his labours in the Gospel-field.'

In 1857, after almost twenty years in Blairgowrie, Macdonald accepted a call to the Free Church congregation of North Leith (Leith today is part of the city of Edinburgh). He was to remain one of its ministers until his death in 1893. In a sketch of his life and work published in 1881, Robert Cowan, a fellow Free Church minister, gives some interesting details of his Leith ministry. His opening text was Romans 15:29, 'And I am sure that, when I come unto you, I will come in the fulness of the blessing of the gospel of Christ.' So it proved. 'Some of his first sermons at Leith are known to have been blessed to the conversion of souls. The Lord's people have been built up and comforted; and more than one season of special refreshing has been enjoyed. The outward prosperity has also been great. During the first years of his ministry, a beautiful and commodious new church was built ...; the communion roll speedily rose from 450 to its present point of 1,100.'

The Blairgowrie years

Macdonald's Blairgowrie ministry began in June 1837. 'From time immemorial,' writes Cowan, 'the parish had had a seed of the righteous; but a special blessing came to it with the advent of the young pastor, so that the church of Blairgowrie began to be known as a centre of spiritual life and evangelistic work.' It shared largely in the season of revival that began in Kilsyth in 1839. In a letter, undated but evidently from around 1840 or 1841, Robert M'Cheyne says, 'I am sure there never was a time when the Spirit of God was more present in Scotland ... There is the clearest evidence that God is saving souls in Kilsyth, Dundee, Perth, Collace, Blairgowrie.' Other places are also mentioned. William Chalmers Burns was at the heart of this movement. So too was M'Cheyne himself, Andrew Bonar of Collace, and John Milne of Perth. And so also was Robert Macdonald of Blairgowrie. These men, says Cowan, 'and a few others of kindred spirit, were at that time in the heart of Scotland, in their evangelistic work and evangelical influence, "like a torch of fire in a sheaf."'

It was noted in passing that Macdonald and M'Cheyne were close friends. In Bonar's *Memoir and Remains* of M'Cheyne there are a number of M'Cheyne's letters to him, quoted either in part or in full. In one, appalled at what he had seen of the desecration of the Sabbath in Paris, M'Cheyne appeals to him to 'stand in the breach, dear friend, and lift up your voice like a trumpet, lest Scotland become another France.' In a second, written on a Saturday, he says, 'You will be busy preparing to feed the flock of God with food convenient. Happy man! It is a glorious thing to preach the unsearchable riches of Christ.' In a third he exhorts him, 'Never cease to show your people that to be holy is to be happy; and that to bring us to perfect holiness and likeness to God, was the very end for which Christ died.' In a fourth he urges him to 'deal faithfully' with all who come to speak to him about sitting at the Lord's Table, 'especially the young.'

A word about his preaching—and his prayers. In an obituary in *The Free Church Monthly*, Norman L. Walker writes of how Macdonald preached 'with extraordinary vivacity and power,' and how 'his prayers were as bright and, one might almost say, as ringing as his preaching.' He adds, 'His light hair, his fresh complexion, and the sunny expression of his face attracted people to him, and the joyous spirit in which he proclaimed the gospel added greatly to the interest and power of his discourses.'

In a personal reminiscence he says, 'My own earliest recollection of him is at a casual meeting of ministers in the house of Mr Milne of Perth. It was proposed that we should have prayer together, and Dr Macdonald was asked to lead. I shall never forget the impression then produced. One felt at once that here was a man who was well accustomed to pray, and who delighted in the exercise. There was a joyous confidence in the supplications which showed a persuasion that he to whom he was speaking was willing to give, and a fullness and freedom of utterance which spoke of a loving heart and a rich spiritual experience.'

Mention needs to be made of Macdonald's Sabbath school. When leaving Blairgowrie for Leith he confessed, 'The happiest hours I have ever spent have been in my Sabbath school, and no part of my labours has been more abundantly blessed.' The regular Sunday services took place before and after noon. Then in the evening, at six o'clock, up to five hundred children would gather in the church for the Sabbath school. By seven, between six and seven hundred adults had joined them. For forty minutes Macdonald would then catechise the children on the lesson of the previous hour, 'interspersing anecdote, illustration, and appeal, concluding all with praise and prayer.' Cowan says, 'the interest was extraordinary, and the blessing great and continuous.'

Wider work

In May 1843, at the Disruption, Macdonald and most of his congregation severed their connection with the Established Church. A suitable building to house the new Free Church congregation was swiftly erected—and filled. The Disruption led to wider work. For many months prior to the Free Church's General Assembly of May 1844 Macdonald toured the country, preaching the gospel, and raising funds for the building of church schools and teachers' salaries. There was at that time no nationwide, government-funded educational system, and circumstances forced on the Free Church the necessity of doing what it could. Macdonald was extraordinarily successful in his appeals for help; so too in later months when a large sum of money was needed to build the New College in Edinburgh to train men for gospel ministry.

His book From Day to Day

Of the handful of books that came from Macdonald's pen the most popular was *From Day to Day; or Helpful Words for Christian Life*. My attention was first drawn to it by a letter to Macdonald from another close friend, Andrew Bonar. He writes, 'My dear Robert, *From Day to Day* is a book of most pleasant and profitable reading. It is 365 meditations—as many as Samuel Rutherford's Letters—as many as Enoch's years of earthly pilgrimage and walking with God. There is a clearness and pointedness in your style of writing that at once attracts the reader, and, dipping his rod in the honey, he finds his eyes enlightened.' Robert Cowan also refers to its 'clearness, point, and grace of style,' and adds, 'in evangelical savour, in abundance and aptness of illustration, and in home-coming persuasiveness and force, it would be difficult to find a rival to it.'

Norman Walker says of Macdonald that 'he wrote most on the page of the human heart. It was the saintliness of his life, the joyousness of his Christianity, his unfaltering faith, his hopefulness, his benignity and loving sweetness of disposition, that won for him the affection of so many, and will ever make his name fragrant to those who knew him.' It was Walker's conviction, however, that Macdonald's book *From Day to Day* would 'live, both in the original English form and in the various translations, and keep his name from being forgotten.' Since history, by and large, has failed to bear that out, it is a particular joy to see *From Day to Day* in print again and to have the privilege of contributing this introduction. Having used these daily readings both in my own personal devotions and in family worship I can warmly recommend them.

DAVID CAMPBELL
July 2023

CONTENTS

February

March

April

May

July

August

September

October

November

December

FROM DAY TO DAY

JANUARY 1

IT IS GRACE THAT DOES ALL, NOT NATURE.

NEVER was any man more marvellously changed than Saul of Tarsus. In thought and desire, in aim and effort, and in every action and habit of his life, he became so entirely a new creature, that in the end the once chief of sinners became, as it were, the chief of saints.

What wrought the change? Was it any mere effort of his own, or the loving energy of any of his fellows? No, verily, but divine grace alone. He himself again and again emphatically said: 'Not I, but the grace of God which was with me.' 'By the grace of God I am what I am.'

When reading these words, which were so strikingly applicable to his own case, John Newton once remarked: 'I am not what I ought to be, I am not what I wish to be, and I am not what I hope to be, but by the grace of God I am not what I once was.' So is it more or less with all the redeemed. Conscious of their unworthiness and deeply feeling their manifold shortcomings, it is one of the readiest and most heartfelt of their utterances, 'Oh to grace how great a debtor!'

Scripture says, 'A threefold cord is not easily broken'; and nowhere is this seen in diviner form than in the threefold grace and love of the Holy Trinity as revealed in redemption: and verily a salvation in which Father, Son, and Holy Spirit are concerned, cannot possibly miscarry.

Some years ago, an English seaman, who had escaped from a wreck, appeared in the Coroner's Court with his right arm in splints. That broken arm was to his honour. It was a memorial of his generous eagerness to save. As the vessel was sinking, he had grasped the hand of one of the sufferers and held it firmly, till a falling beam fractured his arm, when he was heard to cry, 'My God, I must let go, for I have no more strength!' Here was willingness to save, intense willingness, but ability was wanting; but never is it so with our great Redeemer. He has an arm that is full of power, that cannot be broken, and will never let go, for his promise is express: 'I give unto them eternal life; and they shall never perish, neither shall any man pluck them out of my hand.'

No gospel save that of the grace of God in Jesus Christ can avail for highest ends. After preaching morality in vain to his people for many years, Henry Venn was so discouraged that he was about to give up his ministry in despair. When subsequently, however, led to preach, not mere morality as before, but Christ, he found, to his joy, that his people grew holy, not so much when told to be holy, as when they were gazing on the wounds of him who died to redeem them from all iniquity, and to purify to himself a peculiar people, zealous of good works.

> For by grace are ye saved through faith; and that not of yourselves: it is the gift of God: not of works, lest any man should boast.—Eph. 2:8, 9.
>
> Being justified freely by his grace through the redemption that is in Christ Jesus.—Rom. 3:24.
>
> And God is able to make all grace abound toward you; that ye, always having all sufficiency in all things, may abound to every good work.—2 Cor. 9:8.

January 2

THE SINNER MUST DIE, OR THE SINNER'S FRIEND.

IN no part of the word do we find a clearer revelation of the great truth, that Christ *for* us is as all-essential as Christ *in* us, than in the fifty-third chapter of Isaiah.

It was this chapter that the eunuch of Ethiopia was reading when Philip met him on the desert way, and in which these precious words occur: 'He was wounded for our transgressions, he was bruised for our iniquities: the chastisement of our peace was upon him; and with his stripes we are healed.' Yet though he read them carefully and anxiously, he could not understand them. 'How can I,' he said, 'except some man should guide me?' Then Philip preached to him Jesus, the divine Saviour and loving Substitute, suffering, the just for the unjust, to bring us unto God; and did so with such enlightening and saving power, that the eunuch did not merely heartily believe, but went on his way rejoicing.

Happily, what in the beginning was so dark to the eunuch has since been clearly revealed to many a babe. A poor African put the matter with touching simplicity, yet blessed truthfulness, when he said, 'He die; me no die.' This fact embodies the very essence of the gospel; and no gospel that leaves it out can ever meet the anxieties or satisfy the longings of perishing men. Those words alone which reveal the substitutionary work of Christ can calm the troubled soul when guilt presses, and fears arise that there can be no escape from the threatened doom: 'The soul that sinneth, it shall die.' They show what nothing else can, that forgiveness is not inconsistent with truth or righteousness, and that the pardon which in mercy God bestows upon the sinner is bestowed in justice to the well-beloved Son who accepted and discharged the sinner's obligations.

This is an infinitely precious truth, and the hearts of thousands in every age have been sustained and gladdened by it. A good old Christian woman in humble life so fully realised this, that when a revered servant of God asked her, as she lay on her dying pillow, the ground of her hope for eternity, she replied, with great composure, 'I rely on the justice of God'; adding, however, when the reply excited surprise, 'justice, not to me, but to my Substitute, *in whom I trust.*' In this way mercy and justice alike befriend the sinner who believes. 'If you wish to know,' says Mr Moody, 'the secret of our success, it lies in this, that we have stood fair and square on the Bible doctrine of substitution. Ah! that is what is needed by a dying world.'

For he hath made him to be sin for us, who knew no sin; that we might be made the righteousness of God in him.—2 Cor. 5:21.

Who his own self bare our sins in his own body on the tree, that we, being dead to sins, should live unto righteousness: by whose stripes ye were healed.—1 Pet. 2:24.

Christ was once offered to bear the sins of many; and unto them that look for him shall he appear the second time without sin unto salvation.—Heb. 9:28.

January 3

SAINTS MAY DOUBT ABOUT MANY THINGS, BUT NOT THAT GOD ANSWERS PRAYER.

A MAN of enfeebled mind once became possessed, it is said, with the strange idea that the whole postal system of his country was such an unreal thing that, however many the letters sent, no replies to them could ever be received. His neighbours, of course, merely smiled at his fancies, and went on as before, acting on the facts.

In our time some gifted but prayerless men seem to cherish a similar idea regarding prayer. They hold it to be a mere delusion, and assert that from the fixity of nature's laws they can scientifically prove that prayer never has been answered, and never can be. No Christian man, however, who knows his God and trusts him, prays the less on this account, or is in the least degree influenced by utterances like these. They go for nothing with him, because, while he believes in *laws*, he believes as firmly in a supreme, living, personal, and almighty *Lawgiver*; and that all the laws, which are just the expression of his will, must, from the very perfection of his nature, be ever entirely under his control, and consistent at the same time with his own express teaching, that 'men ought always to pray, and not to faint.'

It would be strange, indeed, were this world so made, and its laws so framed, that God, all wise and all powerful as he is, would in all after-time be so painfully fettered by them as to be unable to render the help his love might prompt or his lips had promised, and be actually less free to aid others than the very creatures of his hand. Surely if, in spite of the alleged fixity of nature's laws, the mother can hear the cry of her babe, and supply in need and protect in danger, how much more must the great God over all be free to hear and bless the children of his love, the adopted heirs of the purchased inheritance!

'You may puzzle me with your reasonings,' said a plain man to a learned objector, 'but I can baffle you with *my facts*.' Indeed, that God answers prayer, in temporal and spiritual things alike, is to countless thousands, from long and varied experience, the very surest of all sure things.

'The law of gravitation,' says Mr Spurgeon, 'I might doubt, but the law that God hears my prayers I cannot doubt. I can say honestly that hundreds of times, about all sorts of things, I have taken my case to God, and have obtained the desires of my heart, or something far better, and that not by mere coincidence, as objectors assert, but in a manner palpably in reply to my pleadings.'

But in the answering of prayer, it is often with the Lord as it is with ourselves. When a skilful harper comes to our door, giving sweet voice to his harp, and waking to the full its richest harmonies, if we have no ear to appreciate, we at once give him the mite he requests and send him away; but if we are pleased, we let him play on, and bid him play more, just because his strains delight us, and then in the end we double our gift. So is it with the Lord. If he delays answering the prayers of his children, it is because *he takes such pleasure in hearing them*, for 'the prayer of the upright is his delight'; and because, too, delays test sincerity, exercise patience, invigorate faith, and deepen the gratitude felt when the blessing prayed for finally comes.

Pray without ceasing.—1 THESS. 5:17.

Verily God hath heard me; he hath attended to the voice of my prayer.—PSA. 66:19.

Because he hath inclined his ear unto me, therefore will I call upon him as long as I live.—Psa. 116:2.

JANUARY 4

A REAL CHRIST, OR NONE.

WHEN the life or property of men is known to be seriously imperilled, any professed physician or legal adviser that may present himself will not be accepted; they must have one thoroughly qualified, and worthy of implicit trust. In dealing, however, with infinitely higher matters—salvation and a Saviour—they take no such careful heed. Anything seems to content them, whether shadow or substance, provided only it bear the name. Much is revealed thereby; for when any kind of Christ or Saviour can thus easily satisfy them, they give unmistakable evidence that they have never realised what sin is, or the greatness of the salvation of which they so openly make light.

The teaching of the word invariably is, that there is but one unspeakable gift—the Son of the living God—and that through no other name can salvation be found. Everything, therefore, depends on the answer that may be given to the great question, 'What think ye of Christ?' If our reply is, that he is man only and not God as well, or an example only and not a substitute, or a martyr only who died but never rose again, then we may have a nominal Christ, but a real Redeemer, almighty to save, we have not.

The Christ who is merely human, so far from saving sinners from their sins, is but the gourd of a night, that withers to the dust when a worm touches it; whereas the true Christ, the Lord Immanuel, is the Rock of Ages, in the clefts of which we can hide forever.

Were guilt and danger *unreal*, redemption might safely be of the same character; but beyond question real sinners must have a real Saviour, else they will be forever undone.

Some time ago, a friend of mine was so impressed with the dying experience of his wife, as revealing *the presence* and all-sufficient grace of the Saviour, that he afterwards said to me, with deep emotion, 'Oh, it was *so real*—so *thoroughly real*, that I can never forget it.' The shadowy soon slips from the memory, but the real abides.

Of a truth thou art the Son of God.—MATT. 14:33.

Lord, to whom shall we go? thou hast the words of eternal life. And we believe and are sure that thou art that Christ, the Son of the living God.—JOHN 6:68, 69.

And Thomas answered and said unto him, My Lord and my God.—JOHN 20:28.

JANUARY 5

EVEN WEAK FAITH IS PRECIOUS FAITH.

MUCH as the Lord approves and commends a strong faith, like that of the Hebrew worthies, it would be a grievous misjudging of him to suppose that he confines his loving interest to it alone. No; even the weakest faith is prized and lovingly cherished by him, and day by day he graciously helps it on.

Of this there are manifold exemplifications. What faith could well be weaker than that of the poor father who came to Jesus with his son? He was not sure that his coming would be of any use. The disciples in their attempts to cure had utterly failed; and it might be so with the Master also, for the malady was the very worst imaginable and of long standing. He had strong desire, but only faint expectancy, and therefore all he ventured to say was, 'If thou canst do any thing, have compassion on us, and help us.' Feeble as the faith was, however, it brought him to Jesus, and drew forth in the end the healing virtue needed: for, as one says, 'A lame foot is still a foot,—he who comes slowly nevertheless comes'; and the Lord makes every comer welcome, even the feeblest.

But his mode of dealing in this case was peculiar. The 'if' of the father was met by the 'if' of our Lord. When the one said, 'If thou canst do anything, help us,' the other replied, 'If thou canst believe, all things are possible to him that believeth,'—words that immediately evoked the blessed response, 'Lord, I believe; help thou mine unbelief.'

This was his prayer, and it should be ours, and that other should be added to it, 'Lord, increase our faith'; for of all the graces, faith is the most helpful to men and the most glorifying to God. We cannot therefore have too much of it. An old writer says quaintly,—

> *'What, Thomas!*
> *Won't thou believe till sense be guide,*
> *And thrust its hand into my side?*
> *Where is thy faith, if it depends*
> *On nothing but thy finger-ends?*
> *But blessed are they the truth who seal*
> *By faith, yet neither see nor feel.'*

'Faith,' says one, 'is nothing else but the soul's venture. It ventures to Christ in opposition to conscious guilt and legal terror, and it ventures for Christ in opposition to all difficulty and danger.'

O thou of little faith, wherefore didst thou doubt?—MATT. 14:31.

Jesus saith unto her, Said I not unto thee, that, if thou wouldest believe, thou shouldest see the glory of God?—JOHN 11:40.

For verily I say unto you, That whosoever shall say unto this mountain, Be thou removed, and be thou cast into the sea; and shall not doubt in his heart, but shall believe that those things which he saith shall come to pass; he shall have whatsoever he saith.—MARK 11:23.

JANUARY 6

WE MUST NEITHER MISPLACE REPENTANCE
NOR EXCLUDE IT.

THERE is not and cannot be any antagonism between faith and repentance. Both are enjoined in the word, and the divine

Giver of the one is the divine Giver of the other; for while it is said, 'By grace are ye saved through faith; and that not of yourselves: it is the gift of God,' it is also said, 'He is exalted to be a Prince and a Saviour, for to give repentance to Israel, and forgiveness of sins."

But though there is no antagonism between them in the word, there is often a serious misplacement of them in actual life. It is no unfrequent thing with anxious inquirers so to put repentance before faith as to make a positive hindrance of it. When urged to look to Christ, and at once accept his freely-offered salvation, they virtually say, 'No; we are not yet worthy of it. Our convictions must be deeper first, and our repentance truer.' By such unbelieving hesitancy, they not only grieve the Spirit, but often lose their convictions altogether.

But if some err by making repentance a hindrance to faith, others err as seriously by setting it aside, as something entirely legal, and with which believers have nothing whatever to do. They forget that gospel repentance always includes, not only grief and contrition, but an apprehension of the mercy of God in Christ; and they forget, too, both the great command, 'Repent, every one of you,' and the sad fact that those who never repent of their sins soon and surely return to them again. None, therefore, who really trust and love the Saviour can ever make light of repentance, or fail themselves to exercise it, when there is a need be.

Their tears as penitents, however, should always have sweet as well as bitter in them, because being in Christ, and therefore children accepted in the Beloved, they are privileged to look on all the discipline and trial their backslidings have occasioned as needed and gracious tokens of wise and fatherly love. Though the remembrance of their sins may well keep them humble and watchful, yet when there is such blood to cleanse and the Spirit to help, it should never be allowed to keep them doleful and doubting. Were it otherwise, their repentance, instead of being true and evangelical, would have a Popish taint in it, and show that, to their Lord's dishonour and their own injury, they were only half-believing in a half-forgiveness.

This would be to resemble Joseph's brethren, who, in spite of all his loving assurances and gracious acts, *were ever fearfully brooding over the past*, and unworthily saying, 'Peradventure he will yet hate us.'

Nothing wounds the Lord like such suspicious fears in his children, or so perpetuates gloom in their own souls. When at any time memories of the past awaken fear and disquiet conscience, the only way of relief is a fresh and believing application to the blood of the Lamb.

> And he said unto them ... that repentance and remission of sins should be preached in his name among all nations, beginning at Jerusalem.—LUKE 24:46, 47.

> Now I rejoice, not that ye were made sorry, but that ye sorrowed to repentance: ... for godly sorrow worketh repentance to salvation not to be repented of: but the sorrow of the world worketh death.—2 COR. 7:9, 10.

> That thou mayest remember, and be confounded, and never open thy mouth any more because of thy shame, when I am pacified toward thee for all that thou hast done.—EZEK. 16:63.

JANUARY 7

TRUE LOYALTY TO CHRIST HAS NO RESERVES.

WHEN all others around them proved false and faithless, it was the grand distinction of Joshua and Caleb that they followed the Lord fully. Though thereby they imperilled all that was dear to them, and were nearly stoned to death, yet they swerved not a hair's breadth from the path of duty.

It was the same with Ruth the Moabitess. While her sister kissed Naomi, and departed,—for 'a little entreaty,' as one says, 'will serve to move nature to be good unto itself,'—she resolutely said, 'Intreat me not to leave thee, or to return from following after thee: for whither thou goest, I will go; and where thou lodgest, I will lodge: thy people shall be my people, and thy God my

God: where thou diest, will I die, and there will I be buried: the Lord do so to me, and more also, if ought but death part thee and me.' Nothing could move her; love so true could abide both fire and anvil.

So, too, was it with Paul and Barnabas. They were true men, who in serving their Lord and Master had no reserves, and made no conditions; hence the testimony borne to them, 'Our beloved Barnabas and Paul, *men that have hazarded their lives* for the name of our Lord Jesus Christ.' 'In our love to God,' says an old writer, 'we but crack and vaunt in vain if we cannot be willing to suffer for him.'

Such whole-hearted consecration is often regarded as an uncalled-for extremeness. But never do true Christians so view it. And why? Because Christ is not only their divine Master, whom they are bound to serve, but also their adorable Redeemer, whom they cannot but love, for he laid down his life for their sake; and therefore even to suffer shame for his name they reckon one of the highest of honours.

Such faithful servants have always more or less of present as well as of future reward, and are often the happiest of men even in sorest extremities, for they have a good conscience, a bright hope, and the spirit of glory and of God resting upon them. When Richard Cameron, one of the noblest of our Scottish martyrs, had fallen mortally wounded on Airdsmoss, he said: 'I am dying, happy, happy; and if I had a thousand lives, I would willingly lay them all down one after another for Christ. Oh, he is near me; I think I see him! I am just coming, Lord Jesus.' And he added: 'Tell my parents not to weep, but continue stedfast in the faith, and *not to fear a suffering lot for Christ.*'

Be thou faithful unto death, and I will give thee a crown of life.—Rev. 2:10.

And they overcame him by the blood of the Lamb, and by the word of their testimony; and they loved not their lives unto the death.—Rev. 12:11.

What mean ye to weep and to break mine heart? for I am ready not
to be bound only, but also to die at Jerusalem for the name of the
Lord Jesus.—Acts 21:13.

JANUARY 8

THE CHAIN OF REDEEMING LOVE HAS NO WEAK LINK.

IN spite of manifold tokens of helpful kindness in the past,
believers often give way to fears about the future, especially when
they reflect on their own inherent weakness, and all the might and
malignity that ever confront them. There would be good grounds
for such fears were salvation merely of man, an earthly device,
planned and schemed by human wisdom only; but this is not its
character, for we are expressly and repeatedly assured that, alike in
its beginning, middle, and end, it belongeth wholly to the Lord.
He is not more surely the Author than the Finisher of our faith.

Man's acts of kindness arise often from mere bursts of momen-
tary feeling; but all such acts in God spring from wise, holy, and
deliberate purpose, and no purpose of his can ever fail. Therefore,
no matter how great may be the difficulties in the way, how intense
the opposition, sore the discouragements, or crushing the seeming
defeats, yet in the end all that the Father hath given to the Son shall
come unto him.

The apostle sets this vividly before us when he says: 'Moreover
whom he did predestinate, them he also called: and whom he
called, them he also justified: and whom he justified, them he also
glorified. What shall we then say to these things? If God be for us,
who can be against us?'

Here is a chain of mercy and grace with many links,—eternal
purpose, divine foreknowledge, effectual calling, gracious acceptance, and final glory,—and all of them so strong that nothing can
weaken or sever them. Moreover, as one sweetly says, 'Each several
link, from the first to the last, is in *his* hand, and that alone renders
the chain an indissoluble one, though reaching from everlasting

to everlasting. At whatever point, therefore, faith lays her hand on that chain, she finds it strong enough to bear all that she can hang on it, even the far more exceeding and eternal weight of glory.' Happily, too, there is one link of this blessed chain always so near as to be within reach of all: 'Him that cometh to me I will in no wise cast out'; and whoever takes hold of it by faith makes sure of eternal life.

'The saints,' says Samuel Rutherford, 'seem to have the worst of it; but it is not so. Providence is not rolled upon unequal, crooked wheels; for "all things work together for the good of those who love God, and are the called according to his purpose." Ere it be long, we shall see the white side of God's providence.'

> The Lord will perfect that which concerneth me: thy mercy, O Lord, endureth for ever.—Psa. 138:8.

> God is faithful, by whom ye were called unto the fellowship of his Son Jesus Christ our Lord … who of God is made unto us wisdom, and righteousness, and sanctification, and redemption.—1 Cor. 1:9, 30.

> There is no wisdom nor understanding nor counsel against the Lord.—Prov. 21:30.

JANUARY 9

CONVERSIONS MAY BE SUDDEN, YET SURE.

MANY look on all sudden conversions with such suspiciousness that they will scarcely admit their genuineness in any case, not remembering that some of the most remarkable instances of saving change recorded in Scripture are of this nature. In these cases the suddenness of the change, so far from interfering with the genuineness of it, only brings out more impressively the riches and efficacy of sovereign grace.

We see this strikingly exemplified in the conversion of Zacchaeus. It was a strange sight,—the chief among the publicans sitting on the branches of a sycamore tree, and waiting patiently till Jesus should pass by: yet not more strange than blessed; for, as Thomas Boston says, 'It is good to be in Christ's way, for he loves to surprise sinners with a cast of free grace.' When he came to the place, Jesus paused and looked up. And what a look! Whatever it may have been to others, Zacchaeus at least could never forget it, for there was kindness in it, and inexpressible tenderness. What the look of Jesus in the hall did for Peter, this look apparently, with the words accompanying it, did for Zacchaeus: it imbittered sin to him, and endeared the Saviour.

In dealing with him, the Lord was lovingly urgent: 'Zacchaeus,' he said, 'make haste, and come down; for to day I must abide at thy house.' And not without reason, for as our Lord's ministry was now nearing its close, he was never again to pass that way. He was there for the last time, and virtually, therefore, it was now or never with Zacchaeus. Assuredly, if ever a man should make haste, it is when the Lord of grace is passing by and inviting in love, and willing to enter in and make his abode with him. Zacchaeus felt it to be so, and therefore gave instant obedience to the Redeemer's loving call.

Doubtless that day of his meeting with Christ was the brightest and happiest of his life, and would ever be cherished as its very sunniest memory; and reasonably so, for while on the morning of that day he awoke an alien and outcast, without help or hope, yet ere the sun had set he was forgiven and accepted, a child of God and an heir of glory.

Why should not this, in large measure, be our experience also? The door of mercy is as open now to us as it was then to Zacchaeus; and the welcome will be as warm, if we only come as he came, and trust as he trusted.

> And he said unto Jesus, Lord, remember me when thou comest into thy kingdom. And Jesus said unto him, Verily I say unto thee, To day shalt thou be with me in paradise.—LUKE 23:42, 43.

> And the same day there were added unto them about three thousand souls. And they continued stedfastly in the apostles' doctrine and fellowship, and in breaking of bread, and in prayers.—ACTS 2:41, 42.

January 10

A TRUE SUPPLIANT.

BRIEF as is the publican's prayer, 'God be merciful to me a sinner,' it yet reveals such a deep sense of sin, and such a sweet hope of mercy, that it is in every way suitable for all, whether the holiest of saints or the vilest of sinners. It is not strange, therefore, that it has been in constant use among the redeemed of the Lord. 'It has formed the living motto and dying words of unnumbered thousands; their latest breath has uttered them.'

It is well to note that it was not a vague, general pity the publican asked, or mere forbearance, like the servant in the parable when he said, 'Have patience, and I will pay thee all,' but forgiving mercy—'God be merciful to me a sinner.' This was his petition; and he not only obtained what he asked, but far beyond it, even all the benefits of a full justification—freedom from condemnation, acceptance in the Beloved, and adoption into the royal family of heaven. And these blessings he received at once, for that very day *he went down to his house justified.*

What the Lord did for him, he is able and willing to do for every one who comes in a like spirit. Blessed are all such. When Hugo Grotius, as he lay dying, had his attention drawn to this very prayer, he said, with great earnestness and deep humility, 'I am that publican,—God be merciful to me a sinner.'

Besides the publican, there was another suppliant, the Pharisee; and the difference between them has been thus strikingly stated: 'The one so gives thanks as to forget to pray, the other so prays that he afterwards gives thanks; the one compares himself with other men, the other observes himself in the mirror of God's law; the one counts up his virtues, the other cannot count up his sins; the one with all his virtues still keeps an evil conscience, the other with all his sins receives the full assurance of forgiveness.'

He that covereth his sins shall not prosper: but whoso confesseth and forsaketh them shall have mercy.—PROV. 28:13.

Let the wicked forsake his way, and the unrighteous man his thoughts: and let him return unto the Lord, and he will have mercy upon him; and to our God, for he will abundantly pardon.—Isa. 55:7.

Let Israel hope in the Lord: for with the Lord there is mercy, and with him is plenteous redemption.—Psa. 130:7.

January 11

CONCERN FOR THE LORD'S HONOUR.

IN every aspect of it the fall of David was peculiarly grievous. It injured others; it injured himself; but in the eyes of Nathan the saddest thing of all was the dishonour done by it to the holy name of God. 'By this deed,' he said, 'thou hast given occasion to the enemies of the Lord to blaspheme.' So, also, when for the wickedness of Israel the Lord threatened to consume them, the main argument of Moses, when interceding for them, and the one on which he most leaned, was the possible dishonour their destruction might bring on God's holy name. So has it ever been with all truly loyal hearts: while anything said against themselves can be borne patiently, any reproach cast upon their Lord touches the very apple of their eye.

Paul could be calm when the men of Lystra were stoning him, for that but wounded himself; but he could not restrain himself when they cried, 'The gods are come down to us in the likeness of men,' and were about to worship him, for that would have wounded and dishonoured his Lord. Wherefore, rushing in among the people, and rending his garments, he cried aloud, 'Sirs, why do ye these things? We also are men of like passions with you, and preach unto you that ye should turn from these vanities unto the living God, which made heaven, and earth, and the sea, and all things that are therein.' A spirit like this is ever one of the surest signs of grace, and is never found save in a regenerate heart.

An aged Christian, in great distress of mind, was once complaining to a friend, of his miserable condition, and among other things said, 'That which troubles me most is, that God will be dishonoured by my fall.' His friend hastily caught at this, and used it for the purpose of comforting him. 'Art thou careful of the honour of God, and dost thou think that God has no care of thee and thy salvation? A soul forsaken of God cares not what becomes of the honour of God: therefore be of good cheer; if God's heart were not toward thee, thine would not be turned to God or toward the remembrance of his name.'

> Help us, O God of our salvation, for the glory of thy name: and deliver us, and purge away our sins, for thy name's sake. Wherefore should the heathen say, Where is their God?—Psa. 79:9, 10.

> Them that honour me I will honour, and they that despise me shall be lightly esteemed.—1 Sam. 2:30.

> If any man serve me, let him follow me; and where I am, there shall also my servant be: if any man serve me, him will my Father honour.—John 12:26.

JANUARY 12

FIRST LOVE IS SO PRECIOUS THAT WE MUST BEWARE OF LOSING IT.

YOUNG disciples are sometimes lightly told that the joyous love they have when first they close with offered mercy in Christ is never long retained, and that sooner or later a time of darkness and lukewarmness is sure to come. But such a statement is wholly unwarranted. There is no evidence to show, nor is there any reason whatever to believe, that John ever lost his first love, or Paul or Timothy theirs; or Epaphroditus, who for the work of Christ was nigh unto death; or Priscilla or Aquila, who for Paul's life laid down their own necks, and unto whom not only he gave thanks, but also all the churches of the Gentiles. Nay, on the contrary, their love to Christ, though not always, it may be, so visibly emotional as at first, yet became year by year warmer and more intense, till in the end there was nothing they would not gladly have done or suffered for his sake.

Doubtless from unwatchfulness and over-intimacy with the world, and the manifold cares and conflicts of life, too many lose in part their early and blessed experience. There is, however, no 'must be' in such a declension. This is very manifest from the way in which our Lord addressed the church of Ephesus. He spoke of their losing their first love, not as a misfortune merely, but as a grievous blemish in their character, as a dangerous symptom, as a sin to be confessed and deplored, and one that called for loving yet earnest rebuke. True, they served and laboured, and were commended for so doing; but as service with decreasing love can never satisfy him who said, 'My son, give me thine heart,' there was rebuke as well as commendation. 'Nevertheless I have somewhat against thee, because thou hast left thy first love. Remember therefore from whence thou art fallen, and repent, and do the first works; or else I will come unto thee quickly, and will remove thy candlestick out of his place, except thou repent.'

It should ever, therefore, be our resolute and prayerful effort, through grace, to keep the love that was warm at the first warm to the last. It was said of Moses that even when an hundred and twenty years old, his eye was not dim, nor his natural force abated; and so has it been from time to time, spiritually, with not a few aged believers. It was noted by his friends as one of the grandest things about Dr Cappadose that, long as he lived, he never lost the ardour of his first love. Indeed, ever and again, as his thoughts turned to the Lord who was so dear to him, his heart seemed to burn.

Sun of my soul, thou Saviour dear,
It is not night if thou be near;
Oh, may no earth-born cloud arise
To hide thee from thy servant's eyes!

Go and cry in the ears of Jerusalem, saying, Thus saith the Lord; I remember thee, the kindness of thy youth, the love of thine espousals, when thou wentest after me in the wilderness, in a land that was not sown.—JER. 2:2.

Because iniquity shall abound, the love of many shall wax cold.—
MATT. 24:12.

Thou hast a few names even in Sardis which have not defiled their
garments.—REV. 3:4.

JANUARY 13

*NOTHING SO SWEETENS SUFFERING AS FELLOWSHIP WITH
CHRIST IN IT.*

ALL who are called to endure suffering for righteousness' sake,
not only rejoice in the midst of it, but rejoice also expressly
on account of it, because it links them more closely to their blessed
Lord, and greatly brightens their future; for 'if we suffer with him,
we shall reign with him.' Indeed, the oneness of the Redeemer and
his people is such that they have fellowship alike in joy and sorrow;
and believers are even said to 'fill up that which is behind of the
afflictions of Christ.'

This does not, of course, mean that the atoning sufferings of
Christ in Gethsemane and on Calvary were not of themselves
sufficient for redemptive ends, without the added sufferings of his
saints. No! for, so far as expiation was concerned, everything was
done and borne by Christ himself with such absolute completeness that nothing was left for others to supplement. The afflictions
referred to, therefore, were not the afflictions of atonement, but
the afflictions of sympathy; and so full, close, and tender is that
sympathy, that all the afflictions of his people are virtually his own
afflictions also.

This blessed truth has been a sweet sustainer of suffering saints in
every age. In former evil days in Scotland, Margaret Wilson, a girl
of eighteen, along with an aged widow of sixty-three, was adjudged
to die because she refused to acknowledge the supremacy of any
other but Christ in the church. The sentence pronounced against
them was, that they should be fastened to stakes driven deep into
the oozy sand that covers the beach at Wigtown, and left to perish

in the rising tide. The stake to which the aged female was fastened was farther down the beach than that of the young woman, in order that, being sooner destroyed, her expiring sufferings might shake the firmness of faith of Margaret Wilson. But they had no such effect; for when a heartless persecutor asked, 'What think you of your friend now?' she calmly and nobly replied, 'What do I see *but Christ in one of his members wrestling there.* Think you that we are the sufferers? No; *it is Christ in us*—he who sendeth us not upon our own charges.' Thus we see, to injure the saints is to injure their Lord. Witness his memorable words, 'Saul, Saul, why persecutest thou *me?*'

> Unto you it is given in the behalf of Christ, not only to believe on him, but also to suffer for his sake.—PHIL. 1:29.

> I have surely seen the affliction of my people which are in Egypt, and have heard their cry by reason of their taskmasters; for I know their sorrows.—EXOD. 3:7.

> In all their affliction he was afflicted, and the angel of his presence saved them.—ISA. 63:9.

JANUARY 14

COMFORT IN THE WILDERNESS.

TO believers, this world is not a home, but only a place of sojourn; a wilderness through which, as pilgrims, oft weary and faint, they are passing onward to their eternal rest. But this is their comfort—if it is a wilderness, they are not to be *long* in it. When a few brief years at most have passed away, they will be out of it, and their weary sojourn in it be but a fading memory.

But, better far, they are *not alone* in it. A Friend is near on whom they can lean day by day—a Friend so mighty that he can uphold to the uttermost, and so precious that he is pre-eminently the Beloved. 'Who is this that cometh up from the wilderness, leaning upon her beloved?' With ordinary friends we can only go a certain length in this dependency. If we lean too heavily on them, or too long, they are apt to get wearied of us. But with our blessed Redeemer, if there is complaint at all, it is not that we lean too much on him, but that we lean too little. When he is the object of it, we can never exceed in trustful dependence. Even permission so to lean would be much, but we have far more; it is not only his desire, but his express command, that day by day as they arise we should cast our every burden and care upon him. 'Be careful for nothing,' says the apostle; 'but in every thing by prayer and supplication with thanksgiving let your requests be made known unto God. And the peace of God, which passeth all understanding, shall keep your hearts and minds through Christ Jesus.'

One other thought is peculiarly sweet and comforting; namely, that when once fairly out of the wilderness, *believers never return to it again*. In the new and better Eden of the redeemed, a second fall or a second expulsion is an eternal impossibility; for the saints are vitally one with the glorified Redeemer, and shall be so forever. 'Though I leave this blessed island for a while,' said the saintly Fletcher of Madeley, when about to go abroad, 'I trust I shall never leave the kingdom of God, the Mount Zion, the New Jerusalem. There I entreat you to meet me. There are no parting seas there, no interposing mountains, no sickness, no death, no fear of loving too much, and no shame for loving too little.'

> They wandered in the wilderness in a solitary way; they found no city to dwell in … And he led them forth by the right way, that they might go to a city of habitation.—Psa. 107:4, 7
>
> Therefore, behold, I will allure her, and bring her into the wilderness, and speak comfortably unto her.—Hos. 2:14.
>
> O God, thou art my God; early will I seek thee: my soul thirsteth for thee, my flesh longeth for thee in a dry and thirsty land, where no water is.—Psa. 63:1.

JANUARY 15

THE HOLIER OUR LIFE, THE HAPPIER.

A LIFE of sin is never other in the long run than a life of sorrow. As soon might we gather grapes of thorns or figs of thistles as get real joy from nature's barren soil. A man without a conscience, indeed, can occasionally seem lighter-hearted than a man with one. Nevertheless these words remain eternally true—'The way of transgressors is hard.' On the other hand, there are not surer promises anywhere than these: 'Obey the voice of the Lord, and it shall be well with thee, and thy soul shall live'; 'Wisdom's ways are ways of pleasantness, and all her paths are peace.'

This peaceful pleasantness usually begins the very moment we believe in Christ, and know experimentally the joyful sound. The burden of sin is lightened then, its power broken, and bright and blessed hopes are kindled that can never die. Our way, it is true, may still occasionally be dark and lonely, and not without conflict; yet every step is lighted from above, and is leading heavenward. Practical godliness, therefore, so far from being associated with gloom, is the one and only thing that can finally and effectually dispel it. It casts a smile on a world of sorrow, and through the fulness of its comfort turns grief into gladness.

In a letter written from Mount Carmel, Robert M'Cheyne said to me, more than six and thirty years ago: 'Never cease to tell your people that to be holy is to be happy, and that to bring us to perfect holiness and likeness to God was the very end for which Christ died'; and then he added: 'Wherever we journey, union to Jesus, and holiness from his Spirit flowing to us, is our chief and only happiness.'

'I must bear him witness,' says another, 'that it is sweet to do his will; and had I done it more perfectly, I would have been happier than I am. But as it is, to have given my heart to him, and to have sought his glory, has conferred upon my life its brightest joy and its deepest satisfaction.'

If it is so even here in the wilderness, what must it be with believers when, in the city of the Great King, they sin no more, and enter fully and forever into the joy of their Lord.

He that keepeth the law, happy is he.—Prov. 29:18.

These things have I spoken unto you, that my joy might remain in you, and that your joy might be full.—John 15:11.

Blessed are they that hear the word of God, and keep it.—Luke 11:28.

January 16

TRUSTFUL STILLNESS.

IN great straits, believers are sometimes sorely tempted to yield to unbelieving haste, and to seek deliverance, not in God's way, but in rash and forbidden ways of their own. Could they be but still at such times, they would be safe.

Never were the Israelites in such extreme peril as when the Egyptians were behind them and the Red Sea before them, with rugged steeps on either side. Escape seemed impossible and destruction certain. Now, in this great emergency, the one and only thing enjoined was trustful stillness. 'Fear ye not,' said Moses, '*stand still*, and see the salvation of God. The Lord shall fight for you, *and ye shall hold your peace.*' They did nothing; the Lord did all, and so marvellously that his doings will be held in everlasting remembrance.

It was the same with Hezekiah when the Assyrians were at the gates. 'Be not afraid,' he said to his people, 'nor dismayed for the king of Assyria, nor for all the multitude that is with him: for there be more with us than with him: with him is an arm of flesh; but with us is the Lord our God to help us, and to fight our battles.' And the people '*stayed themselves on God*,' and thereby found immediate strength and glorious deliverance.

Now, what was true then, is not less true to this day. No matter what our straits may be, or from whatever cause—whether from failing means, or failing health, or failing friendship, or political movements, or from combinations of them all—*sitting still, calmly trustful in God*, ever remains our grand strength.

'The man who in the time of his trouble is a wild bull in the net, tossing and struggling, only makes his case the worse, and adds sorrow to sorrow; but he who waits patiently upon his God has a way of comfort and deliverance opened to him, and a happy issue out of all his troubles.'

> Be still, and know that I am God: I will be exalted among the heathen, I will be exalted in the earth.—Psa. 46:10.

> Fear thou not; for I am with thee: be not dismayed; for I am thy God: I will strengthen thee; yea, I will help thee; yea, I will uphold thee with the right hand of my righteousness.—Isa. 41:10.

> Their strength is to sit still. In returning and rest shall ye be saved; in quietness and in confidence shall be your strength.—Isa. 30:7, 15.

January 17

WHEN TO BE PROMPT.

WHEN evil thoughts and purposes spring up in the soul, the Christian must be prompt to resist them. It is easier to check the rising of evil than to control it when in full flood. But when the thoughts and purposes are gracious, he must be prompt in carrying them out. When offer of mercy is made to us in Christ Jesus, we cannot be too immediate in accepting it, because it may be the last offer to be given, or the last time the Spirit is to strive. It was because the Bereans welcomed at once the gospel message that it was said of them, 'These were more noble than those in Thessalonica, in that they received the word *with all readiness.*' They made haste, and delayed not.

Further: when intercession is our duty, there should be like promptitude. This was beautifully exemplified in Abraham, God's friend. As soon as it was revealed to him that the cities of the plain were about to be destroyed, his very first act thereafter was to pour out his soul in their behalf. He pleaded for them with a fervour and fulness rarely equalled. So should it be with us. Whether pleading for friends or neighbours, the church or the world, we should do so with eager readiness. 'When anyone asks your prayers,' said an aged and revered friend, 'and you promise to grant them, trust no tomorrow, but kneel down at once and pour out your heart in supplication.' Were this oftener done, it would prevent many a broken promise, and bring down many a rich and needed blessing; especially if to promptitude in the prayer persistency were added.

What is true of supplication, is true also of liberality. For all such giving we have the authority of our blessed Master, who said, 'Freely ye have received, freely give'; but prompt giving is often of essential moment, and in an emergency, to give quickly is often to give doubly. Dr Wilson of Bath once requested a friend to take £50 to a poor minister. He said he would take the money next day. 'Oh, my dear sir,' said the doctor, 'take it to him tonight. Only think of the importance to a sick man of one good night's rest.' But with all our giving of earthly gifts, let us be prompt in giving to the needy and perishing the word of truth—the glorious gospel—and lovingly press it on their immediate acceptance.

> Whatsoever thy hand findeth to do, do it with thy might; for there is no work, nor device, nor knowledge, nor wisdom, in the grave, whither thou goest.—ECCLES. 9:10.

> Now is the accepted time; behold, now is the day of salvation.— 2 COR. 6:2.

> He becometh poor that dealeth with a slack hand: but the hand of the diligent maketh rich.—PROV. 10:4.

JANUARY 18

STUMBLING OVERRULED FOR STABLISHING.

WE may learn not a little from the somewhat peculiar history of Mark, sister's son to Barnabas. At first everything apparently was bright and hopeful about him. He journeyed with God's

servants, preached and laboured with them, and willingly encountered difficulties and trials. This, however, did not continue; for,
by-and-by, either through indolence or cowardice, he quite unexpectedly forsook Paul and Barnabas, and 'went not with them to
the work.'

After such manifest instability, Paul, losing all confidence in
him, would not allow of his further fellowship in the service of the
Lord; while Barnabas, on the other hand, though greatly saddened
by his nephew's backsliding, was yet resolutely bent on giving him
another trial. The unhappy result was a contention so hot between
the two good men, that they finally separated.

It is hard to say with whom lay the right in this matter; perhaps
both erred, in some degree, in overkeenness of feeling and expression. But, however this may be, in all likelihood the fears of the one
and the hopes of the other, with the very sharpness of the contention
that followed, were all used for the saving good of Mark. Doubtless,
ever after he would be more distrustful of himself, more dependent
on his Lord, and more decided in purpose to follow him fully. Thus
the stumbling in the first instance was graciously overruled for stablishing in the end; and so has it been in innumerable cases.

Happily, there is every reason to believe that there was the
fullest reconciliation afterwards, not only between the two great
evangelists, but also between Paul and Mark; for, subsequently, the
apostle said, with much cordiality, 'Marcus, sister's son to Barnabas
... if he come unto you, receive him'; and again, 'Take Mark, and
bring him with thee; for he is profitable to me for the ministry.'

As this recorded incident but too clearly shows that the best of
men are but men at the best, they never cease to need our prayers;
and it is certain that were Christian people to pray more for their
ministers, they would profit more by them.

> Restore unto me the joy of thy salvation; and uphold me with thy
> free spirit. Then will I teach transgressors thy ways; and sinners
> shall be converted unto thee.—PSA. 51:12, 13.

> For behold this selfsame thing, that ye sorrowed after a godly
> sort, what carefulness it wrought in you, yea, what clearing of

yourselves, yea, what indignation, yea, what fear, yea, what vehement desire, yea, what zeal, yea, what revenge! In all things ye have approved yourselves to be clear in this matter.—2 COR. 7:11.

JANUARY 19

EVEN FINDERS MAY STILL BE SEEKERS.

IN reading the words, 'Hearken unto me, ye that follow after righteousness, ye that seek the Lord,' we might at first suppose that the persons addressed were rather anxious inquirers in search of salvation, than actual believers who had already found it; but from the context we clearly see it was otherwise, for it is afterwards said to them, 'Hearken unto me, ye that *know* righteousness, the people *in whose heart* is my law.' Believers only could be so addressed, for they alone have the saving knowledge of righteousness, and the law divinely written on the heart. It is true they are still called seekers of the Lord; but this involves no real difficulty, as there are many ways in which believers may be said to seek the Lord even after finding him, and to pursue righteousness even after securing the righteousness that justifies through faith in Christ Jesus.

It might be otherwise had there been in Christian life a stereotyped fixity that admitted of no varying degrees of grace and attainment in different believers, and even in the same believers at different times. So far, however, is this from being the case, that there is, or should be, from the very first, a progressive advancement in the divine life; for the path of the just is said to be like the shining light, that shineth more and more unto the perfect day. Such advancement requires constant watchfulness and prayerful pursuit; and thus to the very end they need to be seekers after God, and followers after righteousness.

'The true heart,' says one, 'should echo the will of God, as the rocks among the mountains repeat in sweetest music the notes of the peasant's horn.' It was so with the Psalmist, as these words clearly show: 'When thou saidst, Seek ye my face; *my heart said unto thee,*

Thy face, Lord, will I seek.' It is seeking like this, heart-seeking, that the Lord most prizes, and ever most richly rewards.

There have been few more enlightened seekers after God than the saintly Rutherford. 'Every day,' he said, 'we may see something new in Christ, for his love hath neither brim nor bottom. What would I refuse to suffer if I could get a draught of it at my heart's desire; yet I desire grace and patience, that I may wait on and lie on the brink till the waters fill and overflow.'

> Not as though I had already attained, either were already perfect: but I follow after, if that I may apprehend that for which also I am apprehended of Christ Jesus. Brethren, I count not myself to have apprehended: but this one thing I do, forgetting those things which are behind, and reaching forth unto those things which are before, I press toward the mark for the prize of the high calling of God in Christ Jesus.—PHIL. 3:12-14.

JANUARY 20

THE LORD TRIES HIS PEOPLE, BUT NEVER OVER-TRIES THEM.

WHEN in obedience to the divine command Gideon had gathered an army, and was about to go forth against the Midianites, his one fear was that he had *too few* to meet the multitude against him. Yet the Lord's first word to him was, that he had *far too many*; and he was straightway enjoined to proclaim in the ears of the people, 'Whosoever is fearful and afraid, let him return and depart early from mount Gilead.' The result was that there remained of the people ten thousand. This to Gideon was a heavy blow and sore discouragement. But a harder trial yet awaited him. There were still too many, the Lord said; and by another sifting, nine thousand and seven hundred more were withdrawn from his ranks. Three hundred only now remained to face Midian's countless host; and they were to do so, not with swords and spears, but with trumpets, and lamps, and empty pitchers. This was purposely setting weakness against strength, and folly against wisdom, not only to weaken mere creature confidence, but to show that the church has arms of which the world knows nothing. Yet to Gideon, at the time, it was a trial of peculiar severity.

Nevertheless the trial was not allowed to be greater than he could bear. To encourage him in his extremity, the Lord gave him a sign without being asked for it. He bade him go down to the camp alone, taking no one with him but his armour-bearer Phurah. Coming near one of the outposts, he heard one Midianite telling another a singular dream. 'Behold,' he said, 'I dreamed, and, lo, a cake of barley bread tumbled into the host of Midian, and came unto a tent, and overturned it, that the tent lay along.' This was the dream; and as there is often 'a providence in our sleeping fancies,' it was so emphatically here, for his neighbour immediately replied, 'This is nothing else, save the sword of Gideon: for into his hand hath God delivered Midian, and all the host.' This was enough for Gideon; and straightway, without fear or misgiving of any kind, he did as the Lord enjoined, and won a victory of unparalleled completeness.

So has it been, more or less, with believers in every age. They may have trial upon trial, but never over-trial; for in due season the Lord, with loving tenderness, either lightens their burden or increases their strength. His promised grace is made sufficient for them. They may be often pressed above *their* human, but never above *his* divine and heavenly might.

> *Oh cheer thee, cheer thee, suffering saint,*
> *Though worn with chastening be not faint;*
> *And though the night of pain seem long,*
> *Cling to thy Lord, in him be strong;*
> *He marks, he numbers every tear,*
> *Not one faint sigh escapes his ear.*

There hath no temptation taken you but such as is common to man: but God is faithful, who will not suffer you to be tempted above that ye are able; but will with the temptation also make a way to escape, that ye may be able to bear it.—1 COR. 10:13.

The Lord knoweth how to deliver the godly out of temptations.— 2 PET. 2:9.

The Lord shall deliver me from every evil work, and will preserve me unto his heavenly kingdom.—2 TIM. 4:18.

JANUARY 21

THE SACRED FIRE THAT MUST NOT BE QUENCHED.

JOHN said of Jesus—'He shall baptize with the Holy Ghost, and *with fire*'; and on the day of Pentecost the Spirit was so marvellously outpoured, that 'there appeared unto them cloven tongues like as of fire, and it sat upon each of them. And they were all filled with the Holy Ghost, and began to speak as the Spirit gave them utterance.'

Here the Spirit is compared to fire; and there is a peculiar appropriateness in the imagery. Where there is fire, there is usually light; so is it where the Spirit of the Lord is. He is the great Enlightener of darkened souls, and so effectually reveals Christ to them, in all the fulness of his grace and glory, that multitudes in every age have been able to say, from blessed experience, 'One thing I know, that whereas I was blind, now I see.'

Like fire also, the Holy Spirit softens what is hard. Even when all other influences have utterly failed, yet in his hands the very flintiest of hearts become contrite and tender.

Moreover, as fire refines and purifies by separating the dross from the gold, so also is it with the Spirit. He is the great and gracious Refiner, and purifies the soul, and makes it meet for the inheritance of the saints in light. Accordingly, it is ever found that the more we get filled with the Spirit, the more we get free from corruption.

And this purity is ever associated with peace and joy; for as fire imparts warmth and glow, so does the blessed Comforter. He kindles in the soul a zeal, and love, and gladsome hope that are ever precious in themselves, glorifying to God, and helpful to the world.

As we thus owe so much in every way to the Holy Spirit, we must constantly see to it that what he kindles we do not quench, either by worldliness and unbelief or heedless neglect. And we can only succeed in this by much watchfulness on the one hand, and much prayerfulness on the other. 'If we consider,' says Thomas Boston, 'that our hearts are like wet timber, which is unfit for keeping fire, and that there are so many temptations, like rain from the clouds, we will soon see that there is no keeping the fire in if we give over watching.' 'Walk with God,' he adds, 'as if men's eyes were on you, and with men as having God's eyes on you.'

Quench not the Spirit.—1 Thess. 5:19.

Grieve not the holy Spirit of God, whereby ye are sealed unto the day of redemption.—Eph. 4:30.

My spirit shall not always strive with man.—Gen. 6:3.

January 22

SICKNESS AND SIN.

THOUGH all sin is more or less a fruit of transgression, it would yet be a grievous error to suppose that in every case special sickness is traceable to special sin, and is only laid upon sinners, but never upon saints. Such views find no countenance either in the teachings or facts of Scripture. We are told of Epaphroditus that 'he was sick nigh unto death'; yet, instead of being a noted sinner, he was an eminent saint, whose praise was in all the churches, and of whom Paul said, 'Receive him therefore with all gladness, and hold such in reputation.' We see the same thing in the touching message sent by the sisters of Bethany when their brother Lazarus was at the point of death: 'Lord,' they said, 'he whom thou lovest is sick.'

It would preserve us from this error if we would keep in mind that meanwhile we are under a dispensation of grace, one happy effect of which is, that everything is made to work together for good to those who love the Lord,—the dark and the bright alike, the bitter and the sweet, losses and gains, joys and sorrows, health and sickness. Instead, therefore, of fretting and fearing when affliction comes, true believers are enabled to be submissive and trustful; just because, in spite of all its present grievousness, they regard it, not as a judicial infliction, but as a fatherly chastening and blessed privilege of adoption.

A good and faithful preacher of the word was once lying dangerously ill, and the members of his church were praying earnestly at his bedside that the Lord would raise him up and preserve him unto them. In doing so, they made mention, among other things, of his tender watchfulness in feeding the lambs of the flock, and used the expression, 'Lord, thou knowest how he loves thee.' At this the sick man turned to them, and said, 'Ah, children, do not pray thus! When Mary and Martha sent to Jesus, their message was not, "Lord, he who loveth thee is sick," but, "he whom thou lovest." It is not my imperfect love to him that gives me comfort, but his perfect love to me. "There is no fear in love; but perfect love casteth out fear."'

Plainly, it is not always the worst who are most afflicted, but often the very best, in tenderest love, and for the most gracious ends. The sickness in the outer man tends to give health to the inner, and make that matter of blessed experience which had been before only matter of faith.

> When Jesus heard that, he said, This sickness is not unto death, but for the glory of God, that the Son of God might be glorified thereby.—JOHN 11:4.

> Suppose ye that these Galilaeans were sinners above all the Galilaeans, because they suffered such things? I tell you, Nay: but, except ye repent, ye shall all likewise perish.—LUKE 13:2, 3.

JANUARY 23

HE IS BEYOND MEASURE RICH WHO CAN SAY, 'MY GOD.'

ONE of the things that give peculiar sweetness to the promise, 'My God shall supply all your need according to his riches in glory by Christ Jesus,' is the 'my' with which it begins. It is not said,

'God,' or the 'great God,' or the 'gracious God' shall supply, but, 'my God' shall do it. Before his conversion, the apostle could not in sincerity and truth have so spoken. But it was altogether different after it. His whole relationship became changed, for, having obtained mercy through Jesus Christ, the condemnation without and the alienation within were completely gone, and therefore, like Thomas, he could now say from the very heart, 'My Lord and my God!' Having now a soul-satisfying possession of unlimited fulness, mere outward troubles were never allowed to disturb his peace. In every varying circumstance he could still, as it were, say,—

> *These surface-troublings come and go,*
> *Like rufflings of the sea;*
> *The deeper depth is out of reach*
> *To all, my God, but thee.*

This was Paul's experience; and as it may be ours also, none should be content without it. We do not say that such an assured and appropriating faith is absolutely essential to salvation; far from it. There have often been timid, trembling ones in the church of Christ, 'bruised reeds,' who, in speaking of their God, would fain say 'my,' but are afraid to say it, and who consequently go on their way with saddened heart and weeping eye; but they are God's jewels notwithstanding, and shall yet sit down with Abraham, and Isaac, and Jacob in the kingdom of heaven. But though not indispensable to safety, such an assured hope is yet so essential in many respects to strength, and joy, and blessed usefulness, that we are ever urged to give all diligence to secure it.

When Dr Fisher, bishop of Rochester, came out of the Tower of London, and saw the scaffold on which he was to be beheaded, he took out of his pocket a Greek Testament, and, looking up to heaven, he exclaimed, 'Now, O Lord, direct me to some passage which may support me through this awful scene.' He opened the book, and his eye glanced on the text, 'This is life eternal, to know thee the only true God, and Jesus Christ, whom thou hast sent.' He instantly closed the book, and said, 'Praised be the Lord! this is sufficient for me and for eternity.'

O God, thou art my God; early will I seek thee: my soul thirsteth for thee, my flesh longeth for thee in a dry and thirsty land, where no water is.—Psa. 63:1.

The Lord is my rock, and my fortress, and my deliverer; my God, my strength, in whom I will trust.—Psa. 18:2.

JANUARY 24

THE TRUE SECRET OF STRENGTH.

IT was one of the marked peculiarities of Samson's history to have his birth announced beforehand by an angel of the Lord: 'Lo, thou shalt conceive, and bear a son; and no razor shall come on his head: for the child shall be a Nazarite unto God from the womb: and he shall begin to deliver Israel out of the hand of the Philistines.' He was thus from his very birth consecrated to the Lord for worship and service; and in all likelihood this consecration, in the beginning, at least, was inward in part as well as outward. When reading and thinking of his marvellous exploits, we almost instinctively invest him in our minds with the outward characteristics of some mighty son of Anak, for this seems the readiest and easiest way of accounting for his mighty deeds.

In judging thus, however, we miss entirely the real secret of his strength, which lay, not in the mere shape or build of his physical frame, but in the helpful presence of his God. It is not from mere uncertain inference we gather this, but from express declaration. Thus it is written: 'The Spirit of the Lord began to move him at times in the camp of Dan'; 'The Spirit of the Lord came mightily upon him, and the cords that were upon his arms became as flax that was burnt with fire.' It is plain from this that he was a mighty man mainly because he was a consecrated Nazarite, set apart for God's service, and relying on God's help.

So is it more or less still. If we are to be spiritually vigorous and helpful, we must be heartily the Lord's, and thoroughly consecrated. So long as we thus feel and act God will be with us, and make gracious use of us. Though in ourselves utterly feeble, and in the world's eyes, it may be, the very weakest of weaklings, yet united to the Lord, on whom we lean, we become giants in spiritual might, and can remove mountains.

Blessed are they who can so trust the Lord. 'With men,' says Bishop Hall, 'it is a good rule to try first, and then trust; with God it is the contrary. I will first trust him as most wise, omnipotent, merciful, and try him afterwards. It is as impossible for him to deceive me as not to be.'

If a man therefore purge himself from these, he shall be a vessel unto honour, sanctified, and meet for the master's use, and prepared unto every good work.—2 TIM. 2:21.

Be strong in the Lord, and in the power of his might.—EPH. 6:10.

I can do all things through Christ which strengtheneth me.—PHIL. 4:13.

JANUARY 25

HOPEFUL THIRST.

THERE is an inward want in all men which is ever prompting the cry, 'Who will shew us any good?' They themselves may be unable to define this craving, but it exists, and is inseparable from their very nature. It characterises the worst no less than the best of men; even when they are breaking through every restraint, and violating every law, the one main thing ever stimulating to this is a burning thirst for imagined happiness.

But besides this thirst which all feel, there is a thirst of another kind peculiar to the awakened. Having their eyes opened in some degree, they not only see the world's emptiness and insufficiency, but realise the existence of something truer and better, which if possessed would forever satisfy their every longing. It is, therefore, life they now long for, more than pleasure—a place in the kingdom, more than social elevation or evanescent glory. A thirst like this is always hopeful and full of interest, because it is so usually a near precursor of blessing. It is like the refreshing greenery occasionally met with in the desert, and which is ever the gladdening token to the weary traveller that water is near. Of all such thirsters it may be emphatically said, 'They are not far from the kingdom.'

But there is another thirst still, which is peculiar to those who have already found pardon and acceptance through the blood of the Lamb. It mainly consists in an intense and continuous longing for a fuller knowledge of God, and a closer intimacy with him, and a more entire conformity to his mind and will. It is of this thirst our Lord speaks when he says, 'Blessed are they who hunger and thirst after righteousness, for they shall be filled'; and, generally speaking, its intensity in believers is in proportion to their growth in grace. 'The next best thing to living in the light of the Lord's countenance,' says one, 'is to be unhappy till we have it, and to pant hourly after it.'

> As the hart panteth after the water brooks, so panteth my soul after thee, O God. My soul thirsteth for God, for the living God: when shall I come and appear before God?—Psa. 42:1, 2.
>
> Oh that I knew where I might find him! that I might come even to his seat!—Job 23:3.
>
> My soul longeth, yea, even fainteth for the courts of the Lord: my heart and my flesh crieth out for the living God.—Psa. 84:2.

JANUARY 26

THOUGH WE KNOW LITTLE, OUR LOVING LORD KNOWS ALL.

IF we are made sure of anything it is of this, that as nothing is too hard for the Lord Jesus, so nothing can be hid from him: 'He knoweth all things.' This great fact of our Lord's omniscience is one of no ordinary weight and impressiveness, especially when linked in our thoughts with human responsibility and the great day of account, of which again and again such decisive mention is made in utterances like these: 'We must all appear before the judgment seat of Christ; that every one may receive the things done in his body, according to that he hath done, whether it be good or bad.' 'And I saw the dead, small and great, stand before God; and the books were opened: and another book was opened, which is the book of life: and the dead were judged out of those things which were written in the books, according to their works.' Being omniscient, the Judge will know the secrets of every soul, and none can void the summons that calls to his judgment-seat.

There is peculiar solemnity in this thought, and it may well prove powerfully operative in preserving from sin, and in stimulating to duty. But there is also peculiar sweetness in it, especially in seasons of bitter reproach and persecution, when men say all manner of evil against us falsely for Christ's sake. Looking up at such times, and appealing from the erring creature to the unerring Lord, maligned believers can calmly and trustfully say, 'The world misjudges, but thou, Lord, knowest all things.'

This was many a time a precious and sustaining comfort to Paul. Every evil thing was said of him. He was denounced as a ringleader of the sect of the Nazarenes, a pestilent fellow, a mover of sedition, a rebel against Caesar, and therefore in every way worthy of death. But such falsehoods did not disturb him. On the contrary, with the most blessed calmness he simply said, 'With me it is a very small thing that I should be judged of you, or of man's judgment (yea, I judge not mine own self ... but he that judgeth me is the Lord). Therefore judge nothing before the time, until the Lord come, who both will bring to light the hidden things of darkness, and will make manifest the counsels of the heart: and then shall every man have praise of God.'

In the year 1660, Samuel Rutherford, after being deposed from all his offices, was summoned to answer at next Parliament on a charge of high treason. But it was too late; he was already on his death-bed, and on hearing of the charge, calmly remarked that he had got another summons before a superior Judge and judicatory, and sent the message: 'I behove to answer my first summons, and ere your day arrive I will be where few kings and great folks come.' Soon after, he fell sweetly asleep in Jesus.

Thine eyes are open upon all the ways of the sons of men: to give
every one according to his ways, and according to the fruit of his
doings.—JER. 32:19.

All the churches shall know that I am he which searcheth the reins
and hearts: and I will give unto every one of you according to
your works.—REV. 2:23.

JANUARY 27

TO BE UNFORGIVING IS TO BE UNFORGIVEN.

WE are told that when the woman who was a sinner found
mercy of the Lord, she loved much because she had much
forgiven. So is it, to a greater or less extent, with all who through
faith become the blessed recipients of pardoning mercy. The
fulness and tenderness of it not only completely overcome them
for the time, but make them loving, tender, and forgiving in turn.
This should be the spirit of all who bear the Christian name. Our
Lord enjoins it, and expects it; and, as the parable shows, when it is
wanting he utters words of sternest rebuke: 'O thou wicked servant,
I forgave thee all that debt, because thou desiredst me: shouldest
thou not also have had compassion on thy fellow-servant, even as I
had pity on thee?' Then follows the weighty utterance: 'So likewise
shall my heavenly Father do also unto you, if ye from your hearts
forgive not every one his brother their trespasses.'

The true experience of forgiveness, and a readiness to exercise
it, cannot be separated. Indeed, deliberately and continuously to
refuse forgiveness is, as one has expressed it, 'to break the bridge
over which he himself must pass, and provoke the wrath both of
heaven and earth.' When the Governor of Georgia said in a passion
to Mr Wesley, 'That vile servant of mine misbehaves, though he
knows I never forgive'; then said Mr Wesley, 'I hope you never
sin.' The ready and skilful reproof overcame the angry governor.
Indeed, the worst of men do not so much need *our* forgiveness,
as the best of men need the forgiveness of God. Truly, then, it ill

becomes those who are daily needing forgiveness to be persistently slow in the forgiving of others; all the more if they profess to be followers of him who pleaded for his very murderers and said with his latest breath, 'Father, forgive them; for they know not what they do.' They, more than any others, should ever strive to remember and exemplify these brief counsels—*Bear, Forbear, and Forgive.*

Forgive us our debts, as we forgive our debtors.—MATT. 6:12.

Be ye kind one to another, tenderhearted, forgiving one another, even as God for Christ's sake hath forgiven you.—EPH. 4:32.

Put off anger, wrath, malice ... forbearing one another, and forgiving one another, if any man have a quarrel against any: even as Christ forgave you, so also do ye.—COL. 3:8, 13.

JANUARY 28

THE PERFECT LOVE.

WE are so familiar with the statement of God's love to men that it scarcely strikes us as at all remarkable; yet, when thoughtfully and believingly considered, nothing is more wonderful. Had we remained unfallen and pure, like the angels before the throne, a warm and complacent kindness on his part might not have seemed strange; but our condition being the very reverse of all this—fallen, alienated, depraved, and utterly repellent to affection, instead of attractive—we may well marvel at the grace of it, and say, 'Behold what manner of love the Father hath bestowed upon us.'

Usually in creature affection there is something in the objects of it to call it forth. But there was nothing of this kind in our case; for we are expressly told over and over again that it was when we were enemies and ungodly, unloving and unlovable, that God showed his love to us. Now, it is of this love, and not of ours, that John speaks when he says, 'Perfect love casteth out fear.' It would be poor comfort to tell us that if we loved God perfectly, with all our heart and strength and mind, this would cast out fear; for how can we either kindle or sustain in our souls a love like this? The thing is utterly beyond us. But as one has sweetly said—'The Father is the Perfect One: his knowledge is perfect knowledge, his power is perfect power, and his love is perfect love; and just as the sunbeams cast out the darkness wherever they fall, so does this love cast out fear.'

We cannot say of any saint, however eminent, that he is 'love'; we cannot say that even of John, the most loved and loving of the Twelve. But John emphatically says this of God—'God is love; and he that dwelleth in love dwelleth in God, and God in him.'

Not only so: but in all the unfoldings of it, from first to last, God's love is seen to be, not merely forgiving and tender and full of sympathy, but without variableness or shadow of turning; for his own gracious assurance is—'The mountains shall depart, and the hills be removed; but my kindness shall not depart from thee, neither shall the covenant of my peace be removed, saith the Lord that hath mercy on thee.'

Nay, more: besides setting forth his love, he longs that we should fully open our hearts for the reception and enjoyment of it. 'I have declared unto them,' said our Lord, 'thy name, and will declare it: that the love wherewith thou hast loved me may be in them, and I in them.' 'O that Christ,' said a saintly man, 'would but open up the infinite plies and windings of his soul-delighting love, and give me leave to stand beside it, to get my fill of wondering as a preface to my fill of enjoying!'

> That ye may be able to comprehend with all saints what is the breadth, and length, and depth, and height; and to know the love of Christ, which passeth knowledge.—Eph. 3:18, 19.

> But God, who is rich in mercy, for his great love wherewith he loved us, even when we were dead in sins, hath quickened us together with Christ, (by grace ye are saved).—Eph. 2:4, 5.

JANUARY 29

NO KING REWARDS THE LOYAL LIKE CHRIST.

IF, in ordinary circumstances, none are so poor as to be unable to present to the needy a cup of cold water; on the other hand, scarcely any are so rich as to gift away a crown. So great is the power of the Lord Jesus, however, and so unbounded his resources, that he makes promise of crowns to those who loyally serve him more freely than we can make promise of the commonest things. 'Christ,' says Thomas Brooks, 'is a noble and liberal paymaster, and no small things can fall from so great a hand as his is.' Moreover, his love being as infinite as his power, he not merely can do this, but in the fulness of time *will* do it; for to each individual believer his word is this: 'Be thou faithful unto death, and *I will give thee a crown of life.*' This crown has many notable peculiarities.

First of all, it is a purchased crown. Before the Redeemer could confer it on his people, he had first to win it for them, by himself wearing a crown of thorns, and dying a death of agony: this of itself will ever give to it an unspeakable preciousness in their eyes.

Further, it is a crown that will never sadden the wearer. Usually on earth a crown brings so many cares and anxieties with it, that the emblem of King Henry the Seventh was deemed a fitting one—'A crown in a bush of thorns'; and the poet's saying has passed into a proverb, 'Uneasy lies the head that wears a crown.' But it is not so with the crown of life. The moment it is put upon the head, sorrow and sighing will flee forever away; and thus, for gladness and rejoicing, the final crowning day will be the very day of days to all the redeemed.

Again, it is a crown that never fades. In ancient times crowns were frequently given as rewards to those who excelled in racing or wrestling; and they were prized so highly, that there was scarcely anything men would not do or endure to obtain them. Yet, at the best, they were nothing more than mere fading wreaths of laurel or of pine. But the crown the Lord holds out in promise never fades;

for, being a crown of life, it is as imperishable in its nature as in the end will be the redeemed who wear it.

Nor can they ever be despoiled of it. In a world of change like ours, we can count securely on nothing; even crowns and king-doms here are often lost just like other things. But, happily, come what may, believers can never lose their crown, for it is to be worn where enemies never enter, and revolutions are unknown, and love and joy unutterable glow in every heart. Verily, then, what manner of persons ought believers now to be in all holy conversation and godliness? 'Oh, thrice fools are we,' said one, 'who, like new-born princes in the cradle, know not that there is a kingdom before them!'

> I have fought a good fight, I have finished my course, I have kept the faith: Henceforth there is laid up for me a crown of right-eousness, which the Lord, the righteous judge, shall give me at that day: and not to me only, but unto all them also that love his appearing.—2 TIM. 4:7, 8.

> When the chief Shepherd shall appear, ye shall receive a crown of glory that fadeth not away.—1 PET. 5:4.

JANUARY 30

SHALL WE KNOW EACH OTHER IN HEAVEN?

WHATEVER doubts some may have as to saints knowing each other in heaven, Paul seemingly had none; for had he not confidently expected in the future a full and mutual recog-nition, it is hard to see how he could reasonably have said to the Thessalonians, 'What is our hope, or joy, or crown of rejoicing? *Are not even ye* in the presence of our Lord Jesus Christ at his coming?' He knew them well on earth, and loved them warmly, for they were his own spiritual children, and it would be strange beyond measure if this gladdening knowledge were to be limited exclusively to time; and all the more, as in the nature of things a lessened knowledge in the future would lead to a lessened interest and lessened delight and joy now. 'I am fully persuaded,' said Richard Baxter, 'that I shall love my friends, and therefore know them. And this principally binds me to them on earth. And if I thought that I should never know them more, nor therefore love them, after death, I should love them comparatively little, as I do all other transitory things. But I now delight in conversing with them, as believing I shall commune with them forever.'

Being social in our nature, if we did not know each other in heaven, some of the great elements of perfect happiness would be entirely wanting. It would imply an unnatural isolation, wholly foreign to all that is revealed of the blessedness of our eternal home. Indeed, our whole being craves for such recognition; and on this account, when a beloved relative is seriously ill, there are few things more trying to our feelings than his inability, through failing powers, to recognise us, or to make it manifest that he does so.

Besides, as the Redeemer expressly says, 'I *know* my sheep, and am *known* of mine'; and as this knowledge is mutual and loving, and will ever be growing intenser and fuller through all eternity, we may reasonably infer that what is true in their case will be true of the whole family of the redeemed, and that, instead of knowing each other less in heaven, they will know and love each other immeasurably more. In truth, it seems next to inconceivable that Peter, James, and John, who knew Moses and Elias on the Mount of Transfiguration, should yet fail to know each other in the city of the Great King, or that Paul and Timothy, so lovingly united on earth, should be wholly unknown to each other in heaven.

Just before his death, Dr Emmons said: 'I want to go to heaven; I want to see the old prophets, Isaiah, Daniel, Elijah, and also the apostles; but I want to see Paul more than any other man I can think of.' 'There are others of us,' says Dr Cuyler, 'who will go far to get a glimpse of the author of the eighth chapter of the Romans.' And he adds: 'What a thrill will the meetings and the greetings in the world of glory send through our souls, when we shall rush toward each other in the glow of heavenly love!' Coming forth

> *From this dark world of tears,*
> *From earthly bonds and fears,*

each believer may say,—

> *I go to see his glory*
> *Whom we have loved below;*
> *I go the blessed angels,*
> *The holy saints to know.*
> *Our lovely ones departed*
> *I go to find again;*
> *And wait for you to join us:*
> *Good-night till then.*

Now we see through a glass, darkly; but then face to face: now I know in part; but then shall I know even as also I am known.— 1 Cor. 13:12.

I would not have you to be ignorant, brethren, concerning them which are asleep, that ye sorrow not, even as others which have no hope. For if we believe that Jesus died and rose again, even so them also which sleep in Jesus will God bring with him. Wherefore comfort one another with these words.—1 Thess. 4:13, 14, 18.

JANUARY 31

THE BIBLE OF OUR LORD.

WHATEVER may be the world's thoughts regarding Christ, all true Christians, on grounds that cannot be shaken, believe him to be the Son of God, and therefore so infinitely wise and holy that he can neither sin nor err. Doubtless it is utter mockery to ascribe infallibility to any man, however exalted, or to any church on earth, however pure; but it cannot be so to ascribe it to him in whom dwelleth all the fulness of the Godhead bodily. In his case it is an absolutely essential attribute of his divine nature, and Scripture uniformly speaks of it as such. It is thus written: 'He whom God hath sent *speaketh the words of God*: for God giveth not the Spirit by measure unto him.' And our Lord himself said: 'As my Father hath taught me, I speak these things'; and, 'I do always those things that please him.' His every utterance, therefore, is divinely true, because ever in complete harmony with the mind of the Father, and with his own exalted claim, 'I am the light of the world.' On this account believing men rely with absolute confidence, not on his power only, but also on the certainty of his every word and testimony, and would deem themselves guilty of God-dishonouring unbelief if they did otherwise. Indeed, the very thought of charging their divine Lord and Saviour—who is dearer to them than life, in whom their every hope centres, and before whose judgment-seat all must appear—with jot or tittle of sin or error is utterly abhorrent to them.

On this account, in spite of the intensified scepticism of modern times, the simple fact of our Lord's testimony to the truth of the sacred record gives them an assuredness of trust in the Book of books which nothing can disturb. If he, the Son of God, believed the Bible, how can they doubt it?—all the more as their Bible was also their Lord's Bible—the very Bible which he himself used and expounded and ever appealed to as a decisive authority. Whether quoting from the law or from the prophets, 'It is written' was ever final with him. Indeed, the absolute and enduring certainty he ascribed to his own words he invariably ascribed also to the words of Scripture, and declared them to be all-sufficient. 'If they believe not Moses and the prophets, neither will they be persuaded though one rose from the dead.'

Many now begin to speak as if the varied narratives in the Pentateuch—of the Fall, the Deluge, the call of Abraham, the brazen serpent, the smitten rock, the manna in the desert—were opposed to the ascertained facts of science and historic probability, and must therefore be mere myths and fables. Such statements in no degree influence believers, not merely because even on scientific and historic grounds they deem them wholly unwarranted, as *perfected* investigation, they doubt not, will clearly show, but specially because the Son of God, the Truth, the Life, who cannot err and cannot lie, expressly and emphatically *authenticates* them all by ever referring to them as *undeniable historic facts*. Speaking of the Deluge, he says: '*As the days of Noe were*, so shall also the coming of the Son of man be. For as in the days that were *before the flood* they were eating and drinking, marrying and giving in marriage, *until the day that Noe entered into the ark*, and knew not until the flood came, and took them all away; so shall also the coming of the Son of man be.' Speaking of the manna, he said: '*Your fathers did eat manna in the wilderness*, and are dead … I am the living bread which came down from heaven.' Once more, speaking of the brazen serpent, he says: '*As Moses lifted up the serpent in the wilderness*, even so must the Son of man be lifted up.'

Indeed, all the great events recorded in the Pentateuch, from the beginning of Genesis to the end of the wilderness journey, are mentioned by our Lord, and authenticated *as facts*. Nay more, our Lord, as Dr Porter forcibly puts it, not only attests their reality, but he weaves them up in his grand scheme of doctrine, thus uniting type with antitype and shadow with substance—so blending, in fact, the law and the gospel, the history in the Pentateuch and the doctrines of Christianity, that we cannot possibly reject the one without rejecting the other.

There is thus every reason for holding fast the faith, and not one for letting it go; and therefore, though for a time the whole world were to abandon it, we must, for the honour of our Lord and our own salvation, resolutely cling to it, even unto death. We should do this all the more confidently, because the views and speculations of men are ever varying from age to age, and occasionally to such a degree that what with almost all men of science is *certain truth* one year, and emphatically declared to be such, may through some fresh discovery or new theory be *despised error* with them the next; whereas the word of the Lord standeth forever. Accordingly, enlightened Christian men, instead of fearing science and discovery, and the widest extension of knowledge in every department, cordially welcome them for the beneficent service they render, and the fuller light they are sure to bring: all the more because the God of nature and the God of revelation being one and the same, they feel thoroughly assured that, in spite of all appearances or boastings, or even for a season seemingly general consent to the contrary, not a single fact of science *fully ascertained* will ever *in the end* be proved to be in opposition to a single statement of Scripture *rightly interpreted*. 'To ask a believer,' said the saintly Leighton, 'How know you the Scriptures to be divine? is the same as to ask him, How know you light to be light? He feels as sure of it as of his own existence.'

> Lord, to whom shall we go? thou hast the words of eternal life. And we believe and are sure that thou art that Christ, the Son of the living God.—JOHN 6:68, 69.

> All flesh is as grass, and all the glory of man as the flower of grass. The grass withereth, and the flower thereof falleth away: but the word of the Lord endureth for ever.—1 PET. 1:24, 25.

FEBRUARY 1

THE HEALER AND THE HEALED.

IT is said of Jesus that they 'brought unto him all that were diseased; and besought him that they might only touch the hem of his garment: and as many as touched him were made perfectly whole.' It is instructive to note here that it was not as many as were nigh Christ who were made whole, nor as many as heard and admired him; for mere outward nearness availed nothing, and multitudes freely declared, 'Never man spake like this man'—'He hath done all things well,' who yet continued strangers to his healing power.

The real statement of the sacred historian is this, and nothing could be more cheering: '*As many as touched him* were made perfectly whole.' Of these, it may be, some might only touch feebly, others tremblingly, and even perhaps stealthily; nevertheless, if they had but faith to touch at all, the healing virtue came flowing out to them. Even so is it in the salvation of the soul. Everything depends on the touch or look of faith; and as the dimmest eye that ever looked at the brazen serpent found healing, so the feeblest touch of faith draws forth from Christ life everlasting.

> *'Tis knowing thee that heals,*
> *'Tis seeing thee that seals*
> *Comfort and peace;*
> *Show me thy cross and blood,*
> *My Saviour and my God,*
> *Then troubles cease.*

We see this touching in faith strikingly exemplified in the woman who had an issue of blood. Hearing of Jesus, and needing him, she came in the crowd behind and touched his garment; for she said, 'If I but touch his clothes, I shall be whole.' And immediately, it is added, 'she felt in her body that she was healed of that plague.' The sequel is full of interest. Jesus, knowing that virtue had gone out of him, turned round and said, 'Who touched me?' It was not because he was ignorant of the hand that touched, or grudged the healing virtue thereby drawn forth, that he so questioned, but simply because hidden faith must come to light, not for the glory of the Lord only, but also for its own confirmation and for the encouragement of others. There was need of open confession, as well as real faith; and as soon as she learned this great lesson, he immediately and tenderly calmed her fears by adding, 'Daughter, thy faith hath made thee whole; go in peace, and be whole of thy plague.'

Jesus seeing their faith said unto the sick of the palsy; Son, be of good cheer; thy sins be forgiven thee.—MATT. 9:2.

O woman, great is thy faith: be it unto thee even as thou wilt. And her daughter was made whole from that very hour.—MATT. 15:28.

FEBRUARY 2

THEY ARE BLESSED WHO CAN SAY, 'WE HAVE HEARD HIM OURSELVES.'

THE heart is never selfish that is truly filled with grace. What it itself enjoys, it longs to share with others, and says with eager interest to all, 'O taste and see that the Lord is good.' Before the woman of Samaria met the Lord at Jacob's well, it was for herself only she cared, and the perishable things of time. No sooner, however, did she receive from the hands of Jesus the first draught of the water of life, than she so rejoiced in the gift, and so intensely desired to share it with others, that forthwith she said to everyone she met, 'Come, see a man which told me all things that ever I did: is not this the Christ?' Her loving effort was not in vain, for many in Sychar, through giving heed to her words, soon obtained a like blessed experience, and were able to respond: 'Now we believe, not because of thy saying: *for we have heard him ourselves, and know* that this is indeed the Christ, the Saviour of the world.'

This was knowing religion experimentally, and as in no other way can it be known truly, none should ever be satisfied with anything short of it; for till our convictions rest on direct and personal knowledge, they have neither intensity nor strength, and never result in blessed assuredness. It is here where so many fail. Anything they know about Christ is from the testimony of others only. In spite of all his invitations, precious and loving though they be, they never make direct and personal application to him, or in real faith commit their souls to his gracious keeping. Yet till this is done, however near they may be to the great Fountain, they can never really taste of the living water. What is needed in any case is to hear Christ ourselves, to make personal trial of his goodness and grace, and to take him at his word when he says, 'If any man thirst, let him come unto me and drink.' He who, having so come, has an experimental knowledge of the Lord, with peace of conscience, renewal of nature, and an assured hope of a blissful immortality, is never shaken even by the subtlest of sceptical assaults, however much he may be grieved by them.

'If it please God,' says Dr Dykes, 'to grant to our age ample demonstration, *through the actual experience of many living men*, that regeneration is a possibility and prayer a power, and the gospel of pardon through Christ crucified an answer to the deepest requirements of conscience, then indeed not only shall the tide of unbelief be on the ebb, but a tide of returning faith will have begun to flow.'

> Come and hear, all ye that fear God, and I will declare what he hath done for my soul.—Psa. 66:16.

> We cannot but speak the things which we have seen and heard.—Acts 4:20.

> How excellent is thy lovingkindness, O God! Therefore the children of men put their trust under the shadow of thy wings.—Psa. 36:7.

February 3

*NONE BUT THE TWICE-BORN ENTER
THE KINGDOM.*

THOUGH Nicodemus was a master in Israel, he could form no conception of what our Lord meant when he declared, 'Except a man be born again, he cannot see the kingdom of God.' Had it been simply said, 'Except a man be baptized, or educated, or reformed, he cannot see the kingdom,' he could have understood it; but the need to be born again was such a mystery to him, that he asked, in utter amazement, 'How can a man be born when he is old? can he enter the second time into his mother's womb, and be born?' The regeneration that was so mysterious to him then, is mysterious to multitudes still; nevertheless, nothing less thorough can ever meet the necessities of our case. 'That which is born of the flesh is flesh,' says our Lord; and the flesh, treat it and improve it as we may, is flesh still, and never can be anything else. A new nature, therefore, and a new life are absolutely essential. This is not a may be, but a *must be*. 'Marvel not that I said unto thee, Ye *must* be born again.' As sinners, we require not to do something new only, but, first of all, ourselves to become new; for, as one says, 'It is not merely the bad fruit of our sinful life, but it is also the rotten tree of our corrupt nature, which shuts us out from his kingdom.'

But how is this great change to be accomplished? It is wrought by the Spirit of God, through our coming to Christ in simple faith. As the looking of old to the brazen serpent at once brought healing to the wounded Israelite, so the very looking in faith to Christ invariably brings regenerating influence. Faith and the new birth are absolutely simultaneous. The instant a man is born again, he believes; the instant he believes, he is born again. 'Believing is our side of the matter, while the new birth is the work of God alone; and, therefore, what we have to do is to receive and believe in Christ.' When this is done, the Lord admits us at once to the position of sons of God; for it is expressly said: 'As many as received him, to them gave he power to become the sons of God, even *to them that believe on his name*: which were born, not of blood, nor of the will of the flesh, nor of the will of man, but of God.'

Dr Leifchild tells how, on one occasion, he met a poor lad, eleven or twelve years of age, with a New Testament in his hand. On being asked, 'Can you read?' he answered, 'To be sure I can.' Turning to these words in the third chapter of John, 'Except a man be born again, he cannot see the kingdom of God,'—'What is that?' it was asked. 'It means,' he promptly replied, 'a great change'; and repeated the words, 'Except a man be born again, he cannot see the kingdom of God.' 'And what is that kingdom?' He paused, and, with an expression of seriousness and devotion, placing his hand upon his bosom, he said, 'It is something here,' and then, raising his eyes, he added, 'and something up yonder.'

> For in Christ Jesus neither circumcision availeth any thing, nor uncircumcision, but a new creature.—GAL. 6:15.
>
> Verily I say unto you, Except ye be converted, and become as little children, ye shall not enter into the kingdom of heaven.—MATT. 18:3.

FEBRUARY 4

THE FOLLY OF THE FOOLISH.

I N the parable we are told that while some of the virgins were
wise, others of them were foolish. For a time, apparently, the
latter were not known to be foolish. Nor was it easy at first to
discover the fact; for were they not named alike?—all were virgins;
and dressed alike?—all wore the same bright festal robes; and
provided alike?—all had lamps in their hand; and, moreover, did
they not purpose alike?—for all went out professedly to meet the
bridegroom. Nevertheless, of the ten virgins who went out, no less
than five were foolish. Their folly appeared in this: they provided
everything but the main thing. Each of them had a lamp and
a vessel; and this, so far as it went, was well. But here was their
error—they were so satisfied with the mere possession of a lamp,
as wholly to forget the all-essential oil, without which their lamp
would go out when most it was needed.

Now, there is no singularity in this folly, for to this day we see
the same thing on every side. The lamp symbolises a Christian
profession; and this, doubtless, is not desirable only, but needful.
But the fatal mistake of many is, that they think of nothing but
the profession—the mere externalities of religion—the name, the
form, the visible rite, or, at most, the aesthetic emotion. Thus, with
all their religiousness, they have no religion, no spiritual vitality,
no renewal of nature, and no union to Christ. It is recorded of a
certain Spartan in olden times that he tried hard to make a corpse
stand; but utterly failing to do so, in spite of every effort, he said,
'I see it wants something *within*.' And so is it with those of whom
we speak,—they want something within. They want life and grace,
and the Spirit, and everything of which the oil is the emblem; and
so, sooner or later, when the call comes, being found unready, they
are left in final darkness.

Now, it is all-important to remember, that to get the something
needed within, we must look to something provided without.

'Look unto me,' saith the Lord, 'all ye ends of the earth, and be saved.' To their grievous loss, many forget this; and so, instead of looking without at Christ, the grand object of faith, they are ever looking within at themselves, to see whether they have yet convictions enough to warrant their coming to him. They thus entirely reverse God's order, which is not, 'Live and look,' but, 'Look and live'; not feeling first, and then faith, but faith first, and then feeling.

> He is not a Jew, which is one outwardly; neither is that circumcision, which is outward in the flesh: but he is a Jew, which is one inwardly; and circumcision is that of the heart, in the spirit, and not in the letter.—ROM. 2:28, 29.

> And as Moses lifted up the serpent in the wilderness, even so must the Son of man be lifted up: that whosoever believeth in him should not perish, but have eternal life.—JOHN 3:14, 15.

FEBRUARY 5

THE FOLLY OF THE WISE.

THOUGH there was a marked difference between the wise virgins and the foolish—for while the latter had lamps only, the former had oil as well, and so were ready to enter in before the door was shut—nevertheless, even they too, for a time at least, were foolish enough to slumber and sleep, and to need the rebuke, 'Why sleep ye? rise and pray, lest ye enter into temptation.' In this they strikingly typify the spiritual condition of many believers who are wise only in part. Though divinely quickened, and possessed of real oil, the Spirit of God, yet their works and ways are often such as forcibly to recall our Lord's words,—'The children of this world are wiser in their generation than the children of light.' They are neither so wakeful nor so prayerful as they might be; and so, through the wiles of the ever-sleepless adversary, they are often taken unawares, and thereby their graces lose their brightness, and once forsaken sins almost regain the mastery.

When Legh Richmond, one of the most devoted of men, was nearing his end, he had such realising views of eternal realities, and of the need of doing with utmost might what the hand findeth to do, that he said to a ministerial friend, 'Brother, we are only half awake.' It was a weighty utterance, and one well fitted to rouse the slumbering soul to more earnest thought and energetic action. This serious defect was strikingly exemplified in the case of Lot. He was wise unto salvation, and righteous; but had not folly largely mingled with his wisdom, he would not have gone so readily to Sodom, or have tarried so long in it, or have so narrowly escaped with his life in coming out of it. So has it often been since. Even the wise go where they should not, and become perilously entangled with the world and the things of it.

'A Christian in the world,' said John Newton, 'should be like a man transacting his affairs in the rain. He will not suddenly leave his client because it rains, but the moment the business is done he is gone; and, as it is said in the Acts, "Being let go, they went to their own company."'

> For it came to pass, when Solomon was old, that his wives turned away his heart after other gods: and his heart was not perfect with the Lord his God, as was the heart of David his father.— 1 KINGS 11:4.

> I will hear what God the Lord will speak: for he will speak peace unto his people, and to his saints: but let them not turn again to folly.—PSA. 85:8.

FEBRUARY 6

WHEN GOD IS FEARED, NO OTHER FEAR NEED BE.

THE words of our blessed Lord have not been unneeded, 'Fear not them which kill the body, but are not able to kill the soul'; for in all ages there has been more or less of persecution for righteousness' sake. 'There has been a killing time,' says one, 'in the experience of most Christian countries: the Waldenses and the Albigenses during the middle ages; the Netherlands under the Duke of Savoy; St Bartholomew's Day in France; England's killing time under Mary; Scotland's under the Stuarts,—its moors blossom with its martyr graves.' Such events, however, in spite of all the severities with which they were mingled, need not dismay us. The very worst that wicked men can do is to kill the body. To a man of the world this may seem much; but to a true believer it is nothing more than a temporary disrobing of him, a little shortening of the pilgrimage, an earlier home-going, an absence from the body, to be forever with the Lord.

Happily, no sword can separate the saint from the Saviour, nor fire consume the cords of love that bind them. 'I am persuaded,' says the apostle, 'that neither death, nor life, nor angels, nor principalities, nor powers, nor things present, nor things to come, nor height, nor depth, nor any other creature, shall be able to separate us from the love of God, which is in Christ Jesus our Lord.'

When Latimer was royal chaplain, he one day exclaimed, 'Thou art going to speak before the high and mighty King Henry the Eighth, who is able, if he thinks fit, to take thy life away. But Latimer, Latimer, remember, also, thou art about to speak before the King of kings and Lord of lords; take heed that thou dost not displease him.'

When in lonely and desolate circumstances a martyr loses his life for righteousness' sake, his end seems a hard one, but it is really blessed, the deepest natural anguish being lost in heavenly joy.

> *Changeful his lot, like yon vexed sky*
> *When moorland breezes wildly blow,*
> *His weary soul now rests on high,*
> *His body sleeps below.*
> *Rest, weary dust, lie here an hour;*
> *Ere long, like blossom from the sod,*
> *Thou shalt come forth a glorious flower,*
> *Fit for the eye of God.*

Fear not them which kill the body, but are not able to kill the soul: but rather fear him which is able to destroy both soul and body in hell.—MATT. 10:28.

Fear none of those things which thou shalt suffer: behold, the devil shall cast some of you into prison, that ye may be tried; and ye shall have tribulation ten days: be thou faithful unto death, and I will give thee a crown of life.—REV. 2:10.

Fear thou not; for I am with thee: be not dismayed; for I am thy God: I will strengthen thee; yea, I will help thee; yea, I will uphold thee with the right hand of my righteousness.—ISA. 41:10.

FEBRUARY 7

SALVATION BY GRACE IS NOT INCONSISTENT WITH VARIETY OF REWARD.

IT is thought by some that because persons and services find acceptance solely in Christ, and in unmerited grace, reward is thereby, in every form of it, necessarily excluded. But this is not the case, and the one great truth is in entire harmony with the other. In the parable, all the labourers received the same sum at the close of the day, though some began early and others late. This, apparently, is designed to show that whatever other differences there may be, yet all who believe in Christ and rest upon him are alike forgiven, alike accepted, alike adopted, and finally saved. Without exception, all of them, whatever their time of call, the first hour or the eleventh, not only enter within the gate, but are warmly welcomed there.

But this *equality* in the great essentials is in no degree inconsistent with the inequality in the reward elsewhere set forth. Indeed we are expressly told that if, through grace, our pound gains five pounds, then rule shall be given us over five cities; and if, through still richer grace, our pound gains ten pounds, then rule shall be given us over ten cities. Yes, the greater the grace, fidelity, and devotedness here, the greater and brighter will be the glory hereafter.

Doubtless, after all they have done, even the holiest and best of men must yet say, and do say it, 'We are unprofitable servants'; but not the less is it expressly written, 'God is not unrighteous to forget your work and labour of love, which ye have shewed toward his name, in that ye have ministered to the saints, and do minister.' The world may forget the services of God's saints, and they themselves, too, may forget them, as is evident from the questions put, 'Lord, when saw we thee an hungred, and fed thee? or thirsty, and gave thee drink?' but the Lord cannot forget them, not merely because they are the blessed product of his own grace, in which he delights, but also because, in nature, purpose, and act, he is so overflowingly generous.

Even in ordinary life, after long years of faithful service, a generous master, in dealing with a trusted servant, never limits himself merely to what bare law or rigid justice might measure out, but often lovingly gives in addition very varied reward. So is it, only in an infinitely higher degree, with our blessed Lord in dealing with his servants; for in spite of all their shortcomings, he is loving and generous to them, beyond the power of words to express.

It has been said, 'What better or sweeter reward can God give us than to keep us faithful, to sustain us to the end, and to shed abroad his love in our hearts?' True, this is a marvellous manifestation of grace; but if, in addition, God has been pleased to hold out further reward, in proportion as his own grace is rightly used for his glory—and this he has emphatically done—who shall say that we have not therein the highest incentive to increased and unreserved devotedness to his service? A military gentlemen once said to an excellent old minister in the north of Scotland, who was becoming infirm, 'Why, if I had power over the pension list, I would actually have you put on half-pay for your long and faithful services.' He replied, 'Ah, my friend, your master may put you off with *half-pay*, but my Master will not serve me so meanly; he will give me full pay. Through grace I expect "a full reward."'

> Behold, I come quickly; and my reward is with me, to give every man according as his work shall be.—Rev. 22:12.

> Rejoice, and be exceeding glad: for great is your reward in heaven: for so persecuted they the prophets which were before you.—MATT. 5:12.

If any man's work abide which he hath built thereupon, he shall receive a reward. If any man's work shall be burned, he shall suffer loss: but he himself shall be saved; yet so as by fire.— 1 Cor. 3:14, 15.

FEBRUARY 8

COMPELLING IN LOVE.

IT is one of the emphatic words of the great Master, 'Go out into the highways and hedges and compel them to come in.' It need scarcely be said that there is no warrant here for the employment of force in the conversion of men. Force may make hypocrites, but it cannot make true and genuine disciples of Jesus Christ. It may compel a profession of faith, but faith itself it can neither implant nor mature. Nay, the more force is used for such an end, the more unbelieving does the soul become, and the harder grows the heart and the more stubborn the will. Plainly, then, the compulsion referred to here is moral and spiritual—that of wise, loving, earnest, and prayerful persuasion. Nevertheless there are weighty reasons to justify the strong language used, 'Compel them to come in.'

One reason may be to remind us of the intense unwillingness to be overcome. When we consider the need of man and the bounty of God, and the fulness of grace and all the marvellous blessings of redeeming love, we might have thought, like young Melanchthon, that no pressing would be required, but that all, as soon as the glad tidings were made known to them, would believe and rejoice. But it is not so, for the unconverted heart, when left to itself, instinctively says, 'Let us alone; what have we to do with thee, Jesus of Nazareth?' As, notwithstanding the certainty of his peril, Lot needed a compelling hand as well as an inviting word, else he would have perished in Sodom, so is it in every case of true conversion. The compulsion of love is indispensable.

Another reason may be to show that no means are to be left untried. When we know that every Christless soul is under the curse, and condemned already, we dare not give them up till every argument, appeal, and earnest effort have finally and unmistakably failed. 'It is a rule I fixed long ago,' said John Wesley, 'never to give up anyone till I had tried him at least ten years.'

In seeking to save others, therefore, we are acting in full conformity with our Father's loving will. Whoever may have pleasure in the death of the sinner, he has not.

> As I live, saith the Lord God, I have no pleasure in the death of the wicked; but that the wicked turn from his way and live: turn ye, turn ye from your evil ways; for why will ye die, O house of Israel?—EZEK. 33:11.

> The Lord is not slack concerning his promise, as some men count slackness; but is longsuffering to us-ward, not willing that any should perish, but that all should come to repentance.—2 PET. 3:9.

FEBRUARY 9

EXCLUDING IN RIGHTEOUSNESS.

MEN sometimes speak as if God were indifferent to the treatment he received, and as if with impunity they could reject both the message and the messenger. The very opposite of this, however, is the case; for though he may bear long with the rebellious and unbelieving, he will not bear always; hence the solemn utterance, 'I say unto you, that none of these men which were bidden shall taste of my supper.'

Now, with regard to the excluded, it is important to note that they were all *bidden men.* The inviting servant had been, as it were, at all their doors; yet, though bidden then, they were forbidden now; though told of the supper, not one tasted it. And why? Just because when they might have come, and ought to have come, and were urged to come, they all with one accord declined to come. This clearly shows that it is not the getting of gospel invitations that saves men, but the accepting them.

But further, the excluded were all *well-intentioned men.* Seemingly, it was not in their thoughts finally and persistently to reject the invitation. They meant only civilly to decline the present call, and to delay accepting it till a more convenient season. It never entered their minds that this call might be the last they would ever receive. Yet so it was, for no other messenger ever knocked at their door, or again invited them to the feast.

So is it with many still. When they refuse to believe in Jesus and to repent, it is not their purpose to do so always. Though they decline this call, they will accept the next; utterly forgetting that the call they are getting now may be their very last. There is nothing more perilous than trusting to another day; all the more, as to be once excluded is to be ever excluded. 'The first Adam,' said an old writer, 'closed the door upon us, but there was a second Adam to open it; but if the second Adam close the door, there is no third Adam to open it.' Therefore delay now may be exclusion forever.

How shall we escape, if we neglect so great salvation?—HEB. 2:3.

See that ye refuse not him that speaketh. For if they escaped not who refused him that spake on earth, much more shall not we escape, if we turn away from him that speaketh from heaven.—HEB. 12:25.

Seeing ye put it from you, and judge yourselves unworthy of everlasting life, lo, we turn to the Gentiles.—ACTS 13:46.

FEBRUARY 10

WHEN WARM TO THE MASTER, OUR LOVE WILL NOT BE COLD TO THE SERVANT.

WE are sometimes tempted to imagine that a believer so dead to the world as Paul, and entirely consecrated, would be but little affected by the temporal supplies sent to him from time to time by the Philippian believers. His grateful words to them, however, in his epistle, clearly show that it was far otherwise. 'Even in Thessalonica,' he said, 'ye sent once and again unto my necessity. I rejoiced greatly that your care of me hath flourished again.' Small as such tokens of kindness might seem, they yet gladdened him greatly, and anew refreshed and strengthened him for his arduous labours.

What specially touched him on such occasions was not so much the gift itself, or its seasonableness, as the pure and elevated motive of those who gave it. It was because love prompted it that he prized it so greatly,—love to the Master, and love to the servant for the Master's sake. Such kindness to the servant is kindness to the Lord, and he remembers it as such, and will one day crown it with open acknowledgment and gracious reward. 'Then shall the righteous answer him, saying, Lord, when saw we thee an hungred, and fed thee? or thirsty, and gave thee drink? When saw we thee a stranger, and took thee in? or naked, and clothed thee? Or when saw we thee sick, or in prison, and came unto thee? And the King shall answer and say onto them, Verily I say unto you, Inasmuch as ye have done it *unto one of the least of these my brethren, ye have done it unto me.* Come, ye blessed of my Father, inherit the kingdom prepared for you from the foundation of the world.'

After telling us of the arrival of himself and his companions at a heathen village on the banks of the Orange River, Dr Moffat says: 'We had travelled far, and were *hungry, and thirsty, and fatigued.* We asked water, but they would not supply it. I offered three or four buttons that still remained on my jacket for a little milk. This also was refused. We had the prospect of another hungry and thirsty night. When twilight drew nigh, a woman approached from the height beyond which the village lay. She bore on her hood a bundle of wood, and had a vessel of milk in her hand. She laid them down, and returned to the village. A second time she approached with other and larger supplies. We asked her again and again who she was. She remained silent, till affectionately entreated to give us a reason for such unlooked-for kindness to strangers. The solitary tear stole down her sable cheek when she replied, "*I love him whose servants ye are; and surely it is my duty to give you a cup of cold water in his name.* My heart is full, therefore I cannot speak the joy I feel to see you in this out-of-the-world place." I asked her how she kept the life of God in her soul, in the absence of all communion with saints. She drew from her bosom a copy of the Dutch New Testament she had received in a school some years before. "This," she said, "is the fountain whence I drink; this the oil which makes my lamp burn."'

Thus does the Lord sustain and gladden the hearts of his servants in their times of need.

> Whosoever shall give you a cup of water to drink in my name, because ye belong to Christ, verily I say unto you, he shall not lose his reward.—MARK 9:41.

> I have shewed you all things, how that so labouring ye ought to support the weak, and to remember the words of the Lord Jesus, how he said, It is more blessed to give than to receive.—ACTS 20:35.

FEBRUARY 11

WITH MANY THE BLOSSOM SEEMS TO COME, BUT NEVER THE FRUIT.

AT this moment, in India, there are thousands of those trained in our great missionary institutions who, from intimate acquaintance with the evidences of Christianity and its fundamental doctrines, are almost persuaded to renounce idolatry, and cast in their lot with the people of God. But there, alas! to the grief of those who are thirsting for their salvation, they deliberately and persistently pause. And why? Not because of lacking evidence, or any remaining doubts, but simply because they shrink from the cross and the shame and persecutions that would follow. They have light enough to be almost persuaded, but not strength enough to be thoroughly decided.

With multitudes in our own land, alas! it is just the same. Their faces seem Zionward, their convictions are frequent, and many an anxious inquiry comes from their lips. But they never get beyond this. They are almost, but never altogether Christians. There is always something they will not give up. Though expressly told that they cannot both close with Christ and continue in sin, they still attempt the impossibility. Some evil things, perhaps, after considerable struggle, they might surrender; but to give up the wedge of gold, the Babylonish garment, or, to speak without figure, to give up besetting and long-cherished sins, would be like rending asunder body and spirit; and rather than consent to such a severance, they go on risking their eternal all.

With others the hindrance is not so much something they will not give up, as something they will not accept, and that something is salvation as a gift—free, full, and absolutely unmerited; and so, when the door is finally shut, it is not within that they are found, but without.

In the life of a tree, one sometimes sees a little ivy shoot gradually entwine itself around the stem. For years they grow together, and the stately tree seems almost to be more luxuriant clad in the green foliage of the ivy. But at length the vital resources of the tree become exhausted; it withers and dies. Many forget that sin is an ivy more fatal still; for what it ruins is an immortal soul. To spare the one is eternally to destroy the other.

> Then Agrippa said unto Paul, Almost thou persuadest me to be a Christian. And Paul said, I would to God, that not only thou, but also all that hear me this day, were both almost, and altogether such as I am, except these bonds.—ACTS 26:28, 29.
>
> Ye cannot serve God and mammon.—MATT. 6:24.
>
> Seek ye the Lord while he may be found, call ye upon him while he is near.—ISA. 55:6.

February 12

IN SPITE OF ITS DARK LOOK, TEMPTATION
OFTEN SERVES A BRIGHT END.

O F the many temptations and trials which beset God's children, some are light and transient in their nature, others severe and prolonged; some are mainly outward in their character, others inward and spiritual; some peculiar to youth, while others belong exclusively to age.

Though often linked together, there is yet a difference between temptation and trial. With the former we invariably associate the idea of incitement to sin, through the wiles of our adversary, but not with the latter. It is true that every trial is in one sense a temptation to murmuring, hard thoughts, and distrust. It is true, besides, that every temptation is a trial of the sincerity of our profession, and the thoroughness of our loyalty to our great Lord and Master. But whatever the difference in these respects, this much can be said of all of them, that though never in themselves joyous, but grievous, they are yet divinely permitted, and can be so graciously overruled as to work together for highest good. Indeed, for a good man anything is good that strips the world of its charms, abases his pride, teaches him the meaning of Scripture, exercises his faith, brightens his hope, and thereby makes him long more ardently for his heavenly home. Accordingly, James, when writing to the twelve tribes scattered abroad, said, 'My brethren, count it all joy when ye fall into divers temptations; knowing that the trying of your faith worketh patience.'

It is said of a saintly man in mediæval times that in a season of temptation the great adversary suggested to him that he was a reprobate, and persuaded him to take his fill of all the pleasures of this life, because he was excluded from every future joy with God in heaven. 'No,' replied the good man; 'not so, Satan. If I must not enjoy God after this life, let me enjoy him as much as I can in this life.'

Watch and pray, that ye enter not into temptation: the spirit indeed is willing, but the flesh is weak.—MATT. 26:41.

Lead us not into temptation.—MATT. 6:13.

God is faithful, who will not suffer you to be tempted above that ye are able; but will with the temptation also make a way to escape, that ye may be able to bear it.—1 COR. 10:13.

FEBRUARY 13

OUR FAITH MAY FAIL, BUT NEVER GOD'S WORD.

OUR blessed Lord put great honour on the word. It received special mention from him in prayer: 'Holy Father, keep through thine own name those whom thou hast given me, that they may be one, as we are. ... I have given them *thy word*; and the world hath hated them, because they are not of the world, even as I am not of the world. ... Sanctify them through thy truth: *thy word* is truth.' It was his chosen weapon in conflict; and by a simple 'It is written' he foiled the adversary in every assault. Besides, it was his daily delight to expound it to men, and apply it to their hearts, and carefully to note its varied fulfilment.

So should it be with every disciple. They should love the word, and meditate on it, and treasure it up both in memory and in heart; for it is only as they obtain a growing knowledge of it, and a growing faith in it, that they can rightly do the will of their Father, and go on their way rejoicing. But it is here where so many come short. Wanting faith, instead of taking God at his word like Abraham, and thereby glorifying his name, they are like Cleopas and his friend—'slow of heart to believe *all* that the prophets have spoken.'

Samuel Rutherford says: 'We too often believe the promises as the man that read Plato's writings concerning the immortality of the soul. So long as the book was in his hand, he believed what was said; but as soon as he laid it down, he began to imagine that his soul was only an airy vapour that perisheth with the expiring of the breath. It would greatly help to preserve us from this, and strengthen our faith, if we oftener compared Scripture with Scripture, and prediction with fulfilment.'

Two rabbis, we are told, approaching Jerusalem, observed a fox running up the hill of Zion. Aged Rabbi Joshua wept, but Rabbi Eliezer laughed. 'Wherefore dost thou weep?' demanded Eliezer. 'I weep because I see what was written in the Lamentations fulfilled: "Because of the mountain of Zion which is desolate, the foxes fall upon it."' 'And therefore do I laugh,' said Rabbi Eliezer; 'for when I see with my own eyes that God has fulfilled his threatenings to the letter, I have thereby a pledge that not one of his promises shall fail, for he is ever more ready to show mercy than judgment.'

> The grass withereth, the flower fadeth: but the word of our God shall stand for ever.—ISA. 40:8.

> Ye know in all your hearts and in all your souls, that not one thing hath failed of all the good things which the Lord your God spake concerning you; all are come to pass unto you, and not one thing hath failed thereof.—JOSH. 23:14.

FEBRUARY 14

THROUGH INTENSITY OF UNBELIEF, GREAT JUDGMENTS ARE USUALLY GREAT SURPRISES.

GOD has no pleasure in the death of the sinner, and therefore he is slow to anger; yet being righteous as well as gracious, holy as well as loving, though he bears long with transgressors, he will not bear always. Judgment is his *strange* work, yet it is his work, as will be clearly seen when the fitting time has come.

The saying, that it is the unexpected which happens, is not more familiar than true; and in nothing is its truthfulness more strikingly illustrated than in God's righteous visitations for sin. As events, they are almost invariably unexpected.

It was so with the Flood. Though clearly predicted beforehand and forcibly used to stir up repentance, yet when it came in the end, it was in no man's thoughts; and as none heeded the warning, so none escaped the judgment, save Noah and his household. 'They did eat,' our Lord tells us, 'they drank, they married wives, they were given in marriage, until the day that Noe entered the ark, and the flood came, and destroyed them all.'

Equally unexpected were the judgments which befell the Cities of the Plain. When the fire came down and consumed them utterly, not one of the inhabitants ever dreamt of such a thing or sought to flee from it, save Lot only.

John, in the Apocalypse, tells us that there will be a like experience at the predicted fall of Babylon. Notwithstanding manifold warnings, so far from expecting such a thing, she will be saying in her heart, 'I sit a queen, and am no widow, and shall see no sorrow.' Yet what is added? 'Therefore shall her plagues come *in one day*, death, and mourning, and famine; and she shall be utterly burned with fire: for strong is the Lord God who judgeth her.'

So in the end will it be with the coming of the Lord. Though prophets have clearly predicted it, and good men have all along expected it, and many concurrent signs will immediately precede it, yet through the intensity of men's unbelief, down to the very day of the Lord's advent, the conviction will be general and assured that the whole thing is a mere dream of superstition, an idle myth, to which no man of sound mind would give the least heed. It will thus, at the last, come on the world as the most terrible of all surprises; for, 'when they shall say, Peace and safety; then sudden destruction cometh upon them, as travail upon a woman with child; and they shall not escape.'

The realisation of all this should not only increase our own watchfulness, but quicken and intensify our every loving effort to save the perishing.

> Because sentence against an evil work is not executed speedily, therefore the heart of the sons of men is fully set in them to do evil.—ECCLES. 8:11.

> Despisest thou the riches of his goodness and forbearance and longsuffering; not knowing that the goodness of God leadeth thee to repentance?—ROM. 2:4.

He, being full of compassion, forgave their iniquity, and destroyed them not: yea, many a time turned he his anger away, and did not stir up all his wrath.—Psa. 78:38.

February 15

OUR EVER-LIVING HEAD.

TO all believers Christ Jesus is not the helper only, but the great and sole head of all authority, power, and saving grace, on whose presence and loving favour everything depends. 'The husband,' says the apostle, 'is the head of the wife, even as Christ is the head of the church: and he is the saviour of the body.' So intimate is this relationship to his redeemed people, that he is head to them individually; for it is expressly written, 'The head of every man is Christ.'

There is much to encourage in this, for sometimes his people are apt to fear that their individuality may be lost in the vastness of their numbers. But no; each and every believer has direct and immediate access to Christ, and can personally commune with him, and continuously draw from his overflowing fulness. Nay, so closely and tenderly are they related to him as members, that their sorrows are his sorrows; their cares, his cares; and to touch them is, he says, to touch the apple of his eye. 'From being so united to him,' says an old writer, 'they cannot but be his Father's Jedidiahs, Beulahs, and Hephzibahs, dearly accepted in the Beloved. They are to him as a seal on his arm, a signet on his right hand. He carries their names on his breast continually.'

But besides being the head of each believer, the Lord Jesus is the head of the church at large, yea, also the head for his church over all things and over all persons. In ordinary life the headship sometimes given to men is merely honorary. They may have the title in full and all the insignia of office, but it is not *their* hand but another's that has the power and uses it. It is otherwise with the Lord Jesus. His headship is no mere thing of title only, but real, supreme, and eternally abiding. Were we oftener to remember this, and that the government is on *his* shoulders and not on ours, instead of yielding to despondency, we would, even in darkest and most perilous times, be able to lift up our heads with joy; indeed, not unfrequently it is by those very events we deem the most adverse he is most effectually carrying out the grand and glorious purposes of his love.

> Christ is the head of the church ... and loved it, and gave himself for it; that he might sanctify and cleanse it with the washing of water by the word, that he might present it to himself a glorious church, not having spot, or wrinkle, or any such thing; but that it should be holy and without blemish.—EPH. 5:23, 25-27.

> He is the head of the body, the church: who is the beginning, the firstborn from the dead; that in all things he might have the preeminence.—COL. 1:18.

FEBRUARY 16

OUR BITTER THINGS.

IN this vale of tears there is no day in which there is not bitter weeping somewhere. Sicknesses have largely to do with this, and disappointments in life, and fruitless struggles, and straitened circumstances, and, above all, the sore and crushing bereavements that finally sever us from those nearest and dearest to our heart's affections. Yet, in the riches of his grace, out of all such bitter God often brings a marvellous sweet. Samson said, in his riddle to the Philistines, 'Out of the eater came forth meat, and out of the strong came forth sweetness.' And so is it here. If through faith in his Son we become really his, the Lord will not only lovingly sustain us in our trials, but so graciously overrule them as to make them yield the very choicest fruits of righteousness. This was so fully realised by David in his own experience, that his pen, as one says, never wrote more sweetly than when dipped in the ink of affliction. It was so with Luther. 'I never knew,' he said, 'the meaning of God's word until I came into affliction: I have always found it one of my best schoolmasters.' Yes; truly 'affliction under this divine teaching explains many a hard text, and seals many a precious promise.'

On one occasion a beloved brother said to an eminent Puritan minister, when much depressed through varied persecution and trial, 'Son, son, when affliction lieth heavy, sin lieth light.' This saying, by reminding him how God could make affliction minister to sanctification, gave him great comfort; and he was wont to say afterwards that sanctified afflictions are spiritual promotions. Thus the Lord ever and again, in the riches of his grace, sweetens the bitter Marahs of his people, and makes sorest trials choicest mercies.

Blessed is the man whom thou chastenest, O Lord, and teachest him out of thy law.—Psa. 94:12.

The Lord will not cast off for ever: but though he cause grief, yet will he have compassion according to the multitude of his mercies. For he doth not afflict willingly nor grieve the children of men.— Lam. 3:31-33.

Now no chastening for the present seemeth to be joyous, but grievous: nevertheless afterward it yieldeth the peaceable fruit of righteousness unto them which are exercised thereby.—Heb. 12:11.

February 17

GOLDEN OPPORTUNITIES SHOULD INSTANTLY BE TURNED TO GOLDEN ACCOUNT.

WHEN on one occasion the men of Gennesaret found that Jesus was in the midst of them, straightway they sent to the diseased on every side, and urgently pressed them to come at once to the Great Physician. It was a rare opportunity, and they were lovingly determined to make the very most of it for the good of others. So should it be with us when we feel promptings within us of a similar but higher kind. Happily the Great Physician still is near; and as the spiritually diseased and perishing abound on every side, it is at once our duty and privilege to make known the fact, and lovingly urge an immediate application to him.

Through the grace of the Lord this has been largely done in late years, for with many there has been a peculiar yearning for souls, and much prayerful effort. Mothers, in particular, have wrestled for their children, friends for their friends, and brothers for their brethren, as if feeling that Jesus of Nazareth was passing by, and it might be now or never with them. The result in numerous cases has been, that what was before but a temporary relationship of nature, has become a blessed and enduring relationship of grace.

In awakening times, many a golden opportunity for such soul-winning has been found in the after-meeting. 'The Bible,' says Dr Mackay, 'is the sword of the Spirit; and we should not merely talk of its sharp edge and glittering metal, but in love pierce the sinner's heart with it.' Once, at the close of a meeting in Dr Bonar's church, a sceptic said to me, 'Sir, I do not believe there is a God.' It was 10 p.m., and no time for argument. I cast the burden on the Lord in prayer, and looked so happy that he said, 'You are laughing at me.' 'No; but I was thinking if all the grasshoppers on earth were to say, "There is no sun," it would not alter the matter. The Bible declares, "The fool says in his heart, There is no God."' 'Well, that is so,' he said. I then showed him that God calls every man who does not believe in him a liar. The man went home, seemingly much impressed; and when, some months after, I happened to meet him, referring to our former conversation, he said, 'I found out that I was a fool and a liar, and I have now come to Christ.' Had we more faith in the word, and more reliance on the Spirit to apply it, such blessed results would not be so rare.

> As we have therefore opportunity, let us do good unto all men, especially unto them who are of the household of faith.—GAL. 6:10.
>
> Whatsoever thy hand findeth to do, do it with thy might; for there is no work, nor device, nor knowledge, nor wisdom, in the grave, whither thou goest.—ECCLES. 9:10.

February 18

PRAYER HAS FULNESS OF POWER ONLY WHEN IT HAS
BELIEVING PERSISTENCY.

PRAYER may not be needed in heaven, but on earth it is a lifetime duty and privilege; and it is ever found that as soon as true life enters the soul, true prayer comes from the lips. It is the express teaching of our Lord in the parable, 'that men ought always to pray, and not to faint'; and to every disciple it is emphatically said, 'Pray without ceasing.'

This, it need scarcely be said, does not mean that men are to be ever in their closets and on their knees, and so continuous in supplication as to leave neither time nor place for other engagements. We are not 'to stain one duty with the blood of another,' which we would be doing were we so constant in daily devotions as to neglect daily business and the needed oversight of family and household. Besides, to be always in prayer would be in reality to be never in prayer; it would be mere vain repetition. But though not to be always in the very act and exercise of prayer, we should be ever in the spirit of it. As one puts it, 'If there is not always iron in the furnace, yet let there always be the fire to melt it. If not always shooting the arrow up to heaven, yet always keep the bow well stringed; so shall you always be archers, though not always shooting, and always be men of prayer, though not always praying.'

In spite of all the contempt often thrown upon it, believing prayer still remains the mightiest of agencies. It can still, as of old, bring down from opened heavens showers of blessing; and, if need be, scatter foes and remove mountains. In order to this, however, there must be importunity—seeking and knocking as well as asking; and a patient, trustful waiting, whatever the delay. 'The method appointed for the attainment of the blessing,' says John Newton, 'is the most simple imaginable. It is only, "Ask, and ye shall receive"; but then we are not to give a runaway knock at Wisdom's gate, but humbly and patiently wait till it is opened.'

Continue in prayer, and watch in the same with thanksgiving.—
Col. 4:2.

Rejoicing in hope; patient in tribulation; continuing instant in
prayer.—Rom. 12:12.

We give thanks to God and the Father of our Lord Jesus Christ,
praying always for you.—Col. 1:3.

February 19

*THINGS ABOVE SHOULD EVER HAVE THE FIRST PLACE
WITH US.*

WITH many, this world is avowedly all in all. Their every
thought is centred in it, and their every affection; but as
they know nothing higher, and possess nothing better, we are more
saddened than surprised at their acting. Very different, however, is
our feeling when those who bear the name of Christ and profess
discipleship cherish such a spirit, and instead of cleaving to the
Lord, begin to look down only and cleave to the dust. This awakens the fear that in the end they are about to prefer the red pottage
to the birth-right, and the land and the oxen to the divinely royal
feast.

In this matter, what is required at our hands is nothing
extreme—not any transcendental contempt of the world, nor any
hermit-like separation from it, but simply that the heart be not
injuriously set upon it. The Christian pilgrim is not to despise the
comforts he may meet with on the way—this would be ingratitude
for helpful kindness; but he is not to tarry among them, or leave
them with regret when the Master calls.

Nor should this be deemed a hard thing, for, at the best, earthly
things have no sufficiency; for 'a man's life consisteth not in the
abundance of the things which he possesseth,' and it not unfrequently happens that those who possess most of this world are
the very persons who most feel its utter emptiness. What seemed
to be substance at a distance, is found to be only shadow when

near. But even if earthly things had some sufficiency, they have no permanency. They are constantly changing places; they come today, and depart tomorrow. It is a good old rule, 'Set not your heart on anything on which one could write, *Passing away*.'

Things above have a totally different character. Though meanwhile unseen, they are not shadowy, but real, glorious, and abiding; and the more vividly our faith realises this, the brighter and happier will our experience be. All our highest and most enduring relationships are above, for the Redeemer and the redeemed are there; and there, too, are our richest possessions—the place prepared for us, the home, the inheritance, and the glory.

On one occasion, when the sailor-preacher, Father Taylor, found that his sentences were getting tangled and confused, he quaintly remarked, 'My nominative has lost its verb, and knows not how to find it; but I am bound for the kingdom all the same.' He sought the kingdom first, and so should we.

> If ye then be risen with Christ, seek those things which are above, where Christ sitteth on the right hand of God. Set your affection on things above, not on things on the earth.—COL. 3:1, 2.

> For our conversation is in heaven; from whence also we look for the Saviour, the Lord Jesus Christ: who shall change our vile body, that it may be fashioned like unto his glorious body.—PHIL. 3:20, 21.

FEBRUARY 20

THE NEEDED SHELTER.

IN ancient times, the cities of refuge, being Levitical, were not only sacred in character and quiet in aspect, but were so arranged as to be conveniently near when their shelter was needed. Three were on the east and three on the west side of Jordan; and their very names had more or less of sweet significance, as if for the very purpose of encouraging a trustful and speedy entrance into them. But still further to increase their accessibility, the roads to them were not only good, but in summer and winter alike were kept in thorough repair. Moreover, Jewish writers tell us that, to prevent all uncertainty as to the way, posts were erected in conspicuous places, with these words visibly inscribed on them—'Refuge, Refuge.' Thus everything was done to direct and facilitate the flight of the unhappy homicide.

There is something interesting in this, even as a bare matter of history, but it becomes specially striking and impressive when viewed typically; for all that was true of the type, the city of refuge, is still more true of Christ, our divinely-provided Hiding-place. To him there is not only access for the poor and perishing, but access of the most open, direct, and immediate kind. We need no 'go-betweens,' no priestly mediation to secure us a welcome, but can go at once and directly to Christ himself, at any time and under any circumstances; for it is from his lips the invitation flows, 'Come unto *me*, all ye that labour and are heavy laden, and I will give you rest.' This, too, should be remembered, that near as the cities of refuge may have been to those who needed them, Christ to every troubled soul is nearer still—so near, that the cry of faith, *wherever uttered*, and however faint, instantaneously reaches him and wins his help. We may be at the very end of the earth, but anywhere and everywhere the Redeemer is near, as 'our Refuge and strength, a *very present help* in trouble'; and so absolutely secure that we shall never need another.

It was once said to John Vine Hall, the venerable author of the 'Sinner's Friend,' 'You don't mean to say that you have any doubts?' 'Well,' he replied, 'I have no doubts, because Christ came to save sinners, and I am one. If I get up to the gate of heaven, and any there should object to such a sinner going in, I can fancy another one saying, "Oh, but you must let him in; he has got a drop of the Master's blood upon him, and that cleanseth from all sin."' His favourite seal expressed his only and habitual confidence—the cross, an anchor, and the words, 'Other refuge have I none.'

> And a man shall be as an hiding place from the wind, and a covert
> from the tempest; as rivers of water in a dry place, as the shadow
> of a great rock in a weary land.—Isa. 32:2.

In whom we have redemption through his blood, the forgiveness of sins, according to the riches of his grace.—Eph. 1:7.

FEBRUARY 21

WE ARE NEVER SO CHRISTLIKE AS WHEN, WITH LOVING SYMPATHY, WE REMEMBER THE POOR.

WHEN the prophet Agabus stood up at Antioch and signified by the Spirit that there should be great dearth throughout all the world (which came to pass in the days of Claudius Caesar), there was a remarkable outflow of generous sympathy and help. In its spirit and method it affords a perfect model for imitation; for we are told, 'Every man according to his ability determined to send relief unto the brethren which dwelt in Judaea: which also they did, and sent it to the elders by the hands of Barnabas and Saul.' How resolute they were!—they '*determined*'; how unanimous!—'*every man*'; how ungrudging!—each gave '*according to his ability*'; and how promptly practical!—'*which also they did*,' and sent it to the elders by the hands of Barnabas and Saul.

In this case the striking thing is that the contributors were mainly Gentiles, while the recipients were almost wholly Jews;—a beautiful evidence of the fulness of grace in them, and the strength of the new affection, and that, in Christ Jesus, Jew and Gentile were becoming one.

The poverty in Judaea, which was so generously relieved, naturally suggests to us that word of the Lord, 'The poor shall never cease out of the land: therefore I command thee, saying, Thou shalt open thine hand wide unto thy brother, to thy poor, and to thy needy, in thy land.' No command could be more lovingly considerate, and it beautifully reveals the gracious kindness and tender sympathy of our heavenly Father.

Nevertheless, this continuance of the poor has occasionally been to some a sore perplexity, especially when the needy are not the poor simply, but the saintly poor who fear the Lord and do his will.

It seems strange to them that a people declared to be so precious to him, and dear as the apple of his eye, should yet from time to time be left in such straits. They forget, in their perplexity, that these occasional straits are never accidental. There is wise and loving purpose in them, and they are made mightily helpful in invigorating every Christian grace. And in a very special degree they help to wean them from earth and ripen them for heaven. They forget, moreover, that these trials often serve the further end of being helpful to the rich as well as to the poor, by calling forth their loving sympathy and aid, and thereby saving them from the deadening influence of prosperity, and giving them the opportunity and privilege of ministering to Christ in his members: 'Inasmuch as ye did it unto them, ye did it unto me.' 'Do good to the poor and needy, while your estates are your own; when you are dead, your estates belong to others. God is pleased with no music below so much as with the grateful songs and thanksgivings of relieved widows and supported orphans.'

> Only they would that we should remember the poor; the same which I also was forward to do.—GAL. 2:10.

> Blessed is he that considereth the poor: the Lord will deliver him in time of trouble.—PSA. 41:1.

> For it hath pleased them of Macedonia and Achaia to make a certain contribution for the poor saints which are at Jerusalem.—ROM. 15:26.

FEBRUARY 22

FALSE JOY AND TRUE.

AS so many realities in this world have their counterfeits, it need not surprise us to find that if holiness has its delights and joys, so has sin. Were it otherwise, it could not have been said of Moses that he chose rather to suffer affliction with the people of God than to enjoy the *pleasures of sin* for a season. These pleasures, indeed, are just the bait that covers the hook, the gilding on the fetter that hides the iron. Such joys, however, have nothing in common with the joy of the Lord. The one kind of joy is from beneath, spurious and unreal, the other from above, genuine and blessed; for it is not only a joy from the Lord, but a joy in the Lord, and which meets our every want and longing. It is the only joy which fully satisfies the soul; and it is so satisfying, that even when stripped of every earthly comfort the believer can still rejoice. When he has much, he enjoys God in all things; and when he has little, he enjoys all things in God.

They, then, are blind who would prefer the world to Christ. 'Believe me,' said Samuel Rutherford, 'this world, which the Lord will not have to be yours, is but the dross, the refuse of creation—the portion of mere hired servants—a hard bone, whereon men rather break their teeth than satisfy their appetite.' It is wholly otherwise with those who prefer Christ to the world. When Mr Gardiner of Aberdeen was dying, he said: 'The valley is not dark, for Jesus is here. I know nothing of the bitterness of death. I have had a happy life preaching Christ, and now I am having a happy death, going to be with him.' He had but one thought, the love of Christ; but one feeling, the joy of his presence.

> O Jesus! Friend unfailing,
>   How dear art thou to me!
> Are cares or fears assailing?
>   I find my strength in thee.
> Why should my feet grow weary
>   Of this my pilgrim way?
> Rough though the path and dreary,
>   It ends in perfect day.

Rejoice in the Lord alway: and again I say, Rejoice.—Phil. 4:4.

Happy is the man that findeth wisdom, and the man that getteth understanding. Her ways are ways of pleasantness, and all her paths are peace.—Prov. 3:13, 17.

Stolen waters are sweet, and bread eaten in secret is pleasant. But he knoweth not that the dead are there; and that her guests are in the depths of hell.—Prov. 9:17, 18.

FEBRUARY 23

NEEDED 'BEWARES.'

IT is somewhat remarkable that in one brief verse we have no less than three emphatic cautions: 'Beware of dogs, beware of evil workers, beware of the concision.'

The first of these cautions, 'Beware of dogs,' reminds us of another somewhat remarkable thing,—namely, the frequency with which in Scripture the good, and especially the evil qualities of men are set forth under animal symbols, as in passages like these: 'Go ye, and tell that *fox* [Herod], Behold, I cast out devils, and I do cures to day and to morrow, and the third day I shall be perfected.' Again: 'I know that after my departing shall grievous *wolves* enter, not sparing the flock.' And once more: 'Be sober, be vigilant; because your adversary the devil, as a roaring *lion*, walketh about, seeking whom he may devour.'

The 'dogs' warned against were false teachers, evil workers; the concision, those who, by preaching both Christianity and Judaism, as alike essential, corrupted the gospel, and thereby imperilled the highest interests of men. Such teachers are more to be dreaded than open persecutors. The latter may wound and kill the body, but the former do fatal injury to the soul, by poisoning the very food designed for its spiritual nourishment. As truth, and especially truth as it is in Jesus, is the Spirit's special instrument in saving and sanctifying men, so deadly error is the chosen instrument of Satan in corrupting and destroying them.

Doubtless the language is strong: 'Beware of dogs; beware of evil workers.' Nevertheless it is not too strong when used against those who, by artful wiles and a perverted gospel, would draw away the flock from the faith and the fellowship of God's redeemed. 'It is a right thing,' says an old divine, 'to take off the vizard of seeming virtue under which the spreaders of error do usually lurk. Pretended piety is but the sheep's clothing, and it is never a wrong thing to take it off, if need be even with a rough hand, and let the wolf be seen.' Few are more dangerous than good men holding false doctrine.

> Beware of false prophets, which come to you in sheep's clothing, but inwardly they are ravening wolves.—MATT. 7:15.

> Beware lest any man spoil you through philosophy and vain deceit, after the tradition of men, after the rudiments of the world, and not after Christ.—COL. 2:8.

> Beware lest ye also, being led away with the error of the wicked, fall from your own stedfastness.—2 PET. 3:17.

FEBRUARY 24

THE REVEALED METHOD OF REDEMPTION.

IN unfolding redemption, Scripture always puts these things together—Bethlehem and Calvary, the cradle and the cross, the incarnation birth and the atonement death; and what it hath joined we dare not put asunder, especially when told so emphatically by one apostle: 'Without shedding of blood is no remission'; and so impressively by another: 'The blood of Jesus Christ his Son cleanseth us from all sin.' If anything less precious than this could have satisfied the claims of justice, and have taken away sin,—tears, or sweating toil, or costliest gift, or all combined,—we may rest assured that not one drop of the blood of the Son of God would have been shed. We often waste means; the Lord never does.

> *Jehovah bade His sword awake,—*
> *O Christ, it woke 'gainst thee!*
> *Thy blood its flaming blade must slake,*
> *Thy heart its sheath must be:*
> *All for my sake, my peace to make;*
> *Now sleeps that sword for me.*

Yes, we owe everything to the atoning sufferings and death of Christ. It is because he wept, we rejoice; because he died, we live; because he bore the curse, we shall ever enjoy the blessing: for it is expressly written, 'Christ hath redeemed us from the curse of the law, being made a curse for us.'

All this was variously and strikingly typified in Old Testament times; yet when the true Paschal Lamb appeared, to whom John pointed and said, 'Behold the Lamb of God, which taketh away the sin of the world,' how few believed on him! It is the same still with multitudes.

Not long ago an aged Jew said: 'I have fasted for seven and twenty hours, praying with all possible earnestness, and trembling too, and after all I feel that my sins have not been atoned for.' No; without shedding of blood there is no remission. 'The only plank between the believer and destruction is the blood of the incarnate God.' To make light of the blood, therefore, is to make light of salvation, and miss it forever.

> In whom we have redemption through his blood, the forgiveness of sins, according to the riches of his grace.—EPH. 1:7.

> Unto him that loved us, and washed us from our sins in his own blood.—REV. 1:5.

> Ye were not redeemed with corruptible things, as silver and gold, … but with the precious blood of Christ, as of a lamb without blemish and without spot.—1 PET. 1:18, 19.

FEBRUARY 25

WHERE THERE IS TRUE FAITH THERE WILL BE EVANGELISTIC ENERGY.

THE apostle bore beautiful testimony to the Thessalonians when he said: 'For from you *sounded out the word* of the Lord not only in Macedonia and Achaia, but also in every place your faith to God-ward is spread abroad; so that we need not to speak anything.'

This language calls to mind the trumpet blown in the year of jubilee, which proclaimed liberty to the captive, remission of debts, restoration of inheritances, with manifold attendant blessings. It was a joyful sound to all Israel, as the gospel now should be to all the world; for it brings to us the glad tidings of a Saviour's love and a completed redemption, and gives freest offer of full, immediate, and everlasting forgiveness even to the chief of sinners.

This gospel is here called 'the word of the Lord'; and fittingly so, for the Lord is the author of it, and the subject of it, and the dispenser of it, and it is by the efficacy of his grace that it becomes the power of God and the wisdom of God to everyone that believeth.

It is said to have sounded out from them, not only in Macedonia and Achaia, but also in every place. The central position of Thessalonica was helpful to this; for being a commercial city and a seaport, those who went into it and those who went out could the more readily receive and diffuse a blessed Christian influence. So should it ever be with all who are similarly placed. They should be directly and actively missionary in their efforts, and do what in them lies to carry out their Lord's command, 'Go ye into all the world, and preach the gospel to every creature.'

Not only should every church be thus missionary, but so should every individual Christian. 'As a scented ointment,' says Chrysostom, 'keeps not its fragrance shut up within itself, but sends it afar; so likewise noble men keep not their virtue shut up within themselves, but through their reputation are of good service to many.' The first act of Bunyan's pilgrim, after experiencing the blessedness of pardon, was an effort to rouse the ungodly men whom he saw by the way. Indeed, were good men but thoroughly in earnest, they might each of them become the light and salt of a neighbourhood, and prove, in their own homes at least, blessings unspeakable. When a little boy, the son of a Christian merchant in New York, was dying, he said: 'O father, don't weep for me; don't cry, father. When I die I am going to heaven; and when I get there I will go right up to Jesus, and tell him that it was through you I came there.' More sweetly soothing words to the disconsolate parent he could not have uttered.

> Holding forth the word of life; that I may rejoice in the day of Christ, that I have not run in vain, neither laboured in vain.—PHIL. 2:16.

Only let your conversation be as it becometh the gospel of Christ: that whether I come and see you, or else be absent, I may hear of your affairs, that ye stand fast in one spirit, with one mind striving together for the faith of the gospel.—PHIL. 1:27.

FEBRUARY 26

THOUGH ETERNITY IS NEAR, HOW MANY THINK ONLY OF TIME.

THE Scriptures never allow us to think only of *the now*, but are full of *the everlasting*. The term 'ever and ever' very often occurs, and is at once the saddest and the sweetest word in the Bible.

When applied to the divine perfections and promises, and our own interest in them, there is no expression like it for comfort: 'This God is our God for ever and ever'; 'They that turn many to righteousness shall shine as the stars for ever and ever'; 'The kingdoms of this world are become the kingdoms of our Lord, and of his Christ; and he shall reign for ever and ever.' What could be more cheering than these utterances! 'Oh, sweet word, *ever!*' says an old writer; 'thou art the crown of the saints' crown, and the glory of their glory. They want nothing but to have their portion fixed; and lo, thou art the welcome dove to bring this olive-branch in thy mouth, "This God is our God for ever and ever."'

On the other hand, when the term is applied to those who have made light of redemption and rejected Christ, and deliberately put away from them eternal life, what can be more awful than the thought of their being shut out forever and ever from the light of God's presence and the glories of heaven!

Believers should often ponder the word 'eternity' in both these relations—at once to deepen their own gratitude for redeeming mercy, and to intensify their compassionate efforts for those still unsaved.

After the serious illness which was the turning-point of the spiritual life of Dr Chalmers, he said: 'My confinement has fixed on my heart a very strong impression of the insignificance of time—an impression which I trust will not abandon me, though I again reach the heyday of health and vigour. This should be the first step to another impression still more salutary—the magnitude of eternity. Strip human life of its connection with a higher scene of existence and it is the illusion of an instant, an unmeaning farce, a series of visions and projects and convulsive effort which terminate in nothing.'

The world passeth away, and the lust thereof: but he that doeth the will of God abideth for ever.—1 JOHN 2:17.

For our light affliction, which is but for a moment, worketh for us a far more exceeding and eternal weight of glory.—2 COR. 4:17.

But this I say, brethren, the time is short: it remaineth, that both they that have wives be as though they had none; and they that weep, as though they wept not; and they that rejoice, as though they rejoiced not; and they that buy, as though they possessed not; and they that use this world, as not abusing it: for the fashion of this world passeth away.—1 COR. 7:29-31.

FEBRUARY 27

THE MORE THE HEART IS FILLED WITH GRACE, THE MORE IT GLOWS WITH GRATITUDE.

IN multitudes of instance, the expression, 'Thank God,' is only a form of speech, without any corresponding emotion. The mouth says it, but not the heart. In the temple, the first utterance that came from the Pharisee's lips was a thanksgiving: 'God, I thank thee, that I am not as other men are, extortioners, unjust, or even as this publican.' Instead, however, of thanking the Lord, he was in reality only praising himself. But with Paul, outward expression and inward feeling always corresponded. Indeed, so real was his gratitude that it was continually welling up in his heart, and flowing over in fervent thanksgiving. Moreover, as he never allowed his own things to shut out the things of others, his gratitude was not only thorough in its sincerity, but all-embracing in its objects. He took such large and loving interest in all the churches and in all believers, that every blessing vouchsafed to them, and every grace seen in them, and every Christian effort made by them, called out expressions of grateful emotion. 'I thank my God always,' he said, 'on your behalf, for the grace which is given you by Jesus Christ.' 'I cease not to give thanks for you, making mention of you in my prayers.' And, finally: 'We give thanks to God and the Father of our Lord Jesus Christ, praying always for you, since the day we heard of your faith in Christ Jesus, and of the love which ye have to all the saints.'

'Every night, as I fall on my knees,' said Mr Moody, '*I thank God* for the friends he has raised up in this country. I know that I am speaking to many who will never hear my voice again in this world. If I shall be permitted to return, many of you will be gone; but I pray that you may die, with your eyes on the Master, with your feet on the race-course, and that you may not fall out by the way. There are two lives that every Christian should live: one life he should live alone with God, a life that nobody but himself and God knows, that inner life, that constant communion, whereby he draws strength from God; and then he can live the outer life before the world, adorning the doctrine of Jesus Christ.'

> In every thing give thanks: for this is the will of God in Christ Jesus concerning you.—1 THESS. 5:18.
>
> Giving thanks always for all things unto God and the Father in the name of our Lord Jesus Christ.—EPH. 5:20.
>
> Thanks be unto God for his unspeakable gift.—2 COR. 9:15.

FEBRUARY 28

THE LORD'S SECOND ADVENT IN ITS PRACTICAL BEARINGS.

FROM a misunderstanding of the apostle's words, afterwards made clear to them, many in Thessalonica were led to expect an immediate coming of the Lord from heaven, or rather to think that the day of Christ was already present; and the thought so excited them, that apparently they were ready to drop interest and effort in all usual occupations. They thus fell into a great practical error; for even should the Lord come, as they expected, and find them with the sweat of toil on their brow, they would suffer neither loss nor shame thereby. Nay, rather, 'Blessed is that servant whom the Lord, when he cometh, shall find so doing.' If we are really in Christ and saved, we could not be found in a better state for his coming than just faithfully discharging the daily and ordinary duties of life.

About a hundred years ago, there was in America a day of such unaccountable darkness, that it was supposed by many that the day of judgment had come. The Legislature of Connecticut was in session, and its members shared in the general awe and terror. Someone, in the consternation of the hour, moved an adjournment. Then there arose an old Puritan legislator and said that, if the last day had come, he desired to be found at his post, doing his duty, and therefore moved that the candles be brought in, so that the house could proceed with its business. In this he judged rightly; for our Lord's express command is, 'Occupy till I come,'—a command applicable to every department of duty.

It is important to note that, in correcting the error of the Thessalonians as to the absolute immediateness of the Advent, never did the apostle cast any doubt on the event itself, or speak of it as if, after all, it might turn out to be a mere myth and not a reality, a fancy and not a fact. Nor did he ever speak of it as *so certainly distant and remote* as to deprive it of all immediate and practical influence on the hearts and consciences of men. How could he, when our Lord's words are so express: 'Watch ye therefore: for ye know not when the Master cometh, at even, or at midnight, or at cock-crowing: *lest coming suddenly* he find you sleeping.' Nor, further, did he ever suggest that, to avoid undue excitement, it should be a theme rarely dwelt on. On the contrary, he not only invariably gave it a place in his teaching, but spoke of it as 'the blessed hope,' and made constant and impressive use of it in rousing the heedless and in stimulating and cheering believers in all the duties and conflicts of life. It was the same with the other apostles.

The biographer of Mr Hewitson says of him: 'The "blessed hope" took its place, not only in his understanding, but in his heart. He not only believed in the speedy "appearing"; he loved it, waited for it.' 'Faith,' we find him saying, 'looks to the cross, and is at peace; it looks forward to the crown, and pants for glory. Oh, to have more of the life and power of such a faith!'

That blessed hope, and the glorious appearing of the great God and our Saviour Jesus Christ.—Titus 2:13.

Unto them that look for him shall he appear the second time without sin unto salvation.—Heb. 9:28.

Be ye also patient; stablish your hearts: for the coming of the Lord draweth nigh.—James 5:8.

Therefore be ye also ready: for in such an hour as ye think not the Son of man cometh.—Matt. 24:44.

March 1

DEATH MAY BE EARNED, NOT LIFE.

AS it is through men's own working death comes to them, they often imagine that life and salvation must become theirs in a similar way; forgetting that, though all may readily be their own destroyers, not one can ever be his own saviour. The first is easy; the latter is impossible. Even one man may let in the sea, but millions cannot drive it back again. The whole teaching of Scripture shows that life and death are not similarly obtainable. Death comes as wages—wages out and out earned, by every servant of sin; whereas life comes as a free, unmerited gift of grace through Jesus Christ our Lord. Putting himself as Substitute and Saviour in our room and stead, he not only bore the awful penalty incurred, but, for our sakes also, he merited the needed and promised life. He bought it for us with his own blood, for nothing less precious could avail; and having bought it, no price is asked at our hands; nor must any price be offered, lest it should be said to us, as it was said to Simon Magus, 'Thy money perish with thee, because thou hast thought that the gift of God may be purchased with money.'

Many years ago, after much seemingly fruitless dealing with an anxious inquirer, who had been wearily toiling for months to make himself worthy of salvation, I at length said, 'Friend, you entirely mistake the whole matter. You forget that salvation is a *gift*, and that, so far from you having to press God to give it, he, on the contrary, is pressing you to take it.' 'A gift!' he exclaimed, with surprise,—'a gift! Is salvation really a gift?' 'Yes,' I replied; 'it is yours for the taking.' Without further hesitancy, and with deeply grateful heart, he took what the Lord offered, and as he offered it; and all through his later years, when at any time temptation pressed, and faith was like to fail, the remembrance that salvation was a gift cheered and sustained him. His after-life was holy, and his end perfect peace.

'I beseech you,' said Edward Fisher, 'be persuaded that here you are to work nothing, but only to receive by faith the treasure which is Jesus Christ, although you be never so great a sinner. So shall you obtain forgiveness of sins, righteousness, and eternal happiness, not as an agent, but as a patient—not by doing, but receiving.' It is well to remember, however, that though we must not work *for* life, we cannot too much or too heartily work *from* life.

> The wages of sin is death; but the gift of God is eternal life through Jesus Christ our Lord.—ROM. 6:23.

> For by grace are ye saved through faith; and that not of yourselves: it is the gift of God: not of works, lest any man should boast.— EPH. 2:8, 9.

MARCH 2

THE MORE LOWLY THE SAINT, THE MORE LOVELY.

WHEN high-mindedness for the time seems wholly gone, yet how easily does it again spring up, in the form either of pride of life, or pride of intellect, or pride of spiritual attainment,—for this sin, unhappily, can mingle even with holiest services, and feed on choicest spiritual experiences. Believers, therefore, cannot be too constantly and prayerfully on the watch against it; all the more as while, on the one hand, nothing is more offensive than pride, so nothing, on the other, is more attractive than humility. How beautiful was the unenvious lowliness of Jonathan. 'Fear not,' he said to David; 'for the hand of Saul my father shall not find thee; and thou shalt be king over Israel, and I shall be next unto thee'; and the grateful lowliness of David afterwards: 'Who am I, O Lord God, and what is my house, that thou hast brought me hitherto?'

There is a wide difference between the lowly and the proud. They differ in self-estimate. The lowly look carefully for faults in themselves, and just as carefully for excellences in others, and so are able honestly to esteem others better than themselves; but the proud, reversing this method, look for excellences in themselves, and for faults only in others. They differ also in feeling. Whatever their circumstances, the lowly, in the warmth of their gratitude, say, 'What are we, to receive so much?' while, even in abundance, the proud fretfully whisper, 'Why do we receive so little?' Moreover, they differ in dependence. Knowing their own weakness and liability to fall, the lowly make the Lord alone their confidence, and their daily prayer is, 'Hold thou me up, and I shall be safe'; whereas, vainly self-reliant, the proud almost disdain to seek guiding or upholding of any kind. Finally, they differ in motive. The grand animating motive of the lowly is not their own glory, but the Lord's: 'He must increase; I must decrease'; whereas the things ever uppermost with the proud are their own name, and fame, and exaltation.

'He that has much grace,' said Jonathan Edwards, 'apprehends much more than others that great height to which his love ought to ascend; and he sees better than others how little a way he has risen towards that height. And therefore, estimating his love by the whole height of his duty, he appears astonishingly low and little in his own eyes.'

Here is my heart; it trembles to draw near
  The glory of thy throne.
Give it thy shining robe thy servants wear
  Of righteousness thine own;
Its pride and folly chase away,
And all its vanity, I pray.

'I can never,' says George Herbert, 'do too much for him that hath done so much for me. And I will labour to be like my Saviour, *by making humility lovely in the eyes of all men.*'

Though the Lord be high, yet hath he respect unto the lowly: but the proud he knoweth afar off.—Psa. 138:6.

God resisteth the proud, but giveth grace unto the humble.—James 4:6.

I am not worthy of the least of all the mercies, and of all the truth, which thou hast shewed unto thy servant.—Gen. 32:10.

March 3

A HUMBLING EXPERIENCE OFTEN BECOMES A HELPFUL MERCY.

THE Twelve frankly allowed that what the demoniac's father said of them was true: 'I brought my son to thy disciples, and they could not cure him.' Still the failure was very perplexing to them. If they had been always thus helpless, and had never on any occasion cast out an unclean spirit, they would not have wondered. But it was not so; for wherever they had gone hitherto, this was their uniform testimony, 'Lord, even the devils are subject to us.' Yet now, though in all likelihood they tried hard and tried long, and tried separately and tried unitedly, they could do nothing whatever, but were completely baffled. What made this all the more painful was the publicity of it. Every one in the neighbourhood knew of the failure, and some, it may be, laughed them to scorn.

No experience could have been more humbling than this; nevertheless it was both a needful and helpful one, and afterwards, doubtless, when riper in grace and wisdom, they would not fail to regard it as such. It would teach much that otherwise they might never have learned. In particular it would give a decisive blow to any rising pride or self-complacency, or any over-trustfulness in their own strength, and make them lean more simply and exclusively on the power and grace of their Lord and Master.

Occasionally, when favourite plans are baffled, and the most cherished hopes are seemingly blighted forever, the depressing fear arises, that because there has been such marked failure once, there will be marked failure always. But not so; for these very failures in the beginning are often, under God, the very things that prove the best preventives of all like failures in time to come. An eminently prosperous merchant, when referring to a business event in the past, once said: 'That heavy loss in early life was the very making of me. It checked in time the over-speculativeness that might have been my ruin.'

So has it often been with believers. Under God, their failures have humbled them, their stumblings have steadied them, and their losses have enriched them. Indeed, but for these varied and seemingly adverse things, they might never have been such lights and blessings in their day and generation. God cannot work with proud instruments, but never does he refuse to employ lowly ones.

> Lest I should be exalted above measure through the abundance of the revelations, there was given to me a thorn in the flesh, the messenger of Satan to buffet me. ... For this thing I besought the Lord thrice, that it might depart from me. And he said unto me, My grace is sufficient for thee: for my strength is made perfect in weakness. Most gladly therefore will I rather glory in my infirmities, that the power of Christ may rest upon me.—2 Cor. 12:7-9.

MARCH 4

IF SAINTS LOVED MORE, THEY WOULD DOUBT LESS.

IN days of declining love to Christ, we see little in professing Christians of the holy confidence and boldness of the early church. In spite of divine utterances, both clear and unmistakable, they never get beyond a maybe. They think, they desire, they hope, but that is all; and therefore they can rarely say, with blessed assuredness, '*I know* that my Redeemer liveth'—'*I know* whom I have believed.' What makes this the more sad is, that with some it was once very different. Indeed, not till over-intimacy with the world and over-cleaving to earthly things had turned them from their first love, did darkness and doubt gain any mastery. But now, even with an opened Bible before them, they can neither see the promises as once they saw them, nor take firm hold of them. On this account, though in offer it is the held-out privilege of all believers to know the safety and blessedness of their relationship to God, yet instead of enjoying it, they are always seemingly in Doubting Castle, and full of discomfort and fear. 'Such doubts and fears,' says Thomas Boston, 'are no friends to holiness of heart and life. It is little faith that breeds them, and little faith always makes little holiness.' And as doubts hinder holiness, so they hinder usefulness.

'A man,' says Martin Luther, 'can never move the world that lets the world move him. If he is not certain about something, let him step forth; we cannot have "ifs" and "ands" where the soul is concerned, and heaven or hell at issue.' What is needed in such cases is a renewed application to the blood of sprinkling, a fresh baptism of the Spirit, a thorough coming out from the world, and a resolute return to first love and obedience. This would speedily dispel a thousand doubts and fears, and change cloud into sunshine.

The early Christians, having no chilled affection, had no doubting hesitancy. They believed and were sure that Christ was the Son of the living God, and gladly received the word, and continued stedfastly in the apostles' doctrine and fellowship. Faith like this, as it is ever honouring to God, is ever honoured by him in turn. It often secures blessed secrets for its possessor, and Pisgah glimpses of the coming glory, of which others know nothing.

> *Faith can sing through days of sorrow,*
> *'All is well!'*
> *On our Father's love relying,*
> *Jesus every need supplying,*
> *Or in living, or in dying,*
> *All must be well.*

Hereby we know that he abideth in us, by the Spirit which he hath given us.—1 JOHN 3:24.

We know that we have passed from death unto life, because we love the brethren.—1 JOHN 3:14.

Now are we the sons of God, and it doth not yet appear what we shall be: but we know that, when he shall appear, we shall be like him; for we shall see him as he is.—1 JOHN 3:2.

MARCH 5

THE LIFE OF THE CHURCH IS A MYSTERY TO THE WORLD.

IN all ages true believers have been 'men wondered at,' and often so strangely misunderstood, that their wisdom of grace has been declared to be folly, and their loving earnestness, insane fanaticism. In apostolic times, when the great preacher in bonds was proceeding to set forth the truth as it is in Jesus, with illustrative confirmations from Christian life, his utterances seemed so wildly delusive, that Festus, in the excitement of the moment, exclaimed, 'Paul, thou art *beside thyself*; much learning doth make thee *mad*.'

Like thoughts and feelings are common still. Indeed, there are in Christian experience such contrasts and opposites, that it is always a mystery to the world, and not unfrequently also to believers themselves. When we read such words as these,—'As deceivers, and yet true; as sorrowful, yet always rejoicing; as poor, yet making many rich; as having nothing, yet possessing all things,' they are ready to say, How can such things be, save in idle dream or mystic imagining? Nevertheless, they were true to the very letter in the lives of the apostles; and are true more or less still in the lives of all God's saints. They are poor, yet rich; weak, yet strong; sad, yet joyous; rarely out of conflict, yet never without victory. It was once said of David Brainerd: 'Most wonderful man, what conflicts, depressions, desertions, strength, advancement, and victories are within thy torn bosom! I cannot express what I think when I think of thee.'

This seeming contrariety of experience is not sufficiently borne in mind by believers; and so, when they find that it is not one battle they have to fight, but many, and that their whole life is a warfare—nature ever warring with grace, the flesh with the spirit—they are often at their wits' end, and know not what to do. Amid all this trial and buffeting, however, when trusted, the Lord so lovingly sustains and comforts them, that they not only hold on, but find even in severest conflicts their sweetest experiences. A well-known missionary tells us of a poor African woman, who once said to him, groaning heavily, that she had two hearts, a new and an old, and they were so constantly contending,—the one saying, 'Come to Jesus,' the other saying, 'Stay away'; the one bidding her do good, and the other bidding her do evil,—that she knew not what to do. He read to her the seventh chapter of the Romans, and showed that the apostle felt the same things. When he came to the verse, 'O wretched man that I am! who shall deliver me from the body of this death?' she said, 'Ah, massa, that me; and me know not what to do.' And when he afterwards added the words, 'I thank God, through Jesus Christ,' and explained them, she burst into tears of grateful joy. What comforted her may well comfort all similarly tempted and sorrowing ones.

> Walk in the Spirit, and ye shall not fulfil the lust of the flesh. For the flesh lusteth against the Spirit, and the Spirit against the flesh: and these are contrary the one to the other: so that ye cannot do the things that ye would ... If we live in the Spirit, let us also walk in the Spirit.—GAL. 5:16, 17, 25.

For if ye live after the flesh, ye shall die: but if ye through the Spirit do mortify the deeds of the body, ye shall live.—ROM. 8:13

MARCH 6

GOD UNKNOWN, YET WELL KNOWN.

A CHRISTIAN sailor, when referring to his conversion in early life, once told me that, when he was a boy about twelve years of age, his brother, who had never before spoken to him on religious subjects, gave him this advice: 'If you want anything, ask God for it, and he will give it you.' This greatly surprised him; all the more as never before had the thought entered his mind that prayer was a reality, and not a mere form. As it so happened, however, that at that very time there was something on which his heart was greatly set, he resolved to act on the counsel given him. He prayed, and God answered. This, which proved the turning-point of his whole life, was such a new experience to him, that, young as he was, he said to himself, 'There is a God, and I have not known him.'

It is still so with multitudes. With all their knowledge, they know not God; but this ignorance, so far from being a surprise to them, or a sadness, as with the sailor boy, or a motive for seeking after him, is contentedly accepted,—for they desire not the knowledge of his ways. In these times, God, to large numbers, is little more than a great, resistless, impersonal Force, without love or sympathy, with whom they cannot have communion, and from whom, in their difficulties and sorrows, they can get no help. How strange such darkness, and how mournful! 'That which to us is the greatest reality,' says Mr Saphir, 'appears a vague and doubtful abstraction to unbelief: it regards as obscure what is to us light, manifesting itself and making all things manifest; it deems inadmissible and far off what is constantly around us, nay, lives within us,—a well of water springing up into eternal life.'

Yes; though the unbelieving may not know him, God is well known to others; so well known, indeed, that as children with their Father they daily commune with him, and trust him and love him, and in answer to their prayers continually receive from him blessed sympathy and aid. They would as soon, therefore, doubt their own existence, as doubt the being, faithfulness, sympathy, and tender lovingkindness of their God. Like the Psalmist, they can confidently say, 'This God is our God for ever and ever: he will be our guide even unto death.' When he had reached his last hours, Mr Day of Bristol said: 'O my God, my portion, my all! Blessed be thy name, thou hast said unto me, "I am thine," and never hast thou failed me.' Then stretching out his hand to his family around his bed, like a patriarch on the threshold of heaven, he added: 'Shine forth in thy glory on these dear ones. Thou wilt never leave them.'

> God doth not leave his own:
> This sorrow in their life he doth permit,
> > Yes, chooseth it,
> To speed his children on their homeward way.
> He guides the winds. Faith, love, and hope all say,
> 'God doth not leave his own.'

This is life eternal, that they might know thee the only true God, and Jesus Christ, whom thou hast sent.—JOHN 17:3.

Acquaint now thyself with him, and be at peace: thereby good shall come unto thee.—JOB 22:21.

MARCH 7

WHEN REQUESTS ARE RASH, DENIALS ARE KIND.

NEVER was suppliant more rash than Elijah when 'he requested for himself that he might die; and said, It is enough: now, O Lord, take away my life; for I am not better than my fathers.' He had too much light and godly fear, himself to take away life. Doubtless the very thought of such a thing would have been utterly abhorrent to him. But in his sore disquietude he had not submission and faith enough calmly to wait and say, with the patriarch, 'Though he slay me, yet will I trust in him.' He demanded instant relief, and in his own way. 'O Lord God,' he said, 'take away my life; for I am not better than my fathers.' How strange to be so fearless once, and so fearful now; so lately contending for the truth and honour of God before many enemies, and now setting up his own thoughts against God's thoughts, and rashly declaring, 'It is enough,' when it was not enough!

Elijah had yet many lessons to learn, fuller testimony to bear, and richer privileges to enjoy. 'If the Lord,' as one says, 'had taken him at his word, and also said, "It is enough," Elijah's history would have wanted its crowning glory.' When, therefore, with fretful impatience, he asked for a speedy termination of his seemingly fruitless labours, the Lord in very kindness denied his request.

He might have been excused, in some degree, had high spiritual reasons alone influenced him; but vehemently to desire death through mere vexation and disquietude was entirely unworthy of him. Though it may not be wrong to say, 'Oh that I had the wings of a dove, that I might fly away, and be at rest!'—for the desire is a very natural one, and it is a relief at times to the weary spirit to give utterance to it—yet we should take heed lest there be more of nature than of grace in a too frequent expression of such feeling. Paul longed to depart, for to be with Christ is far better; yet he was heartily willing to abide, because it was more needful for others. So should it be with us.

At a private meeting of friends, on one occasion, George Whitefield, after adverting to the difficulties attending the gospel ministry, said that he was weary with the burdens of the day, and declared it to be his great consolation that in a short time his work would be done, and he should depart and be with Christ. He then appealed to the ministers present, and asked if they had not entirely similar feelings. They generally assented, with the exception of Mr Tennent. On seeing this, Mr Whitefield, tapping him on the knee, said: 'Well, Brother Tennent, you are the oldest man among us; do you not rejoice to think that your time is so near at hand when you will be called home?' Mr Tennent bluntly answered that he had no wish about it. Being still further pressed for some opinion more definite and decided, he then added: 'I have nothing to do with death. My business is to live as long as I can, and as well as I can, and serve my Master as faithfully as I can, until he shall think proper to call me home.' It proved a word in season to the great evangelist, helping him more calmly and patiently to hold on his way.

> For I am in a strait betwixt two, having a desire to depart, and to be with Christ; which is far better: nevertheless to abide in the flesh is more needful for you. And having this confidence, I know that I shall abide and continue with you all for your furtherance and joy of faith.—PHIL. 1:23-25.

> I pray not that thou shouldest take them out of the world, but that thou shouldest keep them from the evil.—JOHN 17:15.

MARCH 8

THE LORD SEES COUNTLESS WAYS OF RELIEF WHEN WE CAN SEE NONE.

USUALLY it is when men are unexpectedly beset with sore difficulties that we best know their real character, and whether faith or unbelief is their ruling principle. We see this strikingly exemplified in the history of the Israelites. So long as outwardly things went well with them, even they could believe his words and sing his praise; but no sooner did any new emergency or pressing want arise, than, forgetful of all his marvellous and loving interpositions in the past, they said, in bitter unbelief, 'Can God furnish a table in the wilderness? Can he give bread also? Can he provide flesh for his people?' Thus, simply because they lost sight of the means, they lost hope in their God; altogether forgetting that when there is real need, 'with means, or without means, or contrary to all means,' he can supply. How frequently is it still so, even with God's own children, especially in temporal straits and difficulties! The moment supplies begin to fail, they begin to fear, and too often to fret as well; as if he who feeds the fowls of the air, and clothes the lilies with such beauty, could ever forget seasonably to supply his people.

When the disciples went forth at their Lord's command, taking nothing for their journey, neither staves nor scrip nor bread, were they allowed to want, and put to shame? No, verily; for when afterwards the question was put to them, 'Lacked ye anything?' they answered, 'Nothing, Lord.' So has it been in every age. The Lord is a generous provider; and in answer to trustful prayer, supplies often come from his gracious hand in an unlooked-for way. We may be at a loss how to supply, but he never is. There may be no miracles now, strictly so called; but there are still assuredly, from time to time, many marvels of loving providence in times of need, as not a few believers can happily testify.

Such experiences greatly refresh the spirit, and are peculiarly strengthening to faith. There are few more interesting examples of this than the one narrated by Mr Spurgeon. Speaking of his grandfather's experience, he tells that when the family cow died, and the poor pastor's children were left without their staff of life—'"What will you do now?" said my grandmother. "I cannot tell what we shall do, but I know what God will do. God will provide for us. We must have milk for the children." The next morning there came £20 for him. He had never made application to the fund for the relief of ministers; but on that day there was £5 left when they had divided the money, and one said, "There is poor Mr Spurgeon down in Essex; suppose we send it to him." The chairman—Mr Morley of his day—said, "We had better make it £10, and I will give £5." Another £5 was offered by another member, if a like amount could be raised to make it up to £20—which was done. They knew nothing about my grandfather's cow; but God did, you see, and there was the new cow for him. And those gentlemen were not aware of the importance of the service they had rendered.'

He who sits upon the throne of grace knows what things we have need of, and knows the best way to help us.

It may not be my way,
It may not be thy way;
But yet in his own way,
The Lord will provide.

Your Father knoweth what things ye have need of, before ye ask him.—MATT. 6:8.

My God shall supply all your need according to his riches in glory by Christ Jesus.—PHIL. 4:19.

Verily, I say unto you, Whatsoever ye shall ask the Father in my name, he will give it you.—JOHN 16:23.

MARCH 9

DEFEAT, YET VICTORY.

ONE of the marked peculiarities of the Bible is, that it gives not only the history of the past, but not a little also of the history of the future. These are the words of the Lord to John: 'Write the things which thou hast seen, and the things which are, and the things *which shall be hereafter.*' Though this is done with much brevity and frequently in symbolical terms, it has nevertheless mightily strengthened the faith, hope, and courage of the church of God in every age. In part of the prophetic unfolding of the future it is thus written of the saints: 'The beast made war against them, and overcame them.' Here defeat is intimated, but such a defeat as to be itself a victory; for elsewhere it is written that, loving not their lives unto the death, '*they overcame him* by the blood of the Lamb, and by the word of their testimony.' And so complete was the triumph, that they are thereafter described by John as having 'gotten the victory over the beast, and over his mark, and over the number of his name,' and as singing 'the song of Moses the servant of God, and the song of the Lamb.' This illustrates the blessed fact that martyrs may be silenced, and yet through grace be victors after all, as history has amply proved.

Ignatius, who was martyred in the year 107, said: 'Let fire and the cross, let wild beasts, let all the malice of the devil come upon me; only may I enjoy Jesus Christ. It is better for me to die for Christ, than to reign over the ends of the earth. Stand firm,' he added, 'as an anvil when it is beaten upon. It is part of a brave combatant to be wounded, and *yet to overcome.*' In losing life, he found it.

So has it been with many all down the centuries. Perhaps when finally overborne by their persecutors, they have said, like Savonarola, 'Nothing now remains but to lament silently, and to hold fast the hope of a better future'; and like him, too, it may be, they have been slain, and their bodies burned by the executioners, but in dying they triumphed, and their martyr-blood became the seed of the church.

Such seeming defeat, yet real victory, is beautifully set forth by Bunyan when describing the martyrdom of Faithful: 'Then they brought him out to do with him according to their law; and first they scourged him, then they lanced his flesh with knives, after that they stoned him with stones, and last of all they burned him to ashes at the stake. Thus came Faithful to his end. Now I saw that there stood behind the multitude, a chariot and a couple of horses waiting for Faithful, who, as soon as his adversaries had despatched him, was taken up into it, and straightway was carried up through the clouds, with sound of trumpet, the nearest way to the celestial gate.

> *Sing, Faithful, sing, and let thy name survive;*
> *For though they killed thee, thou art yet alive.'*

Truly, then, 'It is better,' as one says, 'to weep with Jerusalem in the forenoon, than with Babylon in the afternoon. Our day of laughter and rejoicing is coming.'

I know thy works, and where thou dwellest, even where Satan's seat is: and thou holdest fast my name, and hast not denied my faith, even in those days wherein Antipas was my faithful martyr, who was slain among you, where Satan dwelleth.—Rev. 2:13.

Nay, in all these things we are more than conquerors through him that loved us.—Rom. 8:37.

Gad, a troop shall overcome him: but he shall overcome at the last.—Gen. 49:19.

March 10

*THOSE WHO BEST KNOW THE SOUL'S WORTH, MOST FEAR THE
TEMPTER'S WILES.*

FROM the day of his conversion to the end of life Saul of
Tarsus was so keenly bent on winning souls, that he would
fain have no service barren and no labour lost. He was ever on
the watch, therefore, and far more concerned himself about the
inward spiritual state of professed disciples than about their
outward condition. He was too unselfish and generous, indeed, to
be indifferent to the latter, or to fail in tender sympathy with them
in all the trials and persecutions that befell them for the gospel's
sake. Still, his anxiety was not so much about the possibility of
their suffering, as about the possibility of their sinning and falling,
through subtle temptation. 'For this cause,' he said, 'when I could
no longer forbear, I sent to know your faith, lest by means the
tempter have tempted you, and our labour be in vain.'

Some make light of this great enemy here called the Tempter,
and speak as if he were rather a myth than a reality. They cannot do
this, however, without entirely ignoring the fact that the existence
and personality of Satan are recognised by all the sacred writers,
and that under various names his nature, character, and agencies
are very fully revealed. Indeed, we have just the same evidence
for the real personality of Satan, as we have for the existence
and personality of the Holy Spirit and of the angels of God. The
Christian men who in every age have most nobly battled for the
truth, have ever had the liveliest sense of the reality and ceaseless
counter-working of the great adversary of God and man, and of
the need of continued prayer and watchfulness lest he should get
an advantage over them. Never have they forgotten the apostle's
words: 'We wrestle not against flesh and blood, but against principalities and powers, and the rulers of the darkness of this world.'

But though we have such enemies, we are not to flee in dismay
from them. 'Poor Christian,' Bunyan tells us, 'was hard put to it in
the Valley of Humiliation, for he had gone but a little way before

he espied a foul Fiend coming over the field to meet him—his name is Apollyon. Then did Christian begin to be afraid, and to cast in his mind whether to go back or to stand his ground. But he considered again that he had no armour for his back, and therefore thought that to turn the back to him might give him greater advantage with ease to pierce him with his darts. Therefore he resolved to venture and stand his ground; for, thought he, had I no more in mine eye than the saving of my life, 'twould be the best way to stand.' After sore conflict, he overcame by one stroke with the sword of the Spirit, which is the word of God. His example is fitted to encourage us who are now in the battlefield. There must be no yielding to the Tempter, however fierce the assault or subtle the wile.

Resist the devil, and he will flee from you.—JAMES 4:7.

Neither give place to the devil.—EPH. 4:27.

Put on the whole armour of God, that ye may be able to stand against the wiles of the devil.—EPH. 6:11.

MARCH 11

THE USUAL MODE OF THE SPIRIT'S OPERATION.

WHATEVER the instrumentality employed, the Spirit alone is the real and efficient agent in every conversion, and he works in varied mode. There have been times when thousands have been simultaneously convinced of sin and brought to Christ, as on the memorable day of Pentecost; for then, through one sermon of one ambassador, and he a poor illiterate fisherman of Galilee, no less than three thousand souls were converted at one and the same time. Nor was this conversion either feigned or feeble, for not only did they gladly receive the word and were baptized, but, it is added, 'they continued stedfastly in the apostles' doctrine and fellowship, and in breaking of bread, and in prayers, and did eat their meat with gladness and singleness of heart, praising God.'

Not unfrequently, however, the Spirit begins with a single case, an individual sinner, and awakens, enlightens, and converts him, before, as it were, directly dealing with any other. It was so in Achaia. The first singled out there, and effectually called, was Epenetus; and so the apostle said, 'Salute my well-beloved Epenetus, who is *the first-fruits of Achaia unto Christ*'; and then followed the household. In this way the word of the Lord passed from individual to individual, and from family to family, till a church of believers was gathered in.

So is it still, both at home and abroad. In the riches of his grace, the Lord gathers one here and one there, and adds them to the number of such as shall be saved. Never, therefore, must we despise the day of small things. If it is said, 'What is one Epenetus, or one household of Stephanas, or one mission church, amid the countless thousands of heathenism?' Not much, doubtless, in themselves, or for boastful utterance before men; yet very much when viewed as a token of the Spirit's presence and power, and as an earnest and pledge of what is coming. They are not simply fruits, but *first-fruits*, rich in promise, and sure precursors of a plentiful and glorious harvest when the fulness of time shall come.

When some one, discouraged in the day of small things, once said to Dr Judson, 'Do you think the prospect bright of the speedy conversion of the heathen?' 'Yes,' he nobly replied; 'as bright as the promises of God.' True faith is never staggered, though sense may often be.

> There shall be an handful of corn in the earth upon the top of the mountains; the fruit thereof shall shake like Lebanon: and they of the city shall flourish like grass of the earth. His name shall endure for ever: his name shall be continued as long as the sun: and men shall be blessed in him: all nations shall call him blessed.—PSA. 72:16, 17.

> It shall come to pass in the last days, that the mountain of the Lord's house shall be established in the top of the mountains, and shall be exalted above the hills; and all nations shall flow unto it.—ISA. 2:2.

MARCH 12

DARKNESS PREFERRED TO LIGHT.

THERE is something very saddening in the apostle's words when describing the state of the Gentile world: 'They became vain in their imaginations, and their foolish heart was darkened. Professing themselves *to be wise, they became fools,* and changed the glory of the uncorruptible God into an image made like to corruptible man.'

In not a few respects, this mingling of professed wisdom and exhibited folly is as strikingly exemplified now as in early times. In his rich grace God has been pleased to give a full revelation of himself in his word and in his Son; but instead of thankfully availing themselves of its blessed light, many would rather seemingly go back to the darkness, and find some void where God is not.

Scripture opens with these words: 'In the beginning God created the heaven and the earth.' This utterance, at once simple and sublime, commends itself alike to reason and to conscience, and its truth is confirmed by countless evidences on every side of wise and beneficent design. Many of the professedly wise, however, prefer to believe that, without a personal, all-wise, almighty God at all, 'somehow or other,' as one forcibly puts it, 'innumerable atoms assembled themselves on the fields of primeval chaos, and were violently shaken together; and that from the uncaused commotion of these uncreated atoms there sprang up all the green things under heaven, all the fishes of the sea, all the fowls in the air, and all the thinking, feeling children of human kind.'

Could anything be more utterly incredible? And yet this is a favourite speculation of modern unbelief. What condition of mind could be sadder! God is, and he is the rewarder of all who diligently seek him; but they know him not. From him cometh down every good and perfect gift; but they thank him not. At sundry times and in divers manners he has spoken in time past unto the fathers by the prophets, and in later days unto us by his Son from heaven; but they heed him not. In fine, in him they live, and move, and have their being; but, ignoring all this, they say, 'Who is Lord over us?' Yet death is nearing, and judgment and eternity, and at any moment the message may come, 'Prepare to meet thy God.'

Fully to know this great God and Father, we must know the Son; for, 'This is life eternal, to know thee the only true God, and Jesus Christ, whom thou hast sent.' 'Sages of the earth,' says Vinet, 'Christ is the key of your problems; troubled hearts, he is your peace; lovers of wealth, he is your treasure; men, he is the Word which solves the enigma of life. He alone rebinds us to the Author of our being and to universal order.'

> The wisdom of this world is foolishness with God. For it is written, He taketh the wise in their own craftiness. And again, The Lord knoweth the thoughts of the wise, that they are vain.—I COR. 3:19, 20.

> For after that in the wisdom of God the world by wisdom knew not God, it pleased God by the foolishness of preaching to save them that believe.—I COR. 1:21.

MARCH 13

CONTENTED LUKEWARMNESS.

THAT speech cost him dear who uttered it: 'Soul, take thine ease, eat, drink, and be merry.' Yet, in spirit and aim, how many are like him! Instead of being loyally zealous for truth and righteousness, they sit at ease even when both are imperilled. Nay, worse still, what is manifestly sin they change into virtue by calling it moderation. They go to no extremes, they allege, and take no side. They are friendly to truth, but they are not with any keenness unfriendly to error; and while giving one hand to Christ, they yet do not refuse to give the other to the world. In fine, they try in vain to serve two masters. John Trapp, the commentator, was wont quaintly to say: 'They resolve to keep on the warm side of the hedge, to sleep in a whole skin, to suffer nothing and do nothing that may interfere with their hopes and preferments.'

This by many may be deemed prudence, but the Lord condemns it as a heartless lukewarmness which he utterly loathes. 'I would thou wert cold or hot,' he says. 'So then because thou art lukewarm, and neither cold nor hot, I will spue thee out of my mouth.' Need we wonder at the sternness of such rebuke, when we remember the greatness of the love wherewith he loved us, in that he laid down his life to save us; and consider also what grievous dishonour such coldness brings on his name and cause.

We cannot possibly serve both God and mammon. 'When you see a dog following two men,' says Ralph Erskine, 'you know not to which of them he belongs while they walk together; but let them come to a parting-road, and one go one way, and the other another way, then will you know which is the dog's master. So while a man may have the world and a religious profession too, we cannot tell which is the man's master, God or the world; but stay till the man come to a parting-road. God calls him this way, and the world calls him that way. Well, if God be his master, he follows truth and righteousness, and lets the world go; but if the world be his master, then he follows the flesh and the lusts thereof, and lets God and conscience go.' It is always so. The lukewarm can never be trusted, but the heartily-loving are ever loyal.

> Elijah came unto all the people, and said, How long halt ye between two opinions? if the Lord be God, follow him: but if Baal, then follow him.—1 KINGS 18:21.

> Ye cannot serve God and mammon.—MATT. 6:24.

> He that is not with me is against me; and he that gathereth not with me scattereth abroad.—MATT. 12:30.

MARCH 14

WE MUST BOTH TAKE HOLD AND HOLD FAST.

I T is not more necessary to come to Christ than to cleave to him; and if for any reason we fail to do so, we not only imperil our comfort and usefulness, but our very salvation. It is emphatically written, 'If any man draw back, my soul shall have no pleasure in him'; 'No man, having put his hand to the plough, and looking back, is fit for the kingdom of God.' This was the sin of Lot's wife: she was on the very brink of being saved, but looked back, and perished. There must therefore be neither a looking back on our part nor a going back, but a steady, resolute holding on.

Doubtless this is no easy thing, just because there are so many snares, difficulties, and temptations on every side; but why should any of us fail on this account, or let go the profession we have been privileged to make? We may be weak and our adversary mighty, but what of that when we have one to uphold who is mightier far? The battle is not ours, but the Lord's, and we know that, through him, in the end victory is sure. Those who have Jesus for them and Jesus in them have nothing whatever to fear, though encompassed by enemies on every side.

In the persecuting days of the English Queen Mary, a good man of the name of Palmer, when condemned to die, was earnestly persuaded to recant, and among other things, a friend said to him, 'Take pity on thy golden years and pleasant flowers of youth, before it is too late.' His reply was not more conclusive than beautiful: 'Sir, I long for those springing flowers which shall never fade away.' When in the midst of the flames, he exhorted his companions to constancy, saying, 'We shall not end our lives in the fire, but make a change for a better life; yea, for coals we shall receive pearls.'

And now we fight the battle,
But then shall wear the crown

Of full and everlasting
And passionless renown;
And he whom now we trust in
Shall then be seen and known;
And they that know and see him
Shall have him for their own.

Let us hold fast the profession of our faith without wavering; for he is faithful that promised.—HEB. 10:23.

Seeing then that we have a great high priest, that is passed into the heavens, Jesus the Son of God, let us hold fast our profession.—HEB. 4:14.

The Lord is faithful, who shall stablish you, and keep you from evil.—2 THESS. 3:3.

MARCH 15

IF THE MIGHT OF THE LORD IS MARVELLOUS, STILL MORE IS HIS MERCY.

ONE of the briefest prayers in the word, and one of the best, is that of the publican, 'God be merciful to me a sinner,' just because it so emphatically expresses what everyone needs, and what, too, everyone may find who truly seeks it. However much men may differ in other respects, yet as sinners *needing mercy* they are all on an equality, and must inevitably perish without it.

When this need begins to be felt—and every truly awakened sinner feels it—it is a frequent fear that divine mercy may not prove ample enough to meet their case, and cover iniquities so great and manifold. In cherishing any such feeling, they forget all the wondrous light that Bethlehem and Calvary throw on the character and mercy of God, and the words so solemnly proclaimed in the hearing of Moses, 'The Lord God, merciful and gracious, longsuffering, and abundant in goodness and truth, keeping mercy for thousands, forgiving iniquity, and transgression, and sin,' and they forget the multitudes unnumbered who are already monuments of the mercy that redeems.

When referring to the well-known words of the Psalmist, 'He is merciful and gracious, slow to anger, and *plenteous in mercy,*' an old writer once said: 'Here are four properties in God, and all so necessary that we could not miss one of them. If he were no more than merciful, we could hope for no more but pardon; but when, besides being merciful, he is also gracious, this gives us further hope of a donative, not what we are worthy to receive, but what it is fit for him to give. If he were not so slow to anger, we could expect no patience; but when, besides his slowness to anger, he is full of compassion, this makes us expect that he will be the Good Samaritan, and not only bind up our wounds, but take care also for our further curing.'

> *My soul, repeat his praise*
> *Whose mercies are so great,*
> *Whose anger is so slow to rise,*
> *So ready to forgive.*

God, who is rich in mercy, for his great love wherewith he loved us, even when we were dead in sins, hath quickened us together with Christ.—EPH. 2:4, 5.

I will be merciful to their unrighteousness, and their sins and their iniquities will I remember no more.—HEB. 8:12.

Let Israel hope in the Lord: for with the Lord there is mercy, and with him is plenteous redemption.—PSA. 130:7.

MARCH 16

AIMLESS WORKING IS USELESS WORKING.

PAUL was too intensely set on the salvation of men to be satisfied with the mere preaching of the truth, apart from a direct and personal application of it. He therefore combined admonition with exposition—'warning *every man* and teaching *every man* in all wisdom.' Having a distinct and practical aim, he did not deal with men merely in the general, but individualised them, as it were, and dealt with them as each might need.

So must it be with all workers who would effectually glorify the Lord and serve their generation. In seeking the good of others, they must be special alike in aim and in effort, just because each one has his own special responsibilities, trials, and wants. A mere vague love to humanity is a poor, purposeless, and inoperative thing. It dreams and speculates only, but never puts its hand to real work, or goes forth with deliberate design to lift the fallen, guide the erring, and cheer the downcast.

But true Christian workers are not only special in their aim to save; they are equally special in their aim to elevate, and strive, like the apostle, as far as possible, 'to present every man *perfect* in Christ Jesus,'—perfect in relationship, and 'accepted in the Beloved'; perfect in character, 'holy and unblamable in his sight'; perfect in knowledge, 'filled with the knowledge of his will in all wisdom and spiritual understanding'; and perfect in gladness, knowing that 'the joy of the Lord is their strength.' 'Heaven,' says one, 'begins when faith in Christ drops the seed of eternal life into the soul; increases when the soul quits its earthly tabernacle; and is perfected when, at the Lord's coming, the soul is united to a glorified body.'

> The God of peace, that brought again from the dead our Lord Jesus, that great shepherd of the sheep, through the blood of the everlasting covenant, make you perfect in every good work to do his will, working in you that which is wellpleasing in his sight, through Jesus Christ; to whom be glory for ever and ever. Amen.—Heb. 13:20, 21.

> That he might present it to himself a glorious church, not having spot, or wrinkle, or any such thing; but that it should be holy and without blemish.—Eph. 5:27.

MARCH 17

NOT ONE IN TRIBE, YET ONE IN CHRIST.

THERE are great diversities among men,—diversities in nationality, in civilisation, and religious rite,—and these, too, of long standing, and visible to every eye. Nevertheless, when the gospel comes in power through the Spirit of all grace, the strange diversity is lost in a marvellous unity. There is then 'neither Greek nor Jew, circumcision nor uncircumcision, Barbarian, Scythian, bond nor free: but Christ is all, and in all.' Yes; whatever a man's tribe, or tongue, or outward circumstances, the gospel comes to him, not merely in freest offer, but with such special adaptation and completeness that, when it is embraced, he will feel its quickening and sanctifying power.

From age to age this saving and uniting gospel continues to be the power of God and the wisdom of God to everyone that believeth; yea, to the very lowest of the bond, as well as to the free. Some years ago a poor miner, who had almost been given up as a castaway, was mercifully brought to experience the saving power of the gospel. After his conversion he said: 'I praised God with all my heart for what he had done for a poor sinner like me. Everything looked new to me,—the people, the fields, the cattle, the trees. I was like a man in a new world; and I was so joyous that some said I was a mad-man: but what they might well mean was that I was a glad-man; and, glory be to God! I have been glad ever since.'

Never, perhaps, were two men in the beginning more widely apart in position, character, and cherished interests than Paul and Onesimus. Onesimus was but a servant, yea, lower still, a slave; yet if he had been one of the nearest and dearest of relatives, Paul could not have pleaded for him with more touching affection or persuasive earnestness: 'I beseech thee,' he said, 'for my son Onesimus, whom I have begotten in my bonds: which in time past was to thee unprofitable, but now profitable to thee and to me: ... that thou shouldest receive him; not now as a servant, but above a servant, a brother beloved, specially to me, but how much more unto thee, both in the flesh, and in the Lord?' Such tender and loving words from the lips of a once proud, stern, Gentile-hating Pharisee beautifully illustrates the purifying and ennobling influence of grace. It is only a vital Christianity that can win such triumphs, and unite men in warmest brotherhood in spite of every diversity of tribe and tongue.

There is no difference between the Jew and the Greek: for the same Lord over all is rich unto all that call upon him.—ROM. 10:12.

By one Spirit are we all baptized into one body, whether we be Jews or Gentiles, whether we be bond or free; and have been all made to drink into one Spirit.—1 COR. 12:13.

Let the brother of low degree rejoice in that he is exalted: but the rich, in that he is made low.—JAMES 1:9, 10.

MARCH 18

REPETITIONS MAY BE NEEDFUL.

AN unbroken sameness of discourse soon ceases to be edifying, and therefore, either in matter or form, there must usually be more or less of change. This indispensable characteristic is beautifully seen in the word of God. It contains not only all that is necessary to be known and believed in order to salvation, but there is in it such fulness of gracious truth, in such varied and interesting aspects, that in almost every page we meet with something new. In presenting the new, however, it never allows us to forget the old, or to give but a secondary place to the grand essential truths that centre in Christ, and are linked to salvation: hence the apostle's well-known words, 'To write *the same things* to you, to me is not grievous, but for you it is safe.' Plainly, it was not because his range was a narrow one that he did this—for in his writings we find things deep and glorious, as well as simple and practical; food for the strong, as well as milk for the babes—but mainly that he might the better impress upon men the things that belonged to their peace.

Such repetition and reiteration are at times an absolute necessity. What we hear but once we are apt to underestimate as a thing of but little account, and apt also speedily to forget. 'Why,' said one, 'do you tell that dull boy the same thing twenty times over?' 'Because,' replied the mother, 'nineteen times would not do. If I told him that but nineteen times, my labour is lost, but the twentieth time secures the object.' It is just so with us: we need line upon line, and precept upon precept, to make us permanently remember; and what we need our gracious Lord lovingly bestows.

'Those of us,' says Mr Spurgeon, 'who have been preaching for five and twenty years sometimes feel that the same work, the same subject, the same people, and the same pulpit, are together apt to beget a feeling of monotony, and monotony may soon lead to weariness. But then we call to mind another sameness, which becomes our complete deliverance,—there is the same Saviour, and we go to him in the same way as we did at the first, since he is the same yesterday, today, and forever. Beneath his smile our long-accustomed work grows new, and wears a brighter charm than novelty could have given it. We gather new manna for our people every morning; and as we go to distribute it, we feel an anointing of fresh oil distilling upon us: "They that wait upon the Lord shall renew their strength."'

> I will not be negligent to put you always in remembrance of these things, though ye know them, and be established in the present truth. Yea, I think it meet, as long as I am in this tabernacle, to stir you up by putting you in remembrance.—2 Pet. 1:12, 13.

> Nevertheless, brethren, I have written the more boldly unto you in some sort, as putting you in mind, because of the grace that is given to me of God.—Rom. 15:15.

MARCH 19

ENTRANCE AND CONTINUANCE.

THERE is much in the old saying, 'Well begun is half done.' Nevertheless, hopeful as is a good beginning, it is never of itself enough, either in temporal or in spiritual matters. In a race, men may be first at the start, and yet be last at the goal, and thus miss the prize so eagerly coveted; in a warfare, an army may be victorious in one campaign, and yet be crushingly defeated in the next; and in ordinary business, men may be very prosperous in their first transactions, and yet come to utter bankruptcy through their last.

It is the same in highest things. Rarely is it safe to build with absolute assuredness on any mere beginnings, however hopeful. At the outset, Demas had seemingly so much faith, zeal, and hope that believers never doubted that he was really and truly one of themselves. It was so, too, with the Galatians. How hopefully they began! 'Ye did run well,' said the apostle; 'ye received me as an angel of God.' Yet ere long Paul was constrained to say of them: 'O foolish Galatians, who hath bewitched you, that ye should not obey the truth, before whose eyes Jesus Christ hath been evidently set forth, crucified among you?'

It is not without reason, therefore, that so many earnest cautions are from time to time given us. Some may perhaps imagine that such language is scarcely consistent with the blessed doctrine of the perseverance of the saints. But it is not really so. In the storm, though Paul had an assured belief that not a man in the ship would be lost, because the safety of all had been expressly promised, he did not on this account idly neglect the use of means. On the contrary, he emphatically said, 'Except these abide in the ship, ye cannot be saved'; and by this warning, their lives were preserved and the promise fulfilled. So with believers;—though safe the very moment they come to Christ and enter in, nonetheless are they warned in varied utterances like these: 'If a man abide not in me, he is cast forth as a branch, and is withered'; 'No man, having put his hand to the plough, and looking back, is fit for the kingdom of God'; 'But if any man draw back, my soul shall have no pleasure in him.' Indeed, *the fear of their coming short* is made, through the Spirit, one of the most effective means of preventing it, and of securing their continuance in the faith stedfast to the end.

With regard to the apparently exceptional cases of those who once seemed to be saints, but have afterwards gone wholly back, we can safely use the words of John: 'They went out from us, but they were not of us; for if they had been of us, they would no doubt have continued with us.' 'Never is it well with me,' said John Berridge, 'but when I am at home with Jesus.'

Little children, abide in him; that, when he shall appear, we may
have confidence, and not be ashamed before him at his coming.—
1 JOHN 2:28.

If ye abide in me, and my words abide in you, ye shall ask what ye
will, and it shall be done unto you.—JOHN 15:7.

MARCH 20

*ONLY THOROUGHLY BIBLE CHRISTIANS CAN BE
THOROUGHLY STABLE ONES.*

SCRIPTURE is fittingly called by the apostle 'the word of
Christ,' because it speaks so fully of his person, character,
sufferings, and glory. He is the body of all its shadows, the reality
of all its types, and the Yea and Amen of all its promises.

Now, rightly to honour this word, we must not deal with it
coldly and suspiciously, as we might deal with a stranger, but must
welcome it within, and allow it to reign there and entirely regulate
the life; for so does the apostle enjoin when he says, 'Let the word
of Christ dwell in you richly in all wisdom.' To secure such an
indwelling of the word, we must read it, not occasionally only, but
steadily and systematically; yea, and strive to find day by day our
delight and pleasure in it, even as the Psalmist did. 'O how love I
thy law!' he said; 'it is my meditation all the day'; 'The law of thy
mouth is better unto me than thousands of gold and silver; yea,
sweeter than honey and the honeycomb.' The word, indeed, was
all in all to him: his lamp in darkness, his guide in perplexity, his
armour in conflict, and the very food and refreshment of his soul
in every season of fainting or weariness.

Happily for us, where his word dwells thus richly in any heart,
there the Lord himself dwells also, in all the blessed fulness of
his love and power. In this way, the weak become strong and the
wavering stable; and when times of trouble and temptation come,
instead of turning their back upon the Lord and letting go the
faith, they resolutely cleave to him with purpose of heart, and, if
need be, prove faithful even unto death.

The word of the Lord, therefore, is very precious, and its truths not only cheer the soul, but are its indispensable nourishment. 'The first source of life,' says Dr Cuyler, 'is food; and it must be nutritious enough to produce spiritual bone, blood, and muscle. A Christian's bread is the truth of God. His diet is God's word—whether studied at home or heard in the sanctuary—and solid books, and heart communings with Jesus. No soul can wax fat on syllabub. All the athletic Christians have been huge and hungry feeders on the word.'

> Thy word have I hid in mine heart, that I might not sin against thee.—PSA. 119:11.

> If ye continue in my word, then are ye my disciples indeed.— JOHN 8:31.

> To the law and to the testimony: if they speak not according to this word, it is because there is no light in them.—ISA. 8:20.

MARCH 21

THE INJURED SHOULD NOT INJURE IN TURN.

WHATEVER may be the world's maxim as to forbearance, this is emphatically the Lord's: 'See that none render evil for evil unto any man; but ever follow that which is good, both among yourselves, and to all men.' This is the Christian law, and it is an all-important one; but it runs so contrary to all the instincts of our fallen nature, that it requires no common grace heartily to comply with it. In ordinary everyday life, indeed, it usually finds but little place in the thoughts of men, and still less in their practice.

This gracious spirit of requiting good for evil was ever exemplified by our Lord and Master. 'When he was reviled, he reviled not again; when he suffered, he threatened not; but committed himself to him that judgeth righteously.' Yea, on the very cross his last and touching words were, 'Father, forgive them; for they know not what they do.' Accordingly, in the word this is the spirit everywhere enjoined,—'Recompense to no man evil for evil.' 'Say not thou, I will recompense evil; but wait on the Lord, and he shall save thee.' 'Dearly beloved, avenge not yourselves, but rather give place unto wrath: for it is written, Vengeance is mine; I will repay, saith the Lord. Therefore if thine enemy hunger, feed him; if he thirst, give him drink: for in so doing thou shalt heap coals of fire on his head.'

No one ever conquered an enemy's heart by revenge, but many have done so by love. Few hearts are so obdurate as not to melt, in some degree at least, under the mighty energy of patient, self-denying, burning love. Would that there were more everywhere ready to heap such coals of fire on the heads of those who injure them. It was once said of a saintly man, who had much of this excellent spirit, that the surest way to obtain a kindness from him was to do him an injury. 'When Christian charity,' said Leighton, 'is not encountered by the world's malignance, it hath an easier task, but assaulted and overcoming, it shines the brighter and rises higher; and thus it is when it renders not evil for evil.' He adds: 'It is a poor glory to vie in railings or in returns of evil; but it is the glory of man, one of the noblest of victories, to pass by a transgression.'

It would make the cherishing of such a spirit all the easier, were we oftener to remember how continuously through life we ourselves have been indebted to the forbearing and forgiving lovingkindness of the Lord. Verily, 'It is of the Lord's mercies we are not consumed.' Those who need mercy themselves should never be slow to show it to others.

> Thou shalt not avenge, nor bear any grudge against the children of thy people, but thou shalt love thy neighbour as thyself: I am the Lord.—Lev. 19:18.

> Let every man be swift to hear, slow to speak, slow to wrath: for the wrath of man worketh not the righteousness of God.—James 1:19, 20.

> And when his disciples James and John saw this, they said, Lord, wilt thou that we command fire to come down from heaven, and consume them, even as Elias did? But he turned, and rebuked

them, and said, Ye know not what manner of spirit ye are of.—
LUKE 9:54, 55.

MARCH 22

CHRIST'S DOUBLE SONSHIP.

THOSE who truly realise their lost condition, and would fain be redeemed, will not lightly trust any helper; and reasonably so, because the adequacy of the redemption entirely depends on the sufficiency of the Redeemer. Now, to this sufficiency the double Sonship is all-essential.

Had Jesus not been the son of Mary, he could not have been the Messiah of promise, or the Messenger of the covenant, and these scriptures could not have been fulfilled,—'Behold, a virgin shall conceive, and bear a son, and shall call his name Immanuel'; and again, 'Thou, Bethlehem Ephratah, though thou be little among the thousands of Judah, yet out of thee shall he come forth unto me that is to be ruler in Israel; whose goings forth have been from of old, from everlasting.' There was much, it is true, that was humbling about the time and place of Christ's birth; nevertheless, this very humiliation was not only a fulfilment of Scripture, but was a first and absolutely needful step in the redemption of our race.

Had this been all, however, that could have been said of Jesus, whatever his willingness, *the power* to save would have been wholly wanting in him. But the son of Mary was also the Son of God. In a voice from heaven, the Father said of him, 'This is my beloved Son, in whom I am well pleased.' And he himself said, 'God so loved the world, that he gave *his only begotten Son*, that whosoever believeth in him should not perish, but have everlasting life.'

This all-important fact is one of the most marvellous in the Bible. Indeed, 'God manifest in the flesh' is expressly declared to be the great mystery of godliness; and it is only through divine aid and teaching that any can rightly realise it. Accordingly, when

Peter, in reply to the question of his Lord, said, 'We believe and are sure that thou art the Christ, the Son of the living God,' Jesus answered and said, 'Blessed art thou, Simon Bar-jona: for flesh and blood hath not revealed it unto thee, but my Father which is in heaven.' Indeed, among the early Christians so great a thing was it for a poor sinner to acknowledge that the only begotten of the Father was made flesh and dwelt among us, and died for our salvation, that whenever any one among the Jews or idolaters openly said, 'I believe that Jesus is the Son of God,' they were ready almost at once to baptize him. What need we more? they seemed to think,—the great secret has been revealed to his soul; God has come to him, and dwelleth in him, and he in God.

> *He, the mighty God, has come,*
> *Making this poor earth his home;*
> *Come to bear our sins' sad load,—*
> *Son of David, Son of God.*
> *He has come whose name of grace*
> *Speaks deliverance to our race;*
> *Left for us his glad abode,—*
> *Son of Mary, Son of God.*

'The hand,' said Augustine, 'that was nailed to the cross built the universe.'

Unto us a child is born, unto us a son is given: and the government shall be upon his shoulder: and his name shall be called Wonderful, Counsellor, The mighty God, The everlasting Father, The Prince of Peace.—ISA. 9:6.

Unto you is born this day in the city of David a Saviour, which is Christ the Lord.—LUKE 2:11.

MARCH 23

*THE LORD BOTH KNOWS HIS PEOPLE AND DELIGHTS
IN THEM.*

THOUGH God bears with godless and unsanctified men, and makes his sun to shine and his rain to descend on them as on others, yet he never looks on them with benign complacency, or expresses delight in their persons or ways. He could not, for it is his very nature to shun and loathe everything morally vile. He is not a God that hath pleasure in wickedness; neither shall evil dwell with him. As a refined ear, for which music, with all its rich and varied harmonies, has special charms, cannot possibly delight in jarring discords, so neither can the Lord, from the very perfection and purity of his nature, delight in those who scorn his mercy and go on in sin.

Very differently, however, does the Lord regard those who accept his offered love and grace in Jesus Christ, and walk in his fear. They are precious in his sight, a peculiar treasure, dear as the apple of his eye, the objects of his constant care; even as the prophet says: 'The Lord thy God in the midst of thee is mighty; he will save, he will rejoice over thee with joy; he will rest in his love, he will joy over thee with singing.'

This precious truth, however, is not always realised by them, just because, though the Lord's promises are ever clear, his providences are often dark. At such seasons they are sorely tempted either to say fretfully with the patriarch, 'All these things are against me,' or to ask despondingly with the Psalmist, 'Hath God forgotten to be gracious? hath he in anger shut up his tender mercies?' At other times, again, it is not so much outward as inward things that perplex them; such as the deceitfulness of their own hearts, the waywardness of their affections, and all their deeply-felt shortcomings in daily life.

Yet, in spite of these varied fears, there is never on the part of the Lord any forgetting or forsaking of those who trust in him. It is a proverb among the serfs in Russia, who feel as if they had none to care for them, 'God is high above us, and the Czar is far away.' But no genuine believer has ever reason for any such utterance. It is true no voice may be heard from heaven, nor divine footstep be seen on earth; but he needs no such outward signs to assure him, for he has the word of the Lord on which to rest, and knows that wherever his lot may be cast, or however remote from creature fellowship or sympathy, his God will be with him, keeping his soul in peace, and making even the roughest of paths the very highway to heaven.

> *God will protect to heaven,*
> *And every good that meets thee is*
> *A blessing wisely given.*
> *If losses come—so let it be,*
> *The God of heaven remains with thee.*

If the Lord delight in us, then he will bring us into this land, and give it us; a land which floweth with milk and honey.—Num. 14:8.

The steps of a good man are ordered by the Lord: and he delighteth in his way.—Psa. 37:23.

Thou shalt be called Hephzibah, and thy land Beulah: for the Lord delighteth in thee, and thy land shall be married.—Isa. 62:4.

March 24

THE TRUE PLACE OF APPOINTED ORDINANCES.

THOSE who are prone, from mystical tendencies in their nature, to undervalue outward ordinances, forget that, when kept in their true and intended place, so far from being antagonistic to spiritual religion and the inner life, they are, on the contrary, sweetly helpful in every way. Had it been otherwise, never would the Psalmist have said: 'How amiable are thy tabernacles, O Lord of hosts! My soul longeth, yea, even fainteth for the courts of the Lord.' Others, again, have a tendency to rely unduly on things external, and to make more of the courts of the Lord than of the Lord of the courts. The church gets greater prominence than Christ, and more is expected from the administration of the sacraments than from the preaching of the gospel of the grace of God.

We see this in the case of Paul, who, in the days of his darkness, gloried in mere externals—such as his Hebrew origin, his peculiar training, and his Pharisaic exactness in all matters of the law, though these were of no avail whatever for justification. So was it with his nation. Never, perhaps, were the Jews more ceremonially rigid than in the time of our Lord. They gloried in their ancestry, their exclusiveness, the splendour of their temple, and the multiplicity of their services; yet all the while they were in reality profaning the temple, making void the law, and filling up the measure of their iniquity, till, by the rejection of the Son of God, wrath came upon them to the uttermost. Mere ritualism did not save the Jews, neither will it save the Gentiles.

While guarding, however, against this fatal error in regard to ordinances, we must beware of falling into another not less so, and, alas! still more common—the neglect of ordinances altogether. 'When I thought myself a dying man,' said Robert M'Cheyne, 'the souls of the perishing thousands in my own parish *who never enter any house of God*, have lain heavy on my heart.' He felt that their misery was all the greater, and their need the deeper, that such neglected souls had no wish for help, and would never ask it for themselves. This made him not only labour much for more churches, but *pray much for faithful men to fill them*. He thus summed up his views in lines penned by himself:—

> *Give me a man of God the truth to preach,*
> *A home of God within convenient reach;*
> *Give these, and give the Spirit's genial shower,*
> *Scotland shall be a garden all in flower.*

He is a Jew, which is one inwardly; and circumcision is that of the heart, in the spirit, and not in the letter; whose praise is not of men, but of God.—ROM. 2:29.

We are the circumcision, which worship God in the spirit, and rejoice in Christ Jesus, and have no confidence in the flesh.—PHIL. 3:3.

MARCH 25

TRIAL IS OFTEN A BLESSED 'NEED BE.'

WHEN about to leave the disciples whom he had been revisiting, the apostle's last word to them was not, The worst is now over, and henceforth all trouble will cease; but rather, Trouble will come, and must come, for the pathway to the kingdom is through much tribulation.

This *must*, linked as it is with trial, has a very sad sound to our ears; but there is this to comfort in connection with it,—it is not the 'must' of a cold and grinding fate, which wholly excludes sympathy and forbids prayer, but the 'must' of a Father's will, wise, loving, and tender, and by which gracious ends are served. The vine cannot flourish without the pruning-knife, and as little can the believer be effectually delivered from all the corruptions of the flesh and spirit without painful discipline. 'Thinkest thou,' says an old writer, 'that thou wilt come into the kingdom without the cross and tribulation, which Christ neither would nor could permit even to one of his dearest friends? It is through the cross we reach the glory. Carry it willingly, then; so will it carry thee and conduct thee to that place where there is the end of all thy sorrows and the goal of all thy longings.'

These divinely permitted trials are very varied in their nature. Sometimes it is grievous disappointment that occasions them, or sore bereavement, or the buffetings of the adversary, or the bitter enmity of a hostile world; hence the forewarning yet comforting words of the great Master: 'In the world ye shall have tribulation: but be of good cheer; I have overcome the world.'

Besides thus counselling good cheer, he has again and again *imparted it*, and so fully that even the gloomiest prisons have often resounded with gladsome songs. When Joseph Alleine and seven other ministers, and forty private Christians, were committed to the prison of Ilchester about two hundred years ago, that saintly man said much to cheer them. Among other sweet things, he said: 'Shall I tell you a story I have read? "There was a certain king that had a pleasant grove, and that he might make it every way delightful to him, he caused some birds to be caught, and to be kept in cages till they had learned sundry sweet and artificial tunes. And when they were perfect in their lessons, he let them abroad out of their cages into the grove, that he might hear them singing those pleasant tunes, and teaching them to other birds of milder note." Brethren,' he added, 'the Lord is that king, this grove is his church, these birds are yourselves, this cage is the prison; and God hath sent you hither that you should learn the sweet and pleasant notes of his praise.'

> Confirming the souls of the disciples, and exhorting them to continue in the faith, and that we must through much tribulation enter into the kingdom of God.—ACTS 14:22.

> Wherein ye greatly rejoice, though now for a season, if need be, ye are in heaviness through manifold temptations: that the trial of your faith, being much more precious than of gold that perisheth, though it be tried with fire, might be found unto praise and honour and glory at the appearing of Jesus Christ.—1 PET. 1:6, 7.

MARCH 26

OVERLOVING THE PERISHABLE.

THOUGH at conversion the power and mastery of sin are broken, nevertheless it still lurks in the soul, and unless constantly watched and kept under, it will gather strength again, and break forth, it may be, into open transgression. Even believers, accordingly, were thus exhorted by the apostle: 'Mortify therefore your members which are upon the earth … inordinate affection, evil concupiscence, and *covetousness, which is idolatry.*'

This last-named sin, covetousness, or overlove of the world, is not only sadly common, but perilous in the extreme, and called forth a special warning from our Lord to his disciples in these words: 'Take heed, and beware of covetousness: for a man's life consisteth not in the abundance of the things which he possesseth.'

Indeed, there is no sin more firm in its grasp, or longer lived. When through age, it may be, or sickness, or satiety, or a regard to reputation, the vices of the flesh are forsaken, covetousness still keeps hold. It never seems to know frailty, like other sins, but is ever young. Moreover, it is a sin peculiarly offensive to the Lord, because to all intents and purposes it is idolatry. It puts mammon in the place of God, and consecrates to mere perishable vanities the thoughts, desires, and affections that should ever be centred in him alone; yet, from assuming so many artful disguises, and being compatible often with much outward respectability, the danger of being fatally ensnared by it is on this account all the greater.

'Covetousness,' says Mr Spurgeon, 'is like the silting up of a river. As the stream comes down from the land, it brings with it sand and earth, and deposits all these at its mouth, so that by degrees, unless the conservators watch it carefully, it will block itself up, and leave no channel for ships of great burden. Many a man, when he begins to accumulate wealth, commences at the same time to ruin his soul. And the more he acquires, the more closely he blocks up his liberality, which is, so to speak, the very mouth of spiritual life. Instead of doing more for God, he does less; the more he saves, the more he wants; and the more he wants of this world, the less he cares for the world to come.'

There is no cure for this overlove of money but the generous using of it for the glory of God and the good of others.

> They that will be rich fall into temptation and a snare, and into many foolish and hurtful lusts, which drown men in destruction and perdition. For the love of money is the root of all evil: which while some coveted after, they have erred from the faith, and pierced themselves through with many sorrows.—1 TIM. 6:9, 10.

> Charge them that are rich in this world, that they be not highminded, nor trust in uncertain riches, but in the living God, who giveth us richly all things to enjoy.—1 TIM. 6:17.

MARCH 27

SAINTS ARE SOMETIMES FOUND WHERE LEAST EXPECTED.

THERE was a Joseph in Pharaoh's court, a Jonathan in Saul's, an Obadiah in Ahab's, and a Daniel in the royal halls of Babylon; and, not less remarkable, there were saints even in Caesar's household. As no details are given and no names mentioned, it is impossible to tell who these saints really were, or to whom they belonged—whether to the imperial family, or to the guards or courtiers, or humbler servants. Nevertheless, the fact remains, and it is one of deepest interest, that the Lord Jesus had true and faithful servants even in the palace of one of the greatest of persecutors. It strikingly reveals at once the sovereignty and the omnipotence of grace, and shows that we should never despair either of the worst of places or the worst of persons, should a door of access be given us to them in the providence of God. 'O Rome, Rome!' says one, 'how greatly hast thou changed! Formerly thou hadst true saints even in the household of a pagan and cruel emperor, but now thou hast false saints round the so-called chair of Peter, and at the court of his supposed successors.' However great the discouragements, therefore, we should be slow to give up even the most hopeless, knowing what grace can do, and that the Lord ever takes pleasure in those who hope in his mercy.

> *Hope through the watches of the night,*
> *Hope till the morrow brings the light,*
> *Hope till thy faith be lost in sight,—*
> *Abound in hope.*

Not long ago, a well-known and useful minister said: 'Now I will tell you how I found the Lord. It is fourteen years ago, and I was at a meeting in the house of that good old man, Captain Blackford, where they sang that night the hymn ending with, "I will believe, I do believe, that Jesus died for me." I was asked to go there by the young lady who afterwards became my wife and who died a year ago. The words rang in my ears as I went home, and drove me wild.

Drawing a circle round me with a stick, I said, "A short life and a merry one, though I should perish at last!" But all that night I walked my room in torment. Next day, taking "The Sinner's Friend," I went to the Crystal Palace, and on a seat under a tree read the first page. Springing up upon the seat I said, "I, a wild, reckless young man, take thee, O Christ! as my Saviour for life." And now, after fourteen years, Jesus is more precious to me than ever he was.'

God is able of these stones to raise up children unto Abraham.—MATT. 3:9.

But they had heard only, That he which persecuted us in times past now preacheth the faith which once he destroyed. And they glorified God in me.—GAL. 1:23, 24.

MARCH 28

LOVE IN PART, AND LOVE IN FULL.

BROTHERLY love has for its objects mainly the brotherhood of Christ's people, the family of the redeemed, who have one Spirit, one hope, and one home; yet it never dwells alone in any breast. If really Christians ourselves, besides thus loving all brethren in Christ with the love of complacency or delight, we will cherish also love to all men, whatever their character—the love of benevolence, at least—and seek to do them good as we have opportunity.

This twofold affection is always a great power in men, and energetically influences their whole life and character. To have it in part even is a great blessing, but still more to have it in full. The apostle had so much of it in his own heart, that he intensely longed to see it glowing also in the hearts of others. 'The Lord,' he said, '*make you to increase and abound in love* toward one another and toward all men, as we do towards you.'

He felt it would be vain to enjoin such a thing unless he prayed for it also; for it is only as the Lord works in men to will and to do of his good pleasure that a grace like this can be harmoniously developed. Indeed, so precious is it, and so helpful to man as well as honouring to God, that it should be the intense desire of everyone to possess it in utmost fulness.

It is only complete when wide enough to embrace the whole Christian brotherhood, whatever their diversity in name or tongue or attainment; and intense enough to show itself not in word only but in constant and generous outflow of tender lovingkindness; yea, and mature enough as to be visibly Christlike, and a living embodiment of all that is so beautifully said of charity in the First Epistle to the Corinthians.

This further only need be added, that *the new life*, which ever brings with it *the new love*—for hereby 'we know that we have passed from death unto life, because we love the brethren'—invariably produces a great change, even on our common affection. It gives it a refinement and purity, a moral elevation, it never had before. When referring to this peculiarity, one says, after having himself tasted that the Lord is gracious: 'There is not one of those I love now, as I used to do; the wife of my bosom, the child of my house, the stranger within my gates, the beggar at my door, the queen reigning over me, the companion of my leisure, the partner of my business, the holy man of God, the wretched prodigal—it is, in many aspects of it, a new affection that I feel to every one of them.'

> But as touching brotherly love ye need not that I write unto you: for ye yourselves are taught of God to love one another.—I Thess. 4:9.
>
> And above all things have fervent charity among yourselves.—I Pet. 4:8.
>
> And now abideth faith, hope, charity, these three; but the greatest of these is charity.—I Cor. 13:13.

MARCH 29

LOSING ALL FOR CHRIST.

IN the days of his alienation the great apostle put *all* before Christ; but when light and grace entered his soul he put *Christ* before all, and not in profession only, but in reality. While he could speak for Christ, and never failed to do so on every fitting occasion, he could also unweariedly labour for him, and suffer also. So thorough, indeed, was the surrender made by him, that he not only suffered the loss of all things, but did so joyfully; though in these 'all things' were included, not his goods only, but also his prospects, his friendships, and his very life.

Nor was there anything fanatical in this; for the heaviest losses for Christ ever in the end bring the richest gains. An old commentator says: 'Christ is to be sought and bought at any hand and at any rate. We cannot buy this gold too dear. Paul is well content to part with a sky full of stars for one Sun of Righteousness.' And then he asks: 'Esteem we Christ as the people did David, "worth ten thousand of us"; as Naomi did Ruth, "better than ten sons"; or as Pharaoh did Joseph, "none so wise or worthy as thou"?'

Great as the apostle's sacrifice for Christ was, he never changed his mind regarding it. Having thoroughly counted the cost before he paid it, there was no after regretting, or murmuring, or wishing that what he had done could yet be undone. 'I would like,' says Mr Moody, 'to have been in Rome when Paul walked down its streets. Rome never before saw such a conqueror. "Paul, you are going to execution: are you not sorry you gave your life to the Lord? You have had to suffer so much,—stoned, persecuted, beaten with many stripes, in many dangers in the wilderness, in perils by sea and by land,—are you not sorry? Would you give your life to Christ if you had it to do over again?" "Yes," he replies; "if I had ten thousand lives, I would willingly give them all for his dear sake." He has nothing to regret, nothing to be sorry for. "Sorry!" he cries; "I thank God a thousand times a day that I ever gave myself to him."'

Be thou faithful unto death, and I will give thee a crown of life.—REV. 2:10.

He that findeth his life shall lose it: and he that loseth his life for my sake shall find it.—MATT. 10:39.

I have fought a good fight, I have finished my course, I have kept the faith: henceforth there is laid up for me a crown of righteousness, which the Lord, the righteous judge, shall give me at that day: and not to me only, but unto all them also that love his appearing.—2 TIM. 4:7, 8.

MARCH 30

OUR ADVOCATE WITH THE FATHER.

HIS people are very dear to Christ, and he never forgets them. True, being no longer on earth, we cannot now, like the disciples of old, sit with him, and walk with him, and joyously commune face to face. Nevertheless, we live in his memory and in his heart, and have ever a place in his prayers: 'It is Christ that died; yea rather, that is risen again, who is even at the right hand of God, *who also maketh intercession for us.*' The butler in his exaltation forgot Joseph in the prison, and all about the promise he had so freely made to him. But the Lord Jesus never forgets any of his saints. It is not more true that he ever liveth, than that he ever intercedeth; and not for their safety only, but for their comfort, and usefulness, and final glory.

His prayers, which are ever efficacious—for he can *will*, as well as ask—have no narrow limits, but in their ample sweep embrace both heaven and earth, eternity and time. Yea, he so delights in his people, that though meanwhile he may say, 'I pray not that thou shouldest take them out of the world, but that thou shouldest keep them from the evil'; yet at the last, where he is, there they must be, for these are his own express and blessed words: 'Father, *I will* that they whom thou hast given me be with me where I am; that they may behold my glory, which thou hast given me.'

We often say that heaven would not be heaven to us if the Redeemer were not in it; and rightly, for he is our light and life, our strength and joy, yea, our all in all. But our Lord's petition clearly shows, that neither would it be heaven to him if those were not in it for whom he died.

In most great festive assemblies usually some of the invited are absent, and some seats vacant. But no such blanks in the end shall ever meet the Redeemer's eye; for so all-prevailing is his advocacy, that from the great company of the ransomed not one shall be missing. All that are in him now shall unfailingly be with him hereafter; else the joy which sustained him on the cross would not be realised, nor would he see of the travail of his soul and be satisfied.

A poor old slave, when nearing his end, was asked where he expected to go. 'I think I shall go to the good land.' 'Why do you think so?' 'I cannot tell; but the nearer I come to death, somehow Jesus and I get nearer together.' Happy experience! May it also be ours; for it is only as Jesus is near that we can have safety and peace.

> *I feel thine arms around,*
> *Saviour ever near:*
> *With thee let me be found;*
> *So shall I never fear,*
> *Whatever ills abound,*
> *Saviour ever dear.*

If any man serve me, let him follow me; and where I am, there shall also my servant be: if any man serve me, him will my Father honour.—JOHN 12:26.

If I go and prepare a place for you, I will come again, and receive you unto myself; that where I am, there ye may be also.—JOHN 14:3.

Then we which are alive and remain shall be caught up together with them in the clouds, to meet the Lord in the air: and so shall we ever be with the Lord.—I THESS. 4:17.

MARCH 31

SAINTS CANNOT LOSE THEIR TREASURE.

IN a world like this, where nothing is safe or certain, those who have their portion in this life only are necessarily fearful and anxious, especially in troublous times. When disasters befall them they are ready to say, with Micah, 'Ye have taken away my gods, and what have I more?'

Very different is the experience of true believers when in full fellowship with their Lord. Even in such trying circumstances they are calm and peaceful, because they know that, come what may, they can never lose their promised inheritance. These precious words assure them of this: 'Who hath begotten us again unto a lively hope by the resurrection of Jesus Christ from the dead, to an inheritance incorruptible, and undefiled, and that fadeth not away, reserved in heaven for you.'

It is divinely kept for them; and when they are of full age, and their training complete, they shall surely and eternally possess it. What is laid out upon believers is nothing to what is laid up for them in heaven. Now they have but a few foretastes of the heavenly Canaan—a grape or two, as it were, from Eshcol's clusters. But what of that, when all the grand, precious, and abiding fruits of redemption are securely preserved for them where no enemy can enter, or thieves break through and steal!

Heaven, therefore, should be often in their thoughts. Their true home and blessed resting-place is there; the best and holiest of every age and clime are there: many loved ones of their own, it may be, are already there; above all, their loving Lord and Saviour— their hope, their joy, their treasure, yea, their all in all—is there. And very soon they themselves will be there: for happily there is a double keeping—not only is the inheritance kept for them, but they through the mighty power of God are kept for the inheritance. With such things before them, so sure and blessed, what manner of persons ought they to be in all holy conversation and godliness?

'Dear old saint,' said Richard Knill to the author of 'The Sinner's Friend,' 'I bless God that you were ever born; and that you are born again; and that you have written for the glory of God and the good of souls. While I was preparing to preach in the fields at Tintworth I ruptured a blood-vessel; and though since then able to preach once a week again, I have lost my youthful buoyancy, and wish to stand in a waiting posture every day to obey the summons to depart and to be with Christ. I hope to see you coming after me, if I go first. And what a meeting we shall have! Shall I sing louder than you? I should like to do so. Farewell till we meet in glory.'

Martin Luther once said, 'that a man may lift up his head toward heaven; he must find nothing on earth on which to lean it.'

The hope which is laid up for you in heaven.—COL. 1:5.

For where your treasure is, there will your heart be also.—MATT. 6:21.

For here have we no continuing city, but we seek one to come.—HEB. 13:14.

APRIL 1

THE FIRST WORK TO BE DONE.

WHEN the Jews came to our Lord, and said, 'What shall we do, that we might work the works of God?' the answer they received not only surprised them but deeply offended them: 'This is the work of God,' he said, 'that ye believe on him whom he hath sent.' They would gladly have welcomed any new legal injunctions, however rigid or burdensome, and have done their utmost to carry them out; but simply to believe on Jesus of Nazareth they utterly scorned. It is the same with multitudes still. The enjoined believing is the very last thing they think of; and yet, if ever they are to be saved, it must be the very first. This stands to reason, just because there is no Redeemer but Christ, and no way of acceptance but through his finished work. Till we believe in him, therefore, we are yet in our sins,—lost, helpless, condemned; for it is expressly written, 'He that believeth not is *condemned already.*' In this state, any works wrought by us, whatever their number or excellence, can have no acceptance with God; nor can they lighten the pressing burden of our guilt even by a feather's weight.

Beyond question, then, to trust in Christ is God's first and great commandment of salvation, and until we obey it we are utterly undone. This was the very first thing the awakened jailer of Philippi had to do, and, blessed be God, he did it, and did it too, not on any after-morrow, but then and there. Yea, that very hour he believed on the Lord Jesus Christ, and found salvation. So ought it to be with all, for there should be no lingering in a matter so vital. If none can be too soon forgiven, sanctified, and blessed, then none can too soon close with offered mercy in Jesus Christ.

'The work demanded of the sinner himself,' said Dr Joseph Alexander, 'is only hard because it is so easy. It is hard to do little, when we think we must do much; hard to do nothing, when we think we must do all; hard to believe that we have only to believe, when we expected to achieve our own redemption. When once the soul, however, is brought to believe that this is truly God's plan of redemption—that the Son of God is able and willing to save, and that this salvation is sufficient and secure—and besides this general belief, accepts of this salvation for himself—the work is done; the man is justified, and safe forever.'

This is his commandment, That we should believe on the name of his Son Jesus Christ.—1 JOHN 3:23.

For by grace are ye saved through faith; and that not of yourselves: it is the gift of God.—EPH. 2:8.

He that believeth on me hath everlasting life.—JOHN 6:47.

APRIL 2

THERE IS A SLEEP THAT IS EASY,
BUT NEVER SAFE.

IT was when Samson slept that he was shorn of his locks; it was when Christian slept that he lost his roll; and it was because the virgins slept that they were found unready when the bridegroom came. So, from a like spirit of slumber, multitudes to this very hour are neither safe nor happy. Even believers are showing drowsy tendencies, which injuriously affect their labours, their prayers, their fellowships, and heavenly longings. Yet never before, perhaps, was a thoroughly wakeful, believing spirit more urgently needed; for perils are great on every side, and the witchery that of old beguiled the Galatians, and drew them away from the truth as it is in Jesus, seems now to be showing itself everywhere.

'Satan,' says Bishop Hall, 'always rocks the cradle when we sleep at our devotions. If we would prevail with God, we must wrestle first *with our own dullness.*' And if this be needful, even in ordinary times, how much more so in the perilous days on which we are entering?

Whatever we come short in, let it not be in watchfulness. None like to slumber who are expecting a friend or fearing a foe. How, then, should it be with us, when we have the Friend of friends to look for, and the very worst of enemies to guard against? We are bid beware of our great adversary, who goeth about as a roaring lion, seeking whom he may devour; but like many beasts of prey, he doeth most in the night, and is afraid when he finds a believer armed and on the outlook.

Bunyan tells us 'that when Hopeful came to a certain country, he began to be very dull and heavy of sleep. Wherefore he said, "Let us lie down here, and take one nap." "By no means," said the other, "lest sleeping, we wake no more." "Why, my brother? Sleep is sweet to the labouring man; we may be refreshed, if we take a nap." "Do you not remember," said the other, "that one of the shepherds bid us beware of the Enchanted Ground? He meant by that, that we should beware of sleeping."'

'Therefore let us not sleep, as do others; but let us watch and be sober.' Slumbering and backsliding are closely allied.

> Why sleep ye? rise and pray, lest ye enter into temptation.—LUKE 22:46.

> While the bridegroom tarried, they all slumbered and slept. Watch therefore, for ye know neither the day nor the hour wherein the Son of man cometh.—MATT. 25:5, 13.

> And that, knowing the time, that now it is high time to awake out of sleep: for now is our salvation nearer than when we believed.— ROM. 13:11.

APRIL 3

GO WHERE WE MAY, WE ARE NEVER OUT OF OUR FATHER'S TERRITORY.

WHEN Jacob reached Bethel at sunset, and lay down to sleep with only a stone for his pillow, he was weary, fearful, and faint. Nor can we wonder at this; for not only had his brother threatened his life, and his mother urged him to flee, but the land he was going to was strange and the people unknown. If all human help, however, failed him, the God of his fathers did not; for in a vision by night he graciously said to him, in spite of all his unworthiness: 'Behold, I am with thee, and will keep thee *in all places* whither thou goest, and will bring thee again into this land; for I will not leave thee, until I have done that which I have spoken to thee of.'

This was the promise, and one more full of grace and kindness we cannot easily conceive; and after varied and trying vicissitudes it was fulfilled to the letter. And what God did then for Jacob, he has since done again and again in every age for his trusting people. Amid all their wanderings and perplexities in this vale of tears, he keeps them, guides them, provides for them, blesses them, and never leaves them till he has finally brought them to their heavenly inheritance. In the length and in the breadth of it, the whole earth is the Lord's, for it is the creation of his hand; and, therefore, dwell where his people may, they are never out of his territory, or beyond his loving eye.

Just because of this, when sending his servants to do his work, our Lord asked no man's permission. 'Go ye,' he said, '*into all the world*, and preach the gospel to every creature'; 'I am with you alway, even unto the end of the world.'

> *When on the mighty deep,*
> *He will their spirits keep,*
> *Stayed on his word;*
> *When in a foreign land,*
> *No other friend at hand,*
> *Jesus will by them stand,*
> *Jesus their Lord.*

'O my God, give me but thy presence,' said a good man once, 'and I will not ask thee what road I shall travel, nor dare nor desire to dictate to thee, whether the path shall be rough or smooth. If it be smooth, I may be blessed with thy smile; if it be rough, thou hast given "shoes of iron and brass," and the result is no matter of doubt.'

The Lord is thy keeper: the Lord is thy shade upon thy right hand. The Lord shall preserve thee from all evil: he shall preserve thy soul. The Lord shall preserve thy going out and thy coming in.—Psa. 121:5, 7, 8.

And they shall fight against thee; but they shall not prevail against thee; for I am with thee, saith the Lord, to deliver thee.—Jer. 1:19.

The Lord shall deliver me from every evil work, and will preserve me unto his heavenly kingdom.—2 Tim. 4:18.

APRIL 4

WE MAY DO LOFTY SERVICE EVEN IN
A LOWLY SPHERE.

THERE are few counsels of the word less heeded than that given by the prophet, 'Seekest thou great things for thyself? seek them not.' Instead of not seeking such things, *greatness* in one or other of its forms—a great name, a great position, a great income, a great sphere—seems with many to be their all in all. Yet neither peace nor usefulness is in any way dependent on it. Indeed, in choosing his instrumentality for carrying out his grand and saving designs, it is the feeble rather than the strong, the mean rather than the mighty, that the Lord selects. 'God,' says the apostle, 'hath chosen the foolish things of the world to confound the wise; and God hath chosen the weak things of the world to confound the things which are mighty; and base things of the world, and things which are despised, hath God chosen, yea, and things which are not, to bring to nought things that are: that no flesh should glory in his presence.'

Besides, it frequently happens that the Lord is more glorified in humble positions than in elevated ones. The greatness of the sphere may be a main thing with us, but *faithfulness* in it is the main thing with the Lord. Accordingly, it is not the great servant in the great sphere that is specially commended at the last, but the faithful one in any sphere, even the lowliest. 'Well done, thou good and *faithful servant*: thou hast been *faithful over a few things*, I will make thee ruler over many things: enter thou into the joy of thy Lord.'

'With the sphere of our work we have nothing to do. That is arranged for us from the first. Our only business is to shine where we are. And he whose consistent holy life and simple loving words make him the light of his own family, of his own village, of his own fellow-workmen, of his own fellow-servants, is doing work for Christ in which Gabriel himself would consider it an honour to be employed.'

Be brave my brother;
He whom thou servest slights
Not e'en his weakest one.
No deed, though poor, shall be forgot
  However feebly done;
The prayer, the wish, the thought,
  The faintly-spoken word,
The plan that seemed to come to nought,
  Each has its own reward.

Whosoever therefore shall humble himself as this little child, the same is greatest in the kingdom of heaven.—MATT. 18:4.

Be clothed with humility: for God resisteth the proud, and giveth grace to the humble.—1 PET. 5:5.

And Jesus said, Let her alone; why trouble ye her? ... She hath done what she could: she is come aforehand to anoint my body to the burying. Verily I say unto you, Wheresoever this gospel shall be preached throughout the whole world, this also that she hath done shall be spoken of for a memorial of her.—MARK 14:6, 8, 9.

APRIL 5

THE LORD'S DAY IS EVER A LOVED DAY WITH
HIS PEOPLE.

THERE was a Sabbath in Eden; and if needful then, how much more now, amid all the manifold toils and conflicts of our present fallen condition! If even with such a day we are so prone to sink into carnality and earthliness, what would we be if entirely deprived of its divine and ever helpful influence? It is well, when at any time tempted to its violation, to bear in mind that the Sabbath, unlike mere Jewish and temporary ordinances, has a central place in the ten commandments; and that these commandments alone had the marvellous honour put upon them of not merely being twice written, by the very finger of God, on tables of stone, but of having been proclaimed, by his own voice, in the hearing of thousands. What could more emphatically intimate the binding obligation of the Sabbath, or show that it was designed, not for Jew only, or for Gentile, but for man in all ages and in all climes?

Doubtless, to many the Lord's day is often a weariness. They are grieved when it comes, and glad when it goes, just because, their eyes being unopened and their hearts untouched, they have no spiritual tastes, no intimacy with God, and no realisation of divine and eternal things. But it is not so with those who, through faith in Jesus, have passed from death unto life. They love everything that is his, and therefore they love his day. It is to them the sweetest day of all the seven. Every hour of it is dear to them, and they readily join with the Psalmist in saying, 'This is the day which the Lord hath made; we will rejoice and be glad in it.'

> *O day most calm and bright!*
> *The week were dark but for thy light—*
> *Thy torch doth show the way.*

'A world without a Sabbath,' says one, 'is like a man without a smile, like summer without flowers, like a homestead without a garden.' Truly, then, whatever it may be to others, the Sabbath of the Lord is a delight to the saints—a true joy, a type of heaven—and brings sweetly to mind their risen Lord, the home he is preparing for them, and the rest eternal on which they are soon to enter. 'I was born on a Sabbath,' says David Brainerd; 'and I was new-born on a Sabbath; and I hope I shall die on a Sabbath-day. I long for the time. Oh, why is his chariot so long of coming!'

Remember the sabbath day, to keep it holy.—EXOD. 20:8.

If thou turn away thy foot from the sabbath, from doing thy pleasure on my holy day; and call the sabbath a delight, the holy of the Lord, honourable ... then shalt thou delight thyself in the Lord; and I will cause thee to ride upon the high places of the earth, and feed thee with the heritage of Jacob thy father: for the mouth of the Lord hath spoken it.—ISA. 58:13, 14.

APRIL 6

EVEN IN THE DARKEST VALLEY GOD CAN
GIVE LIGHT.

S OME through fear of death are all their lifetime subject to bondage. They fear the mystery of it, the loneliness of it, the possible conflict and suffering of it, and the unknown experiences that follow it. Yet, strange to say, not unfrequently when these trembling ones come to the dark valley, and are about to pass through it, they are not disturbed by a single cloud, and of dying struggle they sometimes know absolutely nothing. A brother minister once said to an old Christian, who through this fear had been always more or less in bondage: 'Your Lord will either graciously sustain you in the last conflict, or he will save you from all conflict whatever.' So it proved in the end. One morning, on inquiring for his old friend, the housekeeper said: 'O sir, my master is gone! I called him in the morning, when he spoke to me. About an hour later I went into his room. He was lying calm and peaceful. I spoke to him again, but got no reply. Then looking at him more earnestly, I saw it was the sleep of death.' Thus gently and lovingly the Lord took him home.

One great source of such fear and discomfort, on the part of not a few, is unbelieving haste. Not content with getting grace enough to carry today's burden, they would in their eagerness fain have enough to carry tomorrow's also—yea, and all the burdens that may at any time be laid upon them. They forget that it is not God's way to kindle night-lamps before the sun goes down, or to supply today the wants of tomorrow. Suffering grace comes with the suffering hour, and dying grace with the dying hour, but not earlier. Were this only more firmly and abidingly believed by God's children, they might be spared many a sad and clouded hour.

> When thou passest through the waters, I will be with thee; and
> through the rivers, they shall not overflow thee: when thou
> walkest through the fire, thou shalt not be burned; neither shall

the flame kindle upon thee. For I am the Lord thy God, the Holy One of Israel, thy Saviour.—Isa. 43:2, 3.

Yea, though I walk through the valley of the shadow of death, I will fear no evil: for thou art with me; thy rod and thy staff they comfort me.—Psa. 23:4.

April 7

TO DEAL HOPEFULLY WITH THE FALLEN,
WE MUST DEAL TENDERLY.

IF there are occasions when to be faithful we must be stern in our utterances and rebuke with all severity—as when Paul said to Elymas the sorcerer, 'O full of all subtilty and all mischief, thou child of the devil, thou enemy of all righteousness, wilt thou not cease to pervert the right ways of the Lord?'—there are times, on the other hand, when it is the meekness of wisdom that is specially required, with forbearing gentleness. It is thus written accordingly: 'Brethren, if a man be overtaken in a fault, ye which are spiritual, restore such an one in the spirit of meekness; considering thyself, lest thou also be tempted.'

The restoration of a fallen brother is not to be undertaken in a hard and haughty spirit which dwells bitterly on the sin, and brings its aggravations into undue relief, but rather in wise love and gracious tenderness. The enjoined spirit of meekness compassionates while it blames. Its fidelity is Jesus-like and full of sympathy; it does not break the bruised reed or quench the smoking flax.

It is the very want of such wise tenderness that often renders young disciples less able to deal with such cases. From not realising their own weakness and the terrible power of subtle temptation, they are apt to become unduly harsh in their judgments; and thus while they may intend to help and win, in reality they only repel and harden. It is very different with experienced believers. That caution is seldom forgotten by them, 'Considering thyself, lest thou also be tempted'; and, therefore, instead of being, as perhaps once they were, severe on others and tender to themselves, they now judge others with charity and themselves with severity. Exhibiting this spirit, at once lowly and loving, they more readily win the ear of the fallen and gain access to their heart.

It is thus all-important, if we are to deal hopefully with the erring, to keep in abiding remembrance our own liability to fall, and constant dependence on the Spirit of all grace. When Legh Richmond was once conversing with a neighbour on the case of a poor man, who had acted inconsistently with his Christian profession, his friend, after some severe remarks on the conduct of such persons, concluded by saying, 'I have no notion of such pretences; I will have nothing more to do with him.' 'Nay, brother,' replied Mr Richmond, 'let us be humble and moderate. With opportunity on the one hand, and Satan on the other, and the grace of God at neither, where should you and I be?' These are weighty words, and may well find place in every memory.

'Let me not forget,' said an old Christian, 'either my continual liability to fall if left to myself, or the faithful engagements of my God to keep me from falling. While I stand by faith, still the exhortation is most needful—"Be not high-minded, but fear."'

Brethren, if any of you do err from the truth, and one convert him; let him know, that he which converteth the sinner from the error of his way shall save a soul from death, and shall hide a multitude of sins.—JAMES 5:19, 20.

We then that are strong ought to bear the infirmities of the weak, and not to please ourselves.—ROM. 15:1.

Wherefore let him that thinketh he standeth take heed lest he fall.— 1 COR. 10:12.

APRIL 8

MANY OFTEN MISS THE GREAT BY OVERLOOKING THE LITTLE.

IT was well for Naaman, when wroth with the prophet, that he had among his servants one who could wisely say to him, 'My father, if the prophet had bid thee do some great thing, wouldest thou not have done it? how much rather then, when he saith to thee, wash, and be clean?' The simplicity of the remedy offended Naaman, and through unbelieving pride he was nearly missing forever the cure of his body and the conversion of his soul. So it is with many to this day. The way of salvation seems to them foolishly simple and offensively free—'Wash, and be clean'—'Look unto me, all ye ends of the earth, and be ye saved'; and thus, instead of believing in Jesus, they turn away from him in the pride of their heart, and thereby finally and forever miss the gift of gifts—eternal life.

But besides this difficulty before conversion, there is often a somewhat similar stumbling after it, by which not a few entirely miss the great in holiness by overlooking the little. As nothing is insignificant in sin, so neither is anything insignificant in right-eousness. Complete conformity, therefore, to the mind and will of God in everything—in the small as well as in the great, in word as in deed—must ever be our constant aim and prayer.

Nowhere is the importance of this more seen than in the family circle, where the kind look, the soft answer, the willing help, not only gladden like sunshine, but are powerfully influential in winning to higher things. Without this we cannot be Jesus-like in spirit, or be helpful and honoured witnesses for his name in evil times.

The young merchant who takes care of his pounds, but is utterly heedless of his pence, is not likely to become rich. And so, the young Christian who is very careful about great duties, and very careless about what he thinks small ones, is not likely to become eminent in holiness. Even little foxes spoil the vines, and need therefore to be carefully guarded against. 'A holy life,' as Dr Bonar beautifully says, 'is made up of a number of small things: little words, not eloquent speeches or sermons; little deeds, not miracles or battles; not one great heroic act or mighty martyrdom, make up the true Christian life. The little constant sunbeams, not the lightning—the waters of Siloah, that go softly in their meek mission of refreshment, and not the waters of the rivers, great and many, rushing down in torrent noise and force—are the true symbols of a holy life.'

> Whosoever therefore shall break one of these least commandments, and shall teach men so, he shall be called the least in the kingdom of heaven: but whosoever shall do and teach them, the same shall be called great in the kingdom of heaven.—MATT. 5:19.

> And the very God of peace sanctify you wholly; and I pray God your whole spirit and soul and body be preserved blameless unto the coming of our Lord Jesus Christ.—1 THESS. 5:23.

APRIL 9

THERE IS NO SAFER SEAT THAN AT
THE FEET OF JESUS.

THOUGH Martha complained of Mary, it was without just reason; for in reality Mary was not indifferent to her sister, or unwilling to share with her in domestic duties and responsibilities. She was only anxious at such a special time, when she might both learn and receive so much, to give such duties a subordinate place. She judged wisely in this; for when revealing himself, and ready to bestow with generous hand, our Lord would rather see receivers by his side than givers. Mary, knowing this, kept very near him, with open ear and open heart. Never was she happier than when sitting at the feet of Jesus, drinking in his blessed words of grace and truth. He was everything to her,—friend and helper, prophet and priest, guide and guard; yea, a very tree of life, beneath whose shadow she could sit with joy unspeakable. To be in his presence was like Beulah to her, like heaven begun; and to have a continuance of this, and be forever with the Lord, was the intensest longing of her heart. She was ever, as it were, ready to say, 'Tell me, O thou whom my soul loveth, where thou feedest, where thou makest thy flock to rest at noon?'—'Teach me: for thou art the God of my salvation.'

So should it be with all who have been delivered from the burden of guilt and dominion of sin; they should be found sitting at the feet of their Redeemer, with glowing gratitude filling their hearts and rising to their lips: 'What shall I render unto the Lord for all his benefits toward me?' Their meditation of him should be continuous and sweet, until the day break and the shadows flee away.

> *Lord, leave not me,*
> *Though full of sin I be,*
> *But love me yet.*
> *Oh, take me to thy breast,*
> *For there I'll find true rest,*
> *And with thy love possessed,*
> *All else forget.*

Such was Mary; but even she and others of like spirit are not without their danger. Unless specially watchful, they are apt in some degree to lose the practical in the contemplative, and to have too much of the quietist and too little of the worker. In the early Christians both were seen in blessed combination, and it was sweetly said of them by Clement: 'Their peace was profound and beautiful, and in doing good they were insatiable.'

She had a sister called Mary, which also sat at Jesus' feet, and heard his word.—LUKE 10:39.

As the apple tree among the trees of the wood, so is my beloved among the sons. I sat down under his shadow with great delight, and his fruit was sweet to my taste.—SONG OF SOL. 2:3.

To him that overcometh will I grant to sit with me in my throne, even as I also overcame, and am set down with my Father in his throne.—REV. 3:21.

April 10

OUR NEED, AND GOD'S SUPPLY.

IN human history failure of supply is no rare occurrence. Streams run dry, harvests are blighted, riches take wings, and just when help from them is most needed, friends droop and die. But while earthly sources like these may fail, there is no failure with the Lord. He is never to his people a waterless well in a desert land, but, 'according to his riches in glory by Christ Jesus,' he supplies their every recurring need.

How unlike is this to all mere human beneficence! Creature supplies are often so fitful, so coldly given, and so utterly inadequate as to be little more than the crumbs that fall from the table. Not so the gifts of our God. They are bestowed with fatherly love, in covenant faithfulness, and with a continuous fulness that meets our every want. Nor need this surprise us, for 'He that spared not his own Son, but delivered him up for us all, how shall he not with him also freely give us all things?'

It must ever be borne in mind, however, that what he promises to supply is not our imaginary but our real need, and not so much mere outward and temporal things, as those that are spiritual and eternal; for, as an old writer says, 'It is our necessities he consults, not our wishes: but these he meets with royal munificence, for "no good thing will he withhold from them that walk uprightly."'

Some Christians there are who, while they have no misgivings as to supply for spiritual needs, have always heavy and doubting hearts when any temporal straits befall them. But why should this be? Do they not remember what our loving Lord said on this very point?—'Behold the fowls of the air: for they sow not, neither do they reap, nor gather into barns; yet your heavenly Father feedeth them. Are ye not much better than they? Consider the lilies of the field, how they grow; they toil not, neither do they spin: and yet I say unto you, That even Solomon in all his glory was not arrayed like one of these. Wherefore, if God so clothe the grass of the field, which to day is, and to morrow is cast into the oven, shall he not much more clothe you, O ye of little faith?'

> *Who doth the birds supply,*
> *Who grass, and trees, and flowers*
> *Doth beautifully clothe through ceaseless hours,*
> *Who hears us ere we cry,*
> *Can he my need forget?*
> > *Nay, though he slay me, I will trust him yet.*

The God which fed me all my life long unto this day, the Angel which redeemed me from all evil, bless the lads.—GEN. 48:15, 16.

And God is able to make all grace abound toward you; that ye, always having all sufficiency in all things, may abound to every good work.—2 COR. 9:8.

For the Lord God is a sun and shield: the Lord will give grace and glory: no good thing will he withhold from them that walk uprightly.—PSA. 84:11.

APRIL 11

MANY A THING HAS FAILED IN THE TESTING, BUT NEVER A PROMISE OF GOD.

EVER since that fatal word was spoken and believed, 'Ye shall not surely die,' all deceivers have dealt largely in promises, and, alas! not in vain; for, to a large extent, the broken hearts in the world are fairly traceable to the broken promises in it. On the other hand, nothing, through grace, has so greatly contributed to the healing of the broken in heart, and to the cheering and sustaining of them in every trial, as the rich and varied promises of God believed in and realised. Just the other day, in Edinburgh, the testimony of an honoured and much-loved Christian soldier, when he had got nearly through the dark valley, was, 'All the promises of God are true.'

Generally speaking, good men are sparing of their promises, because limited in their resources; and because, moreover, they never make them without honestly purposing to carry them out. But as with God there is no limitation either as to fulness or faithfulness, all his exceeding great and precious promises are freely open to every believer. And as the promises are like the stars in multitude, so like them, also, they are best seen and most prized in our night seasons of sorrow and trial.

'I remember an aged minister used to say,' said Isaac Watts, 'that the most learned and knowing Christians, when they come to die, have only the same plain promises for their support as the common and unlearned; and so,' he continued, 'I find it. It is the plain promises of the gospel that are my support, and I bless God *they are plain*; for I can do nothing now but look into my Bible for some promise to support me, and live upon it.'

> *Jesus, thou Joy of loving hearts!*
> *Thou Fount of life! Thou Light of men!*
> *From the best bliss that earth imparts*
> *We turn unfilled to thee again.*
>
> *Thy truth unchanged hath ever stood:*
> *Thou savest all that on thee call;*
> *To them that seek thee, thou art good;*
> *To them that find thee, all in all.*

When a poor Christian woman was once asked, 'Why are these verses marked?'—'Oh,' she replied, 'these are the promises in my precious Bible. There are many of them, you see, I have *tried*, and so I marked them T.; and many I have *proved*, and I know that they are true, and so I marked them P.' Yes, verily, whoever may prove false, the Lord is ever true; and yet a little while, 'he shall cast the great deceiver out of the earth, and his great lie out of creation.'

> For all the promises of God in him are yea, and in him Amen, unto the glory of God by us.—2 Cor. 1:20.
>
> Having therefore these promises, dearly beloved, let us cleanse ourselves from all filthiness of the flesh and spirit, perfecting holiness in the fear of God.—2 Cor. 7:1.

APRIL 12

THE NOMINAL AND THE REAL.

OCCASIONALLY, when looked at from a distance, the dead branches of a vine hang apparently as gracefully as the living ones, and closely resemble them, too, in colour and foliage. But when observed closely, we soon discover that there is no vital connection with them, no sap in the fibre, and as little fruit as on the barren fig tree on which the curse lighted.

It is thus also in the church of Christ. The nominal Christian sometimes so closely resembles the real that it is hard to discern the difference between them, and to know for certain that the one is a fruitless branch, and the other a fruitful; for in neither may there be any stain of outward immorality, or any deliberately cherished error as to evangelical truth. Persons are daily met with who speak respectfully of religion, and, perhaps, devoutly inquire what good thing they shall do to inherit eternal life. Nevertheless, they are branches that have no spiritual life in them, and they bear no fruit; for they have no living faith in Christ, no saving reliance on his finished work, no true love to his saints, and none of the great essentials of the kingdom,—righteousness, peace, and joy in the Holy Ghost.

This may not be apparent in ordinary times, when the church and world become often strangely intermingled. But let a thorough testing-time come, when neutrality is impossible, and they must be either for Christ or against him, then it becomes abundantly and painfully manifest that the root of the matter has never been in them, and that all along, so to speak, they have been 'spies, and not true men'; for Christ is deliberately forsaken and the world embraced.

The end of such Christless and fruitless professors, if they so continue, is a very mournful one; for it is our Lord himself who says, 'If a man abide not in me, he is cast forth as a branch, and is withered; and men gather them, and cast them into the fire, and they are burned.'

'If you feel at any time "death working in you,"' says Mr Spurgeon, 'and withering the bloom of your piety, remember he who first quickened you must keep you alive. The Spirit of God is like the sap that flowed into your poor branch, because you were grafted into Christ; and as by that sap you were first made green with life, so is it by that sap alone you can ever bring forth fruit unto God.'

> Not every one that saith unto me, Lord, Lord, shall enter into the kingdom of heaven; but he that doeth the will of my Father which is in heaven.—Matt. 7:21.

> Having a form of godliness, but denying the power thereof.—2 Tim. 3:5.

> I know thy works, that thou hast a name that thou livest, and art dead. Be watchful, and strengthen the things which remain, that are ready to die: for I have not found thy works perfect before God.—Rev. 3:1, 2.

April 13

SAFE PROSPERITY.

MUCH that is called prosperity is often more seeming than real; for when suddenly tested, it completely gives way. From time to time, however, there have been many cases of genuine prosperity, and none more striking than that of Jacob's favourite son; for it is written of him, 'The Lord was with Joseph, and he was a prosperous man.' Apparently it mattered not where, or how, or with whom he was placed, Joseph, just because the Lord was with him, uniformly prospered. He prospered even as a slave in Potiphar's house. Everything went so well with his service and management that he was unreservedly intrusted with all that was his master's. He prospered also in the Egyptian jail. He was not long a prisoner there for righteousness' sake, till he became a light and blessing in it,—yea, the most influential man within its walls. And he prospered in the palace as no man in Egypt had ever prospered before, for he was made ruler over all the land, and everywhere they cried before him, 'Bow the knee.' He was thus led on step by step, till at length he reached the very summit of attainable greatness.

Prosperity so exalted was doubtless peculiarly perilous, but in Joseph's case it was rendered safe by the many and sore trials that had preceded it. These kept him near his God, so that, when the full tide of prosperity came, he neither forgot the source from which it flowed, nor the end for which it was given. So is it with believers still. As nothing roots the oak so firmly as the rough winds that occasionally beat upon it and shake it, and strain trunk and branch in every fibre, so nothing roots believers in Christ, and strengthens their hold, and fits them for after positions of honour and usefulness, so much as the early discipline of sanctified trial.

In connection with this subject, it ought never to be forgotten that the most real of all prosperity is prosperity of soul.

> And he shall be like a tree planted by the rivers of water, that bringeth forth his fruit in his season; his leaf also shall not wither; and whatsoever he doeth shall prosper.—PSA. 1:3.

> And David behaved himself wisely in all his ways; and the Lord was with him.—1 SAM. 18:14.

> Beloved, I wish above all things that thou mayest prosper and be in health, even as thy soul prospereth.—3 JOHN 2.

APRIL 14

THERE IS NO WAY OF PEACE BUT GOD'S WAY.

NOTHING so touched the heart of Paul as the mournful condition of his kinsmen according to the flesh. 'I bear them record,' he said, 'that they have a zeal of God, but not according to knowledge. For they being ignorant of God's righteousness, and going about to establish their own righteousness, have not submitted themselves unto the righteousness of God.' Through a like fatal pride and unbelief, it is the same with many still. They have a kind of religiousness about them, a desire to be saved,—yea, and sometimes a willingness to secure needed peace almost at any price; but they will on no account accept it as a gift solely of grace and through the blood of the Lamb, though in no other way can it be found.

Indeed, one of the marked tendencies in our times is to put more reliance on the church than on Christ, and to make union to the former more essential than union to the latter. This is to prefer shadow to substance,—a broken, empty cistern to a fountain ever-springing and divine. No mere rites or services of the church, however multiplied or continuous, can ever meet the anxious fears and pressing wants of a dying soul. Nothing can effectually do this but the precious blood of the Lamb; and of its blessed efficacy for this end there have been countless exemplifications in every age. Indeed, let their previous guilt be what it may, it is the privilege of all true believers who make Christ alone their trust, to be so cleansed by his precious blood from all their sins as to have peace of conscience and peace with God as an enduring possession.

Would that, when the end approaches, the experience of each of us could be like that of one who is reported to have said: 'Though of sinners I am chief, I can do nothing but just lie at my Saviour's feet and let him robe me with his righteousness, sprinkle me with his blood, and load me with his loving gifts.'

When Thomas Bilney was a Romish student in Trinity College, he carried, like Luther, a burdened mind in a body emaciated by penances which afforded him no relief. Hearing his friends one day talking about Erasmus's Testament, he felt a strong desire to possess it. But it was a prohibited book, and when he saw it at first he did not dare to touch it. Hoping, however, he might find something in it to ease his troubled soul, he secretly purchased a copy, and then, hastening to his room, shut himself in. With a trembling heart he opened it, and read with astonishment: 'This is a faithful saying, and worthy of all acceptation, that Christ Jesus came into the world to save sinners; of whom I am chief.' Then, laying it down, he exclaimed, 'What! Paul the chief of sinners, yet Paul sure of being saved!' He read it again and again, and broke out into an ecstasy of joy, 'At last I have heard of Jesus—Jesus Christ. Yes, Jesus Christ saves.' And falling on his knees, he prayed, 'O thou who art the Truth, give me strength, that I may teach it and convert the ungodly, by means of one who has been himself ungodly.'

Verily, it is through Christ alone we can have pardon and peace.

Preaching peace by Jesus Christ.—ACTS 10:36.

And, having made peace through the blood of his cross, by him to reconcile all things unto himself.—COL. 1:20.

Therefore being justified by faith, we have peace with God through our Lord Jesus Christ.—ROM. 5:1.

APRIL 15

WHEN WE KEEP NEAR THE LORD, WE NEVER FAIL TO GET HIS EAR.

WHAT words could be more precious than these?—'If ye abide in me, and my words abide in you, ye shall ask what ye will, and it shall be done unto you.' There is a condition here, it is true—an *if*; but then it is a condition, not of hindrance, but of rich encouragement. In ordinary life, petitioners are so rarely welcome, that when they come to any door they have always more or less of misgiving and fear that they may not get in. But at the Lord's door any such fear is utterly groundless; for to every petitioner it is not only said, 'Come in,' but, '*Abide*'; yea, and more wonderful still, the largeness of the receiving is made to depend *on the length and intimacy of the abiding*: 'If ye abide in me, and my words abide in you, ye shall ask what ye will, and it shall be done unto you.'

Herod, in his folly, said to the daughter of Herodias, 'Whatsoever thou shalt ask of me, I will give it thee, unto the half of my kingdom.' But he no sooner made the promise than he bitterly repented of it. How different with our gracious Lord! Full as his promise is—and there is no half in it, as in Herod's—he never regrets giving it, and is never unwilling to fulfil it, even to utmost measure, provided there is no unbelief to hinder. 'Good prayers,' said Bishop Hall, 'never come weeping home. I am sure I shall receive either what I ask or what I should ask.'

'Some time ago, a town missionary,' says Mr Spurgeon, 'had in his district a man who never would suffer any Christian man to come into his house. The missionary was warned by many that he would get a broken head if he ventured on a visit. He therefore kept from the house, though it troubled him to pass it by. He made *a matter of prayer of it*, as was his wont, and one morning ventured into the lion's den; when the man said, "What have you come here for?" "Well, sir," he said, "I have been conversing with people in all the houses along here, and I have passed you by because I heard you objected to it; but somehow I thought it looked cowardly to avoid you, and therefore I have called." "Come in, then," the man said; "sit down. Now you are going to talk to me about the Bible. Perhaps you do not know much about it yourself. I am going to ask you a question, and if you can answer it, you shall come again; if you do not answer it, I will bundle you downstairs. Now," he said, "do you take me?" "Yes," said the other, "I do take you." "Well, then, this is the question: Where do you find the word 'girl' in the Bible, and how many times do you find it?" The city missionary said, "The word 'girl' occurs only once in the Bible, and that is in the book of Joel, the third chapter and the third verse: 'They sold a girl for wine.'" "You are right; but I would not have believed you knew it, or else I would have asked you some other question. You may come again." "But," said the missionary, "I should like you to know how I came to know it. This very morning I was praying for direction from God; and when I was reading my morning chapter, I came upon this passage: 'There shall be boys and girls playing in the streets of Jerusalem'; and I found that the word 'girl' did not occur anywhere else but in Joel." The result of that story, however odd it seems, was that the missionary was permitted to call; and the man took an interest in his visits, and the whole family were the better, the man and his wife and one of his children becoming members of a church some time afterwards. Is not God the answerer of prayer?'

> Whatsoever ye shall ask in my name, that will I do, that the Father may be glorified in the Son. If ye shall ask any thing in my name, I will do it.—JOHN 14:13, 14.

> Whatsoever we ask, we receive of him, because we keep his commandments, and do those things that are pleasing in his sight.—1 JOHN 3:22.

APRIL 16

BRINGING IN, AND BRINGING OUT.

WHEN God begins a good work, he never ultimately leaves it unfinished. He does not bring out from the darkness and the evil, without bringing into the light and the good in fullest measure. It has been so all along in the past, and it is so still. Those delivered from the darkness of nature are brought into the light of grace, and into the kingdom of God's dear Son. This kingdom has a twofold phase—an earthly and a heavenly. There is the kingdom of grace and the kingdom of glory, and all who are savingly converted are brought first into the one, and afterwards into the other.

Not a little of this was typified by the experience of the Israelites in the days of Moses. There were two million of them, cruelly and seemingly hopelessly oppressed; but in spite of all the might and malignity of their enemies, the Lord with a high hand and an outstretched arm brought them forth out of Egypt, and ultimately into Canaan. This was a marvellous deliverance; but not so great as that which God achieves, in the riches of his grace, when he brings even one poor sinner out of the region of sin into the kingdom of holiness and peace. Yes, one of the grandest of God's works is the quickening into life a dead soul, the changing of a bad heart, and the subduing of an iron will; and he is ready to do this for all who will come to him in faith through Jesus Christ.

Should any be tempted to say, 'Whoever may be brought out of darkness into light, or out of death into life, it never can be so with me; mine is a hopeless case,' let them remember, for their comfort, the words of one of the saintliest of men: 'If God had said that there was mercy for Richard Baxter, I am so vile a sinner that I would have thought he meant some other Richard Baxter; but when he says, "*whosoever*," I know that includes me, the worst of all Richard Baxters.'

> These are they which came out of great tribulation, and have washed their robes, and made them white in the blood of the Lamb ... They shall hunger no more, neither thirst any more; neither shall the sun light on them, nor any heat. For the Lamb which is in the midst of the throne shall feed them, and shall lead them unto living fountains of waters: and God shall wipe away all tears from their eyes.—Rev. 7:14, 16, 17.

April 17

THERE IS NOTHING SIMPLER THAN FAITH, YET IN ACTUAL LIFE WHAT IS HARDER?

IF there is one thing in the word clearer than another, it is the absolute necessity of faith in order to salvation. It was Paul's first word to the awakened jailer: 'Believe on the Lord Jesus Christ, and thou shalt be saved'; and it was one of John's last words in his precious Gospel: 'These are written that ye might believe that Jesus is the Son of God, and that believing ye might have life through his name.'

But faith is not only everywhere set forth as absolutely indispensable, but also as a thing peculiarly simple. This feature gets marked prominence in all the varied scriptural representations of it. It is simple as looking: 'Look unto me, all ye ends of the earth, and be ye saved'; or simple as listening: 'Hearken unto me; hear, and your soul shall live'; or simple as leaning: 'Who is this that cometh up from the wilderness, leaning on her beloved?'

But needful and simple as faith is, there is nothing in which, to their own great loss and peril, men are more grievously wanting.

Faith is hard to them because it is easy, and too simple for their pride. Usually what mainly influences them is not what the great God and Father of all expressly declares, but rather what appearances say or mere likelihoods suggest.

This has been very simply and beautifully put forth by Adolphe Monod in these words:—'Two children were standing on the summit of a hill, watching the setting sun. "What a way," said the elder, "the sun has moved since we saw it coming up behind that tree." "And yet, you remember," said the little boy, "we learned, in this morning's lesson *with our father* that the sun never moves at all." "I know we did," replied the first, "but I do not believe it, because I see it is not so. I saw the sun rise there this morning, and I see it there tonight. How can a thing get all that distance without moving?" "But our father," said the other, "told us that it is the earth that moves." "That is impossible too," replied the elder, "for you see it does not move. I am standing on it now, and so are you, and it does not stir; how can you tend to think it moves, while all the time it stands quietly under our feet?" These simple ones,' he adds, 'might divide mankind between them, and carry the banner of their parties through the world from first to last—from the gates of paradise to the judgment-seat. There never has been, and there never will be, any other division, but they that take and they that will not take *their Father's word.*'

Every chapter of the Bible and every page of human history testify to this. Indeed, wherever the gospel is preached in power, such a division almost invariably presents itself as that recorded in the closing chapter of the Acts: 'Some believed the things that were spoken, and *some believed them not.*' If it rarely happens in any place that all reject the message of reconciliation, more rarely still do all accept it.

Jesus answering saith unto them, Have faith in God.—Mark 11:22.

If ye will not believe, surely ye shall not be established.—Isa. 7:9.

O fools, and slow of heart to believe all that the prophets have spoken.—Luke 24:25.

APRIL 18

THOUGH IN THE WORLD, WE MUST NOT BE OF IT.

IN the church of Sardis, so much evil mingled with the good that the Lord had to say, 'Hold fast, and repent. If therefore thou shalt not watch, I will come on thee as a thief, and thou shalt not know what hour I will come upon thee.' It was not so with all, however. There were noble exceptions; hence the cheering words that followed: 'Thou hast a few names even in Sardis which have not defiled their garments; and they shall walk with me in white: for they are worthy.' Notwithstanding the lukewarmness, worldly conformity, and general defection on every side, these few faithful ones kept undefiled, and walked in all simplicity and godly sincerity.

It was through grace they thus kept themselves unspotted from the world. And as it was then so is it still; for till conversion takes place none ever separate themselves from the world and its ways. When, however, that great change is experienced, old things pass away, and all things become new. Not that such renewal is ever immediately complete. On the contrary, because of lingering corruption, that command is never an unneeded one: 'Be not conformed to this world: but be ye transformed by the renewing of your mind, that ye may prove what is that good, and acceptable, and perfect, will of God.'

This does not necessitate any monastic isolation or literal going out of the world; for how, then, could believers be witnesses for Christ, and lights and blessings to those around? In this, as in all other things, our blessed Lord gave to his disciples a perfect example. He did not dwell in the wilderness like John, solitary and apart, but mingled with men, in the streets, and in the synagogues, and also in their homes; and so freely, that his enemies revilingly said of him that he was the friend of publicans and sinners. But though ceaselessly seeking in this way the world's good, he never imbibed the world's spirit or conformed to its ways. 'I have given them,' he said, 'thy word; and the world hath hated them, because they are not of the world, even as I am not of the world.'

Yet how sadly in these latter times is all this forgotten by many who bear the name of Christ. As if wiser than the Master, instead of fearing the friendship of the world, which is declared to be enmity with God, they carefully cultivate it. This they do professedly to win the world over to the church, but invariably in the end it is the church that is won over to the world.

'As I grow older as a parent,' says Dr J. W. Alexander, 'my views are changing fast as to the degree of conformity to this world which we should allow to our children. I am horror-struck to count up the profligate children of pious persons, and even ministers. The door at which those influences enter which countervail parental instruction and influence, I am persuaded, is yielding to the ways of good society; by dress, books, and amusements, an atmosphere is formed which is not Christianity. More than ever do I feel that our families must stand in a kind but determined opposition to the fashions of the world, breasting the waves like the Eddystone Lighthouse. And I have found nothing yet which requires more courage and independence than to rise even a little but decidedly above the par of the religious world around us. Surely the way in which we commonly go on is not the way of self-denial and sacrifice and cross-bearing which the New Testament talks of. Our slender influence on the circle of our friends is often to be traced to our leaving so little difference between us.'

Whosoever therefore will be a friend of the world is the enemy of God.—JAMES 4:4.

Pure religion and undefiled before God and the Father is this, To visit the fatherless and widows in their affliction, and to keep himself unspotted from the world.—JAMES 1:27.

APRIL 19

THE LORD'S GUIDANCE IS SPECIAL AS WELL AS LOVING.

WHEN the Lord gave the command, 'Go ye into all the world, and preach the gospel to every creature,' he also added the promise, 'Lo, I am with you alway, even unto the end of the world.' There is much to encourage in this. It shows that the Lord does not merely send his servants, but that for their protection and blessing he himself goes with them. Almost every page of the Acts of the Apostles gives varied evidence of this, and clearly shows that a special providence was ever guiding and overruling all their journeyings—the when and the where of them, as well as the purpose and the duration. Nor is it different now, for as the old command is still binding on us, happily the old promise is still binding on the Lord, and he delights to fulfil it; for wherever his people in faith and love go forth with his message, he goes with them to cheer their heart and open their way and bless their labours. Yea, the very steps of a good man are ordered by the Lord, especially when doing Christian work and in a Christian spirit.

In almost every record, whether of home or foreign missions, we find the most varied and touching illustration of this. 'Standing one evening behind Mr Moody in the Agricultural Hall,' said Mr Archibald Brown, 'I saw a man before me trying to hide that he was crying, and I determined, when the service was over, to speak to him, hoping that the Lord might make me a blessing to him. Notwithstanding my efforts, I quite lost him in the crowd at the close, and was much disappointed. As I wished to attend the evening service, and it was too far to go home, I walked through several streets, and, selecting a quiet coffee-house, went in and ordered tea. Shortly after, the person asked me to walk into a more comfortable room, which I did; and there sat the man I had seen in the Hall and lost in the crowd! I don't believe in chance, and I thought *it was the Lord's guidance* that led me to pass through many streets and select this particular house, and there find the man I was anxious to see. It does, indeed, require a little tact to break the ice to sinners; and when he gave me the opportunity, and I told him that I had been praying for him all afternoon, his surprise may be imagined. After convincing him, by telling him where he had sat, and how he had tried to hide his tears with his hat, we fell into a long conversation, and he found rest for his soul.'

Thus wonderfully does the Lord gather his own. Nothing can defeat his loving purpose.

> The steps of a good man are ordered by the Lord: and he delighteth in his way.—Psa. 37:23.

> In all thy ways acknowledge him, and he shall direct thy paths.—Prov. 3:6.

APRIL 20

WE MUST KNOW CHRIST'S GREATNESS TO REALISE HIS GRACE.

WHATEVER may be an open question in a true church, it can never be the divinity of Jesus Christ; for without it our every hope for eternity would become utterly foundationless. The very highest humanity conceivable, if no more than humanity, could never say to any perishing soul, 'In me is thine help found.'

It is only a divine arm that can lift our burden, only a divine expiation that can take away sin, and a divine friend alone that can win our confidence when conscience truly awakes and guilt is realised. It is well for us therefore, that in this matter there is no room for misgiving; for the testimony of Scripture to the divine greatness of Jesus is as full as it is express. Peter said, 'We believe and are sure that thou art the Christ, the Son of the living God.' Thomas, bowing adoringly at his feet, exclaimed, 'My Lord, and my God.' In writing to the Romans, Paul says, 'Christ came, who is over all, God blessed for ever'; and in the opening chapter of John's Gospel we have this testimony, 'In the beginning was the Word, and the Word was with God, and the Word was

God. All things were made by him; and without him was not any thing made that was made ... And the Word was made flesh, and dwelt among us, (and we beheld his glory, the glory as of the only begotten of the Father, full of grace and truth.)' Finally, he himself said, 'I am Alpha and Omega, the beginning and the end, which is, and which was, and which is to come, the Almighty.' Had Christ been anything less than these words reveal, he would have failed in sufficiency for his great redemptive work. It was his to conquer sin, swallow up death, and put to flight all the powers of darkness; and who could do this but the Living, Holy, and Almighty One?

Nor is he greater in might than in love and compassionate tenderness. 'Though rich, yet for your sakes he became poor, that ye through his poverty might be rich.' Taking the form of a servant, he came not to be ministered unto, but to minister; and to give his life a ransom for many; yea, to be their everlasting joy and portion.

When his end was near, Dr Grierson of Errol, after various psalms and portions of Scripture had been read to him, asked his children to conclude by singing the hymn, 'Safe in the Arms of Jesus.' After they had sung it, he said, 'I feel I am safe there. Death has no power nor fear for me at all now.' And when told that it was drawing near the morning, he exclaimed, 'Oh, let me go, for the day breaketh! I feel Jesus very near by me.—Dear Lord, let me go!'

For in him dwelleth all the fulness of the Godhead bodily.—COL. 2:9.

But unto the Son he saith, Thy throne, O God, is for ever and ever: a sceptre of righteousness is the sceptre of thy kingdom.—HEB. 1:8.

April 21

*WE ARE NEVER SO REALLY RICH AS WHEN
RICH IN LIBERALITY.*

JUST as there are varied degrees in faith and love, so also are there in liberality. In nothing are some so defective as in this grace. It is the weakest point in their character. They can receive, but they cannot dispense. Even when they do give something, yet, considering their means, it is little compared with what they might give, and with what others give who are similarly placed; and little, also, when compared with what they readily expend on themselves. Above all, it is little when compared with what the necessities of a perishing world demand, and with what the Lord in the riches of his grace hath bestowed upon them. There are many, however, who, to the praise of his grace, exhibit a widely different spirit. Unlike those who give little out of their much, they give much out of their little to the cause of Christ and his people.

This was the case in a very remarkable degree with the early Macedonian churches. Their liberality was unusually great; for the apostle tells us that, 'in a great trial of affliction, the abundance of their joy and their deep poverty abounded unto the riches of their liberality.' When in straits and affliction, we are apt to become selfish, and to think of no one's sorrow but our own. But it was not so with them. Deep as was their poverty, it never found mention, nor did it restrain by jot or tittle the riches of their liberality.

Not unfrequently, when men grow rich in means they become poor in charity, and the heart that was narrow before becomes narrower still. It was not without reason, therefore, that the apostle said, 'Charge them that are rich in this world, that they be not high-minded, nor trust in *uncertain* riches, but in the living God, who giveth us richly all things to enjoy.' The thought of this might well moderate our thirst for riches on the one hand, and intensify our desire for fuller grace on the other. Uncertain things should never be chief things with us; for that would be to grasp the shadow and let go the substance. Nor should we fail to minister to others in their times of need, lest that should befall us which is written, 'There is that withholdeth more than is meet, and it tendeth to poverty.' 'Proportionate thy charity to the strength of thy estate,' says a quaint old writer, 'lest God proportion thy estate to the weakness of thy charity.'

Therefore, as ye abound in every thing, in faith, and utterance, and knowledge, and in all diligence, and in your love to us, see that ye abound in this grace also.—2 Cor. 8:7.

To do good and to communicate forget not: for with such sacrifices God is well pleased.—Heb. 13:16.

The disciples, every man according to his ability, determined to send relief unto the brethren which dwelt in Judaea.—Acts 11:29.

April 22

TRUE FOLLOWING OF THE LORD.

THE time of their utterance gives additional force to the words of our Lord to Peter, 'What is that to thee? follow thou me'; for it was after his death and resurrection they came from his lips, and when, therefore, his claims on the love and loyalty of his disciple were stronger than ever. Though it was to Peter only the words 'Follow me' were addressed in the first instance, they are now emphatically spoken to all; and it is not more our duty than our privilege to give earnest heed to them.

In carrying out the injunction, our aim should be to follow Jesus as Matthew did—*immediately*. As soon as his Lord said to him, 'Follow me,' 'he arose,' we are told, 'and left all, and followed him.' The heartily loyal never linger. Like Caleb, also, we should follow him *fully*. Uninfluenced by the many around who would neither believe nor obey, he cleaved to the Lord with purpose of heart, and held on resolutely, even to the end. And as he honoured God, God in turn honoured him, and enriched him to the full with every blessing. 'All that have Caleb's spirit,' says Matthew Henry, 'follow the Lord universally—without dividing; uprightly—without dissembling; cheerfully—without disputing; and constantly—without declining.' Above all, we should follow as the hundred and forty and four thousand did, of whom it is written, 'These are they which follow the Lamb whithersoever he goeth.' Those who do so ask no questions, and make no conditions, but unreservedly follow wherever the Saviour leads.

This is no easy thing to do; for there is with all men, even the most saintly, an instinctive shrinking from pain and suffering. 'Oh, pray for me,' said Latimer, in one of his letters from prison. 'I sometimes shudder, and could creep into a mouse-hole, and then the Lord visits me again with his comforts.' Another martyr, when being led to the flames, chancing to see his wife and children among the crowd, burst into tears, and said, 'Ah, flesh! you would fain have your way; but I tell thee, by the grace of God, thou shalt not gain the victory.'

> And he said unto me, My grace is sufficient for thee: for my strength is made perfect in weakness. Most gladly therefore will I rather glory in my infirmities, that the power of Christ may rest upon me.—2 COR. 12:9.

> If ye be reproached for the name of Christ, happy are ye; for the spirit of glory and of God resteth upon you: on their part he is evil spoken of, but on your part he is glorified.—1 PET. 4:14.

APRIL 23

WE OFTEN MISJUDGE THE LORD AND HIS WAYS.

THE Lord gives, and with very bounteous hand; but sometimes also he takes away, not health, or substance, or honour only, but our dearest loved ones. Such dealings are sorely perplexing, and, under their first pressure, even saints occasionally judge and speak very unadvisedly; forgetting that, however keen the stroke or deep the wound, it is a loving hand that has inflicted it, and with wise and gracious purpose.

This spirit needs to be carefully guarded against, particularly in those kinds of trial and suffering in which the evil agency of man is distinctly traceable; for then the tendency to sinful irritation becomes very marked. At such times they wholly overlook the fact that even grievous wrongs from the creature have been, again and again, divinely permitted and overruled for highest sanctifying ends. Indeed, few remember as they ought that the Lord's working is so marvellous that, by trials the most diverse in nature and source, direct and indirect, heavy and light, he can purify his people, yea, and effectually sanctify them, even by the wrath of men and malignity of devils.

When the saintly Arndt heard or sung the words in a well-known hymn,—

The world has falsely me abused,—

he was wont to cover his head, and lift up his heart to God; and, on being asked why he did so, he said, 'These words bring back to my mind the grace which my God has shown me through enemies and slanderers, because thereby he is making me to grow in my Christianity, and in my habits of prayer.'

And so, too, with Martin Luther. 'If the devil,' he said, 'could carry out his wicked will, he would slay us with his knife, and choke us with his poison. But God lays hold of him, and says, "It is true, thou art a murderer and a miscreant, but I will employ thee for my own purposes: thou shalt act only as my pruning-knife, and my precious vineyard shall be all the better thereby."'

As many as I love, I rebuke and chasten.—REV. 3:19.

Blessed is the man whom thou chastenest, O Lord, and teachest him out of thy law.—PSA. 94:12.

Every branch that beareth fruit, he purgeth it, that it may bring forth more fruit.—JOHN 15:2.

APRIL 24

TROUBLOUS TIMES FORESEEN AND FORETOLD.

TO win adherents it is usual, with false teachers, to present the bright side of the picture only, and many use fair and flattering words. But it is not thus the great Captain of our salvation deals with men, when he bids them follow him. Never does he conceal what the truly loyal may have to bear for his sake, or leave them to imagine that everything in his service will be easy and pleasant. On the contrary, with the utmost frankness he tells the whole truth to them, and speaks as openly of the cross as of the crown, and bids all calmly and deliberately count the cost and weigh the consequences, before renouncing all to follow him.

When writing to the church of Smyrna, our Lord said: 'Fear none of those things *which thou shalt suffer*: behold, the devil shall cast some of you into prison, that ye may be tried; and *ye shall have tribulation ten days*: be thou faithful unto death, and I will give thee a crown of life.' Whether these 'ten days' meant ten years of severe buffeting from a godless world, as some think, or, as others suppose, merely many days, this much at least is clear, that the sentence contains a distinct forewarning of troublous times that would severely try the saints of God.

The Lord is thus frank in his intimations, just because, as an old writer well puts it, 'Jesus will cross thee first, if he is to crown thee afterwards.' Some imagine that such tribulation is now wholly a thing of the past, and that never again can there be suffering for righteousness' sake, forgetting that so long as Satan is unbound, and the natural heart unsanctified, so long may the saints of God lay their account to more or less of persecution.

'This world,' said Jonathan Edwards, 'is a dark place without Christ, and therefore is dark till he comes and until his kingdom of glory is set up. And the Scriptures represent the last struggles and changes that shall immediately precede this event *as being the greatest of all*.' From such a man these are weighty and solemn words; yet, should it be as many think, that these perilous times are near, none need fear who trust the Lord, especially when they have such an assurance as this to cheer them: 'The God of peace shall bruise Satan under your feet shortly.'

In one of the last notes received from my friend Robert M'Cheyne were these words: 'Press on; we have attained but little; Christ is full of grace and truth. The Lord fit you for troublous times. Ever yours till glory.'

> The great dragon was cast out, that old serpent, called the Devil, and Satan, which deceiveth the whole world: he was cast out into the earth, and his angels were cast out with him. And I heard a loud voice saying in heaven, Now is come salvation, and strength, and the kingdom of our God, and the power of his Christ: for the accuser of our brethren is cast down, which accused them before our God day and night.—REV. 12:9, 10.

APRIL 25

WE CAN NEVER AIM AT TOO HIGH A HOLINESS.

CONVERSION, all-important as it is in bringing life to the dead soul, is yet but the beginning of the Christian course, the first turning from the wrong way into the right; and therefore, however grateful for it, we must never allow ourselves to think that nothing more is needed; all the more as sanctification, alike in principle and in detail, is dwelt on more or less fully in almost every page of the Sacred Volume. Moreover, it is invariably spoken of as an object of special interest to all the persons in the Godhead. It becomes abundantly manifest, therefore, that what we must aim at is, not a half, but a whole sanctification, even an entire and abiding conformity to the mind and will of God in everything,—in thought, desire, and purpose, as well as in every word and action of daily life.

Were we through the Spirit to have in fuller degree these higher aims, we would sooner or later also have higher attainments. If it was said of Stephen and Barnabas that they were men 'full of the

Holy Ghost,' why might not the same be said of us, especially when *the command* is so express: 'Be ye filled with the Spirit'; and *the promise* is so free: 'If ye then, being evil, know how to give good gifts unto your children: *how much more* shall your heavenly Father give the Holy Spirit to them that ask him?'

Meanwhile it is true, so far as uninterrupted completeness is concerned, there must always, in the very nature of things, be a difference more or less marked between sanctification on earth and sanctification in heaven. This is clearly recognised in Scripture. As one says, 'The eighth of Romans is true; so is the seventh. Both truths, contrary though not contradictory, exist together, and we must hold fast each. We must not let one truth hide the other, or weaken the other, but learn with Paul at once in the same breath to say, "O wretched man that I am! who shall deliver me from the body of this death?" and, "I thank God through Jesus Christ our Lord." Even now, if we had but faith and prayer enough, with added care and effort, so full and visible might our spiritual growth be that men would be constrained to take knowledge of us that we had been with Jesus.'

Blessed are they who, from saying, as the expression of their heart's desire, 'All of self and none of thee,' pass on to say, not merely 'Some of self and some of thee,' or 'Less of self and more of Thee,' but sweetly to add,—

> *Higher than the highest heavens,*
> *Deeper than the deepest sea,*
> *Lord, thy love at last hath conquered:*
> *Grant me now my soul's desire,—*
> *None of self, and all of thee.*

As he which hath called you is holy, so be ye holy in all manner of conversation.—1 Pet. 1:15.

Walk worthy of the Lord unto all pleasing, being fruitful in every good work, and increasing in the knowledge of God.—Col. 1:10.

If a man therefore purge himself from these, he shall be a vessel unto honour, sanctified, and meet for the master's use, and prepared unto every good work.—2 Tim. 2:21.

APRIL 26

TYPICAL SIN-BEARING AND REAL.

IT is written in the word, 'And Aaron shall lay both his hands upon the head of the live goat, and confess over him all the iniquities of the children of Israel ... *putting them upon the head of the goat.*' This symbolic act plainly intimated to every Israelite that guilt and liability to punishment no longer rested on them, but on the devoted victim on which the hands and sins were laid. Its teaching to us is precisely similar; for it vividly sets forth the blessed truth, that the Lord laid upon Christ the iniquity of us all, and that the trusting soul therefore has nothing to fear. He is the true sin-bearer, at once divinely chosen and divinely willing; and it was when feeling the weight of his people's iniquities, and the hiding of his Father's face, as he hung on the cross as their substitute, that he uttered the bitter cry, 'My God, my God, why hast thou forsaken me?' How infinite the love that could so have suffered that we might be saved!

In ancient times there were some sins for which no sacrifice was appointed, and which therefore could not be purged away by any ceremonial oblations whatever. But there are no sins, blessed be God, however deep their dye or millionfold their number, from which we may not be justified by faith in Jesus. As *all* the iniquities of the children of Israel which were confessed and laid upon the head of the goat were borne away and heard of no more, so all the sin and guilt laid in faith upon Jesus he taketh entirely away. To mark the blessed completeness of this, the sin-laden goat was not merely sent away beyond the camp, but even beyond all sight and track of man, into a land wild and uninhabited, there to remain unseen and forgotten till it finally perished.

Could brighter picture be given of the full and enduring pardon so graciously secured to us? It is no mere respite we get through Christ, but an eternal acquittal. On believing, our sins are forever put away, and so effectually that even death and judgment, however nigh, should awaken no fear.

The next day John seeth Jesus coming unto him, and saith, Behold the Lamb of God, which taketh away the sin of the world.— JOHN 1:29.

In whom we have redemption through his blood, the forgiveness of sins, according to the riches of his grace.—EPH. 1:7.

Unto him that loved us, and washed us from our sins in his own blood, and hath made us kings and priests unto God and his Father; to him be glory and dominion for ever and ever.—REV. 1:5, 6.

APRIL 27

IN SOUL-WINNING BE SLOW TO DESPAIR.

WHEN the Great Physician came to the land of Gennesaret, it is recorded not only that the men of that place sent out into all the country round about and brought unto him *all that were diseased*, but also that as many of them as touched him were made perfectly whole.

Now, we are repeatedly and emphatically told that what our Lord did then for the bodies of men, he is able and willing to do for their immortal souls. This great fact, however, is often but half believed, even by Christian men who would fain be soul-winners, especially when difficulties arise, and longed-for results do not at once appear. In connection with the young, it may be, they show little or no despondency; but when addressing themselves to the aged, with their confirmed habits and rooted prejudices, hope seems to fail them altogether.

But why should this be? The aged at Gennesaret were sick and diseased as well as the young when the Great Physician was there; yet, when brought to him in faith by kindly friends, they were healed, and effectually, even as others. So it may be with the aged still. In spite of long years of alienation from God, the hoary-headed and infirm, if only brought in faith to Jesus, may become blessed monuments of saving grace. It may be mainly in early life that souls are savingly won, nevertheless there are well-known instances of conversion at seventy, eighty, and even ninety years of age. It is said of the late Lord Lyndhurst, that his saving enlightenment came in his ninetieth year. Not till then did he really bow the knee to Jesus and pass from death to life.

Those, therefore, who would be eminently successful in soul-winning must be slow to despair. This is the testimony of one who recently died in the faith of the gospel: 'Under God, I owe my conversion to you; not through anything special that you said, but *because* you never would give up hope of me.'

Even if inquirers should turn wholly away from us, we may reach them 'by the way of the throne.'

> This is a faithful saying, and worthy of all acceptation, that Christ Jesus came into the world to save sinners; of whom I am chief. Howbeit for this cause I obtained mercy, that in me first Jesus Christ might shew forth all longsuffering, for a pattern to them which should hereafter believe on him to life everlasting.—I TIM. 1:15, 16.

> God is able of these stones to raise up children unto Abraham.— MATT. 3:9.

APRIL 28

ENLIGHTENED GRATITUDE.

THERE are few, save avowed Atheists, who do not sometimes thank God, but for what?—a safe voyage, it may be, a good harvest, a recovery from sickness, an increasing prosperity, or an extending fame; and there they stop, never in any case going beyond the circle of time and sense.

With enlightened believers, however, it is otherwise. While grateful even for the least of God's mercies, it is ever the graces of the Spirit and the grand blessings and hopes of the gospel that mainly evoke their warmest thanksgivings. 'We give thanks to God and the Father of our Lord Jesus Christ,' says the apostle, 'praying always for you, since we heard of your faith in Christ Jesus, and of the love which ye have to all the saints, for the hope which is laid up for you in heaven.'

His thanksgiving was first of all for 'faith in Christ Jesus.' Faith regards all the truth revealed by God in Holy Scripture. This is its general object. But the object of justifying faith is Christ Jesus as set forth in the gospel. 'This is the record, that God hath given to us eternal life; and this life is in his Son.' Faith, therefore, has principally to do with the Saviour; and moved and influenced by it, we not only trustfully look to him, but we build upon him as our foundation, and enter him as our refuge, and glory in him as our righteousness and strength, yea, and as all our salvation, and all our desire.

There is thanksgiving also for 'love to all the saints.' 'We must,' says Matthew Henry, 'bear *an extensive* kindness and good-will to good men, notwithstanding lesser points of difference and many real weaknesses.' This is true; but, alas! many fail to do this. They can love within their own circle, but not without it. They can love in the absence of defects, but not in spite of them. They can love the great and eminent among saints, but not the lowly and obscure. These are sad shortcomings, and we must carefully guard against them.

Finally, there was thanksgiving for 'hope.' This is a grace in which some are greatly wanting, and therefore, though safe, they never have the comfort of their safety, and too often they go on their way songless and with harp untuned. Another reason for this joylessness is, that instead of casting every burden on the great Burden-bearer, they go climbing upwards with some of the heaviest of them on their own shoulders. Cast off thy burden now:

> *So shalt thou climb yon hill*
> *Up to its steepest height,*
> *Like eagle of the rock,*
> *With easy, joyous flight:*
> *So shalt thou bear the toils*
> *Thy God appoints to thee;*

> *So shalt thou serve thy God*
> *In happy liberty.*

I thank my God through Jesus Christ for you all, that your faith is spoken of throughout the whole world.—ROM. 1:8.

Hearing of thy love and faith, which thou hast toward the Lord Jesus, and toward all saints.—PHILEM. 5.

If in this life only we have hope in Christ, we are of all men most miserable.—1 COR. 15:19.

APRIL 29

THE LOVING INTEREST OF LARGE HEARTS.

IN their views and feelings, some are so restricted and narrow that they can think and speak of family and kindred only. This is their world; and little though it be, it bounds all their vision, and they have not a thought beyond it. Others, again, are so diffusively wide and general in their sympathies, that though professedly interested in mankind, they do nothing whatever for individual men. But the great apostle of the Gentiles fell into neither of these extremes. His vision was such that it could take in the distant, and yet not miss the near; it could be wide-reaching, and yet minutely centred. And it was the same with his feelings. He had so large a heart that he yearned for the eternal good of all his fellows. It was not the king only he thought of when he stood before Agrippa, but his whole audience. 'I would to God,' he said, 'that not only thou, but also *all that hear me* this day, were both almost and altogether such as I am, except these bonds.' Yet so minutely and lovingly mindful was he, that he never forgot a single friend. Accordingly, his epistles abound in such special and kindly salutations as these: 'Greet Priscilla and Aquila, my helpers in Christ Jesus. Greet Mary, who bestowed much labour on us. Salute Andronicus and Junia, my kinsmen, and my fellow-prisoners. Salute Rufus, chosen in the Lord, and his mother and mine. Salute my well-beloved Epaenetus, who is the first-fruits of Achaia unto Christ.' Thus mothers, sisters, brothers, fellow-labourers, and fellow-sufferers were all tenderly and affectionately remembered by him.

So should it ever be with all who love the Lord. 'To be in such a list as this,' said Dr Wardlaw, 'is to be in the roll of true honour and lasting fame. It may be little thought of in this world, but it will be envied in eternity. The humblest name here will stand higher in the world to come than that of the mightiest monarch who lived and died without the grace of God. Seek, brethren, to have your names associated with those of the saints of God—among those whom an apostle would have acknowledged as Christ's, and whom Christ will acknowledge as his own.'

> Come thou with us, and we will do thee good: for the Lord hath spoken good concerning Israel.—NUM. 10:29.

> By faith Moses, when he was come to years, refused to be called the son of Pharaoh's daughter; choosing rather to suffer affliction with the people of God, than to enjoy the pleasures of sin for a season.—HEB. 11:24, 25.

APRIL 30

CANAAN, THOUGH A GOODLY LAND, WAS BUT AN IMPERFECT TYPE.

IN all times the land of Canaan has been regarded as a type of our eternal home, and of the rest that remaineth for the people of God. In reality, however, what it typified was rather the present rest of grace than the future rest in glory, for everything in it was strangely mingled.

While there was plenty in it, there was also want. There were famines even in Canaan; and so severe occasionally that multitudes were utterly destitute, and cried in vain for bread either for themselves or their little ones. Even so, though all true believers have found rest in Christ, their experience is still a very mingled one; for fulness is ever alternating with straitness, and brightness with shade, alike temporally and spiritually. Today there may be corn and wine in every store, but tomorrow only a handful of meal in the barrel and a little oil in the cruse. In heaven it is wholly different. The plenty there is not only in overflowing, but in abiding fulness: hence 'they shall hunger no more, neither thirst any more; neither shall the sun light on them, nor any heat. For the Lamb which is in the midst of the throne shall feed them, and shall lead them unto living fountains of waters.' The Master says, 'The poor always ye have with you'; but in the New Jerusalem never shall beggar be seen in any street, nor be heard knocking at any door, nor want of any kind be left unsupplied.

Again, while there was peace in the land of Canaan, there was also conflict. It was with sword in hand the Israelites entered it; and in the end there was scarcely a hill or valley that had not heard the shout of battle or the groans of the dying. It is the same, more or less, with all believers. They have peace in part, and very precious, but they have also tribulation; safety, but also conflict. An old saint once said to a young and inexperienced one: 'Never expect here any quiet, cosy, well-feathered nest; for there is not one of them that has not some roughness under its lining, and some piercing thorns among its twigs.' But never, within all the borders of heaven, shall sword or spear be seen, or disturbing fear be felt; for into that bright land no enemy can enter: 'No lion shall be there, nor any ravenous beast go up thereon, it shall not be found there; but the redeemed shall walk there.'

Finally, while there was life in Canaan, there were also disease and death: side by side with the dwellings of the living were everywhere found graves for the dead. But not one grave shall ever meet our eye in heaven. No inhabitant there shall ever say, 'I am sick,' or bid to weeping friends a sad farewell. Nor have we long to wait for this bright reality. 'Our fair morning is at hand,' said Samuel Rutherford; 'the day-star is near the rising, and we are not many miles from home.'

> Come unto me, all ye that labour and are heavy laden, and I will give you rest.—MATT. 11:28.
>
> There remaineth therefore a rest to the people of God.—HEB. 4:9.

Let us therefore fear, lest, a promise being left us of entering into his rest, any of you should seem to come short of it.—HEB. 4:1.

MAY 1

TO BE LACKING IN ONE IS TO BE LACKING IN ALL.

AS soon as a sinner is thoroughly awakened, his first thought usually is, that as condemnation comes by breaking the law, so justification must come by keeping it. In this belief, and with the express design of thereby obtaining a righteousness that will save him, he makes it his daily effort to keep all the commandments of God. But the more he toils the more he fails, just because he is attempting an impossibility; for never since the world began has anyone of Adam's race found salvation by keeping the law. What it demands is not a large obedience or a sincere obedience merely, but an absolutely complete obedience, in letter and spirit alike; and to fail in this is virtually to fail in all, for it is written, 'Whosoever shall keep the whole law, and yet offend *in one point*, he is guilty of all.' And again, 'Cursed is every one that continueth not *in all things* which are written in the book of the law to do them.'

To challenge any one of God's claims, even the least, or resist any of his demands, or deliberately disobey in a single point, is, as has been well said, 'to strike at the supremacy and glory of the Divine Lawgiver.' He who does so is guilty of all. 'Suppose,' says one familiarly, 'you were to hang up a man to the roof by a chain of ten links; were one of these links to break, down comes the man. What! has he fallen, and yet all the nine links are whole and perfect? Of course he has. One was sufficient to break the whole. He that sins in one point is guilty of all.' There can, therefore, be no salvation by the law. It can be a blessed rule of obedience to the saved, but never in a single case can it give life and safety to the lost.

Is there, then, no hope for perishing men? Far from it; for what we could not do for ourselves, the Lord Jesus, in infinite love and grace, has done for us. He who knew no sin became sin for us, and suffered, the just for the unjust, to bring us unto God; and the moment we believe in him, all our infinite debt becomes cancelled by his sprinkled blood and appropriated merit. If so, why should there be with any a moment's hesitancy in admitting guilt and accepting forgiveness through Jesus Christ our Lord? In no other way can we get safety and peace, and finally join the great company of the redeemed.

All Christian experience, which in spite of diversity of culture and tongue is marvellously harmonious, gives full confirmation of this. In describing his feelings when he heard Mr Turner the missionary telling at a love-feast how he found the salvation of God, Joel Bulu said with much emotion, 'My heart burned within me as I listened to his words, for in speaking of himself he told all I had felt; and I said to myself, "We are like two canoes sailing bow and bow, neither being swifter nor slower than the other." Thus it was with me when he told me of his repentance; but when he went on to speak of his faith in Christ, the forgiveness of his sins, and the joy which he found in believing, then said I, "My mast is broken, my sail is blown away, he is gone clean out of my sight, and I am left here drifting hopelessly over the waves." But while I listened eagerly to his words, telling of the love of Christ, my eyes were opened; I saw the way; I, even I also, believed and lived.'

> *O thou, my soul, forget no more*
> *The Friend who all thy misery bore!*
> *Let every idol be forgot,*
> *But, O my soul, forget him not!*

Wherefore the law was our schoolmaster to bring us unto Christ, that we might be justified by faith.—GAL. 3:24.

For Christ is the end of the law for righteousness to every one that believeth.—ROM. 10:4.

And by him all that believe are justified from all things, from which ye could not be justified by the law of Moses.—ACTS 13:39.

May 2

THE FEEBLE SHOULD BE FELT FOR AND LOVINGLY HELPED.

THERE are few large families that have not one or more weak and sickly ones among them; and it is usually found that these, more than all the others, get the mother's tenderest sympathy and care. So in measure is it with the great family of the redeemed. With all its blessed oneness, there is yet, at the same time, marked diversity. There are, meanwhile, the strong in it and the weak, the bright and the desponding, babes in Christ and the full grown; and while none are overlooked by him, he is specially tender to the timid and feeble. 'A bruised reed shall he not break, and the smoking flax shall he not quench'—'He giveth power to the faint, and to them that have no might he increaseth strength.' Again: 'He shall feed his flock like a shepherd: he shall gather the lambs with his arm, and carry them in his bosom, and shall gently lead those that are with young.' What tender sympathy, and wise yet gentle love, do these words reveal in our gracious Lord!

Besides, this is not only his own blessed character, but he ever enjoins the closest imitation of it on the part of his servants; and therefore he gives the well-known counsel, 'Comfort ye, comfort ye my people'; and this special one in particular, '*Comfort the feeble-minded, support the weak.*'

The feeble-minded, here referred to as needing comfort, are not the intellectually feeble, but rather those who, by reason of persecution, or bereavement, or buffeting temptation, have become disheartened and desponding, and ready to say, 'Will the Lord be favourable no more? Is his mercy clean gone for ever? ... hath he forgotten to be gracious? hath he in anger shut up his tender mercies?' The very strongest sometimes have their seasons of feebleness and fainting, when a word of comfort even from humblest lips is peculiarly cheering.

John Bunyan, in his inimitable allegory, thus beautifully sets forth the character and experience of these feeble ones:—'When

I came,' said Mr Feeble-mind, 'at the gate that is at the head of the way, the Lord of that place did entertain me freely; neither objected he against my weakly looks, nor against my feeble mind, but gave me such things as were necessary for my journey, and bid me hope to the end. When I came to the house of the Interpreter, I received much kindness there; and because the hill Difficulty was judged too hard for me, I was carried up that by one of his servants. Indeed, I have found much relief from pilgrims: though none was willing to go softly as I am forced to do, yet still, as they came on, they bade me be of good cheer, and said that it was the will of their Lord that comfort should be given to the feeble-minded; and so went on their own pace.' Yes, this is the will of our blessed Lord and Master; and happy are they who, through grace, not only know but do it.

> Bear ye one another's burdens, and so fulfil the law of Christ.—GAL. 6:2.

> We then that are strong ought to bear the infirmities of the weak, and not to please ourselves.—ROM. 15:1.

> To the weak became I as weak, that I might gain the weak.—1 COR. 9:22.

> I have shewed you all things, how that so labouring ye ought to support the weak, and to remember the words of the Lord Jesus, how he said, It is more blessed to give than to receive.—ACTS 20:35.

MAY 3

AN ASSURED HOPE IS BOTH ATTAINABLE AND BLESSED.

NOTWITHSTANDING the express injunction, 'Wherefore the rather, brethren, give diligence to make your calling and election sure,' an apostate church has authoritatively declared that 'a believer's assurance of the pardon of his sins is a vain, ungodly confidence—a prime error of heretics.' And, strange to say, there are not a few others who seem to cherish the depressing idea that no man, however anxious, can possibly know whether he is lost or saved till he has finally passed from time to eternity; and therefore they deem it presumptuous in any to profess assurance of salvation. They forget the words of the beloved apostle, 'We know that we are of God ... And we know that the Son of God is come, and hath given us an understanding, that we may know him that is true, and we are in him that is true, even in his Son Jesus Christ'; and the testimony of Paul, 'I know whom I have believed, and am persuaded that he is able to keep that which I have committed unto him against that day.' These words clearly show that they at least had an assured hope; and it need not be otherwise with us.

We would be far from saying that such an assurance is essential to salvation; for just as a child, without being aware of it, may be truly heir to a large inheritance, so, without being aware of it, a timid believer may be a partaker of grace and an heir of glory. Nevertheless, the want of assured hope is a great want, and injurious in many ways, for it is apt to induce a sadness and despondency that invariably enfeeble. 'Peace,' says one, 'is a holy keeper of the heart and mind, and joy is a divine invigorator and refresher, for it is written, "The joy of the Lord is your strength." Usually, therefore, it is when our hope is most assured that we can do noblest things for the honour of our Lord and the saving good of others.'

Some years ago a miner was down with a brother miner sinking a shaft, and for this end they were blasting the solid rock. They had placed in the rock a large charge of gunpowder, and had so fixed their fuse that it could not be extricated. Through some mistake fire was struck, and the fuse began to hiss. On seeing this, both men dashed to the bucket and gave the signal. The man above attempted in vain to move the windlass. Only one could escape, and delay was death to both. One of the miners, a Christian man, looked for a moment at his comrade, and, slipping from the bucket, said, 'Escape; I shall be in heaven in a minute.' The bucket sped up the shaft, and the man was safe. Eager to watch the fate of his deliverer, he bent down to hear. Just then the explosion rumbled below; a splinter came up the shaft and struck him on the brow, leaving a mark that would remind him all his days of his rescue. They soon began to burrow among the fallen rock for the dead body. But to their surprise they heard a voice: their friend was yet alive; the piece of rock had roofed him over, and he was without injury or scratch of any kind. When asked what induced him to let the other escape, he made the memorable reply, 'I knew my soul was safe. I was not so sure of his.' Here was Christian heroism of the noblest kind, and it was a sweet assurance of his own safety that nerved him for it. We may well therefore give diligence to make our calling and election sure.

> We desire that every one of you do shew the same diligence to the full assurance of hope unto the end.—HEB. 6:11.

> The Spirit itself beareth witness with our spirit, that we are the children of God.—ROM. 8:16.

> Our rejoicing is this, the testimony of our conscience, that in simplicity and godly sincerity, not with fleshly wisdom, but by the grace of God, we have had our conversation in the world.—2 COR. 1:12.

MAY 4

SUCCESSFUL WORKING MAY BE MOST PRIZED BY MAN, BUT FAITHFUL WORKING IS THE MAIN THING WITH GOD.

IT is right both to long and pray for success, but without watchfulness we may easily fall into a twofold error regarding it. We may overburden by making ourselves responsible for success as well as for duty, which our loving Lord never does; or we may unduly relax, by ceasing to work when we cease to succeed, as if the one might fairly be made conditional on the other. In all circumstances, however, with success or without it, the command remains equally binding, 'Occupy till I come.' 'Go work to day in my vineyard'; and it should be our daily aim to yield a prompt and hearty obedience.

Go, labour: it is not for nought,
  Thy earthly loss is heavenly gain.
Men heed thee, love thee, praise thee not;
  The Master praises—what are men!

Go, labour on: enough while here
  If he shall praise thee, if he deign
Thy willing heart to mark and cheer;
  No toil for him shall be in vain.

'I am thankful for success,' says Mr Spurgeon, 'but I feel in my heart a deeper gratitude to God *for permission to work for him.* It seems to me to be one of the highest gifts of his grace to be permitted to take any share whatever in his grand enterprise for the salvation of the sons of men.' It is even so; and they are blessed who realise it, for never are they allowed to labour in vain. Indeed, not unfrequently, when all is seeming failure and sore discouragement, great success is near. The Lord has often first to humble before he can greatly use.

It is told of an eminent man that when at one period of his ministry he became, through discouragement, sorely tempted to abandon both sphere and work, he had a singular dream. He thought he was working with a pickaxe on the top of a basaltic rock. His muscular arm brought down stroke after stroke for hours, but the rock was hardly indented. He said to himself at last, 'It is useless; I will pick no more.' Suddenly a stranger stood by his side, and said to him, 'Are you to do no more work?' 'No.' 'But were you not set to do this task?' 'Yes.' 'Why then abandon it?' 'My work is vain; I make no impression on the rock.' The stranger replied solemnly, 'What is that to you? Your duty is to pick whether the rock yields or not. Your work is in your own hands—the result is not; work.' He resumed his task. The first blow was given with almost superhuman force, and the rock flew into a thousand pieces. This was only a dream, but it so impressed him that, through grace, he was able to turn it to good account; for when he awoke he returned to his work with fresh interest and hope, and with greater tokens of his Master's presence and power than ever before.

Then I said, I have laboured in vain, I have spent my strength for nought, and in vain: yet surely my judgment is with the Lord, and my work with my God. And now, saith the Lord that formed me from the womb to be his servant, to bring Jacob again to him, Though Israel be not gathered, yet shall I be glorious in the eyes of the Lord, and my God shall be my strength.—Isa. 49:4, 5.

He shall see of the travail of his soul, and shall be satisfied.—Isa. 53:11.

May 5

SPEECH MUST BE WATCHED AS WELL AS ACTION.

USUALLY man's wit is far more prized than God's grace; nevertheless, it is not the former but the latter that is the true seasoner of speech, and makes it profitable. 'Let your speech,' says the apostle, 'be alway with grace, seasoned with salt, that ye may know how ye ought to answer every man'—'Let no corrupt communication proceed out of your mouth, but that which is good to the use of edifying, that it may minister grace unto the hearers.' Too many, however, entirely ignore these counsels. In truth, they have in their talk no end whatever in view, but are mere aimless archers, whose arrows never hit the mark. The idea of speaking so as to enlighten, edify, and comfort, never seems to enter their mind; and yet, as one truly says, 'The mouth of believers should be a treasury of benediction, and full of grace to the use of edifying.'

It would tend greatly to further the same desirable end were we, in social life, to speak less of persons than of things; and if of persons, to dwell on the good points rather than on the blemishes—on the excellences rather than on the faults—and to err rather in speaking too little than too much, for 'in the multitude of words there wanteth not sin.' Were this oftener remembered, we might be saved many a bitter regret from rash utterance. Who has not sometimes sorrowfully to say, 'Oh that I had not said it!' 'Much talkativeness and much grace,' says an old writer, 'seldom go together. Men of rich grace and sound intellect try to say much in few words; and there is hardly anything they dread more than to be talking much and yet to be really saying nothing.'

But while there may be an error in over-utterance, there may be a no less one in undue silence, when testimony should be given for truth and righteousness; yet too many, in order to escape the world's reproach, become mere night disciples, like Nicodemus in the beginning, and fail in the great duty of witnessing for their Lord. It was said of Robert M'Cheyne that he cared for no question unless his Master cared for it, and his anxiety ever was to know the mind of Christ and make it known. He once said to a friend, 'I bless God I live in witnessing times.' And are not our times such, when the call to every faithful disciple is to be valiant for the truth, and by word and deed openly take our stand on the side of our great Lord and Redeemer?

I said, I will take heed to my ways, that I sin not with my tongue.—PSA. 39:1.

The lips of the righteous feed many.—PROV. 10:21.

Whoso keepeth his mouth and his tongue keepeth his soul from troubles.—PROV. 21:23.

MAY 6

IF SAFE, IT IS BECAUSE WHILE SATAN SIFTS THE SAVIOUR PRAYS.

WHEN the Great Shepherd was smitten and the sheep were scattered, all the disciples were in danger, but Peter most of all. Not knowing his own weakness, and not fearing the enemy's power, he was on the verge of destruction, and would assuredly have perished but for the gracious interposition of his Lord: 'Simon, Simon, behold Satan hath desired to have you, that he may sift you as wheat: but I have prayed for thee, that thy faith fail not.' At first it seemed as if the prayer had been offered in vain, for Peter, almost immediately after, not only fell, but so awfully that, with cursing and swearing, he thrice denied his Lord. Nevertheless, it was a prayer all-powerful in efficacy; for no sooner did he hear the cock crow than, remembering the word of Jesus, he went out and wept bitterly: his faith in God's mercy did not fail him, and he found in the end loving forgiveness and sweet restoration.

Now, what the Lord said to Peter, he still virtually says to all his people: '*I* have prayed for *thee*, that thy faith fail not.' The *I* and the *thee* were not more emphatic then than they are at this hour, and every believer may take the full comfort of them: for though Jesus has passed into the heavens, yet, so far from forgetting his people, he is there for the very purpose of ceaselessly interceding in their behalf, and sending them help in every time of need; for still the great adversary is ceaseless in wile and effort, and neither by the tenderness of youth nor by the infirmity of age is he ever stayed in his fierce assaults.

When Mrs. Winslow was bereaved of an affectionate husband, deprived of fortune, and in a strange land, and friends far away— 'The enemy,' she said, 'seemed to sift me as wheat. I would steal away and weep in agony, for I lost hold and confidence in him who had said, "I will never leave thee nor forsake thee."' This buffeting of the adversary, however, was but for a season, for afterwards, through the helpful grace of her Lord, her faith revived, and she was able to say, 'He is all and everything he said he would be. He is my joy by night and by day, my stay in trouble, my strength in weakness, the lifter-up of my head, my portion forever. God be praised! God be praised!'

Not less touching is the recorded conflict and triumph of a young disciple. A Christian mother, not long ago, finding, as she sat beside her dying boy, that Satan had been dealing with him, said, 'Does he ever trouble you, George?' 'Oh yes; he has been very busy with me, especially when I have been weak, telling me I was too great a sinner and could not be saved.' 'And what did you say?' 'I told him I had a great Saviour'; and then he added, 'I think the tempter is nearly done with me now.' Some weeks before his death he had been saying, 'There is light in the valley'; and turning to his mother, he said very solemnly, 'Ah, it would be a dark valley without a light!' On the last day of his life she said to him, 'Is there light in the valley now, George?' 'Oh, yes, yes!' And when further asked, 'Is Satan done with you now?'—'Well, I think he is almost. He is lurking near, however; but Jesus is *nearer*.'

> I will put enmity between thee and the woman, and between thy seed and her seed; it shall bruise thy head, and thou shalt bruise his heel.—GEN. 3:15.

> Be sober, be vigilant; because your adversary the devil, as a roaring lion, walketh about, seeking whom he may devour.—1 PET. 5:8.

> The God of peace shall bruise Satan under your feet shortly.—ROM. 16:20.

MAY 7

THE HELPS GIVEN IN CHILDHOOD MAY NOT ALWAYS BE GIVEN IN RIPER YEARS.

WHEN faith is weak and danger manifold, we are apt to have a craving for signs. The thought, it may be, arises: If to encourage him, Gideon got a twofold sign—first the fleece wet and the ground dry, and then the ground wet and the fleece dry—why may not we be similarly favoured? In thinking thus, however, we forget the marked difference between Gideon's circumstances and ours. He lived in early Old Testament days, when light was dim, and the veil unrent, and the Seed of promise was yet unborn; whereas we have all the light, liberty, and varied privilege of gospel times. Moreover, we have a larger strengthening experience to appeal to, for we can point to innumerable Ebenezers set up from age to age by grateful pilgrims when on their heavenward way; and now that Jesus is glorified, we can have a larger measure of the Spirit than could possibly have been enjoyed at an earlier era. The visible signs and helps, therefore, occasionally vouchsafed in the infancy of the church, are not needed now, and ought not to be expected.

What God may do in sovereign grace we know not, and it is not for us to limit the Holy One of Israel; but to all appearance the season for signs like those of Gideon has now gone by. It is always safer, therefore, not to ask them even for confirmation of faith. And as to asking them as a *condition of faith*, it is an offensive and perilous unbelief; such as that which the Lord rebuked in the unbelieving Jews when he said, 'Except ye see signs and wonders, ye will not believe.'

But though the season for such signs as they demanded may be past, happily the season has not gone by for special tokens of heavenly love and special answers to prayer. There are no limits to signs of this nature: they may be multiplied indefinitely, and are the most precious and blessed of all. When seeking guidance and direction, believers must ever count it enough to have the sure and unerring word of their Lord. 'Come the enlargement when it will,' said Thomas Chalmers, 'it must come, after all, through the channel of a simple credence of the sayings of God, accounted as true and faithful sayings.' And he added: 'I would learn of thy holy oracles. Let me believe in the midst of heaviness; let me believe in the dark.'

> And the Pharisees came forth, and began to question with him, seeking of him a sign from heaven, tempting him. And he sighed deeply in his spirit, and saith, Why doth this generation seek after a sign? verily I say unto you, There shall no sign be given unto this generation.—MARK 8:11, 12.

> If they hear not Moses and the prophets, neither will they be persuaded, though one rose from the dead.—LUKE 16:31.

MAY 8

WHOM GOD DEFENDS, NONE CAN INJURE.

FEW passages of the word are more precious, or have been oftener quoted, than the eighth chapter of the Romans. Nor can we wonder; for the fears that have been calmed by it, and the hearts cheered, are innumerable. It has not only *No condemnation* for its beginning, and *No separation* for its end, but it is rich in comfort all through. It tells us of assured adoption—'The Spirit itself beareth witness with our spirit, that we are the children of God'; and of the overruling of love—'We know that all things work together for good to them that love God'; and of the certainty of glory—'For I reckon that the sufferings of this present time are not worthy to be compared with the glory which shall be revealed in us.'

A dying minister so prized this portion of the word that when sight was failing he said to a friend: 'Put my finger on these blessed words, for they cheer my soul—"If God be for us, who can be against us? ... Who shall lay anything to the charge of God's elect? It is God that justifieth. Who is he that condemneth? It is Christ that died, yea rather, that is risen again, who is even at the right hand of God, who also maketh intercession for us."' However worthless, therefore, and weak in ourselves, if only united to Christ we become as absolutely safe in the midst of our enemies as if we were already in the midst of paradise.

A well-known incident strikingly illustrates this security. It is the case of a man who had been condemned in a Spanish court; but being an American citizen, and also of English birth, the consuls of the two countries interposed, and declared that the Spanish authorities had no power to put him to death. Being determined to secure his life, they wrapped him in their flags—they covered him with the Stars and Stripes and the Union Jack—and defied the executioners. 'Now fire, if you dare!' they said; 'for if you do, you defy the great nations represented by these flags, and will bring their power upon you.' There stood the man, and before him the soldiery; and though a shot might soon have ended his life, yet he was as invulnerable as though in a coat of triple steel. 'Even so,' says one, 'Jesus Christ has taken my poor guilty soul ever since I believed in him, and has wrapped around me the blood-red flag of his atoning sacrifice.'

> He is near that justifieth me; who will contend with me? let us stand together: who is mine adversary? let him come near to me. Behold, the Lord God will help me; who is he that shall condemn me?—ISA. 50:8, 9.

I, even I, am he that blotteth out thy transgressions for mine own sake, and will not remember thy sins.—ISA. 43:25.

Therefore being justified by faith, we have peace with God through our Lord Jesus Christ.—ROM. 5:1.

MAY 9

IT IS NOT NEW MEANS WE NEED, BUT NEW POWER WITH THE OLD MEANS.

WHEN the rich man in the parable pleaded so earnestly with Abraham, he had evidently a firm conviction that without repentance his brethren would certainly perish. He was right in this; for in spite of all the dreamings of some about universal salvation in the end, final impenitence and final destruction are eternally linked.

There was another thing, apparently, of which the rich man was equally convinced—namely, that there was no hope whatever for his brethren unless something new and extraordinary were done for their sake; and therefore he earnestly entreated Abraham to send a messenger from the dead to warn them. A means so new and startling as this would, he thought, be certain to arouse them to repentance; and probably he imagined also that if he himself had been thus favourably circumstanced, he would neither have lived nor have died impenitent. So it is with many still. When they give no heed to the things that belong to their peace, and would fain excuse themselves, it is their circumstances they blame, or the utter inadequacy of the instrumentalities employed, but never themselves. Having little or no confidence in the ordinary means of grace—the written word and preached gospel—their fixed idea comes to be, that if men are to be roused and quickened, some other methods must be tried; if not dreams by night, or messengers from the dead, yet, at least, a gospel more suited to the present times, and a more gifted ministry to proclaim it. Now, all this is not merely a grievous dishonour to the word, but it is an utter delusion;

for the real obstacle is not in the means, but in the sinner himself. Hence the reply given: 'If they hear not Moses and the prophets, neither will they be persuaded though one rose from the dead.'

What is really needed is not a new word, or a new gospel, but a new faith in the old word, and a new power with the old gospel, through a new effusion of the Spirit of all grace. And this new faith in the word must be in the preacher as well as in the hearer. It is often forgotten that whatever the gifts or learning of the messenger, they will be of little avail if he has not full sympathy with his message, and *thorough faith* in it.

'I remember,' says Professor Bruce, 'a conversation I had some years ago with a respected minister of another church on the lack of fervour in preaching characteristic of the younger generation of ministers compared with the older generation. He remarked that the older ministers were better preachers than the younger, and wondered what might be the reason. I said in reply, "They believed more than we do. We are a sceptical generation." At this date,' he adds, 'I still think there is something in the explanation. The younger ministers know a great deal of the sceptical literature of the age, and the spirit of scepticism has entered more or less into their own blood; and they speak coldly, because they only half believe what they speak, though of conscious insincerity they are entirely innocent. We want men in our pulpits who believe with their whole heart and soul, and who, *believing intensely*, can speak emphatically, vehemently—yea, on needful occasion, with volcanic force. We want such men, just because the spirit of the age is sceptical. But that which creates the need also causes the difficulty of obtaining supply, and the church must bestow both *prayer and means* for the great end of rearing such a ministry.'

> They have Moses and the prophets; let them hear them. And he said, Nay, father Abraham: but if one went unto them from the dead, they will repent. And he said unto him, If they hear not Moses and the prophets, neither will they be persuaded, though one rose from the dead.—Luke 16:29-31.

May 10

SORE QUESTIONINGS FOR GRACIOUS ENDS.

WHEN for the last time together at the Sea of Galilee, the communing between Peter and his Master had no ordinary interest. Proceeding at once to deal closely and searchingly with his disciple, Jesus said to him, not once only, but three several times, 'Simon, son of Jonas, lovest thou me?' This repetition would at once recall his own threefold denying, and would seem to indicate a still lingering suspicion of him in the mind of his Lord. As soon, however, as the gracious spiritual ends designed by this were secured, there immediately followed renewed tokens of confidence and love. His Lord restored him to office, saying, 'Feed my lambs ... Feed my sheep'; and then, lifting in some degree the veil from the future, he added these striking words: 'Verily, verily, I say unto thee, When thou wast young, thou girdedst thyself, and walkedst whither thou wouldest: but when thou shalt be old, thou shalt stretch forth thy hands, and another shall gird thee, and carry thee whither thou wouldest not,' thereby signifying the violent death he should die.

It seems strange, at first, that immediately after the bestowment of fresh forgiveness, restoration, and blessing, so hard a saying as this should come from the lips of Jesus. Usually we like to conceal the worst from those who are dear to us, and especially if the threatened evil is yet in the far distance, feeling that 'sufficient unto the day is the evil thereof.' But here, seemingly, instead of hiding the worst from his servant, he fully reveals it. Passing over the whole intervening part of Peter's life, he goes at once to its close, and minutely specifies the humiliating and painful treatment he would then receive from the hands of hostile men. Yet who can doubt that all this, so far from being an unkindness to Peter, really conferred on him a marked honour, and unmistakably evidenced how fully his Lord believed in the genuineness warmth of his affection. It was a virtual intimation to him, not merely that his ministry would be a lengthened one, but that what he had failed to do in the beginning, he would nobly do in the end—glorify the Lord alike in life and in death.

There is something very touching in the Master's words, 'When thou shalt be old, thou shalt stretch forth thy hands, and another shall gird thee, and carry thee whither thou wouldest not.' And an old historian tells us that, when the prophecy was afterwards being fulfilled, Peter's love to Jesus so completely overcame the *not willing* of his nature, that there was but one thing he would not: he would not be put to death in the same way as his blessed Lord, deeming himself not worthy of such an honour. He begged it, therefore, as a favour that he should be nailed to the cross with his head downwards. His sufferings were great, but his blessedness was greater; for immediately after he departed to be with Christ, which is far better. 'This world,' as one says, 'was never made to be the saints' rest. Like Noah's dove, they cannot rest but in the Ark.'

> Fear none of those things which thou shalt suffer: behold, the devil shall cast some of you into prison, that ye may be tried; and ye shall have tribulation ten days: be thou faithful unto death, and I will give thee a crown of life.—Rev. 2:10.

> These things I have spoken unto you, that in me ye might have peace. In the world ye shall have tribulation: but be of good cheer; I have overcome the world.—John 16:33.

May 11

TILL WE LET GO EVERY FALSE CONFIDENCE, WE CAN NEVER REALISE THE TRUE.

THE delusions to which men cling in matters of salvation are often as strange as they are varied. Of old the Jews thought themselves safe, because they had Abraham for their father. Saul of Tarsus thought himself safer still, because as touching the law he was blameless, and concerning zeal persecuted the church. The Pharisee who prayed in the Temple had neither doubt nor fear of any kind, simply because he was not an extortioner or a publican, and fasted twice every week.

Similar false confidences are prevalent now. The hope of some is their charity and generous kindliness; while of others the main trust is their pious ancestry, or ecclesiastical relationships, or the depth of their convictions and intensity of their self-denials, or, perhaps, all of them combined. Poor and worthless as these confidences are, mere broken reeds, yet multitudes hold on to them as if their life depended on the firmness with which they were grasped. There is nothing, indeed, that even anxious souls more shrink from than to abandon all trust in self, and rely simply and unreservedly on Christ alone; yet in no other way can the lost be saved.

One night an inquirer, long under deep conviction, but still unsaved, dreamt that he was walking along the edge of a terrible precipice, and fell over it into a horrible abyss. As he was falling he grasped a little branch of some bush that was growing halfway down. There he hung, and cried for help. He could feel the branch giving way. He looked into the black yawning gulf beneath, and again cried out for help. Looking up, he saw, in his dream, Christ standing on the edge, and saying, 'Let go the twig, and I will save you.' Looking at the terrible abyss below, he could not. He cried again; and again came the same answer. At length he felt the branch slipping, and, in the utter desperateness of his despair, *he let go the branch*—when, lo! in an instant, the arms of Jesus were about him, and he was safe. He awoke. It was but a dream of the night. Yet from the vividness and instructiveness of its imagery, he was enabled to let go every false confidence, and rely only on the true. Would that every anxious soul would go and do likewise!

> This is life eternal, that they might know thee the only true God, and Jesus Christ, whom thou hast sent.—JOHN 17:3.

> But what things were gain to me, those I counted loss for Christ. Yea doubtless, and I count all things but loss for the excellency of the knowledge of Christ Jesus my Lord: for whom I have suffered the loss of all things, and do count them but dung, that I may win

Christ, and be found in him, not having mine own righteousness, which is of the law, but that which is through the faith of Christ, the righteousness which is of God by faith.—PHIL. 3:7-9.

MAY 12

THE MUCH COMMENDABLE, YET THE MUCH LACKING, IN THE CHURCH OF EPHESUS.

THOUGH our blessed Lord rebuked the church of Ephesus, he was first of all careful to note and commend all that was right and praiseworthy in it. In these times many members of our churches are little more than listeners, and if not idle in the outside marketplace, they are yet strangely idle in the vineyard. But the Ephesians were doers of the word as well as hearers; for it was said to them, not 'I know thy words,' but 'I know *thy works* ... and that for my name's sake thou hast laboured, and hast not fainted.'

Even this, however, was not all their attainment. Many have the active graces in part who are entirely wanting in the passive; for it is often far more easy to do the will of God than to bear it. But the Ephesians had patience as well as activity, and could endure as well as do. 'I know,' the Lord said to them, 'that thou hast borne, and hast patience.'

Moreover, while not a few now would put saving truth and deadly error on the same level, and make everything doubtful, the Ephesians, on the contrary, were so zealous for the truth that they resolutely opposed false teachers, as well as evil-doers, and would not suffer them on any plea whatever to go on deceiving and misleading the unwary and the ignorant. For this also the Lord graciously commended them: 'Thou canst not bear them which are evil: and thou hast tried them which say they are apostles, and are not, and hast found them liars.'

The Christians in Ephesus were thus, in activity, endurance, and zeal for the truth, so far ahead of many professed disciples in these latter times, that the thought very naturally suggests itself: 'If right in so many things, in what could they be wrong?'

The shortcoming was not such as to be easily discernible by the eye of man; yet it was real and mournful, and only too clearly visible to the heart-searching eye of the Lord. 'Nevertheless,' he said, 'I have somewhat against thee, because thou hast left *thy first love*. Remember therefore from whence thou art fallen, and repent, and do the first works, or else I will come unto thee quickly, and will remove thy candlestick out of his place, except thou repent.'

Frequently the inward feelings of servants give little or no concern to masters, provided the work laid to their hands is thoroughly done; but with our Lord it is otherwise: with him it is not the mere outward work of his servants, but the inward motive which prompts it, that is the all in all. As he is infinitely worthy of our love, and claims it, no service on our part can ever be acceptable to him in which affection is wanting. It should be the resolute aim of all believers, therefore, to keep their love to Christ warm and glowing even to the end; and there is no better way of doing this than by keeping ever in remembrance the greatness of his love to us.

> *Thy name is Love! I hear it from yon cross;*
> *Thy name is Love! I read it in yon tomb:*
> *All meaner love is perishable dross;*
> *But this shall light me through life's thickest gloom.*

God is not unrighteous to forget your work and labour of love.— HEB. 6:10.

Hold fast the form of sound words, which thou hast heard of me, in faith and love which is in Christ Jesus.—2 TIM. 1:13.

MAY 13

OUR CORRUPT NATURE.

WHEN referring to some of the closing verses of the fifth chapter of Galatians, John Calvin says: 'If men knew themselves, they would not need this inspired declaration; but such is the hypocrisy belonging to our natural state, that we never perceive our depravity till the tree has been fully known by its fruit.' And verily what an evil tree must that be which yields such bitter and deadly fruits as are here described: 'Adultery, fornication, uncleanness, lasciviousness, idolatry, witchcraft, hatred, variance, emulations, wrath, strife, seditions, heresies, envyings, murders, drunkenness, revellings, and such like.'

Paul represents these things as the work of the unrenewed nature of man. They are such as human nature, when left to itself, has invariably produced in all ages and in all lands, even as Scripture asserts and history confirms. It is not meant by this that all men are equally wicked, nor that any is as thoroughly corrupt as is possible for him to be, nor that men are destitute of all moral virtues. Even the heathen, the apostle teaches, do by nature the things of the law. They are more or less under the dominion of conscience, which approves or disapproves their moral conduct; nevertheless there is an entire absence of holiness, and a total alienation of the soul from God.

This is man's condition by nature. Manifestly the fallen and impure could not possibly find entrance into a home so pure as heaven is declared to be; for 'they that do such things,' says the apostle, 'shall not inherit the kingdom of God.' A new nature, therefore, and a new life are absolutely indispensable; and unless brought to realise this, and to say, with the publican, 'God be merciful to me a sinner,' never can we find deliverance.

But though the finally impenitent shall be excluded, even the very chief of sinners may find welcome and entrance, if only they yield to the Spirit and wash in the blood of the Lamb. Grievous and inexcusable as had been the guilt and impurity of many of the Corinthians, the apostle could yet say: 'Such were some of you; but ye are washed, but ye are sanctified, but ye are justified in the name of the Lord Jesus, and by the Spirit of our God.' How rich is the grace of God, and how omnipotent!

> *Burdened with guilt, wouldst thou be blest?*
> *Trust not the world, it gives no rest:*

Christ brings relief to hearts opprest—
O weary sinner, come!

God, who is rich in mercy, for his great love wherewith he loved us, even when we were dead in sins, hath quickened us together with Christ, (by grace ye are saved).—EPH. 2:4, 5.

For we ourselves also were sometimes foolish, disobedient, deceived, serving divers lusts and pleasures, living in malice and envy, hateful, and hating one another. But after that the kindness and love of God our Saviour toward man appeared, not by works of righteousness which we have done, but according to his mercy he saved us, by the washing of regeneration, and renewing of the Holy Ghost.—TITUS 3:3-5.

MAY 14

GRACE TO THE GENTILES.

THAT the Gentiles should be fellow-heirs and of the same body with the Israelites, was long concealed from the sons of men. For ages the very idea of such a thing never entered the minds of any. It was hid from the Gentiles, and it was hid also from the Jews. Indeed, such an opening of the door to the Gentiles was a thing so little dreamt of, that it needed a special revelation to make it known to the reluctant mind of Peter; and even when he was convinced, others remained so strongly prejudiced, that he was put upon his defence for going in among the uncircumcised.

In Paul's eyes, however, this mystery of the admission of the Gentiles was a very glorious one, and the more it was developed the more he rejoiced. Nor was this to be wondered at, for from the speciality of his mission his main labours were among the Gentiles, and his main successes also. Though wherever he went the Jews always got the first gospel offer, yet comparatively few of them gave it a welcome, or believed it to the saving of their souls; and therefore he solemnly said in the end: 'It was necessary that the word of God should first have been spoken to you: but seeing ye put it from you, and judge yourselves unworthy of everlasting life, lo, we turn to the Gentiles.' Nor did he turn to them in vain, for alike in Corinth, in Ephesus, and Philippi, in Colosse, in Rome, and Thessalonica, yea, and wherever he preached, multitudes gladly received the word of life. Nay, so marked was his success, that he could say: 'Thanks be unto God, which *always* causeth us to triumph in Christ, and maketh manifest the savour of his knowledge by us *in every place.*'

This unveiled mystery should have a special interest to us as belonging to the Gentiles, and because the opened door that let them in eighteen centuries ago is the same door that lets us in now. It is well to remember, however, that the present favoured condition of the Gentiles is a *conditional* one. If they continue to believe, it shall be well with them; but should they cast off the faith, as many even now are openly doing, they shall be as certainly and awfully overthrown at the end of the Gentile dispensation as were the seed of Abraham when, eighteen centuries ago, they finally and deliberately rejected the Son of God.

'No other land,' said Robert M'Cheyne, 'has the gospel preached as we have, free as the air we breathe, as the stream from the everlasting hills. Then think for a moment, you who sit under the shade of faithful ministers, and yet remain unconcerned and unconverted, and are not brought to sit under the shade of Christ—think how like your wrath will be *to that of the unbelieving Jews.*'

> When they heard these things, they held their peace, and glorified God, saying, Then hath God also to the Gentiles granted repentance unto life.—ACTS 11:18.

> Well; because of unbelief they were broken off, and thou standest by faith. Be not highminded, but fear: For if God spared not the natural branches, take heed lest he also spare not thee.—ROM. 11:20, 21.

MAY 15

THE DOUBLE GIFT.

IN Old Testament times, the promise that stood out most prominently was the grand and oft-repeated one of the Messiah, the Hope of Israel, the gift unspeakable of the Father's love. It was the joyous theme of every prophet, and the bright expectancy of every enlightened saint.

Grand as it was, however, that promise was not more essential and blessed than the great promise of the Spirit so often referred to in the word. As promises, they stand side by side in Scripture; and in inherent preciousness and saving value there is no difference between them. Indeed, the gift of the Son, apart from the additional gift of the Spirit, could have done nothing for us effectually and savingly; for what avails a perfect remedy for the dying, if there be no loving hand to apply it? In the cross we have the providing and the purchasing of redemption; and so effectually that the sinner has nothing to pay—Christ has paid it all. But then, the revealing and applying of this purchased possession to our perishing race is the special office and delight of the Spirit. Hence these gracious utterances of the Lord, when speaking of the Comforter whom he would send: 'When he is come, he will reprove the world of sin, and of righteousness and of judgment: of sin, because they believe not on me; of righteousness, because I go to my Father, and ye see me no more.' And again: 'When he, the Spirit of truth, is come, he will guide you into all truth, and shall glorify me: for he shall receive of mine, and shall shew it unto you.' The Spirit is thus so pre-eminently the great enlightener and quickener, that never in any case is there real conviction of sin, or conversion to God, or advancement in holiness, or fulness of peace and joy, without his presence.

The grand hope of believers, then, and of the church, in furthering the Master's cause and kingdom, is the Holy Spirit in outpoured fulness. For this, therefore, should everyone ceaselessly and believingly plead. An eminent servant of God said at a missionary meeting lately that, when he looked at the divisions and the worldliness of the churches, he should despair if he had nothing but past successes to assure him. But he added, with great emphasis, 'I believe in the Holy Ghost, and therefore I fear not.'

> He that believeth on me, as the scripture hath said, out of his belly shall flow rivers of living water. (But this spake he of the Spirit, which they that believe on him should receive.)—John 7:38, 39.

> I will pour water upon him that is thirsty, and floods upon the dry ground: I will pour my spirit upon thy seed, and my blessing upon thine offspring.—Isa. 44:3.

MAY 16

CONVERSION FIRST, BUT NEVER ALONE.

WHEREVER the apostle went, the first and main thing with him ever was the saving conversion of souls; for he felt that, till this was secured, nothing was secured. Whatever may be done with the living in the way of perfecting them, nothing whatever can be done with the dead; and such all are by nature. Apart, indeed, from spiritual vitality, every attempt of the kind is labour wholly thrown away, and as foolish as to expect by mere hard rubbing to convert a common pebble into a priceless diamond.

It is here where so many professedly Christian workers sadly fail. Though their outward organisation is perfect, and they have every variety of agency in operation, yet their labour is vain, because they have neither the right end in view, nor the right object of dependence, even the life-giving Spirit of the Lord. In truth, without being aware of it, they are trying to get fruit from unrooted branches, and Christian growth and development in the entire absence of Christian life.

But even the new birth is not enough, apart from a renewed life following it; for if created in Christ Jesus, it is unto good works. A religion that saves but does not sanctify is not the religion revealed in the word and indissolubly linked with the name of Jesus, nor is it ever powerfully influential in winning others.

When conversing with an excellent man in England many years ago, he told me that he owed his conversion mainly to the marked consistency of a merchant who lived not far from him. His neighbour was a Christian, and professed to carry on his large business on strictly Christian principles. 'This struck me,' my friend remarked, 'and I said to myself, "I am by no means sure that this is the case, but I shall watch him closely for a year; and if at the end of that time I find that he is really what he professes to be, I shall follow his example, and become a Christian also." During the whole of that year I resolutely kept my eye on him, always expecting to find some flaw or inconsistency in his mode of dealing. But no; he stood the test. The result was a thorough conviction on my part that he was a true man, and that religion was a reality. When I told him the whole circumstances, and asked him how much I should give to the Lord as a thank-offering for his great mercy toward me, the good man was filled with gratitude, but at the same time trembled as he thought what might have happened had he stumbled through any unwatchfulness when so observed, and for such an end.'

> Who shall also confirm you unto the end, that ye may be blameless in the day of our Lord Jesus Christ.—1 Cor. 1:8.

> Only let your conversation be as it becometh the gospel of Christ.—Phil. 1:27.

> And the very God of peace sanctify you wholly; and I pray God your whole spirit and soul and body be preserved blameless unto the coming of our Lord Jesus Christ.—1 Thess. 5:23.

May 17

THE SONSHIP OF ADOPTION.

THERE are some who see nothing peculiar in the filial relationship to God so frequently referred to in the word, but regard it as belonging, without limit or exception of any kind, to the whole human race. Whatever their tribe or tongue, their religion or character, all, in their view, are equally the sons and daughters of the Lord Almighty. To hold this is, however, entirely to ignore the clear and emphatic teaching of the word of God. In a secondary sense it is true; all who are God's creatures, even the most alienated of them who openly scorn his grace and reject his offered salvation, may be said to be God's children, as the apostle admitted when he said to the Athenians,—'For in him we live, and move, and have our being; as certain also of your own poets have said, For we are also his offspring.' But to be offspring in this sense is a widely different thing from being children by adoption in the peculiar and scriptural sense.

Such a filial relationship is never one merely of nature. As set forth in the word, it is a fruit of gracious purpose: 'Having predestinated us unto the adoption of children by Jesus Christ to himself, according to the good pleasure of his will.' Moreover, it springs from distinguishing love; hence the words of John: 'Behold, what manner of love the Father hath bestowed upon us, that we should be called the sons of God.' And it is specially testified to by the Spirit: 'The Spirit itself beareth witness with our spirit, that we are the children of God: and if children, then heirs; heirs of God, and joint-heirs with Christ.'

One of the great privileges of this blessed adoption *is freedom of access*. When a beggar knocks at a door, and then waits for its opening, he is all uncertain as to the reception he may meet with; nay, a repulse may be more likely than a welcome. How different with a son! Whether he knocks or rings, it is with the most trustful confidence and heartiness, for it is his father's house; and enter when he may, he knows assuredly he can count upon a welcome. It is even so with the children of God. They have ever the freest and most intimate access to the Lord, and can at all times pour into their Father's ear and heart every anxiety of their souls and every petition of their lips.

This, believers, is your privilege; and rest assured that, if you are once put into God's family, you will never again be put out of it.

Though, in wondrous grace, outcasts innumerable have become children, yet not one of the real children has ever become an outcast again. There may occasionally, it is true, be not a little waywardness among them, and even grievous and humiliating backsliding; and because of this there may be the hiding of God's face and the losing of assurance, and perhaps even bitter and prolonged chastening before the healing comes again. But in no case will there ever be a final disownment or severance; for having loved his own from the beginning, he loves them to the end. Never, therefore, should they cease to say, with all filial confidence, 'Abba, Father.'

The night before his death, Dr Chalmers, while walking in his garden, was overheard, by one of his family, saying, in low but very earnest tones, 'O Father! my heavenly Father!' Sweet close to so noble a life.

> Ye are all the children of God by faith in Christ Jesus.—GAL. 3:26.

> As many as received him, to them gave he power to become the sons of God, even to them that believe on his name.—JOHN 1:12.

> Beloved, now are we the sons of God, and it doth not yet appear what we shall be: but we know that, when he shall appear, we shall be like him; for we shall see him as he is.—1 JOHN 3:2.

MAY 18

USUALLY, AS OPPORTUNITIES ARE IMPROVED,
THEY MULTIPLY.

AFTER giving the general counsel to the believers in Galatia, 'Let us not be weary in well-doing: for in due season we shall reap, if we faint not,' the apostle immediately added the special one: 'As we have therefore opportunity, let us do good unto all men, especially unto them who are of the household of faith.' With such words before them, none need despair of usefulness who have any of the spirit of Robert Hall, when he said, 'How ardently I long to do something which shall convince the world I have not lived in vain.'

No one can do everything in Christian service, because no one has all the talents or all the opportunities; yet, if but willing, all, even the humblest, have talent enough to do more or less for the honour of their Lord and the salvation of souls. If this something, however little, be only done with single eye and resolute purpose, what was said of old will be graciously said again, 'She hath done what she could.'

Not unfrequently, when it seems as if we had no opportunities of usefulness, it is just because there is a want of the watchful eye to see them and of the loving heart to embrace them.

In times of quickening, when faith brightens and love revives, it is marvellous to see how difficulties vanish, how spheres enlarge, and doors that once seemed hopelessly shut become widely open; and to see also how the very humblest and obscurest become lights and blessings to those around them.

That devoted Christian, Harlan Page, spent most of his life in a quiet New England community, toiling from day to day at the carpenter's bench; and yet, before his death, he knew of more than a hundred souls converted through his instrumentality. Under God, all this was accomplished simply by doing good unto all men as he had opportunity. As one said of him, he made every day tell in the work that held the first thought and place in his heart. 'To meet a neighbour was an occasion to do him good. To hear of a wanderer was sufficient to enlist his soul in efforts to reclaim and save him. By words written and spoken, by tract, and consecrated example, in every way he sought to do good. He had caught the spirit of his Lord and Master; and every action said, "I must work the works of him that sent me, while it is day; the night cometh when no man can work."'

What a different world in purity and peace would this soon be, and how much of heaven might be enjoyed on earth, if all who bear the name of Christ had a similar spirit and a like devotedness!

> Finish thy work, the time is short,
>   The sun is in the west,
> The night is coming down; till then
>   Think not of rest.

Whatsoever thy hand findeth to do, do it with thy might; for there is no work, nor device, nor knowledge, nor wisdom, in the grave, whither thou goest.—ECCLES. 9:10.

Therefore, my beloved brethren, be ye stedfast, unmoveable, always abounding in the work of the Lord, forasmuch as ye know that your labour is not in vain in the Lord.—1 COR. 15:58.

MAY 19

THEY ARE FREE INDEED WHOM THE TRUTH SETS FREE.

LOOKED at from a distance, the service of Christ sometimes seems a hard bondage; but when honestly and heartily entered on, it is ever a yoke that is easy and a burden that is light. A worldling is bond anywhere, but everywhere a true Christian is free. To Adam even paradise was gloomy when guilt had filled him with fear; whereas to Paul even the prison was bright and joyous when grace had loosened his bonds and poured peace into his soul.

He is the freedman whom the Truth makes free,
And all are slaves besides.

This freedom which the Lord gives to his people has nothing spurious in it, and therefore, though freed from the penalty of the law, they are not freed from its precepts. They are no more under its curse, but, to their delight, they are still under its conduct. 'The law,' says John Flavel, 'sends us to Christ to be justified, and Christ sends us to the law to be regulated.' Accordingly, every believer gladly says with the Psalmist, 'Thou hast commanded us to keep thy precepts diligently. O that my ways were directed to keep thy statutes!'

But more than this: when once made free by the Son, we become free to every privilege and blessing his blood has purchased—free to enter his house, to sit at his table, to rejoice in his smile, and to draw without limit from his inexhaustible fulness. No freedom, therefore, could be more blessed than this; and, happily, it has its beginning *the very moment we believe.*

'In foreign harbour,' says Dr Moody Stuart, 'a slave followed the footsteps of her mistress into our ship; and I remarked to the captain that on reaching England she would be free. "No," he replied; "*she is free already*. The Queen of England has no slaves; the moment she set her foot on the planks of this ship she was a free woman, and her mistress cannot now bid her return to the shore without her own free consent." It was a grand thought—no, it was a glorious fact—that this dark daughter of Ethiopia, a helpless bondswoman one moment before, was now as free and as safe as our Queen upon her throne; and that until all the guns of England were silenced and her fleets sunk beneath the waves, not a hair of her head could perish.'

So is it with the spiritually bond. No matter how many the years of their bondage, or how intense their bitterness, the very instant they put their foot, as it were, on the plank of grace, and make Christ their trust, they become as free, and safe, and uncondemned as if they were already in heaven. 'There is now no condemnation to them that are in Christ Jesus.'

> If ye continue in my word, then are ye my disciples indeed; And ye shall know the truth, and the truth shall make you free.—JOHN 8:31, 32.
>
> Where the Spirit of the Lord is, there is liberty.—2 COR. 3:17.
>
> Stand fast therefore in the liberty wherewith Christ hath made us free, and be not entangled again with the yoke of bondage.—GAL. 5:1.

MAY 20

WHOM WE LOVE WE LONG TO SEE.

IN writing to his friend, the well-beloved Gaius, the Apostle John said, 'I had many things to write, but I will not with ink and pen write unto thee: but I trust *I shall shortly see thee*, and we shall speak face to face.' So is it with believers and their Lord. Though, meanwhile, unseen by them, they yet warmly love him; and with good reason, for it was he who delivered their souls from death, their eyes from tears, and their feet from falling, and has proved himself to be of all friends the truest, surest, and most abiding. On this very account there is no hope sweeter to them than that of one day seeing him to *face to face*, and being forever with him; and knowing it to be so, it was with this very hope the apostle cheered the bereaved mourners in Thessalonica. When he comes, he said, 'the dead in Christ shall rise first: then we which are alive and remain shall be caught up together with them in the clouds, to meet the Lord in the air: and so shall we ever be with the Lord. Wherefore *comfort one another with these words.*'

When our Lord said to Peter, in reference to John, 'If I will that he tarry *till I come*, what is that to thee? follow thou me'; forthwith, we are told, the saying went abroad among the brethren that that disciple *should not die.* Whatever error mingled with this saying, it yet clearly showed that in thought and loving expectancy, at least, the early Christians linked the coming of the Lord, not with death, but with life. And so should we, for there is the widest of differences between the coming of death and the coming of Christ. Indeed, there is no death where he is; it flees before him. Dead bodies sprang to life the very moment he touched or spoke to them; and when he sets up his kingdom at the last, there is to be life for evermore. Just in proportion, therefore, to the intensity of their love and gratitude is the ardour with which believers long and say, 'Come, Lord Jesus, come quickly.'

Two centuries ago, Andrew Gray, the M'Cheyne of his time, and who, like him, was early called home, once said at a communion season, 'Oh, when shall these blue heavens be rent, and we be admitted to the marriage supper of the Lamb? I long for the day when all the language of heaven and earth shall be, "Come, come, Lord Jesus."' But, in a more marked degree still, this was a theme in which Samuel Rutherford ever specially delighted. 'All is night that is here,' he said; 'therefore sigh and long for the dawning of the morning, and the breaking of that day of the coming of the Son of man! Persuade yourself the King is coming; read his letter sent before him, "Behold, I come quickly." Wait with the wearied nightwatch for the breaking of the eastern sky, and think that ye have not a morrow.'

> Looking for that blessed hope, and the glorious appearing of the great God and our Saviour Jesus Christ.—TITUS 2:13.

> Surely I come quickly. Amen. Even so, come, Lord Jesus.—REV. 22:20.

> Our conversation is in heaven; from whence also we look for the Saviour, the Lord Jesus Christ.—PHIL. 3:20.

MAY 21

THEY WHO PRAY MOST THEMSELVES MOST PRIZE THE PRAYERS OF OTHERS.

IT was a great day in the history of the church when the Lord said to Ananias, 'Arise, and go into the street which is called Straight, and inquire in the house of Judas for one called Saul, of Tarsus: for, *behold, he prayeth.*' This praying on his part, then just begun, was to the very end of his life characterised by a faith, fervour, and holy importunity rarely equalled, and never surpassed.

He was constantly pleading for others: 'Brethren, my heart's desire and prayer to God for Israel is, that they might be saved'— 'For this cause I bow my knees unto the Father of our Lord Jesus Christ ... that he would grant you, according to the riches of his glory, to be strengthened with might by his Spirit in the inner man'—'Night and day praying exceedingly that we might see your face, and might perfect that which is lacking in your faith.'

And as he thus prayed much for others, so he often asked that they in turn should pray for him: 'Withal praying also for us, that God would open unto us a door of utterance, to speak the mystery of Christ'—'Finally, brethren, pray for us, that the word of the Lord may have free course, and be glorified.' Words like these were no mere words of course with him, or a becoming form only, but the fervent utterance of his whole heart, just because he more than most men believed in the power and efficacy of prayer. Indeed, he attempted nothing and expected nothing without it, but ever carried out to the full the blessed counsel, 'In everything by prayer and supplication with thanksgiving let your requests be made known unto God,'—words which sweetly suggest the three-fold duty, to be careful for nothing, prayerful for everything, and thankful for anything.

Ministers and people greatly need each other's prayers; but in this mightily helpful duty how manifold are the shortcomings of all! 'I would rather know,' says Mr Moody, 'how to pray like David than to preach like Gabriel. Prayer moves the hand that moves the universe; and by the wielding of this powerful weapon *some bedridden saint* may accomplish more in the sick chamber than others in the full enjoyment of health, and who are better known.' Usually when there is little prayer in the pew there is little power in the pulpit. On this account, devoted men of God in every age have ever earnestly entreated the prayers of their people.

Not long ago George Müller of Bristol said fervently and lovingly to those who heard him, 'Believers in Christ, pray for me, for I cannot do without your prayers; pray that the last days of my pilgrimage may be the best days of my life; pray that I may be upheld in the ways of God, strengthened in the inner man, and be made helpful to others.'

> Epaphras, who is one of you, a servant of Christ, saluteth you, always labouring fervently for you in prayers.—COL. 4:12.
>
> Ye also helping together by prayer for us.—2 COR. 1:11.
>
> Now I beseech you, brethren, for the Lord Jesus Christ's sake, and for the love of the Spirit, that ye strive together with me in your prayers to God for me.—ROM. 15:30.

MAY 22

WHAT WE MAINLY NEED.

IN times of sickness, depression, or straitened circumstances, the frequent thought of many is that if they could only get change of scene, or higher friendships, or ampler means, all would be well with them. In this, however, they deceive themselves; for true happiness depends not so much on things as on thoughts, even as our blessed Lord himself intimates when he says, 'A man's life consisteth not in the abundance of the things which he possesseth.' Though Solomon had everything that heart could wish, it was 'all vanity' to him and 'vexation of spirit.' On the other hand, though the prophet was thoroughly stripped of all, 'yet he rejoiced in the Lord, and joyed in the God of his salvation.' What we mainly need, therefore, is not so much fuller stores as richer grace; for this would give us sweet contentedness in any sphere, and enable us, as it were, rather to keep looking at earth from heaven than looking at heaven from earth, as though present things were already past and future things already come.

Nothing comes wrong to the soul that is, through grace, at peace with God, and has a trustful, loving confidence in his word and ways; for he feels assured that whether the Lord gives or takes, smites or heals, sends cloud or sunshine, he doeth all things well.

> *The heart that trusts forever sings,*
> *And feels as light as it had wings;*
> *A well of peace within it springs,*
>   *Come good or ill.*
> *Whate'er today or tomorrow brings,*
>   *It is his will.*

'Christians,' said Edward Payson, 'might avoid much trouble and inconvenience if they would only believe what they profess, that God is able to make them happy without anything else. To mention my own case: God has been depriving me of one blessing after another, but as every one was removed, he has come in and filled up its place; and now, when I am a cripple and not able to move, I am happier than ever I was in my life before, or ever expected to be; and if I had believed this twenty years ago, I might have been spared much anxiety.'

They are blessed indeed who, in all circumstances, can give like gladsome testimony.

> Not that I speak in respect of want: for I have learned, in whatsoever state I am, therewith to be content.—PHIL. 4:11.

> In a great trial of affliction the abundance of their joy and their deep poverty abounded unto the riches of their liberality.—2 COR. 8:2.

> Because thou sayest, I am rich, and increased with goods, and have need of nothing; and knowest not that thou art wretched, and miserable, and poor, and blind, and naked.—REV. 3:17.

MAY 23

REMEMBERED GRACES.

THE three root graces are faith, hope, and love, and in the Thessalonians all of them were so genuine and thorough in their manifestation, that the apostle said, 'Remembering without ceasing your work of faith, and labour of love, and patience of hope in our Lord Jesus Christ, in the sight of God and our Father.'

Speaking of the first, he says, 'Your *work* of faith.' 'True faith,' says an old divine, 'is a working grace, and it has such a deal of work to do that its hands are always full.' Now, such was their faith. It was powerfully operative. It took hold of the promises and pleaded them. It drew daily and largely from the divine fulness; and thus, if strong in the beginning, it became stronger still in the end, and could glorify God even in the fires.

But the love of the Thessalonians was as genuine as their faith. It laboured for God and for man, and not for a brief season only, but from year to year continuously. A love in word and in tongue has always been common enough, but not so a love in deed and in truth, which labour as well as speak for Christ—yea, and if need be, die for him also. Instead of waxing cold, our last love to Christ should be warmer than the first, just because every year gives us a fuller knowledge of his character and a richer experience of his bounty and grace.

The hope specified was equally genuine: 'Your patience of hope in our Lord Jesus Christ, in the sight of God and our Father.' It looked beyond all present things with joyous expectancy. 'In the treatment of nervous diseases,' one has said, 'he is the best physician who is the most ingenious inspirer of hope'; and such a physician pre-eminently is the Lord Jesus. Even in the hearts of the most despairing he has again and again kindled a sure and blessed hope, and put a new song in their mouth. When this hope is genuine, it is patient, because it confidently expects all that God has promised, however long it may have to wait for it.

While so working in faith, and labouring in love, and waiting in hope, all believers have much to cheer them day by day. 'Christ's "well done,"' says an old writer, 'is worth a shipful of good days and earthly honours. I have cause to say this, because I find him truth itself.' And another adds, 'It is blessed to be clinging to Jesus with one hand, and to be working for him with the other; but it is more blessed still to be held up in Christ's strong arms, and to be able to use both hands in his service.'

Faith, if it hath not works, is dead, being alone.—JAMES 2:17.

In Jesus Christ neither circumcision availeth any thing, nor uncircumcision; but faith which worketh by love.—GAL. 5:6.

And now abideth faith, hope, charity, these three; but the greatest of these is charity.—1 COR. 13:13.

MAY 24

IT IS NO EASY THING TO BE STABLE.

SUCH is the mutual dependence of pastor and people that the fidelity and stedfastness of the one ever tell powerfully on the faith and joyfulness of the other. 'Now we live,' says the apostle, 'if ye stand fast'; and what he thus felt and said eighteen centuries ago, all true servants of Christ have been virtually feeling and saying also all down the ages. When in Mentone for his health, Mr Spurgeon, in writing to the members of his church, said, 'If anything could conduce more than all else to restore my health and spirits, it would be good news from the Tabernacle.' Such tidings, when they reached him, always made his heart overflow with joy. He added, 'Your telegram, "Monday—Largest prayer meeting ever held in the Tabernacle," set me in a glow of gratitude to God.' Their standing fast was life and strength to him.

Moreover, stedfastness, besides being desirable, is all-important. It is, however, no easy attainment. Even if we had but inward corruption to contend with, it would still be difficult to quit ourselves like men; but when, in addition, we have to resist the pressure of manifold temptation without, the conflict often becomes beyond measure severe. The foolish self-confidence that forgets this is one of the surest precursors of grievous stumbling. If Peter had not thought it so easy to stand, he would not have been left so sadly to fall.

No matter what our knowledge or talents or experience or resoluteness may be, we cannot stand fast *alone*; for what the apostle says is not simply, 'Now we live, if ye stand fast,' but, 'Now we live, if ye stand fast *in the Lord*.' As it is through faith in the Lord that we get life at the first, so it is by abiding in the Lord that we get strength and stability to the last. 'I can do all things through Christ which strengtheneth me.' On this account, the best fighters in the good fight, and the best runners in the race, and the best workers in the vineyard, are always those who best lean on the word and arm of the Lord. To have such a Lord to lean on, so all-powerful and so infinitely gracious, is one of the divinest of privileges; and yet how little do many avail themselves of it!

> Ye therefore, beloved, seeing ye know these things before, beware lest ye also, being led away with the error of the wicked, fall from your own stedfastness.—2 PET. 3:17.

Henceforth be no more children, tossed to and fro, and carried about with every wind of doctrine, by the sleight of men, and cunning craftiness, whereby they lie in wait to deceive.—Eph. 4:14.

May 25

THE PRECIOUSNESS OF GOD'S FAVOUR.

MERE creature favour is the all in all with many, and they toil hard to secure it; yet what is it at its best but a wavering uncertainty, a very reed that any wind can bend and break. But the favour of the Lord is a reality, and everything about it is precious. It is a tree, yielding choicest fruits; a fountain, from which refreshing streams are ever flowing; yea, a blessing so divinely rich, that he who possesses it may joyously say: 'Sing unto the Lord, O ye saints of his ... for in *his favour is life*'—'In the light of the king's countenance is life; and his favour is a cloud of the latter rain.'

As sunshine is never so welcome as after lengthened seasons of cloud and rain, so never is God's favour so prized and valued as after dreary seasons of depression and darkness. What makes it so peculiarly precious is the foundation on which it rests—not creature deservings of any kind, which are merely imaginary, but the finished work of our blessed Redeemer. So founded, it can never give way or fail to satisfy.

When health began to fail, a late eminent prelate became much disquieted from a sense of his unfitness to stand before God in judgment. He expressed a wish to live, not merely for the sake of his children and the church, but, above all, that he might deepen and perfect his own repentance. But as the end drew still nearer, all distressing doubts as to his own fitness and the imperfection of his own repentance seemed to have been rolled away before the rising brightness of the Sun of righteousness; and he was enabled, as he himself expressed it, 'more and more to place his whole confidence in the precious blood.'

So must it be with all who would secure and enjoy this first of blessings—the favour of God. It cannot be bought; but, as a free gift of grace through Jesus Christ, it may be ours for the taking, without measure and without end.

> Remember me, O Lord, with the favour that thou bearest unto thy people: O visit me with thy salvation.—Psa. 106:4.
>
> Thou, Lord, wilt bless the righteous; with favour wilt thou compass him as with a shield.—Psa. 5:12.
>
> Him that cometh to me I will in no wise cast out.—John 6:37.

May 26

THE ONCE DEAD, BUT NOW RISEN.

ON Easter morning it is a custom almost universal in Russia, when two friends meet, to say, 'Christ is risen.' They tell it to each other as good news, that may well gladden every heart. What sweeter salutation can there be or truer? Whoever else may still be in the grave, Christ at least is risen—risen, as he said, risen in spite of every foe; and, better still, risen to give visible and eternal proof that his redemption work was not only divinely completed on earth, but divinely accepted in heaven.

What is true of Christ as to resurrection, is true also of his people. Because he lives, they shall live also; and the glad day is hastening on when he shall come to awaken them out of sleep. Nay, more, because he lives, they live even now; for, spiritually, they become risen with Christ the very moment they believe.

Very frequently when, from very lowly circumstances, men struggle upwards to great wealth and high social status, they are spoken of as men who have *risen*; and while some congratulate, others envy them. But no elevation of this nature, however high, can for a moment be compared with that of those who are risen with Christ; for their rise is not simply from poverty to wealth, from obscurity to distinction, from ignorance to knowledge, but from death to life, and from sin to holiness. Indeed, apart from the great reward held out in the future, there is even now, in a renewed life, such moral elevation of character, such purity of aim and feeling, such conscious peace with God, and blessed aspirations after perfect conformity to the Lord's mind and will, that it might well be chosen for its own sake. But when we remember that the transformation is not merely something so desirable that all should long for it, but a thing so absolutely essential that without it we can neither have part nor lot with the children of God; then to disregard and neglect it, is not unwisdom only, but utter infatuation.

To all who have experienced this blessed change, the apostle says: 'If ye then be risen with Christ, seek those things which are above, where Christ sitteth on the right hand of God.'

> *Brethren, arise!*
> *There is no home for us*
> *Till earth be purified.*
> *We may not here abide,*
> *We were not born for earth;*
> *The city of our birth,*
> *The better paradise,*
> *Is far above the skies:*
> *Upward, then, let us soar,*
> *Cleaving to dust no more.*

Likewise reckon ye also yourselves to be dead indeed unto sin, but alive unto God through Jesus Christ our Lord.—ROM. 6:11.

But God, who is rich in mercy, for his great love wherewith he loved us, even when we were dead in sins, hath quickened us together with Christ, (by grace ye are saved;) and hath raised us up together, and made us sit together in heavenly places in Christ Jesus.—EPH. 2:4-6.

MAY 27

SEEMING DEAFNESS TO ENTREATY.

THE Lord's usually open ear to his people becomes, at times, a seemingly shut one. They supplicate as before, it may be, and say with all earnestness, '*Give ear*, O God of Jacob'; but to their sore discouragement, no response is given and no relief comes. It is as if he heard them not. This was touchingly exemplified in the case of the Syro-phenician woman. No affliction could have been greater than hers, for her daughter, possibly an only child, was grievously vexed with a devil; nor could any prayer have been more intense in its earnestness than the one she offered. Again and again she cried aloud, 'Have mercy upon me, O Lord, thou son of David!' but all to no purpose apparently, for we are expressly told that 'he answered her not a word.'

Nor is this a mere solitary instance of such painful silence. With many of God's children it is often so still; they get a shut ear when they are intensely sighing for an open one, and this, too, at a time when the blessings they ask seem right and good—nay, even when spiritual things alone are the burden of their cry. At such seasons they are ready, with the Psalmist, to say, in sorrowful despondency, 'Why hidest thou thy face, O Lord? Why art thou silent unto me?'

There may be mystery in such dealings, dark and perplexing; nevertheless, to the troubled believer, who calmly waits in patient faith, they will, sooner or later, be found to embody in them the wisest wisdom and the warmest love.

At other times God is silent to his people because, like the disciples of old, they ask amiss. As in ordinary family life, were a son so deluded as to ask from his father not bread but a stone, not an egg but a scorpion, then just in proportion to his wisdom and love would be the resolute persistency with which the father would shut his ear to him. So is it with our heavenly Father; when unwise petitions are presented to him, in very mercy and kindness he will not answer. Such a providence may *seem* frowning, but there is love behind it. Just as Joseph was never more yearning in his affection for his brethren than at the very time when outwardly he was roughest, so often the Lord is never so truly gracious to his children as when seemingly sternest and deafest to all their supplications.

This shutting of the Lord's ear is often the experience of days only, but occasionally it is the experience even of months or of years; but whatever the interval between the prayer and the answer, there is always loving purpose in it, either, it may be, to exercise patience or to test faith.

An old Christian once gave his experience upon this matter very simply when he said: 'When I want anything, I just ask the Lord, and he is sure to send it. Sometimes he does this afore I've done askin', and then sometimes he holds back, *just to see if I trust him.*'

The trying of your faith worketh patience.—JAMES 1:3.

And he spake a parable unto them to this end, that men ought always to pray, and not to faint.—LUKE 18:1.

Because of his importunity he will rise and give him as many as he needeth. And I say unto you, Ask, and it shall be given you.—LUKE 11:8, 9.

MAY 28

*WE HAVE NOT ONLY A SAVIOUR IN CHRIST,
BUT A KING.*

THE Jews, eighteen centuries ago, however unwilling to receive Jesus as a Saviour from sin, were perfectly ready, nay, intensely eager, to take him as a King. We are expressly told, indeed, that when our Lord 'perceived that they would come and *take him by force* to make him a king, he departed into a mountain alone.' In our day many go to the other extreme, for while seemingly willing, in a general sense, to take Christ as a Saviour, on no account will they take him as a King. They may let him save, if it must be, in some shadowy way, but in any true and practical sense they sternly forbid him to rule. They may listen, but they will not bow or conform in any degree their thoughts to his thoughts, or their will to his will. Even a nominal submission to Christ is now, in many parts of Christendom, openly and growingly denied by not a few who bear his name. Indeed, it seems but too evident that the predicted glory of millennial times, when 'the kingdoms of this world are to become the kingdoms of our Lord and his Christ,' will not be consummated until a terrible struggle has convulsed the nations. 'Earth,' says one, 'loves not her rightful Monarch, but clings to the usurper's sway. The terrible conflicts of the last days will illustrate both the world's love of sin and Jehovah's power to give the kingdom to his Only Begotten. Nothing can ever hinder the fulfilment of the promise, "Yet have I set my King upon my holy hill of Zion."'

> *We wait for thee: already thou*
> *Hast all our hearts' submission;*
> *And though the Spirit sees thee now,*
> *We long for open vision,*
> *When ours shall be*
> *Sweet rest with thee.*

'I have lived during the reign of four kings,' said an old man at a missionary meeting on the island of Raratonga. 'In the first, we were continually at war, and a fearful season it was: watching and hiding in fear took up all our thoughts. During the reign of the second, we were overtaken with severe famine, and all expected to perish; then we ate grass and wood and loathsome things. During the third, we were conquered and became the spoil and the prey of the people in the other parts of the island; then, if a man went to fish, he rarely ever returned, or if a woman went any distance to fetch wood, she was seldom ever seen again. But during the reign of the third king we were visited by another King, a good King, a King of love—Jesus, the Lord from heaven. He has conquered our hearts, and therefore, we now have peace and plenty in this world, and hope soon to dwell with him in heaven.'

Happily, the day is hastening on when, in a fuller and more blessed sense than ever, all this shall be visibly realised.

In his days shall the righteous flourish; and abundance of peace so long as the moon endureth ... Yea, all kings shall fall down before him: all nations shall serve him.—Psa. 72:7, 11.

I speak of the things which I have made touching the king: my tongue is the pen of a ready writer. Thou art fairer than the children of men: grace is poured into thy lips: therefore God hath blessed thee for ever.—Psa. 45:1, 2.

MAY 29

THOSE WHO COME TO CHRIST MUST WALK WITH HIM.

IT is the law of the kingdom that if we begin with Jesus we must go on with him. The inner life must, sooner or later, have an outward and progressive manifestation in our daily walk. Full sympathy is required for this; for, in the nature of things, there cannot be fellowship in walk without fellowship in feeling. 'Can two walk together except they be agreed?' On this account we must carefully see to it, not merely that there is a begun reconciliation in our souls, through the blood of the Lamb, but that, through the word and Spirit, it is maintained from day to day in loving, conscious warmth. This is all the more needful, as it is expressly predicted that when 'iniquity shall abound, the love of many shall wax cold.' Alas! how many are there even now who give their whole sympathies to the world and not to Christ.

Further, in order to consistency of walk, there must be constancy in dependence. It is the sweet privilege of believers not merely to be near their Lord, but to lean upon him. This should ever be their relation and attitude—the weak leaning on the Strong, at once trustfully and lovingly. It is heavy walking when this is forgotten. In wisdom's paths it is always found that the best leaner is the best walker.

Moreover, there must be a steady holding on to the very end. 'Enoch did not only take a turn up and down with God,' as one says, 'and then leave him; but he walked with God four hundred years, and then passed sweetly away from earth to heaven.' 'This world,' said Sir Matthew Hale, 'is the place of our travel and pilgrimage, and at the best our inn. I will therefore content myself with the inconveniences of my short journey; for my accommodations will be admirable when I come to my home—the heavenly Jerusalem—the place of my rest, where there are no sorrows, nor fears, nor troubles more.'

> Thus saith the Lord; I remember thee, the kindness of thy youth, the love of thine espousals, when thou wentest after me in the wilderness, in a land that was not sown.—JER. 2:2.

> I therefore, the prisoner of the Lord, beseech you that ye walk worthy of the vocation wherewith ye are called.—EPH. 4:1.

MAY 30

WE SHOULD PRIZE TRUE UNITY, AND PRAY FOR IT.

WHEN men keenly say, 'I am of Paul; and I of Apollos; and I of Cephas,' they put the servant where the Master only should be, and are narrow and sectional when they should be lovingly catholic. Such things ought not to be; for, as their natural tendency ever is to envyings and strifes and bitter divisions, they are necessarily destructive of all true unity. Every man, doubtless, should be fully persuaded in his own mind, and honestly carry out his conscientious convictions; yet this should always be done as much as possible with kindly and considerate forbearance, all the more as there may be real unity without absolute uniformity.

There must never, indeed, be any letting go of the fundamental truths of the gospel for any end whatever, however seemingly desirable. Any unity so secured would be at a fatal price, and would surely and speedily issue in spiritual decay and death. Those who forsake the faith, however seemingly united, will themselves be forsaken, and have Ichabod inscribed on them. What should be mainly aimed at and prayed for in this matter, is to secure 'in essential things, unity; in doubtful things, liberty; and in all things, charity.'

True unity was so dear to our blessed Lord, that it may well be dear to all his people. 'Neither pray I for these alone,' he said, 'but for them also which shall believe on me through their word; that they all may be one; as thou, Father, art in me, and I in thee ... that the world may believe that thou hast sent me.' What thus found a place in his prayers should also find a place in ours. Meanwhile, it is cheering to think that, beneath all the seeming diversity in name and form, there often exists among believers such substantial unity in truth and love.

'I was once permitted,' said Robert M'Cheyne, 'to unite in celebrating the Lord's Supper in an upper room in Jerusalem. There were fourteen present, the most of whom, I had good reason to believe, knew and loved the Lord Jesus Christ. Several were godly Episcopalians; two were converted Jews—one a Christian from Nazareth, converted under the American missionaries. The bread and wine were dispensed in the Episcopal manner, and most were kneeling as they received them. We felt it to be sweet fellowship with Christ, and with the brethren; and, as we left the upper room and looked out upon the Mount of Olives, we remembered with calm joy the prayer from our Lord that ascended from one of the shady ravines after the first Lord's Supper: "Neither pray I for these alone, but for them also that shall believe on me through their word; that they all may be one."'

If such union and communion are so sweet, even on earth, what will they be in heaven, when, without cloud or veil of any kind, believers in countless numbers shall be forever with the Lord!

> *That mighty multitude shall keep*
> *The joyous jubilee!*
> *Unfading palms they bear aloft,*
> *Unfaltering songs they sing,*
> *Unending festival they keep,*
> *In presence of the King.*

I therefore, the prisoner of the Lord, beseech you that ye walk worthy of the vocation wherewith ye are called, with all lowliness and meekness, with longsuffering, forbearing one another in love; endeavouring to keep the unity of the Spirit in the bond of peace.—EPH. 4:1-3.

Above all these things put on charity, which is the bond of perfectness. And let the peace of God rule in your hearts, to the which also ye are called in one body; and be ye thankful.—COL. 3:14, 15.

MAY 31

WE CANNOT BE LOYAL TO THE LORD IF DISLOYAL TO HIS WORD.

THE Lord counts no man his friend who deals lightly with his word. He who, under the guise of being fair and candid, while admitting its unrivalled excellence, denies its inspiration, is betraying it with a kiss. A Bible uninspired, or only half inspired, the value and degree of weight of its statements made matter of each man's discretion,—whatever else it may be, is not the God-given Sword of the Spirit, which is quick, powerful, sharp, piercing to the dividing asunder of soul and spirit, and is a discerner of the thoughts and intents of the heart. It is not the word to which the Son of God referred when he said: 'Sanctify them through thy truth: *thy word is truth.*'

Though it is not given us fully to understand the *mode* of inspiration by the Spirit, we are left in no doubt as to the *completeness* of it. As the human and the divine, in a manner unknown to us, were combined in Christ to constitute him the all-perfect Mediator and Redeemer, so is it with the Bible. The human is in it, for it comes to us through men; and not through the instrumentality of their hands simply, but of their whole nature—mind, heart, conscience, will, imagination, and memory. But the divine is also in it; and so in it, though in a manner unknown to us, as to secure that it shall, notwithstanding human infirmity, be the all-perfect word of God, and be such a rule of faith and practice that it can ever be said of it, 'To the law and to the testimony: *if they speak not according to this word*, it is because there is no light in them.' With our Lord, accordingly, during his ministry on earth, 'It is written,' and, 'Have ye not read in the scriptures?' were always decisive and final words.

Such was ever our blessed Lord's deep reverence for its authority, that rather than even seem to violate it, he renounced all angelic aid in the hour of his sorest conflict and deepest sorrow. 'Thinkest thou,' he said, 'that I cannot now pray the Father, and he shall presently give me more than twelve legions of angels? But *how then shall the scriptures be fulfilled, that thus it must be?*' With him Scripture was the most sacred of sacred things; and well might his reverence for it rebuke the unhallowed lightness of too many of his professed disciples.

Some, in dealing with the word, make much of its discrepancies, altogether overlooking the fact that the great majority of them are only apparent, and yield to careful examination; and not considering, moreover, that not a few of its obscurities and things hard to be understood may have been designedly left in the word for great moral ends. 'God, willing to be revealed,' says Pascal, 'to those who seek him *with the whole heart*, and hidden from those who as cordially fly from him, has so regulated the means of knowing him as to give indications of himself which are *plain* to those who seek him, and *obscure* to those who seek him not. There is light enough for those whose main wish is to see, and darkness enough for those of an opposite description.'

Plainly, then, no loyal-hearted Christians will ever, because of some imagined, or it may be *for the time* real difficulties, hurriedly question the authority of any part of Holy Writ, but will rather calmly and prayerfully *wait for further light*: remembering what is written, 'Unto the upright light ariseth in the darkness'—'He that believeth shall not make haste'; and remembering, too, that not a few statements once *hastily* and unwarrantably given up as inaccurate, have yet, through further light thrown on them by recent discoveries, been found *in every detail* to be in entire harmony with fact.

'I may have to admit,' said the late Dr Candlish, 'that there are difficulties in connection with these precious remains which I have not, in this remote age and country, the means of solving. But I, for one, will be no maker of difficulties, no eager finder of them; nor will I make too much of them when they force themselves upon me. I will not refuse a probable or even a possible explanation, merely because it does not clear up all and make all certain. And most assuredly, even in a desperate case, I shall consider it *infinitely more probable* that there is some mistake on my part, some error in my way of looking at the matter—that the puzzle I am in is owing to my distance from the writers—that a few simple words from them would at once remove it, and will remove it when I meet them in a better world—than that either they should have undertaken or God should have permitted them to handle, as his authorised ambassadors and the authoritative teachers of his church in all ages, the deep things of his righteousness and peace, in any other words than those which his own Holy Spirit sanctioned and approved.'

The scripture cannot be broken.—JOHN 10:35.

All scripture is given by inspiration of God, and is profitable for doctrine, for reproof, for correction, for instruction in righteousness.—2 TIM. 3:16.

Prophecy came not in old time by the will of man: but holy men of God spake as they were moved by the Holy Ghost.—2 PET. 1:21.

If any man shall take away from the words of the book of this prophecy, God shall take away his part out of the book of life, and out of the holy city, and from the things which are written in this book.—REV. 22:19.

JUNE 1

WHATEVER MAY BE LACKING, IT IS NOT FREE INVITATION.

WHEN addressing the multitude on the great day of Pentecost, Peter, quoting from the prophet Joel, said, in the name of his blessed Master, 'Whosoever shall call on the name of the Lord shall be saved.' He could not have uttered any invitation more precious or seasonable, for on that memorable day there were men of every nation and of every tongue before him,—Parthians, Medes, Elamites, Cretes, and Arabians. Nay, more, there were there men of the vilest and most malignant character, even the very crucifiers of the Lord; nevertheless Peter did not hesitate lovingly and boldly to say, 'Whosoever shall call on the name of the Lord shall be saved.' And not in vain, for, through the Spirit, they 'who gladly received his word were baptized: and the same day there were added unto them about three thousand souls.'

Need we say that this invitation was not for that time only, but for all times, and therefore is as directly addressed to us as it was to the Jews in apostolic days. Nor could any offer of pardon and peace be more free or gracious. There is not one restrictive or exceptive word in it all. It is not, Whosoever is sinless among you, or Whosoever has little sin, or some righteousness. No; it has in it only the sweet, all-embracing word 'whosoever,' without anything whatever to narrow it.

Besides, it is so simple. Not unfrequently what is desired by men can only be obtained by long and toilsome effort,—by digging deep, it may be, into the bowels of the earth, or, at the risk of life, scaling some perilous steep. But it is not so in this case, for so simple is the method of obtaining salvation that it is within easy reach of all who really desire it. The strong can get it, and the weak, the aged and the little child, just because all that is needed for this end is to call in faith on the name of the Lord, and take him at his word when he says, 'Him that cometh unto me I will in no wise cast out.' This is what the thief on the cross, the jailer of Philippi, and Mary Magdalene did. They trustfully called on the name of the Lord, and thereby each and all of them were finally saved. If it is certain, as God declares, that not one who finally rejects Christ can be saved, it is equally certain that not one who really believes in him can perish. Happily no preparation is needed beforehand, no previous worthiness; for never are we so welcome as when found at his feet, saying,—

Just as I am—without one plea,
But that thy blood was shed for me,
And that thou bid'st me come to thee,
O Lamb of God, I come!

'My next step,' said an anxious inquirer, 'is to get deeper conviction.' 'No,' replied a Christian friend, 'your next step, and only step, is to go to Christ just as you are. He does not say, Come to conviction, come to a deeper sense of sin, which you have been labouring to get; but he says, "Come unto *me*."' 'Ah,' she exclaimed, 'I see it now. Oh, how self-righteous I have been, really refusing Christ, while all the time I thought I was preparing to come to him.' 'Will you go to Jesus now?' was hastily asked. She looked up, with a smile, and then humbly yet decisively said, 'I will.' And the Lord, in the riches of his grace, enabled her so to do.

Whosoever will, let him take the water of life freely.—Rev. 22:17.

Him that cometh to me I will in no wise cast out.—John 6:37.

God so loved the world, that he gave his only begotten Son, that whosoever believeth in him should not perish, but have everlasting life.—John 3:16.

June 2

EVEN THE STRONG ARE WEAK.

GREAT and good men are precious gifts of God, and we cannot be too thankful for them; but they are not pillars upon which we can lean. Even the best of them have stumbled, and the strongest given way. Few ever wrestled with such resolute earnestness as the patriarch Jacob. 'I will not let thee go,' he said, 'except thou bless me'; and in consequence his name was no more called Jacob, but Israel: for as a prince he had power with God, and prevailed. Nevertheless the same Jacob, who was then so commended for his strength, became afterwards so feeble as to say, in a spirit of utter hopelessness, 'Me have ye bereaved of my children: Joseph is not, and Simeon is not, and ye will take Benjamin away: *all these things are against me.*' But was it really so? On the contrary, these very things were so divinely overruled as to be made to work effectually for his highest good.

So also it was with David, the king of Israel. Usually he was so strong in faith, courage, and sterling loyalty, that he would dare anything for the Lord and the honour of his name; yet even he had his seasons of such deep despondency that for the time he seemed feebler than the feeblest.

Such experiences of buffeting temptation are not only needful for believers themselves, to keep them humble and trustfully dependent, but the very record of them specially helpful to the church of Christ in every age. In afflictive seasons, they have not only comforted many, by showing them that they are not singular in being sorely tried and depressed, even as it is written, 'There hath no temptation taken you but such as is common to man,'—but they have shown them also, by revealing the weakness even of the strongest, the necessity of leaning at all times, not on mere creature instrumentalities, but on their Lord alone.

Of the strong, in his day, Martin Luther seemed pre-eminently the strongest, and very signally did the Lord use and honour him; yet there were times even with him when faith seemed wholly lacking. Once, when nothing apparently availed to comfort him, he was induced to leave home for a few days, in the hope that he might recover his cheerfulness; but he returned with a cloudy and dejected countenance. How great was his surprise on entering the house to find his wife seated in the middle of the room attired in black garments, and with a mourning cloak thrown over her, while she pressed to her eyes her handkerchief, as if weeping bitterly. He eagerly inquired the cause of her distress, which she seemed loath at first to communicate; but on again imploring her to speak, she exclaimed, 'Only think, dear doctor, our Father in heaven is dead. Judge if I have not cause for my grief.' Upon this, immediately comprehending her riddle, he laughed and, embracing her, said, 'You are right, dear Kate; I am acting as if there were no God in heaven.' And from that hour his melancholy greatly abated.

When my soul fainted within me I remembered the Lord: and my prayer came in unto thee, into thine holy temple.—JON. 2:7.

What time I am afraid, I will trust in thee.—PSA. 56:3.

Though he slay me, yet will I trust in him.—JOB 13:15.

JUNE 3

*GOD'S PROMISES, THOUGH OFTEN FORGOTTEN ON EARTH,
ARE NEVER FORGOTTEN IN HEAVEN.*

WHEN Joshua became old and stricken in years, he uttered these memorable words: 'Behold, this day I am going the way of all the earth: and ye know in all your hearts and in all your souls, that not one thing hath failed of all the good things which the Lord your God spake concerning you; all are come to pass unto you, and not one thing hath failed thereof.' This was a remarkable statement, not merely because of Joshua's peculiar circumstances at the time, but specially because it was true to the very letter; for though the good things promised were many, and the obstacles in the way great, yet not even *in one thing* was there any failure. And so in the main has it been with all in every age who have lived near the Lord, and pleaded his promises in confiding trustfulness. Ever and again their grateful song has been, 'Verily God hath heard me; he hath kept his word and fulfilled his promise.' 'Hath he said, and shall he not do it? or hath he spoken, and shall he not make it good?'

'The solvency of a bank,' says one, 'or of a government, gives the value to its notes; so it is *the everlasting faithfulness* of God that makes his every promise exceeding great and precious.' There may often be a lengthened interval between the giving of a promise and the fulfilling of it, but neither promise nor prayer is ever forgotten by the Lord.

The saintly Judson, whose abounding labours among the Burmese were so greatly blessed, once said, that though one soul purchased by the blood of Christ is as valuable as another, he should deem it a peculiar privilege to lead one of the lost sheep of the house of Israel to the Lord Jesus. He made various efforts towards establishing a mission in Palestine, all of which proved unavailing; yet the earnest wish was granted in an unlooked-for way. It was eighteen years afterwards, and only a few days before his death, that tidings reached him of the conversion of some Jews through one of his own tracts. On hearing this his eyes filled with tears, and then he said, with great solemnity: 'I never prayed sincerely and earnestly for anything but it came at some time, no matter at how distant a day—somehow, in some shape, probably the last I should have thought of, it came; and yet I have always had so little faith. May God forgive me, and while he condescends to use me, wipe away the sin of unbelief from my heart!'

> There failed not ought of any good thing which the Lord had spoken unto the house of Israel; all came to pass.—JOSH. 21:45.

> Heaven and earth shall pass away: but my words shall not pass away.—LUKE 21:33.

> All the promises of God in him are yea, and in him Amen, unto the glory of God by us.—2 COR. 1:20.

JUNE 4

EVERY SAINT IS THE SAVIOUR'S, AND A PRIZED POSSESSION.

WHEN we remember all their worthlessness, it may well surprise us to be told that the Lord's portion is his people; yet so it is. 'All thine are mine,' said our Lord, when speaking of them; 'and I am glorified in them.' 'Any man,' says Luther, 'may say, "What is mine is thine," but only the Saviour can say, "What is thine is mine."'

They become the Lord's in many ways. They are his by divine gift. 'I have manifested thy name,' he says, 'unto the men which thou gavest me out of the world: thine they were, and thou gavest me them.' 'Watch thou over thine own gift,' he would seem to say; 'in becoming mine they have not ceased to belong to thee, but have even become more than ever thine.' This fact is full of comfort; for whatever may befall other gifts, nothing can imperil gifts of the Father to the Son. They will never be withdrawn, and can never be lost.

Moreover, they are his by purchase. As their loving Saviour and Substitute, he has paid to the full all that law and justice could possibly demand at his hands for their sakes. Becoming thereby the redeemed of the Lord, they are his, too, by conquest. Till their conversion, instead of bewailing their bondage and giving to the great Deliverer a grateful welcome, they say, like the Gadarenes of old, 'Depart from us.' There is thus need of subduing as well as of redeeming—of a day of power as well as of a day of mercy—of a conquering King as well as of an atoning Priest; and all this they find to the full in and through the Lord Jesus.

To the praise of his grace it may also be added, they are his by deliberate and hearty choice. The unbelief of their hearts being taken away, they now see his beauty and prize his love, and joyously say, 'Whom have I in heaven but thee? and there is none upon earth whom I desire beside thee.'

'Oh,' said Samuel Rutherford, 'what pains and charges it costeth Christ ere he get us! And when all is done, we are not worth the having; but love overlooketh blackness and feebleness. I have been a wretched, sinful man, but I stand at the best pass that ever a man did—"Christ is mine, and I am his."'

> Whether we live, we live unto the Lord; and whether we die, we die unto the Lord: whether we live therefore, or die, we are the Lord's.—Rom. 14:8.

> The Son of God, who loved me, and gave himself for me.—Gal. 2:20.

> For ye are bought with a price: therefore glorify God in your body, and in your spirit, which are God's.—1 Cor. 6:20.

JUNE 5

WHEN GOD IS ABOUT TO WORK GREATLY BY US, HE FIRST
WORKS GREATLY IN US.

AS an instrumentality, nothing apparently could have been simpler or feebler than that of the fishermen of Galilee; and yet the moral transformations thereby accomplished were strikingly great. It is all important to note, however, that before the Lord did great things by these men, he first did great things in them. For this end he said—'Tarry ye in the city of Jerusalem, *until ye be endued with power from on high.*' In calm and prayerful expectancy they did so tarry; and it was only when at length the Spirit came upon them in all fulness and power that they went forth on their divinely-appointed work to preach the gospel to every creature. The effect was marvellous; for so great and continuous was their success that multitudes everywhere were savingly converted and added to the Lord.

And so is it, more or less, still. The vessels most used by the Lord are those most meet and ready for his service. 'If a man purge himself from these,' it is written, 'he shall be a vessel unto honour, sanctified, and meet for the master's use, and *prepared unto every good work*.' From forgetting this, believers occasionally, in spite of excellent gifts and manifold opportunities, have but little usefulness. When the Lord would employ them, he finds them, as it were, so spiritually defiled, through want of due watchfulness and prayer, that he has to pass them by and take others more meet for his use. But for varied discipline and trial, this would oftener be the case with God's children; and if so, instead of murmuring and fretting when trial comes, they should rather be found earnestly praying that thereby the quickening so urgently needed may be secured.

It is said that shortly before Mr Moody began those labours which were so marvellously blessed, he was greatly impressed by the remark made by a Christian friend: 'It remains for the world to see what the Lord can do with a man *wholly consecrated to Christ.*' Why should not all of us aim at such a consecration, seeing that every saving blessing we enjoy we owe to the riches of redeeming love and grace?

> But ye shall receive power, after that the Holy Ghost is come upon you: and ye shall be witnesses unto me both in Jerusalem, and in all Judaea, and in Samaria, and unto the uttermost part of the earth.—ACTS 1:8.

> Stephen, full of faith and power, did great wonders and miracles among the people.—ACTS 6:8.

> If ye have faith as a grain of mustard seed, ye shall say unto this mountain, Remove hence to yonder place; and it shall remove; and nothing shall be impossible unto you.—MATT. 17:20.

JUNE 6

THE RIGHT AND THE WRONG OF ANGER, AND HOW TO DEAL WITH IT.

ANGER is not, in every form and shape of it, necessarily sinful. There is such a thing as righteous anger, and occasions again and again arise in which it would be positive sin not to feel and show it. It is recorded of Moses—not in censure, but in commendation—that when he saw the golden calf 'his anger waxed hot.' Beyond a doubt, therefore, there is not only such a thing as righteous indignation, but the sight of grievous wrongdoing never fails to awaken it in every truly Christian heart. On this account an old divine quaintly says: 'Anger is one of the sinews of the soul; and he that wants it hath a maimed mind, and, like Jacob when the sinews shrank in the hollow of his thigh, must needs halt.'

Nothing, however, is more difficult than to keep this feeling within due and proper limits, and to do as the Lord enjoins in his word, 'Be ye angry, and sin not.' Anger in sympathy with God is the only legitimate anger. In too many instances anger arises from slight causes, and perhaps from no perceptible cause whatever, and there is sad intemperateness in its manifestation. For its right regulation, these counsels may not be unhelpful.

First: when anger arises, beware of nursing it. If we put no fresh fuel on a fire it will soon go out; and so is it with this fiery passion. It will soon be quenched if we do not dwell and meditate on the things that excite it. It is always a blessed thing to have a long memory for kindnesses and a very short one for wrongs.

Again: when anger arises, be slow in expressing it. Silence is never so golden as under great provocation; and it is often of itself a great victory if, instead of replying today, we do not reply till tomorrow. There would be little contention in the world if men could be silent when hot, and speak only when cool.

Finally: when anger arises, never forget how much we all owe to the forbearance of God. Had he not been slow to anger with us, long ere now we would have been undone forever.

'I am naturally as irritable as any,' said an old minister once; 'but when I find anger or any other evil temper arising in my mind, I go to my Redeemer immediately, and, confessing my sins, *give myself up to be managed by him.* This is the way I have taken to get the mastery of my passions.'

> The discretion of a man deferreth his anger; and it is his glory to pass over a transgression.—PROV. 19:11.

> He that is slow to wrath is of great understanding: but he that is hasty of spirit exalteth folly.—PROV. 14:29.

> Let every man be swift to hear, slow to speak, slow to wrath: for the wrath of man worketh not the righteousness of God.—JAMES 1:19, 20.

JUNE 7

THE LORD'S LEADINGS, HOWEVER STRANGE, HAVE ALWAYS WISE LOVE IN THEM.

IN our earthly pilgrimage, we would fain have neither cross nor cloud nor crooked turning; but the wish is a vain one, for strive as we may, thorns spring up, clouds gather, and sorrowful anxiety enters the heart. It is not so of mere chance, but of wise and gracious design, in order to exercise patience, strengthen faith, and promote that healthy moral discipline without which we can neither have fitness for the kingdom nor entrance into it.

It was once said to the Israelites—and the words are memorable—'Thou shalt remember all the way which the Lord thy God led thee these forty years in the wilderness, to humble thee, and to prove thee, to know what was in thine heart … and *to do thee good at thy latter end.*' This is a long period, forty years, and many a tear dropped in the course of it; yet it was not a year, nay, not even a day too long, for *wise love* was leading all through. Doubtless, for mere flesh and blood it would have been pleasanter far if, instead of wandering for forty years in such a desert, they could have passed at once from Egypt to Canaan; but then, for highest interests, it would not have been safe.

Nor is it otherwise with God's spiritual Israel now. Indeed, without more or less of such sorrowful training, pride, unbelief, and earthliness would ever be clinging to us, and heart and conscience become thereby defiled. 'I find,' says an old experienced believer, 'that when the saints are under trials and well humbled, little sins raise great cries in the conscience; but in prosperity conscience is *a pope that gives dispensations with great latitude* to our hearts.' A measure of adversity, therefore, is oftentimes a merciful necessity. As it is not in smooth waters, but rough, that pebbles are rounded and polished, so it is not in easy times, but in trying, that believers, through grace, become holiest and brightest and likest their Lord. Much as we shrink from trials, therefore, how often do they bring us our truest and richest blessings!

> *So help me, Lord, thy holy will to suffer,*
> *And still a learner at thy feet to be;*
> *Give faith and patience, when the way is rougher,*
> *And happy victory at last to me.*
> *Thus grief itself is changed to song*
> *Oft-times on earth, and evermore ere long.*

I will bring the blind by a way that they knew not; I will lead them in paths that they have not known: I will make darkness light before them, and crooked things straight. These things will I do unto them, and not forsake them.—Isa. 42:16.

The Lord will perfect that which concerneth me.—Psa. 138:8.

June 8

WE SHOULD BE PRAISEFUL AS WELL AS PRAYERFUL.

THE Lord so delights in the prayers of his people that he not only lends his ear, but lovingly says, 'Let me hear thy voice; for sweet is thy voice.' Nor is it otherwise with their praises; for these are his own words, 'Whoso offereth praise glorifieth me.' Though nothing can add to God's essential glory, yet by praise we can declare it, and spread abroad the fame of it, and help to multiply those who joyously show it forth. To praise the Lord, therefore, whether singly or unitedly, in the privacy of home or in the great congregation, has ever been to his saints a special delight. 'Methinks,' said Richard Baxter, 'when we are singing the praises of God in the great assemblies, with joyful and fervent spirits, I have the liveliest foretaste of heaven, and I could almost wish that our voices were loud enough to reach through all the world, and to heaven itself.'

Nor is it wonderful that we should thus praise the Lord. Indeed, when we remember who he is—the God and Father of our Lord Jesus Christ, our life, our hope, yea, our all—and think of what he has done and is still doing for us, with all the blessed things awaiting us in the eternal future, the highest praises we can render come infinitely short of what is due.

When referring to David praising the Lord on an instrument of ten strings, an old writer says: 'He would never have told how many strings there were, if he had not made use of them all. God has given all of us bodies—instruments, as it were, of many strings; and can we think it music enough to strike but one string—to call upon him with our tongues? No, no; when the still sound of the heart, by holy thoughts, and the shrill sound of the tongue, by holy words, and the loud sound of the hands, by pious works, all join together, that is God's concert, and the only music wherewith he is affected.'

This is praise in truest form, and we cannot have too much of it; and as everyone has a heart to praise, so everyone has something to praise for.

> Let my mouth be filled with thy praise and with thy honour all the day.—Psa. 71:8.
>
> O God, my heart is fixed; I will sing and give praise, even with my glory.—Psa. 108:1.
>
> Great is the Lord, and greatly to be praised.—Psa. 145:3.

JUNE 9

WE SHOULD NEVER BE STAGGERED BY APOSTASY FROM THE FAITH, HOWEVER MUCH WE MAY BE SADDENED BY IT.

WHILE there is still much around us peculiarly cheering, there is at the same time not a little to awaken grave anxiety and watchful fear. Indeed, it is now freely admitted by thoughtful observers that the current of opinion in cultivated circles is running with a powerful tide in a direction contrary to all that is most central and sacred in Christian belief, and that with large numbers in our own and other lands faith is becoming visibly feebler regarding prayer and providence, sin and redemption, God and Christ. But the other day a professor of note in one of our universities said: 'The struggle into which the church of Christ seems now entering is one as to the very foundations of the faith. God grant that we may all be found faithful to him and to his Son, for many doubtless will fall away.'

All this to many is not merely a sadness, but a surprise, and a surprise so great that they are almost staggered by it; and as Eli trembled for the ark of God, so they begin to tremble for the faith once delivered unto the saints, on which rests their every bright and blessed hope. In yielding to such fears, however, they forget that what is so great a surprise to them is no surprise whatever to their Lord; for he not only foresaw it all, but noted it as one of the marked characteristics of the last days. 'I have told you,' he said, 'before it come to pass, that when it is come to pass *ye might believe.*' So that our faith in the word, instead of being staggered by such things, should rather be confirmed. Is it not written: 'The Spirit speaketh expressly that *in the latter times* some shall depart from the faith, giving heed to seducing spirits and doctrines of devils'—'The time will come *when they will not endure sound doctrine*; but after their own lusts shall they heap to themselves teachers, having itching ears; and they shall turn away their ears from the truth, and shall be turned unto fables'?

The great evangelical truths which constitute the very essence and glory of the gospel of Christ, are now growingly distasteful to many and openly rejected by not a few. This, doubtless, is greatly to be deplored; but their disbelief of evangelical doctrine, however injurious it may be to themselves, in no degree affects the soundness or efficacy of the doctrine itself. It remains as before, 'the power of God and the wisdom of God *to every one that believeth*,' and will eventually bring joy and gladness to all the earth. When the waves dash against the rock, it is not the rock that gives way and is broken to pieces, but the waves. Such a Rock is the truth as it is in Christ Jesus our Lord—nothing can prevail against it.

Dr Chalmers evidently had forebodings of a period of apostasy. When alluding to our Lord's question, 'When the Son of man cometh, shall he find faith on the earth?' he said, 'We are here premonished that a time is coming when faith shall well-nigh disappear from the earth.' But he touchingly added elsewhere: 'Oh, may I be counted worthy to stand before the Son of man! And let me not be discouraged by the frustration, for a season, of all the attempts now making to regenerate our earth, but even in the midst of most adverse visitations lift up my head, for that our redemption is drawing nigh. What a moral victory will then be achieved, when its kingdoms shall become the kingdoms of our Lord and his Christ.'

All the ends of the world shall remember and turn unto the Lord: and all the kindreds of the nations shall worship before thee.—Psa. 22:27.

It was needful for me to write unto you, and exhort you that ye should earnestly contend for the faith which was once delivered unto the saints.—Jude 3.

June 10

THOUGH ALL BELIEVERS ARE RISEN MEN, NOT ONE IS SELF-RISEN.

MEN can neither be saviours of themselves nor of others, for 'none can by any means redeem his brother, or give to God a ransom for him.' The giving of life—the raising up, and the restoring again to divine likeness and fellowship—is not man's work, but the Lord's. He expressly says, 'In *me* is thy help found'; and to him, therefore, must ever be ascribed the undivided glory. Paul, and Apollos, and Cephas were eminent servants of Christ, and unreservedly consecrated their every talent and energy to his service; but not any one of them, nor all of them combined, could quicken a single dead soul to newness of life. Of this they made open avowal everywhere. 'Who then is Paul,' the apostle asks, 'and who is Apollos, but ministers by whom ye believed, even as the Lord gave to every man? I have planted, Apollos watered; but God gave the increase. So then neither is he that planteth anything, neither he that watereth; but God that giveth the increase.' They were as utterly helpless in this matter as was the prophet of old in the valley of vision. When the Lord said to him, 'Son of man, can these bones live?' he could only reply, 'O Lord God, thou knowest.' When, however, *the command* came: 'Prophesy upon these bones, and say unto them, O ye dry bones, hear the word of the Lord'; and *the promise* came: 'Behold, I will cause breath to enter into you, and ye shall live'; and above all when the needed *prayer* came: 'Come from the four winds, O breath, and breathe upon these slain, that they may live,'—straightway the breath entered them, and they lived, and stood upon their feet, an exceeding great army. So is it still when the Spirit of the Lord breathes upon those who are dead in trespasses and sins: they spring to life and gladness as new creatures in Christ Jesus, and consecrate their lives wholly to his service.

On one occasion a visitor was standing alone on a balcony in a lunatic asylum watching the inmates amusing themselves in the garden. He thought he was safe, when suddenly, to his dismay, a great strong man, with a horsewhip in his hand, stepped out of the window on to the balcony, and insanely bade him leap down immediately. Seeing him hesitate, the maniac became louder and fiercer in his demand—'Leap down, leap down at once!' With great presence of mind the gentleman replied, 'Any fool can do that—that's easy enough; but come with me, and I will show you something far more wonderful. Can you leap up?' So he led the maniac to the door, and down the stairs, and out into the garden in front of the balcony, and there left him vainly trying to leap up.

What a touching picture have we here of what the sinner can do, and what he cannot. Ah, it is easy to leap down into guilt and woe—anyone can do that; but who can leap up again to life, righteousness, and peace. Only the Spirit of the Lord can enable us to do this, and we must seek his help. 'Human corruption,' says one, 'proves always too hard for human eloquence; it is ever found to have a strong enough footing in the heart to stand out against all the golden sayings of the tongue.'

And you hath he quickened, who were dead in trespasses and sins.—Eph. 2:1.

When we were yet without strength, in due time Christ died for the ungodly.—Rom. 5:6.

It is the spirit that quickeneth; the flesh profiteth nothing: the words that I speak unto you, they are spirit, and they are life.—John 6:63.

JUNE 11

THOUGH SLIGHTED BY MANY, CHRIST IS EVERYTHING TO
THOSE WHO KNOW HIM.

IT was impressively declared by the prophet: 'He shall grow up before him as a tender plant, and as a root out of a dry ground: he hath no form nor comeliness; and when we shall see him, there is no beauty that we should desire him. He is despised and rejected of men.' It proved even so; for when the fulness of time came these words were fulfilled to the very letter. For a season, indeed, eager crowds enthusiastically followed him everywhere, and spread abroad his fame; but in the end the desertion and turning away became general, and the same lips that once shouted 'Hosanna!' finally cried, 'Crucify him, crucify him!' Nevertheless there were always some, like the inquiring Greeks, ready to say, 'Sirs, we would see Jesus,' or to declare, like Paul, 'I count all things but loss for the excellency of the knowledge of Christ Jesus my Lord.' And it is the same still. The world to this hour makes light of Christ, and makes light to all who trust and love him. His name has no charm for them, nor his work, nor his coming again; and, however tenderly and earnestly he may speak, they turn to him a deaf ear, and think of him with a cold and unloving heart.

But, blessed be God! there are always some differently minded, who not only accept the gospel message but ever make the Subject and the Sender of it their grand hope and joy. He is to them 'the one pearl of great price,' 'the chief cornerstone, elect, precious,' 'the well beloved,' 'the chiefest among ten thousand,' 'the altogether lovely,' 'the great God and our Saviour.'

John Brown of Haddington used to say: 'I have served several masters, but none so kind as Christ. Many a comely person I have seen, but none so comely as Christ. Many a kind friend I have had, but none like Christ in lovingkindness and in tender mercies.'

Verily, then, we can neither overlove Christ, nor overtrust him, nor overserve him.

God forbid that I should glory, save in the cross of our Lord Jesus Christ, by whom the world is crucified unto me, and I unto the world.—GAL. 6:14.

Of him are ye in Christ Jesus, who of God is made unto us wisdom, and righteousness, and sanctification, and redemption.—I COR. 1:30.

Christ is all, and in all.—COL. 3:11.

JUNE 12

MUCH MAY INTERVENE BETWEEN THE SOWING AND THE REAPING.

'THE word preached in any place,' says an old writer, 'doth usually work best at first. After a while men become like birds in a belfry, that can well enough hear the noise of bells and not be frightened.' It was not so, however, at Thessalonica; for while the truth proclaimed worked well at the first, it worked still better afterwards, and the faith, love, and hope of its saints were spoken of everywhere with joyous commendation and delight.

It sometimes happens that, to appearance, the word preached does not work at all for long. Year after year rolls on, and yet no souls awake, no grace reveals itself, no fruit is gathered, and the weary labourer perhaps begins to fear that his every toil has been in vain. Nevertheless, in the very place where all seems so barren showers of blessing may at length come down, and glorious harvests be reaped, in sweet fulfilment of the promise, 'He that goeth forth and weepeth, bearing precious seed, shall doubtless come again with rejoicing, bringing his sheaves with him.'

But even when the faithful sower is not himself the favoured reaper, yet in the time of harvest sower and reaper alike shall join in the song and share the reward. Speaking of one sowing and another reaping, the saintly Bengel says: 'In the divine economy there is a wise arrangement of succession; everything earlier is a sowing out of a harvest to follow. Every man is sower with reference to his successor, and a reaper with reference to his predecessor. Into Christ's *alone meritorious labour* do all his servants enter, and reap what not they have sown, but he; yet, in the mutual interdependency of God's fellow-workers in his field, each one is sower and reaper alike.'

If we had but more faith and patience, all of us would sow more diligently and reap more abundantly.

> Be not deceived; God is not mocked: for whatsoever a man soweth, that shall he also reap … And let us not be weary in well doing: for in due season we shall reap, if we faint not.—GAL. 6:7, 9.

> But this I say, He which soweth sparingly shall reap also sparingly; and he which soweth bountifully shall reap also bountifully.— 2 COR. 9:6.

JUNE 13

SELF-COMPLACENT CONTENTEDNESS.

THOUGH the great apostle of the Gentiles rejoiced in first principles and ever firmly adhered to them, yet he never made the mere elements and primary beginnings a final resting-place; he was ever progressing onward and upward. And so should it be with us; for though we may be satisfied with less, our Lord never will. He expects a growing as well as a rooting in Christ, fruit as well as a blossom, increasing fellowship as well as vital union.

Yet how sadly is this overlooked. Indeed, many dwell so exclusively and self-complacently on experiences and attainments once possessed, that after-backslidings, however grievous, seem never to occasion them much anxiety. They forget that the main thing to be considered is not what they were once, but what they are at present; not how they felt and acted on the day of their supposed espousals to the Lord, but how they feel and act now: for it is written, 'He that endureth to the end, the same shall be saved.' Indeed, a suspicion will justly attach to the whole of our past experience, as after all but a dream and a delusion, if it is not continuous, or at least if there is not a real contrition for any after-backsliding and an earnest and prayerful longing for healing and restoration.

There are others, again, who, comparing themselves among themselves, and not with Jehovah's law and the Redeemer's example, are ever prone to rest complacently in a supposed superiority to those around them. Such measuring is never either wise or safe. Alas! so low often is the standard of spirituality in the church, and so rare a true singleness of eye and simplicity of purpose, that even were our attainments very much above anything existing around us, we would have little to justify our boasting. Besides, even for our own peace, we should avoid all such self-complacent thinkings; for, as one says, 'We can scarcely, even the best of us, bear a word of praise or thought of self-congratulation. It is pleasant, doubtless, to have self flattered, caressed, and humoured; but afterwards it upsets the balance of the spirit, and stings like an adder.' True, it is not required that we should be blind to what the Lord has done either in us or by us, or that we should altogether ignore it; but while humbly thankful for it, we should yet forget the things which are behind, and continually reach forth unto those which are before.

Not as though I had already attained, either were already perfect: but I follow after, if that I may apprehend that for which also I am apprehended of Christ Jesus.—PHIL. 3:12.

We desire that every one of you do shew the same diligence to the full assurance of hope unto the end: That ye be not slothful, but followers of them who through faith and patience inherit the promises.—HEB. 6:11, 12.

JUNE 14

CHRISTIAN CONSISTENCY.

CHRISTIANITY is not a mere speculative theory. All its revealings and teachings are designed to tell practically on the life; and if they are not employed for this end, the so-called

Christianity sooner or later degenerates either into worthless will worship or dreary scepticism. The man whom we call an architect is not merely he who can readily discourse about buildings, but the man who has the skill to plan and erect them. So the man whom we call a Christian is not merely he who knows the duties of believers, and can fluently talk about them, but the man who, on the good foundation, builds up the structure of a Christian life. On this account we are constantly urged in Scripture to be practical as well as devout in our religion, and to maintain a sweet consistency between profession and practice; cultivating all that is true, pure, honest, lovely, and of good report; or, as the apostle expresses it, 'walking worthy of the Lord *unto all pleasing.*'

We are to do this by looking, not at our own things only, but also on the things of others, and by exhibiting in every relation of life the kindness, forbearance, and unselfishness which would not only evidence our own sincerity, but powerfully influence others to follow our example. 'Some believers,' said Robert M'Cheyne, 'were a garden that had fruit trees, and so were useful; but we ought to have spices also, and so *be attractive*. "Come, thou south wind; blow upon my garden, that the spices thereof may flow out."'

Happily it needs neither great gifts nor high social position thus to adorn our Christian profession, but simply *whole-hearted* consecration to Christ.

'Whatsoever thy condition,' says an old Puritan writer, 'thou mayest glorify God in it, and bring praise to his name. He that grinds at the mill may glorify him as well as he that sits upon the throne.'

Walk worthy of God, who hath called you unto his kingdom and glory.—1 Thess. 2:12.

Only let your conversation be as it becometh the gospel of Christ.— Phil. 1:27.

We beseech you ... that as ye have received of us how ye ought to walk and to please God, so ye would abound more and more.— 1 Thess. 4:1.

JUNE 15

FRUITLESS EFFORT.

S IN is so seldom a matter of anxious thought with men, that that most vital of questions very rarely comes from their lips, 'What must I do to be saved?' But when conscience awakes, and the powers of the world to come begin to be felt, it is otherwise; salvation then becomes, in some measure, a real need with them, and if they could only secure it self-righteously, there is nothing seemingly they would not gladly do or suffer. Every effort so made by them, however, is as vain and fruitless as that of the fabled Sisyphus, who had ever hopelessly to begin his weary task anew. They try *perfectly* to keep the law, but ever fail; they shed many a tear, but find no relief; they pray, and fast, and toil, but, in spite of all, their heavy burden still presses.

And so will it ever be with them till they take God's method of justification, and not their own. The way to get acceptance with God is not to work hard for it, or to work long, but to cease to work at all; just because all that is needed for this end Christ has already thoroughly done. He would have us to believe on him who justifieth *the ungodly*; and therefore he does not require us to be godly before we believe, or to be healed before we come to the Physician, but simply to take salvation as the free, unmerited gift of grace, and consent to be saved by Christ alone.

An excellent man was once asked to visit a poor dying sufferer. The messenger could give no account of her state of mind, except that she was a very good woman, and was now at the end of a well-spent life, and therefore sure of going to heaven. He went, and after a few kindly inquiries about her bodily condition, said, 'I have been told you are in a very peaceful state of mind, depending upon a well-spent life.' The dying woman looked hard at him, and said, 'Yes; you are right. I am in the enjoyment of peace, sweet peace, and that from a well-spent life: but *it is the well-spent life of Jesus,*—not my doings, but his; not my merits, but his blood.' Blessed close to life. May our latter end be like hers!

Therefore by the deeds of the law there shall no flesh be justified in his sight: for by the law is the knowledge of sin.—ROM. 3:20.

By grace are ye saved through faith; and that not of yourselves: it is the gift of God.—EPH. 2:8.

Christ is the end of the law for righteousness to every one that believeth.—ROM. 10:4.

JUNE 16

WHEN NEED IS SOREST, COMFORT IS SWEETEST.

THE cup of some is so full that seemingly they stand in no need of comfort; while the spirit of others is so proud that, even when there is such need, they scorn to own it. It was never so with the apostle of the Gentiles. As he was so repeatedly in weariness and painfulness, in hunger and thirst, in cold and nakedness, his need of comfort was often great and pressing; and, from his Christian simplicity and manly frankness, he was never ashamed to own this need or to accept the kindness that met it. 'Therefore, brethren,' he said, 'we *were comforted over you* in all our affliction and distress by your faith.'

This comfort of which he speaks did not arise from any brightening of his outward circumstances, or any softening of the world's enmity, for these remained very much as before. What mainly imparted it was the message of Timothy, and especially the cheering tidings he brought of the love, loyalty, and stedfast faith of his spiritual children: it was a comfort, therefore, pure and unselfish in its nature, and wholly unlike that to which the mere worldling clings.

It came very seasonably; not so early as to interfere with needed discipline and the due exercise of faith and patience, and yet not so late as to be of little practical value in cheering his heart. The Lord's timing of things is often specially tender and gracious. As an old Christian once said, 'He not only knows the best things to send to his children, but the times for sending them.' Besides, the comfort the Lord imparts is so full and all-sufficient that, when we get it, we can be joyous anywhere and in any circumstances.

The day before he died, John Holland, turning with his own hand to the eighth chapter of the Romans, bade Mr Legh read it: at the end of every verse he paused and gave the sense to his own comfort, but more to the joy and wonder of his friends. An hour or two after, on a sudden, he said, 'Oh, stay your reading! What brightness is this I see? Have you lighted any candles?' No, it was replied; it is the sunshine. 'Sunshine!' he said; 'nay, it is my Saviour's shine. Farewell, world—welcome, heaven!'

> Let, I pray thee, thy merciful kindness be for my comfort, according to thy word unto thy servant.—PSA. 119:76.

> Ye believe in God, believe also in me ... I will not leave you comfortless: I will come to you.—JOHN 14:1, 18.

JUNE 17

THE RICHLY FRUITFUL.

IN the religion of the Colossians there was more than mere conviction, or emotional excitement, or visible profession; there was, over and above all this, varied and substantial fruit. Speaking to them of the word of the truth of the gospel, the apostle said, 'Which is come unto you, as it is in all the world; and bringeth forth fruit, as it doth also in you, since the day ye heard of it, and knew the grace of God in truth.' The fruit so commended were those graces of the Spirit which adorn the Christian character, and of which all must more or less be possessed who would really be the Lord's.

Fruit is the Lord's expectation, and it is a grievous sin to disappoint it: 'These three years I come seeking fruit on this fig tree, and find none.' Fruit, too, is the test of discipleship: 'By their fruits ye shall know them.' To remain barren and unfruitful, therefore, decisively falsifies our profession. Moreover, when abundant, fruit is specially honouring to the Lord; for it is expressly written, 'Herein is my Father glorified, that ye bring forth *much fruit.*' From these and similar statements it is clear that when fruit does not spring up in the life, the word has never truly gone down into the heart. This is ever a perilous condition, for though the Lord may bear long with the fruitless, he will not bear always.

With regard to the Colossians, it is an interesting fact that they were not only richly fruitful, but the word produced fruit in them from the first day they heard it. Like the Bereans, they received the word with all readiness of mind, and speedily brought forth the peaceable fruits of righteousness.

We cannot be too soon the Lord's, and live to high and holy purpose.

> *'Tis not for man to trifle: life is brief,*
> *And sin is here;*
> *Our age is but the falling of a leaf—*
> *A dropping tear.*
> *We have no time to sport away the hours,*
> *All must be earnest in a world like ours.*

I have chosen you, and ordained you, that ye should go and bring forth fruit, and that your fruit should remain.—JOHN 15:16.

For the fruit of the Spirit is in all goodness and righteousness and truth.—EPH. 5:9.

Being filled with the fruits of righteousness, which are by Jesus Christ, unto the glory and praise of God.—PHIL. 1:11.

JUNE 18

ALL GOES WELL WITH US WHEN THE LORD IS WITH US.

MERE outward circumstances, however seemingly favourable, are no sure evidence of true welfare. Even when our cup is full to overflowing with earthly blessing, it may yet be going ill with us, simply because the Lord is not with us. On the other hand, if only the Lord be near, though there should be but a handful of meal in the barrel and a little oil in the cruse, it may be thoroughly well; for as we may be full, yet really empty, so we may be empty, yet really full, because rich in faith and love.

Nevertheless, even in this life, God is often pleased so to prosper his people outwardly that they stand out as striking exemplifications of the truth that 'godliness is profitable unto all things, having promise of the life that now is, and of that which is to come.' Like Abraham, having the Lord with them, they are at once rich in goods and rich in grace; hence the old saying, 'Those who would prosper must make God their friend; and those who do prosper should give God the praise.' In doing so they would find that as the Lord was with Abraham and Joseph and Daniel, so would he be with them, perfecting strength in weakness, and guiding in love.

It is well, however, to remember that a time of prosperity is very often a time of spiritual peril; for its natural tendency is to foster pride, even in renewed hearts, and to dull and deaden every heavenward aspiration. 'Build your nest,' said Samuel Rutherford, 'on no tree that grows in the forest of this world, for the whole is doomed and will soon be cut down; but mount up and hide in the clefts of the Rock.'

> *I do not ask that flowers should always spring*
> *Beneath my feet;*
> *I know too well the poison and the sting*
> *Of things too sweet:*
> *For one thing only, Lord, dear Lord, I plead—*
> *Lead me aright,*
> *Though strength should falter, and though heart should bleed,*
> *Through peace to light.*

What man is he that feareth the Lord? Him shall he teach in the way that he shall choose. His soul shall dwell at ease; and his seed shall inherit the earth.—Psa. 25:12, 13.

There shall not any man be able to stand before thee all the days of thy life: as I was with Moses, so I will be with thee: I will not fail thee, nor forsake thee.—Josh. 1:5.

JUNE 19

FLATTERING TO DECEIVE.

BEFORE finding fault or inflicting censure, it was the apostle's usual way to go first as far as he honestly could in saying what was favourable. This was not flattery, but the wisdom of love; for thereby he always got a more willing ear and a more receptive heart for his Master's message. Though he praised, he never on any occasion spoke flattering words for selfish ends. But what he would not do the false teachers of his time readily did, and thereby insinuated their errors, to the injury of the church and the ruin of souls. 'A flatterer,' said good Bishop Jewell, 'maketh it his greatest care to please men, and his greatest fear to displease men. He changeth often as the weather-cock, and dareth not to strive against the stream.'

There still exist many such flatterers, against whom we must guard; and it is not without only they are found, but within also: hence the caution solemnly given, 'He that trusteth in his own heart is a fool.' It is sometimes falsely whispered to them: 'You may have needed watchfulness before, but being in Christ now, and freed from the law, it would be going back to bondage to be still watching and praying'; and thereby they are often but too successful in *misguiding* the steps and *defiling* the garments of the inexperienced and the weak.

'If with a careful and enlightened eye,' says Dr Payson, 'we trace the path of a numerous church, we shall find it strewed with the fallen, the fainting, the slumbering, and the dead, who set out in their own strength, and have been stopped, ensnared, and overcome by various obstacles.' What need, then, of ceaseless and prayerful watching!

> Our exhortation was not of deceit, nor of uncleanness, nor in guile:
> But as we were allowed of God to be put in trust with the gospel,
> even so we speak; not as pleasing men, but God, which trieth our
> hearts.—1 THESS. 2:3, 4.

For they that are such serve not our Lord Jesus Christ, but their own belly; and by good words and fair speeches deceive the hearts of the simple.—ROM. 16:18.

JUNE 20

WE DISHONOUR THE GIVER WHEN WE DESPISE THE GIFTS.

IT would be a mistake to suppose that when the apostle said, 'Despise not prophesyings,' he referred simply or mainly to a foretelling of future events. His words might include that, but they included much more, and in particular the expounding and applying the word for saving and sanctifying ends, as is abundantly evident from what he states elsewhere: 'He that prophesieth speaketh unto men to edification, and exhortation, and comfort.' Therefore to despise the preaching of the word, or the ministry of the gospel, which the Lord has expressly appointed for the body of Christ, is to go directly in the face of the apostle's injunction: 'Despise not prophesyings.' Indeed an evangelical and living ministry is one of the choicest gifts of the Lord to his church and people, for thus it is written: 'When he ascended on high, he gave gifts unto men; some apostles, some evangelists, some pastors and teachers, for the work of the ministry, for the edifying of the body of Christ.' True, the publishing of the glad tidings of salvation is not the duty and privilege of ministers only. All, in their own sphere, not only may, but ought lovingly and heartily to help in this blessed and glorious work. All such additional help, however, can never supersede the preaching of the word by a stated ministry, which, being a divine and peculiarly precious arrangement, should ever be greatly prized and turned to the best account.

Mr Moody, wherever he went, invariably sought and secured the co-operation of ministers; for he strongly felt that, however admirable and useful occasional labourers might be, it would yet be injurious in the highest degree to weaken the hands of the stated ministry, on whose efforts, under God, the systematic and permanent instruction of the people must depend. Though the apostle only forbids the sin of despising, in reality he virtually enjoins the duty of honouring the ministry by giving welcome to messenger and message alike, for the Master's sake.

> The ministry, which I have received of the Lord Jesus, to testify the gospel of the grace of God.—ACTS 20:24.

> We do all things, dearly beloved, for your edifying.—2 COR. 12:19.

> Now then we are ambassadors for Christ, as though God did beseech you by us: we pray you in Christ's stead, be ye reconciled to God.— 2 COR. 5:20.

JUNE 21

APOSTOLIC CONFLICT.

WHEN the apostle said, 'I would that ye knew what *great conflict* I have for you and for them at Laodicea, and for as many as have not seen my face in the flesh,' he probably referred not merely to the weariness and painfulness endured for their sake, but specially to his fervent wrestlings with God in their behalf. The conflict maintained by him was thus partly outward, from the bitter enmity and persecuting violence of men, and partly inward, from the intense anxiety and fear which the bare possibility of their relapse and apostasy awakened within him. So still Christian conflict has more or less of this twofold aspect; but usually we find that when there is most of outward conflict, there is least of the inward, and when the inward is most severe, the outward is greatly modified.

Now in this we see the compassionate tenderness of our Lord. He lays no over-heavy burden on his people; or if he seems to do so, he then graciously perfects his strength in their weakness. It is even as the old proverb says, 'He tempers the wind to the shorn lamb.' Moreover, even if conflict were far sterner than it is, there is this grand fact to cheer—it is limited to time, to the vale of tears: the saints who have gone home know nothing of it; they have now rest with their Lord.

Rest without broken dreams,
Or wakeful fears,
Or hidden tears,
That shall be thine—
All well with thee:
O would that it were mine!

'It needs,' says Lady Powerscourt, 'a great stretch of faith some-times, when the enemy comes in like a flood, to believe that God is as much at peace with me, through Christ, as with those already above—that Abraham now in heaven is not safer than I.' Yet it is even so; if Christ is in the ship with us, we are just as safe in wildest storm as in stillest calm.

We wrestle not against flesh and blood, but against principalities, against powers, against the rulers of the darkness of this world, against spiritual wickedness in high places.—EPH. 6:12.

The night is far spent, the day is at hand: let us therefore cast off the works of darkness, and let us put on the armour of light.—ROM. 13:12.

JUNE 22

HEALING AND HELPING.

BY profession Luke was a physician, and a kindly and skilful one, too, we may infer from the warm and loving way in which the apostle speaks of him. At first he was but a physician of the body; but as soon as grace touched his heart he became, in addition, a wise physician of souls—a loving evangelist, who turned his healing art to saving account; and thus in him we have, as it were, an incipient exemplification of the medical missionary. An evangelist of this kind, who can both teach and heal, has many advantages, and often finds an open door and a warm welcome when others, strive as they may, can find neither.

In connection with this healing and helping of Luke, it is well to remember that, specially gifted as the apostles were, it was not given them to work miracles of healing when and where it pleased them. Even Paul could not always heal, however much he might desire it, else he would not in all likelihood have said, 'Trophimus have I left at Miletum sick'; for, at the time, he not only loved him as a brother, but urgently needed his companionship and service. And as he could not always heal others, so neither could he always heal himself; and very probably, in seasons of infirmity, he needed, from time to time, not merely the helpful sympathy but the healing skill of Luke, the beloved physician.

Happily for us, however, though the servants may sometimes be helpless, the great and blessed Master never is: his skill is never baffled; and it is when our need is greatest that he is ever nearest. 'Let us get well acquainted with our Physician,' said one; 'let us come in the simplicity of sickness, in the helplessness of want: to trust is to be healed.'

> Heal me, O Lord, and I shall be healed; save me, and I shall be saved: for thou art my praise.—Jer. 17:14.

> Bless the Lord, O my soul, and forget not all his benefits: who forgiveth all thine iniquities; who healeth all thy diseases.—Psa. 103:2, 3.

June 23

TRIED YET JOYOUS RECEIVERS OF THE WORD.

WHEN the apostle said, in one of his epistles, '*Our* gospel came unto you not in word only,' it was not because he was the author of it, for it is God's gospel and not man's, nor because he was the subject of it, for he preached not himself but Christ Jesus the Lord. No; his main reason for so speaking was, because he himself needed it, and believed it, and had, in varied experience, fully tested its truth and felt its power. This gospel of the grace of God he proclaimed with such assured faith and blessed efficacy, that he could say, when addressing them, 'Ye became followers of us, and of the Lord, having received the word in much affliction, *with joy of the Holy Ghost*.'

In those early times it was no easy thing for men to become Christians, for their doing so often involved them in much persecution and trial. Nay, more; not unfrequently they had to forsake father and mother, brethren and sisters, houses and lands, for Christ's sake and the gospel's.

In a favoured land like ours, the hearers of the word may not be exposed to such severity of trial; nevertheless, it is still more or less true of all real followers of Christ, that it is through much tribulation they enter the kingdom. But, happily, the much tribulation does not hinder the much peace, because there ever comes with it the much grace to help and the many promises to cheer.

'When you come to the other side of the water,' said Samuel Rutherford, 'and have set down your foot on the glorious shore of Eternity, and look back again to the waters and to your wearisome journey, and shall see, in that clear glass of endless glory, nearer to the bottom of God's wisdom, you shall be forced to say, If God had done otherwise with me than he has done, I had never come to the enjoyment of this crown of glory. Verily, then, whether God come to his children with a rod or a crown, if he come himself with it, it is well.'

> The Holy Ghost witnesseth in every city, saying that bonds and afflictions abide me. But none of these things move me, neither count I my life dear unto myself, so that I might finish my course with joy, and the ministry, which I have received of the Lord Jesus, to testify the gospel of the grace of God.—ACTS 20:23, 24.

JUNE 24

THE ONE OFFERING OF THE ONE PRIEST.

THE sacrifices under the law, being only types, though offered year by year continually, had no real atoning efficacy. Even as the continued application of many and varied medicines gives clear evidence of their powerlessness to heal, so the great variety of Old Testament sacrifices, and their frequent repetition, clearly manifested their utter inefficiency to take away guilt. When, however, in the fulness of time, the true High Priest appeared, the Lord Jesus Christ, with the true offering, all became changed. Nothing more was required; for when he himself bare our sins in his own body on the tree, what he did was *once for all*, because his offering so fully met every demand of law and righteousness as to be all-sufficient for atoning and justifying ends. His finished work on the cross, therefore, needs no additions on our part, and it is perilous to attempt them. What we have to do is simply to rest on the atonement already made, and to wear the robe of righteousness already woven, a robe offered freely, not to the worthy, but to the worthless, and lovingly pressed on their acceptance. It is from forgetting this that many have remained so long in spiritual darkness.

'Many years ago, in a time of spiritual inquiry,' says Dr Moody Stuart, 'a stranger having an air of superior intelligence, called on me, in distress of mind. In speaking to her, I was brought to a stand by her thorough knowledge of the letter and doctrine of the Scriptures; and finding I could add no instruction, I asked no further questions, but briefly opened and pressed the words, "Jesus Christ came into the world to save sinners," and ended with prayer. While I was speaking, a stream of silent tears began to flow, and she looked relieved, but was silent. A week after, she returned, with her face bright with joy, to tell me that she had found that peace with God which she had before been vainly seeking. I asked her, "Why did you weep when you left last day?" "I wept for joy." "And what gave you the joy?" "I saw, as you were speaking, that Jesus came into the world to save sinners." "But you knew that before?" "No." "Then what did you think?" "I always thought that Jesus came into the world to save saints; and I wept for joy when I saw he came to save sinners."'

> So Christ was once offered to bear the sins of many; and unto them that look for him shall he appear the second time without sin unto salvation.—HEB. 9:28.

> But this man, after he had offered one sacrifice for sins for ever, sat down on the right hand of God; For by one offering he hath perfected for ever them that are sanctified.—HEB. 10:12, 14.

JUNE 25

WE MAY RENDER GREAT SERVICE BY SILENT MESSENGERS.

THERE are not a few whose felt difficulty in doing good is precisely that of Moses when the Lord said to him, 'Come now therefore, and I will send thee unto Pharaoh.' They are thoroughly true-hearted, and would fain serve God and be useful to their fellows; but being, like him, 'not eloquent, but slow of speech, and of a slow tongue,' they are apt to shrink back and do nothing. As Moses, however, found a helpful substitute to speak for him, so may they in one or other of the countless little books, or tracts, or leaflets easily found anywhere.

In these times great contempt is often poured upon such silent messengers, as if of weak things they were the very weakest. Nevertheless, they have often proved, in the hands of the Spirit, a marvellous instrumentality for saving good. The man to whom Mr Vine Hall presented the first three copies of 'The Sinner's Friend' rudely pushed them away, saying, 'They are of no use to anybody.' Yet that despised little messenger has since then gone forth to all the world, and been blessed to the conversion of thousands of souls. The author was spared to witness the publication of two hundred and ninety editions of that tract in twenty-three languages, comprised in one million two hundred and sixty-eight thousand copies. And what secured so great a result? Not so much any peculiar excellence in the tract itself, as the continuous love, faith, and prayer with which it was given, and the just as incessant watchfulness lest pride or self-complacency of any kind might unawares creep in and hinder the blessing.

Some time ago, when passing along one of the crowded streets of London, a gentleman was attracted to a corner where, in the midst of some two hundred people, his eye rested upon a man in the dress of a clown, who drew the attention of all the passers-by. Moved with tender pity for the man whose daily bread was earned in such a way, and lifting up his heart in prayer, he pressed through the crowd, and gave him a carefully selected tract. The clown contemptuously took it, and, to the astonishment and dismay of the giver, held it up and commenced reading it aloud. Word after word he read, with wonderful distinctness, till at length his eye rested on its closing sentence: 'Thou fool! this night thy soul shall be required of thee.' His whole frame shook with emotion, and with instant speed he left the crowd. While the people around were looking on in amazement, the gentleman followed, and finding him, drew him aside, and tried to enter into conversation with him; but the only answer he could obtain was, 'I'm lost! I'm lost!' Who can describe the joy that filled his soul when he found that God had by his Holy Spirit brought home to this man's heart and conscience the truth and power of that word which he had despised hitherto! In love and gentleness was the saving power of Jesus set before him. Every word he drank in as living water; all hardness was gone. He had been led to the foot of the cross as a repentant prodigal, and found forgiveness through a crucified Saviour. 'Blessed are they who sow beside all waters.'

> Cast thy bread upon the waters: for thou shalt find it after many days.—ECCLES. 11:1.

> He that goeth forth and weepeth, bearing precious seed, shall doubtless come again with rejoicing, bringing his sheaves with him.—PSA. 126:6.

JUNE 26

THE NEARER WE KEEP TO THE LORD OURSELVES, THE ABLER WE ARE TO GUIDE OTHERS TO HIM.

ONE of the sad results of David's fall was, that it immediately shut his mouth and destroyed his usefulness. With such a sin on his conscience, and such a stain on his life, he could do nothing for a time *but mourn in silence*. It was this that led him to pray so earnestly afterwards, 'Restore unto me the joy of thy salvation; and uphold me with thy free Spirit. Then will I teach transgressors thy ways; and sinners shall be converted unto thee.' Conscious of weakness, he now earnestly sought the upholding presence of the Holy Spirit, that he might be preserved from ever again bringing dishonour on the Lord, or proving a stumbling-block in the way of others.

Nor is the open fall of professed Christian teachers less hurtful to religion in our own day. Is not the name of God thereby dishonoured, his cause injured, the hearts of true disciples saddened, and a scoffing world made more scoffing still? Surely in such grievous cases, even when pardon has been sought and found through the blood of the Lamb, ample time should be given thoroughly to test the reality of their repentance, ere they venture again openly to speak in the name of the Lord.

Even with genuine Christians who have become unwatchful, does it not often happen that when they lose their spirituality and peace they lose their power, and cannot, as before, guide others to the Lord with holy wisdom and yearning tenderness?

'There is no better preparation,' says Dr Culross, 'for entering the inquiry-room than devout and joyful intercourse with God, and a freshened sense of his love. When we have chalked out a line for ourselves beforehand, and prepared the things we should say, we have utterly failed; whereas going forward as those who were in communion with God, it has been given us in that hour what we should speak,—right words have come unstudied to our lips, and the souls we have been dealing with have been blessed. Simplicity, tenderness, wisdom, persuasiveness, holy skill, will not be wanting to those who come forth from the presence-chamber with the atmosphere of the holiest about them, their spirit chastened and hallowed and cleared by intercourse with God. And so, when telling about Jesus, we shall do so, not as if we believed, but, which is a very different thing, *because* we believed.'

Brethren, if any of you do err from the truth, and one convert him; let him know, that he which converteth the sinner from the error of his way shall save a soul from death, and shall hide a multitude of sins.—JAMES 5:19, 20.

Howbeit Jesus suffered him not, but saith unto him, Go home to thy friends, and tell them how great things the Lord hath done for thee, and hath had compassion on thee.—MARK 5:19.

JUNE 27

CORRECTION AND SUGGESTION HAPPILY BLENDED.

THE reply of our Lord to Peter's question as to John's future, 'If I will that he tarry till I come, what is that to thee?' is practically suggestive. It clearly intimates that our tarrying or departing, our having a long life or a short one, rests wholly with him. 'If I will that he tarry,' naturally suggests the thought that our times are in his hand. Therefore it is ever a fitting thing that we should remember and act upon the words of James: 'Go to now, ye that say, To day or to morrow we will go into such a city, and continue there a year, and buy and sell, and get gain: whereas ye know not what shall be on the morrow. For what is your life? It is even a vapour, that appeareth for a little time, and then vanisheth away. For that ye ought to say, If the Lord will, we shall live, and do this, or that.'

It gave rise to a strange misapprehension. The very fact that, from a misunderstanding of what was said, the idea that John should live on till our Lord's second advent obtained such currency even in these early times, shows us how little reliance can be placed on mere tradition, and is fitted to make us deeply thankful that God has given us a written word, pure and precious, and bound us to it. 'If they speak not according to this word, it is because there is no light in them.'

It brings vividly to mind the great event of the future, for he says, 'Till I come.' If in the past the greatest of all events was the first coming of the Son of God, doubtless the grandest of the future will be his second coming, linked as it is indissolubly with resurrection, and triumph, and glory, and all that is brightest in heavenly promise and human hope. There may be uncertainty as to the time,—and purposely so in order to quicken watchfulness and prayer,—but there is nothing surer than the event itself, and it is rapidly hastening on. 'He which testifieth these things saith, Surely I come quickly.'

This thought reminds one of Edward Irving's saying regarding the Revelation: 'My view of the Apocalypse is, that it was intended to be at once the chart, and the pole-star, and the light of the Christian church over the stormy waves of time, until the great Pilot, who walketh upon the waters and stilleth the waves, should again give himself to the sinking ship, and make her his abode, his ark, his glory forever.'

> When Christ, who is our life, shall appear, then shall ye also appear with him in glory.—COL. 3:4.

> For whether we live, we live unto the Lord; and whether we die, we die unto the Lord: whether we live therefore, or die, we are the Lord's.—ROM. 14:8.

JUNE 28

IT IS WELL TO REMEMBER WHAT WE ONCE WERE.

IT has been beautifully said, 'Write injuries in dust and kindnesses in marble'; but too often we reverse this, and remember what we should forget, and forget what we should remember. This is true even of God's children. They are prone to forget the lovingkindnesses of the Lord, to let fade from their memory the sin and misery in which they once were when he looked upon them in redeeming mercy; or, as Scripture presents it, they forget 'the rock whence they were hewn, and the hole of the pit whence they were digged.'

The imagery here employed, 'the hole of the pit,' fittingly sets forth their former condition of darkness, wretchedness, and helplessness, all of which are true and mournful characteristics of fallen humanity. The unsaved are like men in a deep pit, from which the light and comfort of day are entirely excluded. They sit in darkness and in the shadow of death, without peace and joy, because wholly estranged from God.

Nor is their wretchedness greater than their helplessness. When Joseph was cast into the pit by his murderous brethren, he could do nothing whatever for his own deliverance. Help must come from above, and from other hands than his own, else very speedily that pit must become his grave. So is it with all who are still in the pit of corruption and sin. They are not only without righteousness, but also utterly without strength.

But though there is no help in themselves, blessed be his name there is infinite help for them in the Lord. 'Be thy sins never so great,' says an old writer, 'fear not to come: for he that calleth thee hath stretched out his arms of mercy at length; for they are wide open to receive thee; mercy is ready to all who will receive it, and *to them that need it most*, most ready.'

> Ye were without Christ, being aliens from the commonwealth of Israel, and strangers from the covenants of promise, having no hope, and without God in the world.—Eph. 2:12.

> He brought me up also out of an horrible pit, out of the miry clay, and set my feet upon a rock, and established my goings.—Psa. 40:2.

June 29

IN SPITE OF BONDS, PRISON EXPERIENCES HAVE OFTEN BEEN BRIGHT.

WHEN shut up in prison men are apt to settle down into a morbid melancholy, from which nothing can rouse them. Such, however, is the sweetly-sustaining power of grace, that even in closest imprisonments God's saints have often had their most blessed enlargements of heart and soul.

This was strikingly seen in Philippi; for there, even in the darkest cell and at the dreariest hour of night, Paul and his companion were able to sing so loudly and cheerily that all the prisoners heard them. Nor is this strange, for it was not for any wrong they had done they were so confined, but solely and wholly for righteousness' sake. Men might condemn them, but their conscience did not, nor their Lord, and so they were at peace. It may be a terrible thing to suffer in a bad cause, as a thief or as a murderer, but to suffer as a Christian, in the best of causes, is a distinction and honour that even angels might covet.

Besides, however strong may be the bars of any prison where saints are lodged, they have never been able to keep out Christ. He may be rarely in palaces, but he has, in the fulness of loving sympathy and help, been many a blessed day and hour with his saints in prison when suffering for his name.

When in imprisonment in Aberdeen, Samuel Rutherford said: 'No king is better provided for than I am. My chains are over-gilded with gold; for my Lord is kinder than ordinary, and cometh and visiteth my soul.'

And so when Madame Guyon was imprisoned in the Castle of Vincennes, in 1695, she not only sang but wrote songs of praises to her God. 'It sometimes seemed to me,' she said, 'as if I were a little bird which the Lord placed in a cage, and that I had nothing now to do but sing. The stones of my prison looked in my eyes like rubies. My heart was full of that joy which thou givest to them that love thee, in the midst of the greatest crosses.

> 'A little bird I am,
>   Shut from the fields of air,
> And in my cage I sit and sing
>   To him who placed me there;
> Well pleased a prisoner to be,
> Because, my God, it pleaseth thee.'

If ye be reproached for the name of Christ, happy are ye; for the spirit of glory and of God resteth upon you.—1 Pet. 4:14.

They departed from the presence of the council, rejoicing that they were counted worthy to suffer shame for his name.—Acts 5:41.

June 30

HE WHO HAS A GOODLY HERITAGE MAY WELL HAVE
A GLADSOME HEART.

WE like to see fertile fields, even when they belong to another; but the pleasure is greatly intensified when we can call them our own. On this account, apart from the wrongness of the time and motive, when the man in the parable said, 'I have bought a piece of ground, and must needs go and see it,' he said what was both natural and reasonable, and what any other man would have said in similar circumstances. Indeed, for anyone to acquire a property, and not go to see it, would indicate either that he had no interest in his purchase or that he regretted having made it.

An inheritance we value we delight to survey. 'When I look out of my manse window,' said a valued friend, 'I see, beyond the Forth, hills, fertile fields, plantations, and dwelling-houses. Suppose all were declared to be my inheritance, my property, and that as soon as the title-deeds were made out I should be put in possession, I should then look on it with much greater interest. I should direct my telescope to every part of the goodly inheritance, till I became familiar with each house and hedgerow.'

Now, if it is so with us when looking at an earthly and perishable possession, how much more should we delight to contemplate the heavenly inheritance bought for us by our Lord with his own blood, and of which he will eternally be the light and glory—an inheritance not, as here, ours today and another's tomorrow, nor one partially freed from fretting cares. No; the inheritance awaiting us will be one without sadness or care of any kind, and our joy will be enhanced by the presence of all in Christ whom we have best known and loved on earth.

Such an inheritance may be too remote for unbelief, for it cannot see afar off; but happily not for faith, for it is the substance of things hoped for, and the evidence of things not seen. And therefore it can rejoice with joy unspeakable in all that the Lord has promised and will most surely provide.

'Remember,' said Matthew Henry, 'it is life eternal we have in our eye. Better be with a few in that land of the living, than with multitudes in the congregation of the dead.'

> In my Father's house are many mansions: if it were not so, I would have told you. I go to prepare a place for you. And if I go and prepare a place for you, I will come again, and receive you unto myself; that where I am, there ye may be also.—JOHN 14:2, 3.

> In thy presence is fulness of joy; at thy right hand there are pleasures for evermore.—PSA. 16:11.

JULY 1

WE ARE BY NATURE NOT ONLY DEEP BUT DEAD IN SIN.

WHEN speaking of the natural state of men, all the sacred writers are thoroughly at one in representing it, not simply as a state of poverty, or bondage, or banishment, or blindness, or nakedness, but worse far, as *a state of death*. 'To be carnally minded is death,' says the apostle. 'You hath he quickened, who were dead in trespasses and sins.'

The expression 'dead in sin' is one intensely and painfully suggestive. A dead body has no sensibility. Place it where you may, or use what appliances you may, it sees not, it hears not, it tastes not, it feels not. Whether a feather or a stone is put on it, a wreath of flowers or a fetter of iron, it makes no difference; it has no sensibility, just because it has no life.

Now, so is it with unconverted men, who have dead souls in living bodies. They have neither sense of sin nor spiritual perception of any true kind. There may be wondrous things written in the law, and glorious things revealed in the gospel, yet they neither understand nor appreciate them. They see no beauty that he should be desired even in him who is the chief among ten thousand and altogether lovely.

Nevertheless, their case is not hopeless. Dead though they be, and vile, the Lord can quicken them to life, and clothe them with beauty. In truth, there is such a quickening to life through the word and Spirit in every case of genuine conversion. It was once mockingly said to a missionary, when going forth to seek the conversion of the heathen, 'Can you raise the dead?' 'No,' he replied; 'but my blessed Master can. Nothing is ever too hard for him. Of the very stones of the field he can raise up children to Abraham.' In seeking the saving good of others, we would seldomer faint and grow weary if we kept this blessed fact more constantly in mind.

> You, being dead in your sins and the uncircumcision of your flesh, hath he quickened together with him, having forgiven you all trespasses.—COL. 2:13.

> He that heareth my word, and believeth on him that sent me, hath everlasting life, and shall not come into condemnation; but is passed from death unto life.—JOHN 5:24.

JULY 2

EVEN LITTLE ATTENTIONS MAY BE HELPFUL EXPRESSIONS OF GRACE.

IT is somewhat remarkable that one whole chapter of Paul's greatest epistle contains scarcely anything but salutations. Yet what a blank, and what a loss of sweet instruction and Christian experience, would there have been had that chapter been left out! Doubtless, when compared with the great doctrines, promises, and counsels of the word, such salutations might, in one aspect of them, safely be dispensed with. Nevertheless, with all their seeming littleness, they were largely serviceable, not only in revealing the loving sympathy and kindness of the apostle, but also in cheering the hearts of God's saints; for they were proofs to them, amid all their trials, that there were some at least who lovingly remembered and ceaselessly prayed for them.

A salutation is usually considered a very subordinate and unimportant thing, and little more than a mere act of courtesy. But even were it so, it should not be overlooked by Christians. On the contrary, they should make such courtesies real by putting life and love into them. An old divine says: 'Christianity is no enemy to courtesy. God's scholars are taught better manners than to neglect so much as salutations.' They should be the less grudged, because, though they cost little to the giver, they may yet be greatly helpful to the receiver.

When Charles Simeon went first to Cambridge, and preached there the glorious gospel in all its fulness, he was greatly despised and opposed on every side. This continued for several years. He was sorely discouraged. But one day, as he was walking along the street, a man lifted his hat to him. This was the first time such courtesy had been shown him, and it cheered him greatly. It seemed to him a token that the Lord was beginning to bless his labours, and that the tide was turning. What that little attention did then, in sustaining and cheering a discouraged heart, a kindly look, a word of sympathy, or a loving remembrance has in innumerable instances done since. Indeed, nothing gives our Christianity such a winning attractiveness as little things like these, when done seasonably and in genuine love.

Finally, be ye all of one mind, having compassion one of another, love as brethren, be pitiful, be courteous.—1 PET. 3:8.

Be kindly affectioned one to another with brotherly love; in honour preferring one another.—ROM. 12:10.

Our friends salute thee. Greet the friends by name.—3 JOHN 14.

JULY 3

A REAL WORD OF GOD WITHOUT MYSTERIES WOULD BE THE GREATEST MYSTERY OF ALL.

SUCH is the marvellous completeness of the Sacred Volume, that we cannot without peril either take from it or add to it.

Yet in every age men have shown a tendency to make it void in part, either by added traditions on the one hand, or rationalistic exclusions on the other.

Not a few in our time, while admitting that there are mysteries in nature and their own being *which must be believed*, though not fully understood, yet strongly object to any like mysteries in God's word. Indeed, it is a fixed idea with them, that unless the Bible can be wholly stripped of everything miraculous in event and mysterious in doctrine, it can never be a power for good in the world. Such seeming wisdom, however, is destructive folly; unless it be wisdom to perfect food by first extracting from it every nutritive element, or to destroy the root of a tree in order to get more and better fruit from it. Doubtless, the Trinity in unity is a mystery; and so too is the incarnation, and the indwelling of the Spirit, and the cross of Christ, and the resurrection. But if they are great mysteries, they are at the same time such grand and fundamental truths that the greatest of the apostles did not merely believe them, but never ceased to proclaim and glory in them. 'God forbid,' he said, 'that I should glory, save in the cross of our Lord Jesus Christ, by whom the world is crucified unto me, and I unto the world.' He so dealt with the cross, mystery though it was, because he found nothing so powerfully operative for the winning and saving of souls. 'There is one point,' says a saintly man, 'where the eternities meet, and all mysteries become irradiated with the sweet light of peace. It is the little hill outside Jerusalem; it is the cross outside the camp; it is Jesus crucified for us.'

A Bible, therefore, without such practical mysteries as these, would for saving ends be no Bible at all. Speaking of mysteries, one forcibly says: 'As pertaining to matters which are *above our comprehension*, they rebuke our pride of intellect by showing the greatest minds that even for them there are questions farther from their grasp than the deepest problems are from that of a child. As applied to things which are *within our comprehension*, but which God withholds from our knowledge, it calls for the submission and confidence of the heart towards God, as guiding us by ways which we often know not. As applied to matters which are not only comprehensible to the intellect, but which are also intended to be discovered by the use of our own faculties, mystery stimulates curiosity, rouses hope, quickens exertion, and rewards discovery. Thus mystery produces at once adoration, faith, and activity.'

> And without controversy great is the mystery of godliness: God was manifest in the flesh.—1 Tim. 3:16.

> The mystery of God, and of the Father, and of Christ; in whom are hid all the treasures of wisdom and knowledge.—Col. 2:2, 3.

> O the depth of the riches both of the wisdom and knowledge of God! how unsearchable are his judgments, and his ways past finding out!—Rom. 11:33.

July 4

PATIENCE, THOUGH PAINFUL IN EXERCISE, IS PRECIOUS IN RESULT.

IN their present circumstances, so full of trial and conflict, there is perhaps no grace that believers more need than patience; and it is one very frequently enjoined: 'In your patience possess ye your souls'—'Let us run with patience the race that is set before us'—'Be patient therefore, brethren, unto the coming of the Lord.' The word in such places denotes that tenacity which still holds on, and perseveres, and waits God's time, whatever the present pressure of evil, or the delay of expected deliverance. And so serviceable, under God, has it often been in furthering the Redeemer's cause on the earth, that one of the early fathers said of it: 'It defeats all its enemies without toil. Its repose is more efficacious than the movements and deeds of others. It subdues the greatest courage, and converts the most obstinate. It is the strength and the triumph of the church.' It is often even as the prophet saith: 'In returning and rest shall ye be saved; in quietness and in confidence shall be your strength.'

It was so prized by the apostle that he earnestly prayed that the Colossian believers 'might be strengthened unto all patience and longsuffering, with joyfulness.' And in connection with this grace, such strengthening specially needs to be prayed for, because in times of delay, disappointment, and privation, believers have often, silently and unobserved, to wait and not weary, to want and not murmur, to toil and not faint, and to face, if need be, even exile and death for Jesus' sake. Yet all this, through the Spirit, has again and again been beautifully exemplified by the saints in every age. In the patience of faith the Hebrews took joyfully the spoiling of their goods; the apostles rejoiced that they were counted worthy to suffer shame for his name; and others loved not their lives unto the death.

> Ye have need of patience, that, after ye have done the will of God, ye might receive the promise.—Heb. 10:36.

> Be not slothful, but followers of them who through faith and patience inherit the promises.—Heb. 6:12.

> Knowing this, that the trying of your faith worketh patience. But let patience have her perfect work, that ye may be perfect and entire, wanting nothing.—James 1:3, 4.

July 5

A PECULIAR TITLE SOMETIMES YIELDS PECULIAR ENCOURAGEMENT.

JACOB, we would have thought, was the last man to be singled out for any special distinction; for though, without doubt, he had really the root of the matter in him, yet no Old Testament saint, perhaps, had his character stained with so many blemishes. In early life he acted with great selfishness and duplicity, and took most ungenerous advantage of a father's weakness and a brother's folly. In any man such conduct would merit censure, but it was specially offensive in him, because he knew better, and had solemnly vowed to act otherwise. In these circumstances, while quite prepared to hear the Lord addressed as the God of Abraham or Isaac, or Moses or Joshua, it does seem strange to hear him spoken of as the God of Jacob, the man of whom he had such reason to be ashamed. In spite of his unworthiness, however, the Lord assumed this very title. True, he did, with marked severity, visit Jacob's transgression with the rod, and his iniquity with stripes; nevertheless, his lovingkindness he did not utterly take from him, nor suffer his faithfulness to fail. On the contrary, he forgave his iniquities, healed his backslidings, loved him freely, and was not ashamed to be called his God. Such merciful graciousness may well encourage despairing backsliders to return to the Lord in hope.

But the title yields an additional encouragement. In ordinary life, it is no unusual thing to hear it said, 'If he succeeded, why might not I?' Probably the Psalmist had this very thought when he said, 'Give ear, O God of Jacob.' His so using Jacob's name might imply that he had found encouragement in Jacob's example: and well he might, for in trustful supplication Jacob held a high place. Indeed, he had scarcely any superior in this respect; for in pleading with the Lord no delays seemingly could discourage nor difficulties baffle him. He kept resolutely to his purpose: 'I will not let thee go, except thou bless me'; and as 'a prince he had power with God and prevailed.' Happily, we too, through a like persistency and faith, may be privileged with a like honour.

And prayer can still accomplish great things. We are told that when the Diet of Nuremberg were signing the edict which gave deliverance to Protestants, that very moment Luther was kneeling down in his favourite room praying for the accomplishment of the object. Without any communication between their hall and his room, Luther rose from his knees with a shout, rushed out into the street, and cried, 'We have got the victory,—the Protestants are free!' That was prayer getting its answer straight from the throne. It is ever found that when there is faith enough, the Lord not only does wonders for his people, but delights to do them.

> Who is a God like unto thee, that pardoneth iniquity, and passeth
> by the transgression of the remnant of his heritage? He retaineth
> not his anger for ever, because he delighteth in mercy ... Thou

wilt perform the truth to Jacob, and the mercy to Abraham, which thou hast sworn unto our fathers from the days of old.— MICAH 7:18, 20.

JULY 6

MEN MAY BE THOROUGHLY BOND, YET THINK THEMSELVES FREE.

WHEN Jesus said to the Jews, 'If ye continue in my word, then are ye my disciples indeed; and ye shall know the truth, and the truth shall make you free,' they indignantly replied, 'We be Abraham's seed, and were never in bondage to any man: how sayest thou, Ye shall be made free?' So is it still with multitudes. Though doubly enslaved through guilt and corruption, they not only think themselves free, and resent all hints to the contrary, but deliberately put away from them every gracious offer of deliverance through the blood of the Lamb and the Spirit of all grace.

What blindness could be greater? Can he be free who is the servant of sin—who approves better things and follows worse— and who, instead of being ruled by the dictates of conscience, is swayed only by the cravings of lust? As one of the early fathers said: 'A good man, though he were a slave, is yet free; whereas a wicked man, though he were a king, is yet enslaved, and not to one master only, but worse far, to as many masters as he has lusts.' Every sin that rules us is a cruel taskmaster, and many are the stripes they inflict on the spiritually bond.

Now, this much is equally clear and indubitable, that there is no help whatever for us in ourselves. Do what we may, we cannot atone for sin; and strive as we may, we can never, in our own strength, break asunder our bonds and secure the joyous liberty of the sons of God. Indeed, seemingly the more we strive, we only rivet our chains the more. It was once said, and some one, perhaps, may be saying it again now: 'I have been bound with many resolutions, but sin like Samson, has snapped them as though they were but green withes. I have been shut up with many professions, as though once for all I were a prisoner of morality; but I have taken up posts and bars, and every other restraint, and have gone back to my old impurities. Can I be saved from these inbred corruptions?'— Yes, verily, if only you will apply to him who is infinitely stronger than all your corruptions, and who has been anointed for the very purpose of proclaiming liberty to the captives, and the opening of the prison to them that are bound. If the Son of God make you free, ye shall be free indeed.

> Verily, verily, I say unto you, Whosoever committeth sin is the servant of sin.—JOHN 8:34.

> His own iniquities shall take the wicked himself, and he shall be holden with the cords of his sins.—PROV. 5:22.

> The Spirit of the Lord God is upon me; because the Lord hath anointed me ... to proclaim liberty to the captives, and the opening of the prison to them that are bound.—ISA. 61:1.

JULY 7

POVERTY IS NOTHING IF THERE BE PURITY.

IN reading the epistles to the seven churches, we cannot fail to be struck with the wise and loving way in which the Lord mingles commendation and censure. Even in the worst of them there were usually some little things that could be approved; and, on the other hand, even in the best there was more or less of defect to call forth reproof. He warmly commended the church of Ephesus for its works, and labour, and patience; yet he adds, 'I have somewhat against thee, because thou hast left thy first love.' So also, while commending the church of Thyatira for its charity, service, and faith, he adds, 'Notwithstanding I have a few things against thee, because thou sufferest that woman Jezebel to teach and to seduce my servants.'

The church of Smyrna, however, is an honourable exception. In the epistle addressed to it not an error or shortcoming of any kind is specified, nor one word of reproof given; it is throughout laudatory. But though eminently sanctified, it was not sinless. The church militant may be graciously kept from falling; but it is only the church triumphant that is presented *faultless* before the presence of his glory with exceeding joy. Such as it was, however, it was very dear to Christ. 'I know thy poverty,' he said. This poverty was peculiar, and entirely different from that of the church of Laodicea. While the Lord said to the latter, 'Thou sayest, I am rich, and increased with goods, and have need of nothing; and knowest not that thou art wretched, and miserable, and *poor*, and blind, and naked,' he said to the former, 'I know thy poverty, but thou art rich.' It was poor in earthly things—poor, possibly, through its very loyalty and faithfulness; but it was rich in heavenly things, and in the graces of the Spirit,—faith, love, and joyous hope. Thus while in the one church we see *poor* rich men, in the other we see *rich* poor men; hence the beautiful words of an old divine, 'Sweet-smelling Smyrna, thou poorest but purest of the seven.'

The same thing was true of the Macedonian believers: they were poor, but pure, yea, also rich and blessed; for 'in a great trial of affliction the abundance of their joy and their deep poverty abounded unto the riches of their liberality.' The more gracious the heart is, and the more purified through the Spirit, the more generous it is.

> Ye know the grace of our Lord Jesus Christ, that, though he was rich, yet for your sakes he became poor, that ye through his poverty might be rich.—2 Cor. 8:9.

> There is that maketh himself poor, yet hath great riches.—Prov. 13:7.

JULY 8

THE 'COME' AND THE 'DEPART' OF THE GREAT DAY.

NO part of Scripture, perhaps, is more impressive than that which tells of the Lord's advent, and of his sitting on the throne of his glory, and gathering all nations before him. He shall then, it is said, separate them one from another, as a shepherd divideth his sheep from the goats. The righteous shall be set on the right hand, and the wicked on the left, and never more shall they meet or mingle. Even among the Twelve there was found a Judas; but in the blessed family of the redeemed, to be then gathered on the right, will be found only the believing and the true; and to them the King will say, 'Come, ye blessed of my Father, inherit the kingdom prepared for you from the foundation of the world.'

But besides the bright, there is a dark and oft-forgotten side of the picture; for then, also, the King shall say unto them on the left hand, 'Depart from me, ye cursed, into everlasting fire, prepared for the devil and his angels.'

More awful words than these can scarcely be conceived. Yet mercy may be seen in the very recording of them beforehand in all their decisiveness and awfulness; for in the hands of the Spirit they have been the means, in every age, of leading countless thousands, not merely to serious thought, but to flee from the wrath to come, and find safety and peace in the one and only Refuge.

Doubtless it would be easy so to handle and plausibly interpret these words as to take away from them much both of their sternness and their certainty; but would he that uttered them thank us for so doing? or would they then serve their beneficently designed purpose to awaken and save? One ingredient taken out may change the best of medicines into a deadly poison; so one clause dropped from a text, or one word in it softened, may make that destructive which before was saving. On this account, the express injunction of the Lord to Jeremiah was: 'Speak unto all the cities of Judah all the words that I command thee to speak unto them; diminish not a word.'

When of old God said, 'In the day thou eatest thereof *thou shalt surely die*,' it was softer to say, 'God hath said, Ye shall not eat of it, *lest ye die*.' The difference may seem slight between these two sentences, yet it so altered the word of God as at once to change certainty into doubt, and rob *of all its preserving influence* the very first and weightiest of the divine warnings. So would it be with any softening down of the awful words recorded by the evangelist: 'Depart from me, ye cursed, into everlasting fire, prepared for the devil and his angels.'

What intensifies their solemnity is the lips from which they came, and which has so often before entreated and warned, but all in vain. 'It should constrain us,' says one, 'to humility and silence on this subject, that the most solemn and explicit declarations of the everlasting misery of the wicked recorded in the Scriptures, fell from the lips of him who, though equal with God, was found in fashion as a man, and humbled himself unto death, even the death of the cross, *for us men*, and *for our salvation*.'

Seeing that it is so, it should make men tremble to tamper with divine utterances, remembering who it was that said, 'Ye shall not surely die'; and remembering, too, all the ruin and woe which that lie *believed* has brought for ages on our fallen race. Unsaved men are ready enough to quench conviction without being helped to do it by deceitful whisperings that, even if salvation is missed in this world, it may yet in the end be found in the next, or that, at the very worst, all that is meant by perishing is a sleep from which there is no awaking. It will go hard with the misled in such a case, but if we are to believe the great Judge of all, it will go harder still with those misleading; for thus it is written: 'When I say unto the wicked, Thou shalt surely die; and thou givest him not warning, nor speakest to warn the wicked from his wicked way, to save his life; the same wicked man shall die in his iniquity; but his blood will I require at thine hand.' The friendliness is cruel that says, Peace, peace, when there is no peace; whereas the severity is tender and loving that tells of the wrath to come, and fervently urges to flee from it.

A venerable minister, with compassionate earnestness, once preached a sermon on this solemn theme. On the next day some thoughtless men agreed that one of their number should go to him, and, if possible, draw him into a discussion. He went accordingly, and began the conversation saying, 'I believe there is a small dispute between you and me, and I thought that I would call this morning and try to settle it.' 'Ah!' said the good man, 'what is it?' 'Why,' he replied, 'you say that the woe of the finally impenitent will be eternal, and I do not think it will.' 'Oh, if that is all,' he answered, 'there is no dispute between you and me. If you turn to Matthew 25:26, you will find that the dispute is between you and the Lord Jesus Christ, and I advise you to go immediately and settle it with him.'

> Behold, now is the accepted time; behold, now is the day of salvation.—2 COR. 6:2.

> How shall we escape, if we neglect so great salvation?—HEB. 2:3.

> I tell you, Nay: but, except ye repent, ye shall all likewise perish.—LUKE 13:3.

> He that believeth on the Son hath everlasting life: and he that believeth not the Son shall not see life; but the wrath of God abideth on him.—JOHN 3:36.

> Of how much sorer punishment, suppose ye, shall he be thought worthy, who hath trodden under foot the Son of God, and hath counted the blood of the covenant, wherewith he was sanctified, an unholy thing, and hath done despite unto the Spirit of grace?—HEB. 10:29.

JULY 9

THE JOY OF GRACE IS AS SERVICEABLE AS IT IS SWEET.

TOO often from overlooking that precious saying of the word, 'The joy of the Lord is your strength,' believers have been feeble and downcast when they might have been hopeful and strong, and have done little when they might have done much. This joy, from its very nature, invigorates for duty, and such invigoration is never unneeded. Whatever may be true of the beginning, it is often extremely difficult to hold on in well-doing stedfastly to the end, especially when such well-doing involves labour, and sacrifice, and patient endurance. Nevertheless, such is the inspiriting power of the joy of the Lord, that when fully possessed of it men can, as it were, do or bear anything.

All sadness has an impeding effect; and so, even in ordinary life, when men have any work to do requiring energy or courage, they do their utmost to keep both from themselves and others everything that might depress. It has often been noted that sailors give a cheering cry as they weigh anchor, and the ploughman whistles in the morning as he drives his team; and when soldiers are leaving friends behind them, they do not march out to the tune of the 'Dead March in Saul,' but to the quick notes of some lively air. So is it with believers in their Christian work and warfare. With joy in their hearts, they can often do more than double the work they can accomplish if pressed down with despondency. The uniform tendency of the joy of grace is so to clear the moral vision that all difficulties and trials are seen not merely in their true light, as blessings in disguise and tokens of love, but also in their happy issue, as making them meet for the inheritance of the saints in light and the full glory to be revealed.

One stormy winter day a minister was visiting one of his people, an old man who lived in great poverty in a lonely cottage a few miles from Jedburgh. He found him sitting with the Bible open on his knees, but in outward circumstances of great discomfort, the snow drifting through the roof and under the door, and scarce any fire on the hearth. 'What are you about today, John?' was his question on entering. 'Ah, sir,' said the happy saint, '*I'm sittin' under his shadow wi' great delight.*' Truly, here was the joy of grace at once serviceable and sweet.

> The kingdom of God is not meat and drink; but righteousness, and peace, and joy in the Holy Ghost.—ROM. 14:17.
>
> These things have I spoken unto you, that my joy might remain in you, and that your joy might be full.—JOHN 15:11.

JULY 10

THE FEARLESS BECOMING FEARFUL.

WE are told that 'whatsoever things were written aforetime were written for our learning, that we through patience and comfort of the scriptures might have hope'; and among the things written we find these words: 'He himself went a day's journey into the wilderness, and came and sat down under a juniper tree: and he requested for himself that he might die; and said, It is enough: now, O Lord, take away my life; for I am not better than my fathers.'

What a picture have we here of loneliness and deepest despondency. The pilgrim is in the wilderness, hungry, athirst, way-worn, and so weary of life as to ask the Lord that now he might die. The remarkable thing about this is, that the solitary, desolate man was not only a true saint, but an eminent one both in word and deed; for he was no other than Elijah, the prophet of the Lord, and that the time when he made this strange request was immediately after the overthrow of the priests of Baal by the power and visible interposition of the God of Israel.

We might reasonably have expected that after such an experience Elijah would never have fear again, but would face any foe and dare any danger in carrying out the will and purpose of the Lord Jehovah. This was what he ought to have done, but what, alas! he failed to do; for as soon as Jezebel sent a messenger to him, saying, 'So let the gods do to me, and more also, if I make not thy life as the life of one of them by to morrow about this time,' he gave way to fear and unbelief, and instantly fled for his life. The sad result was that soon, in spite of all they had seen on Carmel, the people went back to their old ways and debasing idolatries.

Such a failure at such a time is in some respects a mystery; but possibly Elijah needed some such humbling experience to reveal his nothingness if left to himself, even as Paul needed a thorn in the flesh to prevent undue elation and spiritual pride. God could easily do everything without Elijah, but all the Elijahs in the world could do nothing without God.

When Antigonus heard some of his troops rather despondingly say, 'How many are coming against us?' he asked, 'But, my soldiers, how many do you reckon me for?' So if Christians, when dismayed by their enemies, would only look to the great Captain of their salvation, and realise who he is and what he can do for them, instead of yielding to unbelieving fears, would they not be able confidently to say, More is he that is for us than all that can be against us?

> Why art thou cast down, O my soul? and why art thou disquieted within me? Hope in God: for I shall yet praise him, who is the health of my countenance, and my God.—Psa. 43:5.

> The Lord is my light and my salvation; whom shall I fear? The Lord is the strength of my life; of whom shall I be afraid? … Though an host should encamp against me, my heart shall not fear.—Psa. 27:1, 3.

July 11

EVERY REDEMPTION-BLESSING HAS THE CHARM OF COMPLETENESS.

WHAT the Lord said of old to the man sick of the palsy, he virtually says to every sinner who believes in him: 'Son, be of good cheer; thy sins be forgiven thee.' This divine forgiveness is no mere partial, imperfect thing, but *full and complete*. Our sins may be numerous as the sands on the seashore, but on our believing in Christ, they are remembered no more against us.

Whatever may be true of the forgiveness which men grant, that which comes through the blood of the Lamb has no limitations or exceptions of any kind. It extends to all trespasses, of whatever character, and whether related to heart or life, youth or age; for the Lord expressly says, 'Come now, and let us reason together: though your sins be as scarlet, they shall be as white as snow; though they be red like crimson, they shall be as wool.'

When once in Christ, nothing remains against us, and there is no more condemnation; for it is written, 'Blotting out the hand-writing of ordinances that was against us, which was contrary to us, and took it out of the way, nailing it to his cross.' A handwriting is what one writes with his own hand, and especially a bond or caution, written with the hand of a debtor, that he may never be able to deny the debt. Now, so far as we are concerned, that bond is 'just the law binding us, and proving our debt, and accusing and condemning us for the non-fulfilment of duties required.' In ancient times there were different ways of cancelling a bond. Sometimes it was blotted out, and sometimes it was pierced with a nail, and rendered thereby of none effect. In our case the blessed Redeemer, to give us full assurance that we shall never be dealt with according to the rigour of the law, adopted both these ways of cancelling the handwriting against us. He blotted it out, and he also nailed it to his cross. If so, what a wonderful sight is the cross of Christ! It may be nothing to the eye of sense, but faith sees there the grandest mystery of godliness and love,—sin punished, the law magnified, and yet the sinner saved, righteously as well as graciously.

'Man can live,' says one, 'in God's mercy; not in an abstraction, not in a vapid sentimentality, but in that dying, living, priestly, vicarious, atoning Christ. Flee thither, for by the cross no one dies. By the cross you will find pardon, peace, immortality, and heaven.'

> Having made peace through the blood of his cross, by him to recon-cile all things unto himself; by him, I say, whether they be things in earth, or things in heaven.—COL. 1:20.

> God forbid that I should glory, save in the cross of our Lord Jesus Christ, by whom the world is crucified unto me, and I unto the world.—GAL. 6:14.

JULY 12

WITHOUT WATCHFULNESS, THE WARM EASILY BECOME THE LUKEWARM.

NAZARETH was so noted for its irreligion and wickedness, that when Philip said, 'We have found him, of whom Moses in the law, and the prophets, did write, Jesus of Nazareth,' Nathanael at once unbelievingly replied, 'Can there any good thing come out of Nazareth?' We are ready at first to put a similar question about Laodicea; for its very name has become so associated in our minds with formality and lukewarmness and spiritual degeneracy, that we can scarcely believe that it was ever otherwise with it. Nevertheless, in its first and best days, even Laodicea had warm and loving hearts in it, and obtained honourable mention. We would fain know somewhat more of Nymphas, the Laodicean so specially singled out; for it is natural to suppose that he must have been a Christian of more than ordinary devotedness—one who would, for his Lord's sake, lay down his life, if need be, like faithful Antipas. In speaking of him, the apostle does not simply say, 'Salute the brethren which are in Laodicea, and Nymphas,' but adds, 'and the church which is in his house.' The church here spoken of is obviously not the place of worship, but the persons worshipping, and in particular those of his own household who had passed from death unto life and were truly the Lord's. There was thus not only holy warmth in the heart of Nymphas, Laodicean though he was, but holy warmth also in his home. Yet the church of Laodicea as a whole soon, alas! so completely lost its early ardour as to become hopelessly lukewarm.

When we find any tendency in us to yield to such a spirit, we should remember that nothing so imperils salvation as lukewarmness, or so surely and sadly dims the future glory of believers. 'I have an idea,' says one, 'that there are not a few crownless saints in heaven. They have indeed been redeemed by the blood of the Lamb; but as they have mainly sought their own ease in the world, and not Christ's honour and the saving good of others, there is no brightest glory for them, no place near the throne. They have just got in at the gate; that is all.' The very possibility of such a result in their case might well quicken every believer to redoubled watchfulness and prayer.

'Is my heart made of stone,' said one not long ago, 'that it can read of the sorrows of Christ, and not melt within me? Blessed Lord! smite the rock, and let it pour out new streams of repentance and of affectionate gratitude.'

> I know thy works, that thou art neither cold nor hot: I would thou wert cold or hot. So then because thou art lukewarm, and neither cold nor hot, I will spue thee out of my mouth.—REV. 3:15, 16.

> Nevertheless I have somewhat against thee, because thou hast left thy first love.—REV. 2:4.

> Because iniquity shall abound, the love of many shall wax cold.—MATT. 24:12.

JULY 13

NOTHING IS SO COMMENDATORY OF THE MASTER AS CONSISTENT DISCIPLESHIP.

THERE are always some who never seem to get beyond the borderland in Christian life. Though they accept Christ, it may be, yet in aim and attainment they remain so sadly defective, that none would ever point to them as models for imitation. Others, on the contrary, are so sanctified, live so truly for the Lord, and so adorn their Christian profession, that they are visibly epistles of Christ, known and read of all men. By such consistency they become powerfully influential for good, and do much to recommend the Master and his cause to the favour and acceptance of those who are without. Indeed, nothing speaks so eloquently for Christ as a holy life, or proves such a stumbling-block as an unholy one.

More than thirty years ago there was in the north of Scotland a man who long and resolutely forsook all religious ordinances. When kindly dealt with by a revered minister whom I knew well, he made this remarkable statement regarding a noted professor whom he once greatly honoured for his piety: 'That man's proved hypocrisy, after such a profession, was the beginning of my ruin, and ever after I could neither bear religion nor religious men.' How constant is the need, therefore, for prayerful watchfulness and higher attainments in the divine life! Never, however, can this be accomplished in our own strength; help must be sought from a higher source.

'Once I was sensible of my lameness,' said John Berridge in his own quaint way, 'but did not know that Christ was to be *my whole strength*, as well as righteousness. At length God has showed me that John Berridge cannot drive the devil out of himself; but Jesus Christ, blessed be his name! must say to the legion, "Come out." I see that faith alone can purify the heart, as well as pacify the conscience, and that Christ is worthy to be my all in everything, in wisdom, righteousness, sanctification, and redemption.'

> Be not deceived; God is not mocked: for whatsoever a man soweth, that shall he also reap ... And let us not be weary in well doing: for in due season we shall reap, if we faint not.—GAL. 6:7, 9.

> And God is able to make all grace abound toward you; that ye, always having all sufficiency in all things, may abound to every good work.—2 COR. 9:8.

JULY 14

PENITENCE AND PEACE.

IT is a firmly-cherished idea with many that contrition and repentance, instead of bearing fruits of God's reconciling love, are the causes of it; and as soon therefore as they begin to have religious earnestness, they try to make their peace with God through the fervour of their prayers and the intensity of their penitence.

These things, they imagine, must always come first, and that then God will look on them in mercy.

'How much must a man repent that God may be gracious?' was once asked of our great moralist, Dr Johnson. 'Err on the safe side,' was his reply; 'better repent too much than repent too little.' In reality, however, there can be no true evangelical repentance, either much or little, till God is seen as pacified towards us in Christ Jesus. So long as we regard God as an enemy, and see nothing but his broken law frowning on us as transgressors and threatening us with death, there never can be any real softening of heart or tender contrition. There may be alarm, and fear, and earnestness; but, in the very nature of things, till we apprehend the mercy of God in Christ, and have some believing conception of pacifying on his part, there never can be a true repenting on ours.

'Till I knew God as the God of peace,' said an old minister, 'my heart could no more bleed than a stone. But when I saw his glory in the face of Jesus Christ, and his abundant mercy and the exceeding riches of his grace, not only in sparing me so long, but in being willing to receive me after all my offences, then the stone became flesh, and I sorrowed after a godly sort.'

This is touchingly illustrated in the Lord's parable. The prodigal son had some sense of sorrow and shame when he resolved to return and make confession of sin and unworthiness. But when his father, hastening to meet him, fell on his neck and kissed him, these feelings of contrition doubtless would be intensified a thousandfold. It would then grieve him to the heart, as never before, to think that he could have wounded such a parent. But who can describe the joy that mingled with his tears when the best robe was put upon him and the ring on his finger, and when there came from paternal lips the blessed words: 'It is meet that we should make merry, and be glad … this my son was dead, and is alive again; he was lost, and is found.'

When a poor bricklayer, who had fallen from a great height, was lying fatally injured, he was visited by a minister in the neighbourhood. On entering the cottage he said, 'My dear man, I am afraid you are dying. I exhort you to make your peace with God.' 'Make my peace with God, sir! Why, that was made eighteen hundred years ago, when my great and glorious Lord paid all my debt upon the cruel tree. Christ is my peace, and I am saved.'

> That thou mayest remember, and be confounded, and never open thy mouth any more because of thy shame, when I am pacified toward thee for all that thou hast done, saith the Lord God.—EZEK. 16:63.

> I will forgive their iniquity, and I will remember their sin no more.—JER. 31:34.

JULY 15

FOREWARNINGS OF THE WORD.

THE Lord, seeing the end from the beginning, has in some degree lifted up the veil from the future, that his people, being graciously forewarned of coming dangers, may be in some measure forearmed to meet them. These, among other things, are written in the word: 'There shall arise false Christs, and false prophets, and shall shew *great signs and wonders*; insomuch that, if it were possible, they shall deceive the very elect'—'Then shall that Wicked be revealed, whose coming is after the working of Satan *with all power and signs and lying wonders*, and with all deceivableness of unrighteousness.'

Whatever else may be taught by these words, they clearly intimate a rising up of men in the latter times who, by the wiliness of their teachings, and also apparently by their power to do semi-miraculous things, will draw many away from truth and righteousness. Whether the great signs and wonders spoken of are to be wholly deceptions through sleight of hand or otherwise, or partly also, as some think, directly Satanic, is not said; but this much is clear, that when in full manifestation they will exert so great an influence for evil on men in general that even the very elect of God will, for the time, be imperilled by them.

Some have spoken of modern Spiritualism, with its mysteries and wonders, and professed supernaturalism and communings with the dead, as if it were in part a kind of incipient fulfilment of certain of these prophetic words. Whether it be so or not, it may at least be said that while in some of its aspects it is so altogether contemptible that it may be safely disregarded, yet in other respects, and when looked at in its possible fatal consequences, it becomes serious in the extreme. The whole system proceeds on *the insufficiency* of Scripture as a revelation, and accordingly, from giving heed to its whisperings, not a few have gradually lost all faith in the teaching of the word and in the blessed gospel of the grace of God.

'If you want to see,' said Mr Moody, 'the fruit of Spiritualism, go to our country; it has been a blight on it. I consider it the greatest plague that could come on any nation. I would a good deal rather have some terrible disease sweeping over the land and taking away hundreds, than to have God's people running after spirits. What do we want to know from departed spirits, if we have the Son of God? It must grieve the Master.'

It ought to be kept fixedly in mind that should there be in the future any such signs and wonders as Revelation 13 indicates, so startling in their nature and seemingly supernatural as powerfully to influence beholders, they must yet be resolutely disregarded, because they will be signs not of Christ but of Antichrist, to draw men away from the Redeemer and redemption. Indeed, *the forewarnings* just referred to are mercifully given by the Lord to his people for the express purpose of preserving them from the peculiar perils of such an era.

> Now the Spirit speaketh expressly, that in the latter times some shall depart from the faith, giving heed to seducing spirits, and doctrines of devils.—1 Tim. 4:1.

> Beloved, believe not every spirit, but try the spirits whether they are of God: because many false prophets are gone out into the world.—1 John 4:1.

> Saul died for his transgression which he committed against the Lord, even against the word of the Lord, which he kept not, and

also for asking counsel of one that had a familiar spirit, to inquire of it; and inquired not of the Lord: therefore he slew him, and turned the kingdom unto David the son of Jesse.—1 CHRON. 10:13, 14.

JULY 16

CAN WE MAGNIFY THE LORD?

IN a strict and literal sense, the Lord Jesus cannot be magnified or be made greater than he is, for he is infinitely great already, and possessed of a glory altogether unbounded. But in a secondary sense, he may be magnified and extolled by his saints, and have his greatness rendered more striking and conspicuous in the eyes of others. We find, accordingly, the Psalmist saying, 'O magnify the Lord with me, and let us exalt his name together.' It is in the same sense and application that the apostle's words must be understood when he says, 'According to my earnest expectation and my hope, that in nothing I shall be ashamed, but that with all boldness, as always, so now also Christ shall be *magnified* in my body, whether it be by life, or by death.'

In a world like this it is vain to expect perpetual sunshine and calm; all have some trying experiences which make demands on their fortitude, patience, submission, and Christian charity. It may be feeble health, or failure in business, or loss of friends, or the sudden blighting of the fairest and most cherished of hopes. Now, in all these things the Lord may be magnified or the Lord may be dishonoured by his professing people. He is dishonoured when they fret and repine, and so dwell on past comforts and blessings as to ignore all present ones. On the other hand, he is magnified when they are submissive and calm, and can, even in thorny paths and clouded hours, and in the darkest of valleys, be sweetly trustful.

> *Let good or ill befall,*
> *It must be good for me,*
> *Secure of having thee in all,*
> *Of having all in thee.*

'Nothing,' says one, 'magnifies Christ like a Christian deathbed, when, in spite of languor and disease, there is perfect submission to the will of God, and an entire repose of the heart, all based upon what Christ has promised, and above all upon what Christ is.'

Perhaps no man throughout life ever more resolutely aimed with single eye and loyal heart at magnifying his Lord than President Edwards, and in this he very largely succeeded. When, for the last time, he had taken leave of his family, he looked about, and said, 'Now, where is Jesus of Nazareth, my true and never-failing Friend?' And so he fell asleep, and went to the Lord he loved.

> Whoso offereth praise glorifieth me: and to him that ordereth his conversation aright will I shew the salvation of God.—Psa. 50:23.

> Verily, verily, I say unto thee, When thou wast young, thou girdest thyself, and walkedst whither thou wouldest: but when thou shalt be old, thou shalt stretch forth thy hands, and another shall gird thee, and carry thee whither thou wouldest not. This spake he, signifying by what death he should glorify God.—John 21:18, 19.

And they glorified God in me.—Gal. 1:24.

July 17

THE GREAT HINDERER.

WHEN the apostle heard of the sore and varied trials of the Thessalonian believers, he longed much to visit them again. In this, however, he did not succeed as he desired; and what hindered? Occasionally in such cases we know that the Lord is the hinderer: it is thus written, for example,—'They assayed to go into Bithynia: but the Spirit suffered them not.' We cannot, however, trace his non-return to Thessalonica at this time to any such special divine interposition. What, then, stood in the way? He himself tells us that it was the great adversary: 'We would have come unto you, even I Paul, once and again; but Satan hindered us.'

He did this, as some think, by raising such a persecution against Christians at Berea and other places, that it was deemed prudent by the apostle to delay his visit till the storm had somewhat abated. Or, as others suppose, he hindered by intensifying the antagonism of false teachers, or by stirring up dissensions and discords in the churches. But whatever the outward instrumentality, whether persecution, or heresy, or internal division, this much is clear, that Satan himself was ever the prime mover and hinderer—a fact that strikingly shows the wonderful importance attached to the action of Christian ministers. 'Here,' says one, 'is the master of all evil, the prince of the power of the air, intensely watching the journeying of three humble men (Paul, Silas, and Timothy), and apparently far more concerned about their movements than about the doings of Nero or Tiberius. These despised heralds of mercy were his most dreaded foes. They preached that name that makes hell tremble, and declared that righteousness against which Satanic hate always vents itself with the utmost power.'

As it was then, so is it still. Indeed, in every age Satan has been the great hinderer, compelling God's saints again and again to say, from painful experience, 'We wrestle not against flesh and blood, but against principalities, against powers, against the rulers of the darkness of this world.' But amid all these dangers believers have much to cheer them. They know, for one thing, that neither against Christ nor against any of his people could Satan have any power at all, unless it were given him from above for special and all-important ends. And they know, moreover, that his power is under absolute control, and that their faithful, loving God will not suffer them 'to be tempted above that they are able, but will with the temptation make a way to escape, that they may be able to bear it.' Besides, and best of all, they have the sure and express promise, that 'the God of peace shall bruise Satan under their feet shortly.' Yes; if Satan is strong to hinder, the Saviour is ever infinitely stronger to help.

The Lord knoweth how to deliver the godly out of temptations.— 2 Pet. 2:9.

Because thou hast kept the word of my patience, I also will keep thee from the hour of temptation, which shall come upon all the world, to try them that dwell upon the earth.—Rev. 3:10.

And he laid hold on the dragon, that old serpent, which is the Devil, and Satan, and bound him a thousand years.—Rev. 20:2.

July 18

THE ARROW THAT NONE CAN ESCAPE.

DEATH has an inexhaustible quiver, and never misses his aim when the fated hour has come; hence the question put, 'What man is he that liveth and shall not see death?' Wherever men build houses, they must dig graves; and so numerous are they now, that tread where the living may, the silent dead are beneath their feet. Is, then, death inseparable from God's handiwork? Has it always been so in the past, and will it ever be so in the future? Had we been left to mere human teaching, we could have got no answer to such inquiries, and the whole matter would have remained an inscrutable mystery. God himself, however, has graciously lifted the veil; and now we know that when God first made man in his own image, enlightened, pure, and blessed, he made him to live, and not to die, to rejoice, and not to weep.

How, then, has death entered? The apostle tells us in these words: 'By one man sin entered into the world, and death by sin; and so death passed upon all men, for that all have sinned.' From this statement, which, it is to be observed, speaks of men only, and not of other orders of creatures, it is plain that death is not to be referred either to physical necessity or to arbitrary will, but to a judicial decree, announced from the beginning by God as Judge against man as a transgressor. Yes; death is the fruit, the wages, the penalty, the end and consummation of sin.

When standing in the Père la Chaise, at Paris, a young man once said to me, 'Should it not be a first and a last thing with us to hate death with a perfect hatred?' and then he added, 'O death, death, how I hate you!' I said in reply, 'Would it not be wiser to fix the eye rather on sin than on death? for without the demerit of the one, there would have been none of the sweeping desolation of the other.' And I added, 'Would it not be better still to fix the eye and heart on Christ? for then death would have no sting to us, and the grave no victory, just because he died and rose again for our redemption.'

A firm faith in the Lord Jesus can give sweetest songs even in the valley of the shadow of death. 'Why do you say this is a bed of suffering?' said a saintly dying woman not long ago. 'I never had such joy in all my life, as I have had while lying on this bed. No words can be found to express my joy in the Lord.'

> For the wages of sin is death; but the gift of God is eternal life through Jesus Christ our Lord.—ROM. 6:23.

> If by one man's offence death reigned by one; much more they which receive abundance of grace and of the gift of righteousness shall reign in life by one, Jesus Christ ... That as sin hath reigned unto death, even so might grace reign through righteousness unto eternal life by Jesus Christ our Lord.—ROM. 5:17, 21.

JULY 19

WHAT THE LORD BEGINS HE COMPLETES.

IT is a brief sentence, but an encouraging one: 'Faithful is he that calleth you, who also will do it.' In so writing to the Thessalonians, the apostle virtually said: If your sanctification depended solely on your own wisdom and energy, it could never be yours; or if it depended mainly on the power and efficacy of my ministrations, it would be equally unattainable. It depends, however, on neither, but on the Lord alone, who, having graciously begun this good work in you, will not fail to complete it. 'He will do it.' This was his uniform teaching in all his epistles, whether his aim was to convince sinners of their utter inability to be their own saviour, or to remind saints, for their encouragement, that the Lord will graciously perfect all that concerns them.

The good work begun in effectual calling never terminates there, but goes progressively on till perfected in glory. The many sweet and precious promises, all of them Yea and Amen in Christ Jesus, are given expressly to help and cheer us in pressing on to higher attainments. It is thus written: 'Having therefore these promises, dearly beloved, let us cleanse ourselves from all filthiness of the flesh and spirit, perfecting holiness in the fear of God.' He may indeed take his own time and way to fulfil these promises, but fulfil them he will, for 'faithful is he that calleth you, who also will do it.' 'Hath he said, and shall he not do it? or hath he spoken, and shall he not make it good?'

Purpose, promise, and fulfilment, through unchanging faithfulness, love, and power, make such a chain that nothing conceivable can ever sever it. It is therefore the privilege and joy of every believer to say, 'I am persuaded, that neither death, nor life, nor angels, nor principalities, nor powers, nor things present, nor things to come, nor height, nor depth, nor any other creature, shall be able to separate us from the love of God, which is in Christ Jesus our Lord.' Whatever befalls them is made to work together for good. As an old writer says: 'Every wind, though it blow ever so cross, speeds believers to their port; not a stone thrown at them, but it is to them a precious stone; not a thorn in their crown, but it turns into a diamond.'

> All that the Father giveth me shall come to me; and him that cometh to me I will in no wise cast out.—JOHN 6:37.

> The Lord will perfect that which concerneth me: thy mercy, O Lord, endureth for ever.—PSA. 138:8.

JULY 20

GRACE SEEN IN MARTHA.

NOT a few have dwelt so exclusively on the Saviour's gentle though merited rebuke of Martha, as almost entirely to overlook the many excellences in her Christian character.

She had uncommon faith. Whatever may have been the misgivings of others, such was her confidence in the tender love of the

Lord Jesus, and in his ability to save, that she never for a moment doubted that had he been present during the illness of her brother, he both could and would have spoken the healing word. True, we trace an imperfect recognition of Christ's omnipotence in her limitation of it to his presence: 'Lord, if thou hadst been here.' Yet, on the other hand, there is an immediate acknowledgment of his ever-prevailing intercession: 'But I know, that even now, whatsoever thou wilt ask of God, God will give it thee.' And when Jesus said to her, 'I am the resurrection, and the life: he that believeth in me, though he were dead, yet shall he live: and whosoever liveth and believeth in me shall never die. Believest thou this?'—'Yea, Lord,' she replied: 'I believe that thou art the Christ, the Son of God, which should come into the world.' Could she have said more? Truly, even Peter's confession was not nobler than this.

But Martha had love also as well as faith. Towards the close of our Lord's public ministry, it became a somewhat dangerous thing for anyone to befriend him. But love unfeigned—and such was Martha's—knows no fear, and therefore to the very last she openly welcomed Jesus to her home in Bethany, and with her whole heart gave her very best for his refreshment and comfort.

Now, in all this we ought closely to follow her bright example. Daily should we be seeking to have our faith more firmly rooted in Christ, and, as a blessed fruit of it, to have our love more intense and practically operative. 'Christ wants love,' said Edward Irving, 'and nothing less than love can please him. He is troubled with the falling away of our love, and he laments over it. How beautiful, how sublime is such condescension in God's Anointed One, who ever hath and holdeth the love of God, and of all elect angels, and of all glorified saints, thus to make moan over his turtle dove upon the earth.'

Timotheus ... brought us good tidings of your faith and charity.— 1 Thess. 3:6.

We are bound to thank God always for you, brethren, as it is meet, because that your faith groweth exceedingly, and the charity of every one of you all toward each other aboundeth.—2 Thess. 1:3.

July 21

THE WRONG QUARTER AND THE WRONG TIME.

THOUGH in the beginning the foolish virgins took no thought of the oil, yet did they seek it in the end; for they found in their extremity that they could not get light without it, and to be lightless at such an hour was to be hopeless. So, turning to their companions, they said, with all earnestness, 'Give us of your oil; for our lamps are gone out.' This was a natural impulse on their part, for the wise were near, and well supplied, and generously inclined; nevertheless, it was a mistaken and unavailing one; for what was the reply?—'Not so; lest there be not enough for us and you: but go ye to them that sell, and buy for yourselves.' They sought the right thing, but at the wrong quarter. And there is no singularity in this folly, for the same thing is still seen from day to day. Indifferent as men usually are about what is vital in religion, counting it, it may be, a foolish excitement, or a righteousness overmuch, yet when a serious illness comes that brings eternity near, they sometimes become so thoroughly awakened by it, that the very thing they once despised they would now give worlds to possess. Saving grace is now the main thing with them; but, instead of going to the Lord himself for it, they go to Christian friends or neighbours only, and say, 'Give us of your oil.' They altogether forget that no man can give grace to his fellows. All that believers can do is to point to the true source, even the Redeemer himself; for, apart from him, when the last summons comes, though all the saints on earth stood weeping at our side, they could not put one drop of oil into our expiring lamp.

The foolish virgins took the right course in the end, but took it too late. How many have been like them in every age!—aroused, but not converted; going to buy, but too late to get. The very possibility of such a thing should make all close at once with offered mercy in Christ.

'Make sure of salvation,' said Samuel Rutherford, 'that it be not a seeking when the sand-glass is run out, and Time and Eternity shall tryst together.'

> Behold, now is the accepted time; behold, now is the day of salvation.—2 Cor. 6:2.
>
> Seek ye the Lord while he may be found, call ye upon him while he is near.—Isa. 55:6.

July 22

IT IS ONLY THE WISDOM OF GRACE THAT IS WISDOM INDEED.

WISDOM would not have been described in Scripture as better than gold, and more precious than rubies, were it not a thing of such value as to be absolutely indispensable. It is all-important, therefore, to be careful in this matter, not merely because wisdom is a very plausible word with men, and often used to hide the rankest folly, but because we are expressly told that there is a wisdom from beneath, which is earthly and sensual, as well as a wisdom from above, which is pure, peaceable, gentle, and full of mercy and of good fruits.

In defining wisdom, one has truly said, that it is the choice of the best ends, and the use of the most appropriate means to accomplish these ends. And were we to specify such an end, we could not better do so than in those simple but expressive words with which our Shorter Catechism opens,—'Man's *chief end* is to glorify God, and to enjoy him for ever.' He only is a wise man who aims at this, and he only a happy man who attains to it. Accordingly, those who have the wisdom of grace invariably make this the supreme object of their choice, and resolutely subordinate everything else to its attainment. Whatever misplacement there may be with folly, there is none with true wisdom. It ever gives a low place to self, no place to sin, and to Christ the highest place of all.

When of old the question was asked, 'What think ye of Christ?' generally speaking, the great men of the world, and the wise, made so light of him as virtually to give him no place whatever. But with the lowly wise, the Stone which the builders rejected is the most precious stone of all—their choicest treasure. Speaking of him, John Flavel once said: 'Alas! I write his praises by moonlight; I cannot praise him so much as by halves. Indeed, no tongue but his own is sufficient to undertake the task. His excelling glory dazzles all apprehension and swallows up all expression.'

> Happy is the man that findeth wisdom, and the man that getteth understanding ... She is more precious than rubies: and all the things thou canst desire are not to be compared unto her.—PROV. 3:13, 15.

> Wisdom is the principal thing; therefore get wisdom: and with all thy getting get understanding. Exalt her, and she shall promote thee: she shall bring thee to honour, when thou dost embrace her ... A crown of glory shall she deliver to thee.—PROV. 4:7-9.

> From a child thou hast known the holy scriptures, which are able to make thee wise unto salvation through faith which is in Christ Jesus.—2 TIM. 3:15.

JULY 23

MARY'S LOVE TO HER LORD.

THE offering of affection presented by Mary would get no mention from an ordinary historian; for he would naturally regard it as a mere meaningless incident in the life of an obscure woman in an obscure village of Judaea. The Lord's thoughts regarding it, however, were not as man's; and therefore this seemingly insignificant incident, just because of the rich grace and love it manifested, has found permanent place in the sacred page.

In Old Testament times many offerings were obligatory; but there was no legal injunction of any kind in the case of Mary. Her act was free and spontaneous, and prompted solely by love; and on this account it took everyone by surprise, for none save herself thought beforehand of any such thing. What added to their surprise was the value of her offering: it was the very richest she could bring. Some, like the Israelites of old whom the prophet reproved, offer to the Lord only what is bruised, crushed, or broken—something so valueless that it would be mockery to speak of it as a token either of love or gratitude. But with Mary it was wholly otherwise; she resolved to give, not something merely but *her best*—an alabaster box of ointment, very precious and her only regret was that she had not something more costly still to bestow upon him whom her soul loved. Nay, more, as one has beautifully said: 'All too slowly for her did the spikenard trickle through the narrow mouth; therefore she must break the glass. And as from the broken vessel the precious ointment flowed, filling the house with delicious odours; so her heart was broken, for it was not large enough to contain within itself the fulness of the Lord's love to her, and the sweet savour of her answering love that was gushing forth in return.'

Some may be ready to say, with a sigh: 'I have no such precious token to present. Anything I can bring is so poor and worthless that it would be almost presumptuous to offer it.' But not so: what the Lord regards is not so much the gift itself, or its own inherent value, as the spirit, and specially the grateful adoring love, with which it is offered.

'O thou loving One,' said John Bunyan, 'O thou blessed One, thou hast bought me; thou deservest to have me all. Thou hast paid for me ten thousand times more than I am worth.'

> Whom having not seen, ye love; in whom, though now ye see him not, yet believing, ye rejoice with joy unspeakable and full of glory.— 1 PET. 1:8.

We love him, because he first loved us.—1 JOHN 4:19.

JULY 24

LABOURERS ARE NEEDED, AND HOW TO GET THEM.

A S God has never yet left himself without a witness, so he has never left his church or people without pastors to cheer them in sorrow, and, through the word and Spirit, to build them up in faith and holiness. Accordingly, with their varied gifts and graces, they are ever reckoned part of the prized possessions of the saints: 'All things are yours, *whether Paul, or Apollos, or Cephas*, or the world, or life, or death, or things present, or things to come; all are yours, and ye are Christ's.'

The ministry is sometimes spoken of as a mere human arrangement—a thing to be continued or abolished at pleasure, and which depends for success solely on the talent and genius of the men who discharge its duties. In reality, however, it is a *divinely appointed* instrumentality, an ordinance of Christ. The vessels may be earthen, not golden, yet they are God's vessels notwithstanding; and he has been pleased, in the riches of his grace, to put the treasure therein for saving ends. This ministry is not a priesthood, and no priestly function is ever ascribed to it. The ministers of Christ do not mediate between God and men; they are never said to offer sacrifices for sin; and they have no power as intercessors that does not belong to every believer. All believers are priests in the only sense in which men are priests under the gospel; that is, all have liberty of access to God through Jesus Christ.

A true, living gospel ministry of this nature is so needed in this dark world, that our Lord bids us pray for it: 'Pray ye therefore the Lord of the harvest, that he will send forth labourers into his harvest.' Yet perhaps there is no duty in which Christians more sadly fail than in thus earnestly and continuously pleading for a God-given ministry; and very much just because they fail to realise the fact once expressed by John Newton, that only he who made the world can make a minister of Jesus Christ. Were there more of such wrestling prayer, how soon might we have our pulpits at home and our mission stations abroad filled with men of God, stedfast in the faith, and yearning for souls.

Some years ago, as a young missionary, after bidding farewell to all the loved ones of his family, was passing the threshold of his home, possibly never to recross it, his heart began to fail him, till, looking upward to the heavens, he remembered the words of Daniel, 'They that turn many to righteousness shall shine as the stars for ever and ever.'

> The harvest truly is plenteous, but the labourers are few; Pray ye therefore the Lord of the harvest, that he will send forth labourers into his harvest.—MATT. 9:37, 38.
>
> Finally, brethren, pray for us, that the word of the Lord may have free course, and be glorified.—2 THESS. 3:1.
>
> Praying also for us, that God would open unto us a door of utterance, to speak the mystery of Christ.—COL. 4:3.

JULY 25

THE GOSPEL IN POWER.

TO multitudes the gospel comes in word only. It is a mere unmeaning sound to them, that awakens no interest and makes no impression, but leaves the soul, as before, in all the darkness and misery of nature. Nay, even after hearing it for years together from many lips, its real character as a gospel of grace often remains wholly unknown to them, and they neither believe it nor receive it. Widely different was it with the Thessalonians in the days of Paul, for the gospel came to them not in word only, but in power. It not only reached the ear, but the understanding, and the conscience, and the heart, till their whole nature within and their whole life without became influenced by it. And all this, we are told, was associated in their minds with 'much assurance.' They did not half believe the gospel merely, as if a measure of doubt still rested on it, but with firmest conviction they heartily embraced it as the very truth of God.

'A true and enlightened believer,' says an old writer, 'doth as plainly judge of the word of God, and try out the truth thereof, from the devices and doctrines of men, as a man of clear sight is able to judge of colours, and to know one colour from another: yea, and with more certainty, because colours fade and alter, and often one colour fadeth into another; but the truth of God doth never alter. It continueth one through all ages; it is the word of everlasting life. Heaven and earth shall pass away, but one tittle thereof shall not be lost.'

It is even so. Nevertheless, the word itself is not enough for the conversion of souls, however gifted may be the preacher who expounds or applies it. Whence, then, the power? It was the energy of the Holy Spirit; for what says the apostle?—'Our gospel came not unto you in word only, but also in power and in the Holy Ghost.' Believers, therefore, cannot too earnestly or believingly plead for his presence and power. It is said that an evangelist who has been greatly blessed was so deeply anxious about himself and his work that he was constantly begging his friends to pray for him. There were two very aged saints, in particular, of great faith, to whom he used to go, like a broken-hearted child, and ask them to teach him how to trust wholly in God. This proved a part of the Lord's blessed preparation of him for his great work, by which, through the Spirit, the gospel came, in mighty and saving power, to thousands of souls.

My speech and my preaching was not with enticing words of man's wisdom, but in demonstration of the Spirit and of power.— 1 Cor. 2:4.

For this cause also thank we God without ceasing, because, when ye received the word of God which ye heard of us, ye received it not as the word of men, but as it is in truth, the word of God, which effectually worketh also in you that believe.—1 Thess. 2:13.

JULY 26

THE COMING DAY OF DAYS.

WHEN of old the high priest said to the Lord Jesus, 'I adjure thee, by the living God, that thou tell us whether thou be the Christ, the Son of God,' he solemnly replied, 'Hereafter shall ye see the Son of man sitting on the right hand of power, and coming in the clouds of heaven.' The angels, too, immediately after our Lord's ascension, said to the men of Galilee, 'This same Jesus shall so come in like manner as ye have seen him go into heaven.' The blessed hope of this predicted advent has cheered the saints of God in every age, and Scripture is full of it. Paul often refers to it in his epistles. He does not, indeed, always expressly name or define it; but even when, as is frequently the case, he simply says 'that day,' none can mistake his meaning. In utterances like these, we can think of but *one* day: 'The Lord grant unto him that he may find mercy of the Lord *in that day*'—'I am persuaded that he is able to keep that which I have committed unto him *against that day*'—'Henceforth there is laid up for me a crown of righteousness, which the Lord, the righteous judge, shall give me *at that day*: and not to me only, but unto all them also that love his appearing.' And as that day was so much in his thoughts, it should be much also in ours; for it is the day to which all other days point, of which all the prophets have sung, and for which every believer intensely longs, as the completion of their redemption and the perfection of their joy.

To all who now receive and welcome Christ, that day, when it comes, will be the day of days for brightness, joy, and glory; but to those who now deliberately reject him, it will as certainly be a day of deepest gloom and terror. It is still possible, however, even for the chief of sinners to find refuge and safety from the wrath to come, for the day of grace is not yet ended, nor is the offer of mercy yet withdrawn; but even an hour's delay may be perilous.

When the prairie grass catches fire, and the wind is strong, and the flames hasten onward twenty feet high, what do the frontier men do when they see them coming? Knowing that they cannot outrun them,—the fleetest horse cannot do that,—'They just take a match,' says Mr Moody, 'and light the grass around them, and let the fire sweep it; and then they get into the burnt district and stand safe. They hear the flames roar; they see death coming towards them; but they do not tremble, because the fire has passed over the place where they are, and there is no danger,—there is nothing for the fire to burn. There is one mountain-peak that the wrath of God has swept; that is Mount Calvary, and that fire spent its fury upon the bosom of the Son of God. Take your stand here by the Cross, and you will be safe for time and for eternity.'

> Christ hath redeemed us from the curse of the law, being made a curse for us.—GAL. 3:13.

> For he hath made him to be sin for us, who knew no sin; that we might be made the righteousness of God in him.—2 COR. 5:21.

> So Christ was once offered to bear the sins of many; and unto them that look for him shall he appear the second time without sin unto salvation.—HEB. 9:28.

JULY 27

THE LORD'S TOUCHING BEWAILMENTS.

NOT a few sometimes speak as if it were a matter of little concern to God whether men were wise or foolish in their actings, saved their souls or lost them. Nothing, however, can be more contrary to truth than such a thought, as is abundantly evidenced by his manifold bewailments over their sin and folly. Who can read such touching passages as these without realising this?—'O that there were such an heart in them, that they would fear me, and keep all my commandments always, that it might be well with them, and with their children for ever!'—'O that thou hadst hearkened to my commandments! then had thy peace been as a river, and thy righteousness as the waves of the sea'—'Oh that my people had hearkened unto me, and Israel had walked in my ways! I should soon have subdued their enemies, and turned my hand against their adversaries ... and should have fed them *also with* the finest of the wheat: and with honey out of the rock should I have satisfied thee.' And if more were needed to illustrate the Lord's compassionate interest, we have it, in its most moving form, in the tears and lamentations of our adorable Redeemer when looking down upon Jerusalem from the Mount of Olives: 'If thou hadst known,' he said, 'even thou, at least in this thy day, the things which belong unto thy peace! but now they are hid from thine eyes.' It was not for himself he poured out these tears, but for the city—not for him who was to be crucified, but for the crucifiers; and not for the woes merely of time that would befall them, but for the deeper woes of eternity. But we have more even than tears to point to in evidence that the Lord has no pleasure in the death of the sinner; we can point to Gethsemane and to Calvary, and show there a forgiving and redeeming love, whose height and depth, and length and breadth, are altogether immeasurable. Yes, verily, 'God commendeth his love toward us, in that, while we were yet sinners, Christ died for us.'

'I will bless the Lord,' said Samuel Rutherford, 'that ever there was such a thing as a free ransom given for captive souls. Only, alas! guiltiness maketh me ashamed to apply to Christ, and to think it pride in me to put out my withered hand to such a Saviour. But it is neither shame nor pride for a drowning man to swim to a rock, nor for a shipwrecked soul to run himself ashore upon Christ.'

> The Lord is not slack concerning his promise, as some men count slackness; but is longsuffering to us-ward, not willing that any should perish, but that all should come to repentance.—2 PET. 3:9.

> O house of Israel, every one according to his ways, saith the Lord God. Repent, and turn yourselves from all your transgressions; so iniquity shall not be your ruin ... For I have no pleasure in the death of him that dieth, saith the Lord God.—EZEK. 18:30, 32.

JULY 28

CALLS FOR HELP.

WHEN for the first time Europe was, in the rich mercy of God, and through the ministry of Paul, to be made a partaker with Asia of all the fulness of gospel blessing, it was by special vision that the call was given to the apostle. In the night season, a man wearing the dress and speaking the dialect of a son of Macedonia drew near and pleaded earnestly for needed aid. 'Come over and help us,' was his urgent cry. Such a scene could not fail deeply to interest the great evangelist in Macedonia, and make him resolve to go thither at once.

This vision would have all the more power with the apostle because it was so seasonable. At the time it was given it was a night season with him, both literally and figuratively; for he knew not where to turn his steps, or to what fields he should next go forth to sow broadcast and with liberal hand the good seed of the kingdom. The vision would thus virtually be to him both a fulfilment of the promise, 'Unto the upright light ariseth in the darkness,' and an answer to his prayer for needed guidance. Accordingly, immediately he and those who were with him 'endeavoured to go into Macedonia, assuredly gathering that the Lord had called them for to preach the gospel unto them.'

Nor would the apostle be less impressed by this call when he found that the man who stood before him in the night season was in truth no real man at all, but a mere fleeting phantom. No, never till divinely awakened do lost and perishing men cry for pardoning mercy and saving help. It is their condition that cries, not their lips. In reality, therefore, it was the Lord himself who made the touching appeal which the sacred historian records, and so it ever is more or less. If we begin to seek him, it is because he first sought us. Our following is ever the result of his gracious drawing. From time to time the Lord, by his word and providence, still makes like appeals; and the more true and loyal his church and people are, the more promptly and heartily will they respond.

Churches and men possessed of the true missionary spirit are ever alive to such calls; and when the call has been heard, they are animated by the like spirit. When referring to the time when he was solemnly set apart for mission work, the great missionary Williams said: 'I shall never forget how good Dr Waugh, with heaven beaming on his benevolent countenance, and the big tear of affection glistening in his intelligent eye, said,—"Go, my dear young brother: and if your tongue cleave to the roof of your mouth, let it be with telling poor sinners of the love of Jesus Christ; and if your arms drop from your shoulders, let it be with knocking at men's hearts to gain admittance for him there."'

> How then shall they call on him in whom they have not believed? and how shall they believe in him of whom they have not heard? and how shall they hear without a preacher? And how shall they preach, except they be sent? —Rom. 10:14, 15.

> God, who commanded the light to shine out of darkness, hath shined in our hearts, to give the light of the knowledge of the glory of God in the face of Jesus Christ.—2 Cor. 4:6.

JULY 29

THE TIMING OF EVENTS.

EVENTS not being left to mere blind chance, but guided and overruled by an all-wise Providence, they have all necessarily their definite times and seasons. 'To everything,' says Solomon, 'there is a season, and a time to every purpose under the heaven.' This was emphatically true of the first Advent; for not till the fulness of time had come did God send forth his Son made of a woman, made under the law, that we might receive the adoption of sons. And it will be equally true of the second Advent, the most blessed of all our hopes; for God hath appointed a day, in which he will judge the world in righteousness by that Man whom he hath ordained.

It is natural to us to be interested in the predicted events of the future, especially when, like those just mentioned, they are not only glorious in their own nature, but have a direct and practical bearing on ourselves. Nor does the Lord frown on such a spirit, or discourage in any way prophetic inquiry. On the contrary, in spite of all the seeming mystery of the Book of Revelation, and the dark symbolism that abounds in it, and the many possible mistakes into which interpreters might fall, he expressly says, 'Blessed is he that readeth, and they that hear the words of this prophecy, and keep those things which are written therein: for the time is at hand.'

So also, when the disciples came to him privately upon the Mount of Olives, and put the twofold question, 'Tell us, when shall these things be? [of which he had told them] and what shall be the sign of thy coming?'—instead of rebuking them, our Lord gave a lengthened and profoundly interesting reply. It was veiled indeed, and obscure in certain parts of it, and purposely so for definite ends: meanwhile, therefore, it is not always easy to see what refers to the first question, 'When shall these things be?' and what to the second, 'What shall be the sign of thy coming?'—but it is full of meaning and richest instruction. And doubtless the nearer the time of fulfilment comes, the clearer will its every statement appear, and the brighter all the attendant signs. While the word forbids all light and prying curiosity, for mere talking ends, yet for the quickening of hope and loving effort, it invariably encourages a calm, earnest, and prayerful study of the signs of the times.

'A prophecy,' said George Herbert, 'is a wonder sent to posterity, lest they complain of want of wonders. It is a letter sealed and sent, which to the bearer is but paper, but to the receiver and opener full of power.'

> The children of Issachar, which were men that had understanding of the times, to know what Israel ought to do.—1 CHRON. 12:32.

> When these things begin to come to pass, then look up, and lift up your heads; for your redemption draweth nigh.—LUKE 21:28.

> The grass withereth, the flower fadeth: but the word of our God shall stand for ever.—ISA. 40:8.

July 30

THE REMEDIAL EFFICACY OF THE GOSPEL.

SOME remedies suit but one clime only, and are utterly useless anywhere else. Others, though marvellously efficacious in a former age, have no healing power now. But the gospel of Christ, being everlastingly true, is suited for every clime and age, and for every ailment of the soul; and therefore it is still, as of old, the power of God and the wisdom of God to every one that believeth. All, without exception, need the mercy and grace it proclaims, because all have sinned and come short of the glory of God; and correspondingly ample is the provision made, for the great Master's command is, 'Go ye into all the world, and preach the gospel to every creature.' There is here no narrowing limitation of any kind; and the injunction is still as binding on the disciples of Christ as when first it was uttered eighteen centuries ago. If, therefore, we have any regard for safety and blessing, we cannot too early accept the gospel ourselves, or, after accepting it, too earnestly and lovingly make it known to others.

Mere civilisation, however advanced, can never, as a remedial instrumentality, be a substitute for the gospel. When the seven sons of Sceva tried to cast out devils, the evil spirit answered and said, 'Jesus I know, and Paul I know; but who are ye?' and, falling on them, they had to flee wounded and naked. And so it is now. The evil spirits of our time, the morally debased, the criminal, are subject only to one Power. New houses, good wages, improved education, will not of themselves avail to change their character or drive them out. Nay, as one forcibly puts it, 'Even the prison and the gibbet fail to scare them. There is no healing for the body politic except the gospel of Christ, borne home to the hearts and homes of the outcasts by the self-sacrificing love of them that believe.' To know this, and not compassionately act on it, is a grievous failure of duty.

Arise, shine; for thy light is come, and the glory of the Lord is risen upon thee.—Isa. 60:1.

How beautiful upon the mountains are the feet of him that bringeth good tidings, that publisheth peace; that bringeth good tidings of good, that publisheth salvation; that saith unto Zion, Thy God reigneth!—Isa. 52:7.

July 31

MUCH TO TRY, YET MORE TO CHEER.

AS the vine in Judaea generally grew best on the mountainsides, the steepness of the slopes often greatly increased the owner's toil. On this account, we are not surprised to find the labourers in the parable speaking of 'the burden and heat of the day.' The design of this statement apparently is to show that, noble and blessed as Christian work is in itself, and in the grand results that will ultimately spring from it, it has yet many difficulties connected with it peculiarly trying to flesh and blood. In doing it, we have first of all to go against the grain of our own fallen nature, and to crucify the flesh, even if need be to the plucking out of a right eye or the cutting off of a right hand. Further, in the same line, we have to meet the chill and opposition of a godless world, and to struggle daily against the wiles and snares of our sleepless and malignant adversary. There are times, accordingly when even the holiest of God's saints are ready to faint and grow weary, and almost sink entirely under the heat and burden of the toilsome day. But it should not be so; for if there be much to discourage, there is still more to cheer.

First of all, hard as the work is in which they are engaged, it is nothing to the hard and bitter bondage of the slaves of sin. Nay, in spite of all its difficulties, there is, after all, no work like it, so reasonable, so holy, so elevating, so restful. And why? Because it is the Lord's work—work which he appoints, which he delights in, and which one day he will not only openly commend, but largely reward.

Moreover, hard as it is, they are not asked to engage in it in their own strength. To encourage and cheer them the Lord not only says,

'As thy days, so shall thy strength be'; but he graciously adds, 'Fear thou not; for I am with thee: be not dismayed; for I am thy God: I will strengthen thee; yea, I will help thee; yea, I will uphold thee with the right hand of my righteousness.' Renwick, the last of the Scottish martyrs, speaking of his sufferings for conscience' sake, said: 'Enemies think themselves satisfied that we are put to wander in mosses and upon mountains; but even amid the storms of these last two nights, I cannot express what sweet times I have had, with no covering but the dark curtains of night. Yea, in the silent watch my mind was led out to admire the deep and inexpressible ocean of joy, wherein the whole family of heaven swim. Each star led me to wonder what he must be who is the Star of Jacob, of whom all stars borrow their shining."

Besides, even if the work were far harder than it is, what of that when it so soon terminates? It is only for a day they toil, a brief day—soon over; but the rest that follows is for a whole eternity. There should be no weariness with us therefore, or half-heartedness, or wrapped-up talents, or wasted hours, while doing our appointed work; but rather fresh energy and strength, through renewed waiting on the Lord.

> And he called his ten servants, and delivered them ten pounds, and said unto them, Occupy till I come.—LUKE 19:13.
>
> As every man hath received the gift, even so minister the same one to another, as good stewards of the manifold grace of God.— 1 PET. 4:10.
>
> My yoke is easy, and my burden is light.—MATT. 11:30.
>
> Be thou faithful unto death, and I will give thee a crown of life.— REV. 2:10.

AUGUST 1

STOOPING TO SAVE.

IT is the remark of an old writer, 'He that would lift the fallen, must himself stoop down'; and never was its truth more impressively manifested than in the eventful history of our Lord. From first to last it was one unparalleled humiliation for the redemption of the lost. Most humiliations are compulsory in their nature, things struggled against and bewailed. Except in rarest cases, kings never become throneless and crownless by willing abdication. But with the Lord Jesus humiliation was from first to last free and spontaneous. When he humbled himself, he not only submitted to all the privation, sorrow, and shame it would necessarily involve, but he did so with the most heartfelt willingness.

We read in the word, that though he 'thought it not robbery to be equal with God, yet he made himself of no reputation, and took upon him the form of a servant, and was made in the likeness of men: and being found in fashion as a man, he humbled himself, and became obedient unto death, even the death of the cross'—'I lay down my life … No man taketh it from me, but I lay it down of myself.' Indeed, his murderous enemies were not more eager to take his life than he was in his love to give it; and the best proof of this is his own memorable utterance: 'I have a baptism to be baptized with; and how am I straitened till it be accomplished!'

And for what end was all this? This is not difficult to perceive. When, before the commencement of a journey, the camel of the desert stoops beside its Arab owners, the reason is obvious. It is their great burden-bearer in the sandy wastes, and only by kneeling can it receive its load. Now even so, but in an infinitely higher sense, was it with our great Burden-bearer, the Lord Jesus Christ. But for his humbling himself as he did, our iniquities could not have been laid upon him, nor could he as the Lamb of God have taken them forever away, for it was as a man only he could serve and suffer, and give his life a ransom for many. In this way, and as the Father's servant in the great work of redemption, he accomplished everything for which he had come into the world. The full obedience was rendered, the full debt was paid, and the full penalty borne. 'Wherefore God hath highly exalted him, and given him a name which is above every name.'

No word is sung more sweet than this,
No name is heard more full of bliss,
No thought brings sweeter comfort nigh,
Than Jesus, Son of God most High.

'A poor landlord,' said John Maclaurin, 'thinks it a lasting honour to his cottage that he has once lodged a prince or emperor. With how much more reason may our poor cottage, this earth, be proud of it, that the Lord of glory was its tenant from his birth to his death.'

For ye know the grace of our Lord Jesus Christ, that, though he was rich, yet for your sakes he became poor, that ye through his poverty might be rich.—2 Cor. 8:9.

All things that the Father hath are mine.—John 16:15.

Foxes have holes, and birds of the air have nests; but the Son of man hath not where to lay his head.—Luke 9:58.

August 2

THE FULNESS THAT NEVER LESSENS.

LONG centuries ago, it pleased Pharaoh to commit all the fulness of the land of Egypt into the hands of Joseph, and to the famished people on every side his one word was, 'Go to Joseph.' A wiser counsel could not have been given; and none who acted on it, whatever their extremities, were allowed to perish. While this was true even of the Egyptians, it was more emphatically true still of the children of Israel; and naturally so. Joseph was their brother; and as the fulness of his power was not greater than the fulness of his brotherly love, so long as he lived they never wanted any good thing. Their corn abounded, their cup ran over, and both for life and property they had absolute security. But everything changed when Joseph died. The fulness ended then, and the freedom and the peace, and many a bitter hour thereafter did his kinsmen experience.

Very different is it with the Lord's redeemed; for in Jesus Christ they have an elder brother, infinitely greater and more loving than

Joseph—of whom Joseph was but the faintest of types. He *ever liveth* and changeth not, and in him all fulness dwells—fulness of grace, of strength, and of joy, infinitely more than sufficient to meet their every want. Their necessities are great and manifold: nevertheless, everything needed by them, whether for duty or trial, life or death, time or eternity, is wrapped up in the divine fulness which dwells in Christ; and it is the will of their Father that out of his fulness they should be ceaselessly drawing. So long, therefore, as there is faith to draw, there never can come a last supply.

A benevolent person once gave Rowland Hill a hundred pounds to dispense to a poor minister; and thinking it was too much to send him all at once, he put five pounds in a letter, with simply these words within the envelope, 'More to follow.' Shortly after, the good man received another letter, with the same cheering motto, 'And more to follow.' And again, a little after, came a third and a fourth, and still the same promise, 'More to follow.' Now every blessing that comes from God, as has been well said, is sent with the self-same message: 'I forgive you your sins, but there is more to follow; I justify you in the righteousness of Christ, but there is more to follow; I adopt you into my family, but there is more to follow; I give you grace upon grace, but there is more to follow; I will uphold you in the hour of death, and when passing into the world of spirits my mercy shall continue with you, and when you land in the world to come there shall be still more to follow.'

> *Freely he his grace bestows;*
> *Still there's more to follow,—*
> *More and more, more and more,*
> *Always more to follow.*

And of his fulness have all we received, and grace for grace.—JOHN 1:16.

Blessed are they which do hunger and thirst after righteousness: for they shall be filled.—MATT. 5:6.

Being filled with the fruits of righteousness, which are by Jesus Christ, unto the glory and praise of God.—PHIL. 1:11.

AUGUST 3

THE PRAYERS OF DYING SAINTS HAVE OFTEN UNDYING POWER.

ONE day, eighteen centuries ago, an infuriated crowd was seen hurrying through the streets of Jerusalem, dragging along a calm and saintly man, whose name will be held in everlasting remembrance. To mere sense his end was bitter, for he was stoned to death; but ere the holy martyr fell asleep, two touching petitions came from his lips—the one for himself, and the other for his murderers. 'Lord Jesus,' he said, 'receive my spirit.' And then, in louder tones, he added, 'Lord, lay not this sin to their charge.' The first petition was answered at once, for as soon as he was absent from the body, he was found present with the Lord and in joy unutterable. Nor was it otherwise, save in the matter of time, with the other petition. Saul of Tarsus may not have been in Stephen's thoughts when his dying prayer was offered, but very manifestly he was in the Lord's; for in answer to it, as well as in fulfilment of eternal purpose, he was not only forgiven and saved, but made a preacher of the very faith he had done his utmost to destroy. What, in answer to prayer, the Lord did then, he is ready to do again. No prayer of faith is ever lost. It may go up from the lowest depth, or be the last utterance of dying lips, but sooner or later the answer to it will assuredly come.

In London, some time ago, on a Sabbath evening, Mr Taylor observed among the inquirers a man about thirty years of age, with his face buried in his hands, and weeping bitterly. He was the profligate son of a minister, and had just returned from France, where he had for six years served in the French army. 'Oh, how I blasphemed God's holy name,' he said, 'and went greedily into all sin. God's mercy is great, but I am beyond the line; it cannot reach me.' It came out, in the course of conversation, that his father and mother had both died during his absence from England, and that on his return he received from a relative his mother's farewell message: 'Tell him, if he should ever come back, that I spent my dying hours praying for his salvation.' He continued, says Mr Taylor, for some time much distressed and very hopeless, when it occurred to me to say, 'Do you believe that God hears prayer?' 'Yes, the prayers of his people; I believe that again now.' 'What,' I continued, 'if in you, here humbled and seeking forgiveness, there is an answer to that dying prayer of which you have just spoken!' He became more composed, and after a short silence, said,—'I had not thought of that; it gives me hope.' 'After again reading some of the precious words of grace which have brought peace to so many of the children of God, I offered prayer. When I had prayed, I asked him to pray for himself. I can never forget that prayer. It was the grandest litany to which I ever listened. Such an outpouring of confession, and broken by sobs; such pleadings of the precious promises and the precious blood of Jesus; such trust, hesitating at first, but rapidly growing to strong assurance in salvation to the uttermost, and grace to the chief of sinners; and then such wonder, such quiet joy in salvation, or rather in a Saviour so unexpectedly, so suddenly, and yet so surely found.'

> Therefore I say unto you, What things soever ye desire, when ye pray, believe that ye receive them, and ye shall have them.—MARK 11:24.

> This is the confidence that we have in him, that, if we ask any thing according to his will, he heareth us.—1 JOHN 5:14.

> If ye abide in me, and my words abide in you, ye shall ask what ye will, and it shall be done unto you.—JOHN 15:7.

AUGUST 4

THE SEEN IS THE SHADOWY, THE UNSEEN THE REAL.

THE good things of this life—its riches, honours, and pleasures—are with many their all in all, and to secure them in ever-increasing abundance is their constant aim. They deem this truest wisdom, mainly on the ground that such things are present, visible, and substantially real.

This may be their estimate, but it is not the Lord's; for he expressly says, 'A man's life consisteth not in the abundance of the things which he possesseth.' Neither is it in harmony with facts. Indeed, even at their best, earthly things not only fail to satisfy, but never can they be surely counted on for a single moment; for though ours today, they take wings tomorrow; or if they continue, we ourselves may not: for what is our life? It is even as a vapour, that appeareth for a little while, and then vanisheth away. Yea, the world itself passeth away, and the lust thereof; and only he that doeth the will of God abideth forever.

Verily, then, the things shadowy are the things seen and temporal; while the world to come, the heavenly inheritance, the far more exceeding and eternal weight of glory, unseen though they be, are, nevertheless, the things real and abiding. Moreover, their attractive and sanctifying powers are every day felt by the children of God; and so strongly, that with such a better and enduring substance in prospect, they would deem it utterly unworthy of them to set their eyes or hearts on what, after all, is but a fashion that passeth away.

On one occasion, a passer-by, seeing a blind boy seated on his father's steps, holding in his hand a kite-string,—the kite flying far away in the air,—said to him, 'Is that any satisfaction to you, my lad, to fly that kite when you cannot see it?' 'Oh yes,' he replied; 'I can't see it, but I can feel it pull.' 'So out of this dark world,' says one, 'and amid this blindness of sin, we feel something pulling us toward heaven; and though we cannot see the thrones, and cannot behold the joy, and cannot yet gaze upon the coronation, blessed be God we can feel them drawing us heavenward.'

While here, we should ever feel as strangers, and declare plainly that we are seeking a better country, even a heavenly. 'As you walk through a flower-garden,' said a saintly man, 'you never think of lying down to make your home among its roses; so pass through the garden of this world's best joys. Smell the flowers in passing, but do not tarry. Jesus calls you to his banqueting house; there you will feed among the lilies, on the mountains of spices.'

We walk by faith, not by sight.—2 COR. 5:7.

Faith is the substance of things hoped for, the evidence of things not seen ... By faith he [Moses] forsook Egypt, not fearing the wrath of the king: for he endured, as seeing him who is invisible.—HEB. 11:1, 27.

Whom having not seen, ye love; in whom, though now ye see him not, yet believing, ye rejoice with joy unspeakable and full of glory.—1 PET. 1:8.

AUGUST 5

THOSE WHO RIGHTLY TURN WILL PATIENTLY WAIT.

THE early Christians did not only turn from idols to serve the living and true God, but 'waited' also, we are told, 'for his Son from heaven, whom he raised from the dead, even Jesus, which delivered us from the wrath to come.' It is implied in these words that Christ, who died and rose again, and ascended into heaven, is to return to this earth; and that, meanwhile, it is the duty and privilege of every believer to wait expectantly for his coming.

It has, indeed, been said, Were they not deceived in this expectation? was not their waiting a very fruitless expenditure of desire and patience? for since then eighteen centuries have run their weary course, and still the heavens retain him. To this, however, it has been justly replied: 'Insofar as they or any of them held it as a matter of faith, or even of opinion, that the Lord should certainly return *in that age*, to that extent, of course, they were mistaken. But if they simply believed that his coming was, in general terms, a thing near at hand, and if not knowing precisely how near it was, they felt it to be at once their duty, their interest, and their delight to be ever waiting for it, and preparing for it, then they were not mistaken, but just did what their inspired teacher and the Lord himself required of them.' Accordingly, wherever the grace of God then appeared, it taught men, as one grand motive to all sober, righteous, and godly living, to look for that blessed hope, and the glorious appearing of our great God and Saviour Jesus Christ; yea, to look for it as possibly near, as a thing to be loved, and hastened, and waited for, at all seasons, whether of sorrow or joy.

All are familiar with these passages: 'The coming of the Lord draweth nigh.'—'Now is our salvation nearer than when we believed. The night is far spent, the day is at hand.'—'For yet a little while, and he that shall come will come, and will not tarry.'—'Therefore be ye also ready: for in such an hour as ye think not the Son of man cometh; and what I say unto you, I say unto all, Watch.' The coming of our Lord from heaven, therefore, may well be much in the thoughts and affections of all the redeemed.

'The loving wife longs for her husband's return,' said Angell James. 'Oh, when will he come back! is her frequent exclamation. Wife of the Lamb, church of the Saviour, where is thy waiting, hoping, longing for the second coming of the Lord? Is this thy blessed hope, as it was of the primitive church?' Similar in spirit was the utterance of Thomas Chalmers:—'In the attitude of habitual service and of habitual supplication would I wait for thy coming to our world. Come quickly, Lord Jesus; and, to prepare me for this coming, let thy grace be abundantly bestowed, and thy power rest upon me.'

> Ye men of Galilee, why stand ye gazing up into heaven? this same Jesus, which is taken up from you into heaven, shall so come in like manner as ye have seen him go into heaven.—ACTS 1:11.

> I will come again, and receive you unto myself; that where I am, there ye may be also.—JOHN 14:3.

AUGUST 6

WITH US, BUT NOT OF US.

IT is one of the memorable utterances of John in his First Epistle, 'They went out from us, but they were not of us; for if they had been of us, they would no doubt have continued with us: but they went out, that they might be made manifest that they were not all of us.' These words have something saddening in them, for they clearly show that it is quite possible to have a name to live and yet not be living, and to be mingled with the saints even long and closely without ever being united to the Saviour. It was so with Judas, and with Simon Magus; and it was also so, alas! even with Demas. The name of Demas occurs several times in the Sacred Volume, and in honourable fellowship. 'Luke, the beloved physician, and Demas greet thee'—'Marcus, Aristarchus, Demas, and Lucas, my fellow-labourers.' Manifestly, therefore, Demas not only came out of heathenism, and all evil companionship, and cast in his lot with the Lord's people, but became to all appearance so full of zeal for the cause of Christ and the conversion of souls, that he was openly recognised as a fellow-labourer of Paul himself. In spite of all this, however, Demas in the end forsook the apostle, renounced his ministry, and turned back to his old ways. 'Demas hath forsaken me,' he mournfully said, 'having loved this present world.' Alas! the world was dearer to him than Christ, and time more in his thoughts than eternity. It might therefore have been truly said of him, 'He went out from us, but he was not of us; for if he had been of us, he would no doubt have continued with us.' This case affords a terrible warning: let it not be forgotten that the same love of the world that ensnared him to his ruin, has ensnared multitudes in every age.

It is not without reason, therefore, that the great Dreamer thus writes: 'At the farther side of that plain was a little hill called Lucre, and in that hill a silver mine, which some of them that had formerly gone that way, because of the rarity of it, had turned aside to see; but going too near the brink of the pit, the ground, being deceitful under them, broke, and they were slain. Some also had been maimed there, and could not, to their dying day, be their own men again. Then I saw in my dream, that a little off the road, over against the silver mine, stood Demas, gentleman-like, to call passengers to come and see; who said to Christian and his fellow, "Ho! turn aside hither, and I will show you a thing."'

This narrative is full of instruction, which all should ponder. When commenting on it, Thomas Scott says: 'The love of money does not always spring from a desire of covetous hoarding, but often from a vain affectation of gentility, which is emphatically implied by the epithet *gentleman-like* bestowed on Demas. This often tempts them into a style of living they cannot afford. Thus debts are contracted, and gradually accumulate. In these ensnaring circumstances, professed Christians, if not powerfully influenced by religious principles, will be almost sure to embrace Demas's invitation to turn aside to the hill Lucre, along with By-Ends, Money-Love, and Save-All, and, if they be not drowned in destruction and perdition, will "fall into temptation and a snare, and pierce themselves through with many sorrows."'

No servant can serve two masters: for either he will hate the one, and love the other; or else he will hold to the one, and despise the other. Ye cannot serve God and mammon.—LUKE 16:13.

They are not all Israel, which are of Israel.—ROM. 9:6.

Love not the world, neither the things that are in the world. If any man love the world, the love of the Father is not in him.—1 JOHN 2:15.

AUGUST 7

THE LORD NEVER GIVES HIS EAR ALONE TO TRUSTFUL SUPPLIANTS.

IN ordinary life we meet with many who readily, and, it may be, patiently also, give their ear, but that is all they give. They are hearers only when petitioners come to them, but never prompt and generous givers. It is not thus the Lord deals with believing suppliants. His readiness to listen is never greater than his willingness to help. The ear is but the first of his gifts, and is the earnest and pledge of greater and better to follow. Knowing this, an old believer once said: 'I know that I have got the King's ear, and therefore there can be no lack now.'

Yes; when the Lord gives his ear, he never fails in the end, so to speak, to give his hand and his heart, with all the helpful power of the one and all the tenderest sympathy of the other. Accordingly, there is scarcely any limit to his promises: 'Open thy mouth wide, and I will fill it'—'If ye abide in me, and my words abide in you, ye shall ask what ye will, and it shall be done unto you.' Possessing such amplitude of promise, we might well say, 'Here, O my soul, is a fountain opened; here thy eager thirst may be fully satisfied; thy largest desires filled up, and thy mind be forever at rest.'

One who was very familiar with palaces said: 'Some who know little of courts and courtiers think that the king's ear may be had at any time; but it is a great mistake.' This may be true of earthly princes, but it is never so with our Lord and King. At all times, under all circumstances, and for all supplies, morning or evening, midday or midnight, we may safely count on getting, in God's good time, the relief we need and the blessings we implore; and happily, too, everything we get now is but an earnest of infinitely greater things yet to come.

In every age believers have, from personal experience, borne joyous testimony to this blessed fact; saying with the Psalmist, 'Verily, God hath heard me; and hath not turned away my prayer, nor his mercy from me.'

> *Have you no words? Ah, think again,*
> *Words flow apace when you complain,*
> *And fill your fellow-creature's ear*
> *With the sad tale of all your care.*
> *Were half the breath thus vainly spent*
> *To heaven in supplication sent,*
> *Your cheerful song would oftener be,—*
> *Hear what the Lord has done for me.*

O fear the Lord, ye his saints: for there is no want to them that fear him. The young lions do lack, and suffer hunger: but they that seek the Lord shall not want any good thing.—Psa. 34:9, 10.

He that spared not his own Son, but delivered him up for us all, how shall he not with him also freely give us all things?—Rom. 8:32.

AUGUST 8

UNWISE INQUIRY.

IF, after the partial revelation the Lord made to him of his own future, Peter had, for practical ends, only inquired still more minutely what he had first to do, or where next to go, no fault could have been found. But, not satisfied with knowing his own duty and destiny, he became unduly curious about his fellow-disciple. Pointing to John, he said, 'Lord, and what shall this man do?' To this inquiry the only answer given was, 'If I will that he tarry till I come, what is that to thee? follow thou me.' Had the Lord been dealing with John, as well as with Peter, in searching yet loving scrutiny, there might have been something to justify the question put. But there being nothing of this kind, Peter had no more call in providence to make such inquiries about John than he had to make them about James or Andrew, or any other of the Twelve.

Yet, what Peter did then, multitudes are ever ready to do still. Instead of quietly doing their Master's work in the sphere assigned them, with high aim and pure motive, they busy themselves in other men's matters, to their own injury and their neighbours' disquiet. The duties and responsibilities of others seem more to concern them than their own, and thus they become mere idlers in the Lord's vineyard. They forget what the apostle said to the Thessalonians: 'We hear that there are some which walk among you disorderly, working not at all, but are busybodies.'

So long as, like Paul, and in his spirit, we simply say, 'Lord, what wilt thou have *me* to do?' the guidance needed will not be withheld, nor the daily grace for daily duty.

> *Lord, and what shall this man do?*
> *Ask'st thou, Christian, for thy friend?—*
> *If his love for Christ be true,*
> *Christ hath told thee of his end.*
> *This is he whom God approves,*
> *This is he whom Jesus loves—*

Ask not of him more than this.
  Leave it in his Saviour's breast,
Whether early called to bliss
  He in youth shall find his rest,
Or armed in his station wait
  Till his Lord be at the gate.

What each man is to do, and where and how long, the Lord himself appoints, mysteriously sometimes to us, yet ever, in reality, wisely and graciously.

Foolish and unlearned questions avoid, knowing that they do gender strifes.—2 TIM. 2:23.

Avoid foolish questions, and genealogies, and contentions, and strivings about the law; for they are unprofitable and vain.—TITUS 3:9.

Neither give heed to fables and endless genealogies, which minister questions, rather than godly edifying which is in faith: so do.—1 TIM. 1:4.

AUGUST 9

NONE NEED FEAR THE STRONG WHO HAVE THE STRONGER THAN HE AT THEIR BACK.

WE are told in the word of a broken-hearted father, who, coming to Jesus with his son, and kneeling at his feet said, 'Lord, have mercy on my son: for he is lunatick, and sore vexed: for ofttimes he falleth into the fire, and oft into the water. And I brought him to thy disciples, and they could not cure him.' Moved with compassion, Jesus at once graciously replied, 'Bring him hither to me.' And rebuking the devil, and casting him out, the child was cured from that very hour. Verily, nothing is too hard for our blessed Lord to do. Here was a desperate case. The father could do nothing; the very disciples could do nothing; and it was instinctively felt by every onlooker that vain was the help of man. Yet the very instant that Jesus took him in hand, he was healed, and so effectually and visibly that all men marvelled.

Now the main interest of this to us lies in its typicalness. In ordinary circumstances, the more a benefactor does for one the less he is able to do for another; and when a fresh application is made, he often excuses himself on this very ground. But here it is the very reverse. What was done by our Lord on that occasion emphatically intimates what can be done by him on any and every occasion; for, as the Lord of life—the Seed of the woman, the Stronger than the strong man armed—he can save to the uttermost, for there is no limit whatever to his redeeming power.

As a foe Satan is mighty, and we are weak; but our Lord being mightier far, and ever near in times of conflict, we have nothing whatever to fear. 'It is,' says one, 'a narrow and straight path between overrating and underrating Satan. Underrate him not, for thou art no match for him; overrate him not, for he is no match for Christ. Remember he is a resistible foe; his power, great as it is, is not omnipotence, his cunning is not omniscience.' In our time of need, therefore, we cannot either too trustfully or too hopefully say, 'Jesus, thou Son of David, have mercy upon me.'

> When a strong man armed keepeth his palace, his goods are in peace: but when a stronger than he shall come upon him, and overcome him, he taketh from him all his armour wherein he trusted, and divideth his spoils.—LUKE 11:21, 22.

> Therefore will I divide him a portion with the great, and he shall divide the spoil with the strong.—ISA. 53:12.

> I give unto them eternal life; and they shall never perish, neither shall any man pluck them out of my hand.—JOHN 10:28.

AUGUST 10

LITTLE SUCCESS AND LARGE.

IN our gardens, what is our hope in spring is not always our joy in autumn: there is the early blossom, but not the after fruit. So is it often in the church of God. Even in the worst of times his servants have usually some success; but often, alas! it is sadly mingled with disappointment. Some are their hope in the beginning who fail to be their joy in the end: like Felix, they tremble, but never repent; or like Agrippa, they are almost persuaded, but never altogether; or like the young man in the Gospel, they have many good thoughts about Christ, yet go away sorrowful. Nay, even believers are not always the joy to them they might be: the root of the matter, indeed, is in them, but their backslidings are so frequent and their love so cold that they are rather a grief than a gladness.

Now, labourers in God's vineyard must neither yield to unbelieving despondency, nor sluggish contentedness in such a state of things, but rather prayerfully strive to have the little success turned into the large. In so doing, they may find, if they are to be used by the Lord, that he empties before he fills, and weakens before he strengthens; just the more deeply to impress the great truth that success is not by might or by power, but by the Spirit of the Lord. The most lowly, therefore, if only heartily trustful, are usually the most likely to be greatly honoured in the Lord's service.

Not long before his death, William Grimshaw stood with John Newton on a hill near Haworth, surveying the romantic prospect. He then said, that at the time he first came into that part of the country, he might have gone half a day's journey on horseback, towards east, west, north, and south, without meeting one truly serious person, or even hearing of one. But now, through the blessing of God, not fewer than twelve hundred were in communion with him; most of whom, in the judgment of charity, he could not but believe to be one in Christ. But such was his humility, that when nearing his end he said: 'When I die I shall then know my greatest grief and my greatest joy: my greatest grief, that I have done so little for Jesus; and my greatest joy, that Jesus has done so much for me. My last words shall be, "Here goes an unprofitable servant!"'

Wilt thou not revive us again: that thy people may rejoice in thee?— Psa. 85:6.

Now thanks be unto God, which always causeth us to triumph in Christ, and maketh manifest the savour of his knowledge by us in every place.—2 Cor. 2:14.

AUGUST 11

THE WORTHLESSNESS OF WILL WORSHIP.

NOTHING seems to have surprised or saddened the great apostle of the Gentiles more than the readiness of the Galatians to revert to Judaism. It gave clear evidence to him that they had come under the power of some fatally bewitching influence: for just as their spiritual life became feeble, outward rites increased; as faith decayed and the truth lost hold, mere carnal ordinances and beggarly elements became all in all. The Colossians showed not a little of a similar tendency; for, ignoring the true and the spiritual, they began to make religion very much a thing of times and seasons, and meats and drinks, and to confound the willing worship of grateful love with the mere will worship of slavish fear. They forgot entirely what is so expressly taught in the word: 'Meat commendeth us not to God: for neither, if we eat, are we the better; neither, if we eat not, are we the worse.' 'For the kingdom of God is not meat and drink; but righteousness, and peace, and joy in the Holy Ghost.'

'There is no end,' says an old writer, 'to the scruples of superstition. If it regulate your eating today, tomorrow it will give you laws for your clothing, and afterwards for each part of your life, not leaving so much as your looks and breathing free. It is a labyrinth in which poor consciences go on intricating themselves without any issue; and a snare which first takes them, then binds them fast, and in the end strangles them. The apostle sums the matter up in these words: "Which things have indeed a shew of wisdom in will worship, and humility, and neglecting of the body; not in any honour to the satisfying of the flesh."'

God delights in a humility that is genuine and true, but loathes a humility that is pretended and false. He honours the self-denial that shows itself in sobriety and temperance, and all chasteness and purity; but not the self-denial that neglects the body and degrades it by sackcloth and scourgings. The essence of will worship is virtually a refusing to do in religion what the Lord asks, and a perverse eagerness to do what he asks not. Such self-willed service, however varied or abundant, never can be pleasing to the Lord.

What though a child eagerly brought many gifts to its father, if yet it wilfully refused to bring the only thing the father asked? So, do or bring what we may, we cannot please God till we believe on his Son. 'Behold, to obey is better than sacrifice.' This, however, is the very thing that mere will worshippers entirely forget. Though with much zeal they may do and bring many things to the Lord, they yet do not, as God requires, first and before all, believe and rest on Christ alone for salvation.

Their heart is far from me. But in vain they do worship me, teaching for doctrines the commandments of men.—MATT. 15:8, 9.

Their fear toward me is taught by the precept of men.—ISA. 29:13.

Whether therefore ye eat, or drink, or whatsoever ye do, do all to the glory of God.—1 COR. 10:31.

AUGUST 12

SPECIAL GRACE PREPARING FOR SPECIAL TRIAL.

FEW have been called to bear or suffer more than the Hebrew believers who lived in early days. They were buffeted, tempted, and impoverished, and made a public gazing-stock by manifold reproaches. Nevertheless, instead of letting go the faith, or denying their Lord, or yielding to despondency, they took joyfully the spoiling of their goods, knowing in themselves that they had in heaven a better and an enduring substance.

Now, what enabled them to witness so good a confession and so gladsome? Not, assuredly, their own inherent vigour and firmness of resolve, but only the rich grace imparted beforehand and continued throughout. 'Call to remembrance,' says the apostle, 'the former days, in which, after ye were illuminated, ye endured a great fight of afflictions.' Manifestly the real and precious preparative for the fight was the gracious illuminating that preceded it.

Such preparing beforehand was beautifully exemplified in the case of Stephen. He had a great fight to endure, for he was honoured to be the first of Christian martyrs; but he had a previous and most blessed illuminating to fit him for it; for it was given him to be full of the Holy Ghost, and, when looking upward, to see the glory of God, and Jesus standing on the right hand of the Father ready to receive his departing spirit.

And so in every age has it been more or less with God's tried yet trusting saints. The strengthening grace, when needed, is never wanting; when trouble is near, he is lovingly nearer to fulfil his blessed promise: 'When thou passest through the waters, I will be with thee; and through the rivers, they shall not overflow thee: when thou walkest through the fire, thou shalt not be burned; neither shall the flame kindle upon thee. For I am the Lord thy God, the Holy One of Israel, thy Saviour.'

It is related of Robert Glover that for some time before his death the prospect of martyrdom almost overwhelmed him, and he earnestly pleaded for the light of God's countenance. His darkness continued almost till he was within sight of the stake, when suddenly his whole soul was so filled with consolation, that he could not forbear clapping his hands, and crying out, 'He is come, He is come!' He appeared to go up in a chariot of fire, with little or no apparent sensibility of his cruel death. Here there was, to the glory of God, trial and triumph in one—bitter and sweet, death and life.

'God,' says Thomas Brooks, 'puts the distinction of suffering for Christ only on those who are vessels of honour. By grace he makes men vessels of silver and vessels of gold, and then casts them into the fire to melt and suffer for his name; and a higher honour he cannot put upon them on this side glory.'

Unto you it is given in the behalf of Christ, not only to believe on him, but also to suffer for his sake.—Phil. 1:29.

And they departed from the presence of the council, rejoicing that they were counted worthy to suffer shame for his name.—Acts 5:41.

AUGUST 13

THE REFUGE OF REFUGES.

EVERY sinner as much needs a refuge for his soul as did the manslayer of old for his natural life; for if he has not an avenger of blood at his heels, he has the justice of God and a violated law pursuing him. His danger, therefore, is great and pressing; and so long as he is out of Christ, he is not only on slippery places, but on the very verge of perdition. In ancient times, he who killed anyone unawares had to flee to his refuge at once. Not a moment could he tarry, for on the way he might be slain, near the gate he might be slain, touching the wall his life's blood might flow; but once across the threshold, and within the gate, not a hair of his head could perish. And so it is with every sinner. If it be true that out of Christ there is no safety, it is equally true that in Christ there is no danger. 'There is therefore now no condemnation to them that are in Christ Jesus'; for 'the name of the Lord is a strong tower; the righteous runneth into it, and is safe.'

So fully did the great apostle of the Gentiles realise this that, when once sheltered in Christ, he fearlessly challenged every foe to do his worst. 'Who shall separate us,' he said, 'from the love of Christ? Shall tribulation, or distress, or persecution, or famine, or peril, or sword? Nay, in all these things we are more than conquerors through him that loved us.' When, with the energy of despair, Joab clung to the horns of the altar and pleaded for his life, it was in vain; he perished even there. But none ever perished in the arms of Jesus, or were plucked out of them.

One says, 'There is no refuge like the bosom and wounds of Jesus.' It is even so; there is no softer pillow anywhere for weary head, or safer shelter for imperilled soul. Oh, could we but lean and hide there in simple faith, how little would the things of time and sense trouble us! Even the world's worst things would then seem but little more than the gentle ripplings of a summer sea when winds are hushed.

A Christian elder in Lanarkshire, when trying to show to one in deep anxiety how to be saved by simply coming to Jesus, was met at once with the difficulty, 'Ah, but we canna come richt.' 'That's true,' he replied; 'but we canna come wrang.' We cannot come right, because there is always something defective in our faith in coming; but if it is Christ we come to, we cannot come wrong. Faith saves because it takes hold of a Saviour. From its very nature it looks away from self to its object.

> *It claims no merit of its own,*
> *But looks for all in Christ.*

Come unto me, all ye that labour and are heavy laden, and I will give you rest.—MATT. 11:28.

Him that cometh to me I will in no wise cast out.—JOHN 6:37.

He that believeth on the Son hath everlasting life: and he that believeth not the Son shall not see life; but the wrath of God abideth on him.—JOHN 3:36.

AUGUST 14

YIELDING AT LAST.

WHEN sickness, entering a household, imperils some precious life, earnest prayers often go up for an immediate removal of it; and if, in spite of them, every symptom gets more alarming, the anxious perplexity becomes extreme. Nevertheless, there may be wise and loving design in the very severity of the illness. So long as a sickness seems likely to be a mere slight and transient one, and is not supposed to bring any specific message with it, it makes little or no impression. When, however, it assumes so serious an aspect that it becomes hard to tell what may be the end of it, first things—such as a right relation to God, the forgiveness of sin, and eternal safety—more readily get a first place. In this way, severe sickness has again and again been followed by saving results. In cases innumerable it has been the very first thing to rouse to solemn thought, to a sense of sin, and to a felt need of the Saviour. It may well be reckoned, therefore, among the choicest of our mercies.

But sickness alone, however lengthened or severe, will avail nothing apart from the truth applied by the Holy Spirit. That saintly man, Fletcher of Madeley, when speaking of some of his afflicted parishioners, tells of a collier boy fifteen years of age, who for two years would not so much as cross the way to hear him preach, though often invited to do so. His long and varied afflictions seem to have been entirely lost on him. 'When I visited him,' the good man said, 'I found him worn to a skeleton, with his candle burning in the socket, and no oil seemingly in the vessel. I spent an hour in setting before him the greatness of his sin in this respect, that he had been so long under the rod of God, and had not been driven out of his careless unbelief to the bosom of Jesus Christ. The truth entered; the rebelliousness gave way; the blessing came; and, when he got his feet upon the Rock, he spent his last hours in sweetly comforting his weeping mother. Thus, though long delayed, through rich grace happy yielding came at last.'

It is good for me that I have been afflicted; that I might learn thy statutes.—Psa. 119:71.

I know, O Lord, that thy judgments are right, and that thou in faithfulness hast afflicted me. Let, I pray thee, thy merciful kindness be for my comfort, according to thy word unto thy servant.—Psa. 119:75, 76.

AUGUST 15

HAVE FAITH IN GOD.

WHEN we know that the Lord is a God of truth, who cannot lie, it ought to be an easy thing to trust him; yet it is not, for through the corruption of our nature doubt comes to us more naturally than loving confidence. This is especially the case when our surroundings are unfavourable, and the moral tone and religious feeling have consequently become lowered. 'It is not known,' says one, 'how hard it is to believe in the midst of a crowd that does not believe'; and often, too, it is no less hard to believe in the midst of troubles whose pressure is severe. Even then, however, their blessed experiences in the past, and the sure promises for the future, should enable every true follower of the Lamb to say, 'Though he slay me, yet will I trust in him.'

We are told that on one occasion a swallow having built its nest on the tent of Charles V, he generously commanded that the tent should not be taken down until the young birds were ready to fly. Truly, if he, a rough soldier, could have such gentleness in his heart towards a little bird, how much more will the Lord have it to all those who flee to him for shelter in loving trustfulness. 'He that builds his nest upon a divine promise,' says one, 'shall find it abide and remain until he shall fly away to the land where promises are lost in fulfilments.' Believers should be the more emboldened to do this, from the fact that what God has already done for them is designed to be a sure and blessed earnest of all the grander things to be done for them in the future. He never lifts any from the pit only to cast them in again. Men may do such a thing, but the Lord never does.

In one of his prized letters, my friend Mr Hewitson once said to me: 'Have faith in God: faith will be staggered by loose stones in the way if we look manward. If we look Godward, faith will not be staggered, even by seemingly inaccessible mountains stretching across and obstructing our progress. "Go forward" is the voice from heaven; and faith obeying, finds the mountains before it flat as plains.'

> [Abraham] staggered not at the promise of God through unbelief; but was strong in faith, giving glory to God; and being fully persuaded that, what he had promised, he was able also to perform.—ROM. 4:20, 21.

> If thou canst believe, all things are possible to him that believeth.—MARK 9:23.

AUGUST 16

PROVING FULLY MUST BE FOLLOWED BY HOLDING FIRMLY.

THE apostle did not merely say, 'Prove all things,' but he added, 'Hold fast that which is good.' The latter is as much a duty as the former, and therefore every man who, after full inquiry, has found the truth, is bound to embrace it and hold it fast. He is not at liberty to deal with it as a common thing, which he may keep or throw away at pleasure. On the contrary, rather than abandon it, he must be ready to suffer the loss of all things. The counsellings of the word on this matter are very emphatic: 'Hold that fast which thou hast, that no man take thy crown'—'Stand fast, and hold the traditions which ye have been taught, whether by word, or our epistle.' The world that lieth in wickedness ever did and ever will set itself against the doctrines of the gospel, for it knows not their preciousness and life-giving power; but by whomsoever opposed, the many or the mighty, we must neither abandon nor modify them, but in all their integrity resolutely hold them fast to the very end.

When the pilgrims were in Vanity Fair, one chanced mockingly to say to them, 'What will ye buy?' But they, looking gravely on him, said, 'We buy the truth.' At that there was occasion taken to despise them the more; some mocking, some taunting, and some calling upon others to smite them. Nevertheless, in spite of all the abuse, these good pilgrims would only buy the truth; and when they bought it, not for any price would they sell it again. Usually, in ordinary merchandise, what we buy we are at liberty to sell; but it is not so here, for the command is express, 'Buy the truth, and sell it not.' And a most merciful provision it is; for, as one says, 'Those who sell the truth sell their own souls with it.'

In earlier times, before the word 'Protestant' was known, such as opposed the errors of the Papacy were called 'Fast Men,' in the noble sense of the term, because they held the truth fast in practice and opinion alike,—so fast that they readily imperilled life itself rather than let it go. So should it be with all. Not only the truth, but the whole truth, as the Lord has graciously revealed it, should ever be dear to us. 'You start,' said Vinet, 'at the strange dogmas of Christianity, a crucified God, the punishment of an innocent victim, the mysteries of free will and sovereign grace. They are strange; I dare not make them a little less strange. Yet it was these strange dogmas that conquered the world. It will be all over with Christianity when the world has begun to think it reasonable, or, eliminating the supernatural element, to give it a niche among the philosophies.'

> The kingdom of heaven is like unto a merchant man, seeking goodly pearls: who, when he had found one pearl of great price, went and sold all that he had, and bought it.—MATT. 13:45, 46.

> Abhor that which is evil; cleave to that which is good.—ROM. 12:9.

AUGUST 17

DISAPPOINTED EXPECTANCY.

NEVER was the expectancy of the Israelites brighter than when they found, to their joy, that the Red Sea was no longer before but behind them; yet what disappointment speedily followed! Indeed, scarcely had they finished their song of triumph on the shore, when the Lord, by the hand of Moses, led them out into the wilderness of Shur, and there, for three long days together, not one drop of water could they find. This was no ordinary trial, and it was all the more severe from its being one so entirely new in their experience; for in Egypt, even in the worst of times, water was never a want with them. But though this was their condition on the third day, they had yet bright hope on the fourth, for manifold tokens appeared that at no great distance water would be found in amplest supply. It was even so; but, alas! it was not more plenteous than bitter, and therefore, instead of bringing relief, it only intensified their misery.

All this is peculiarly instructive. It shows not merely how brief sometimes is the interval between seeming triumph and severe trial, but also that sudden changes are often an essential part of the needed discipline by which alone we can be ripened in grace and made meet for glory. Verily, it is vain to dream of unclouded sunshine here. Even when men get what, for years, they have been sighing for, it often proves not an Elim, with its sweet wells and shady palm trees, but a bitter Marah; and they still cry out with disappointed heart, 'Who will shew us any good?' 'What are the breasts of most of us,' says the saintly Leighton, 'but so many nests of foolish hopes and fears intermixed, which entertain us day and night, and steal away our precious hours from us, that might be laid out so gainfully upon the wise and sweet hopes of eternity, and upon the blessed and assured hope of the coming of our beloved Saviour.'

The hope of the righteous shall be gladness: but the expectation of the wicked shall perish.—Prov. 10:28.

My soul, wait thou only upon God; for my expectation is from him.—Psa. 62:5.

August 18

WE MAY AS SURELY LOSE SALVATION THROUGH SELF-RIGHTEOUSNESS AS THROUGH NO RIGHTEOUSNESS.

NEVER were men more madly set against God's way of salvation, or more blindly resolute for their own, than the unbelieving Jews in apostolic days. This was ever a sore grief of heart to Paul, for his countrymen were dear to him, and he yearned intensely for their salvation. 'Brethren,' he said, 'my heart's desire and prayer to God for Israel is, that they might be saved. For I bear them record that they have a zeal of God, but not according to knowledge. For they being ignorant of God's righteousness, and going about to establish *their own righteousness*, have not submitted themselves unto the righteousness of God.' They grudged no effort, or toil, or sacrifice, so long as any hope remained of their thereby securing a righteousness self-wrought, self-approved, and on the ground of which they could claim acceptance with God as a merited reward. But on no other terms would they deign to accept it.

So is it with many still. They are not indifferent, neither do they make light of eternal life; but instead of accepting it as a gift of grace, they insist on toiling for it as the wages of merit. They forget in so doing that transgressors can merit nothing; and just as no exactness in paying future debts can possibly be a payment for debts already incurred, so no exactness of obedience to the law in the future can ever compensate for the violation of it in the past.

On this point Scripture teaching is clear and unmistakable. 'Now we know,' says the apostle, 'that what things soever the law saith, it saith to them who are under the law: that every mouth may be stopped, and all the world may become guilty before God. Therefore by the deeds of the law there shall no flesh be justified in his sight: for by the law is the knowledge of sin.' The law may declare guilt, but it cannot remove it; it may be a schoolmaster, but it cannot be a Saviour. Christ alone is 'the end of the law for righteousness to every one that believeth.' In him the law is magnified, its demands are met, and its curse exhausted.

'I have not time to add more,' said the poet Cowper, in one of his letters, 'except just to say that if ever I am enabled to look forward to death with comfort, which I thank God is sometimes the case with me, I do not take my view of it from the top of my own works and deservings, though God is witness that the labour of my life is to keep a conscience void of offence to him. Death is always formidable to me, except when I see him disarmed of his sting, by having sheathed it in the body of Jesus Christ.'

A man is not justified by the works of the law, but by the faith of Jesus Christ.—GAL. 2:16.

And be found in him, not having mine own righteousness, which is of the law, but that which is through the faith of Christ, the righteousness which is of God by faith.—PHIL. 3:9.

AUGUST 19

*WHEN TRIAL COMES, WE MUST NEITHER DESPISE
NOR DESPOND.*

WE need special watchfulness in an afflictive time, else, instead of being melted and softened by it, we may only be hardened the more; hence the counsel given should never be forgotten by us: 'My son, despise not thou the chastening of the Lord.' This forbidden thing may be variously done.

Men despise chastening when they refuse to own it as God-sent. The words of the Psalmist in this connection are very weighty: 'Because they regard not the works of the Lord, nor the operation of his hands, he shall destroy them, and not build them up.' Yet how many are chargeable with this very thing. Come what may in event or circumstance, they see second causes only, and subordinate instrumentalities, and never recognise a supreme, overruling, and all-wise Providence. Nay, even believers, especially when trials press heavily on them, sometimes look so exclusively to the mere rod that wounds, as almost entirely to ignore the loving hand that lifts it, and therefore, instead of meekly submitting, they fretfully murmur.

Further: chastening is despised when men deem it too slight to be heeded. A blow, when heavy, startles men, and they deem it right to ponder earnestly whence it cometh, and why. But when it is little more than a passing frown, or gentle touch, they make no account whatever of so small a token of displeasure. In judging thus of God's dealings, there is grievous folly as well as sin; for if the Lord begins with gentle measures rather than with severe, it is just because he would rather draw than drive, rather guide with the eye than by bit and bridle.

But it is not merely said, 'Despise not thou the chastening of the Lord'; it is added, 'Nor faint when thou art rebuked of him.' We may sorrow without sin; but when we so morbidly brood over our griefs as to refuse to be comforted, we sinfully faint under them.

There might be some excuse for such fainting if our clouded sky had never any rifts in it to let the blue of heaven be revealed, or our present night had no after-morn. But there is a bright as well as a dark side both in our experience and in God's purposes; hence the well-known saying: 'Fiery trials make golden Christians; and suffering hath kept many a believer from sinning.' If in our deepest perplexities we could be but silent and trustful, how surely would all things come right in the end.

> Behold, happy is the man whom God correcteth: therefore despise not thou the chastening of the Almighty.—JOB 5:17.

> All the paths of the Lord are mercy and truth unto such as keep his covenant and his testimonies.—PSA. 25:10.

AUGUST 20

GOD DELIGHTS IN THE LOWLY.

HOWEVER it may be regarded by the proud and high-minded, humility is peculiarly precious in the sight of the Lord. Alike in connection with command, invitation, promise, and loving approval, it is largely dwelt on in the word. It is written, 'Be clothed with humility'—'God resisteth the proud, but giveth grace to the humble'—'Thus saith the high and lofty One that inhabiteth eternity, whose name is Holy; I dwell in the high and holy place, with him also that is of a contrite and humble spirit, to revive the spirit of the humble, and to revive the heart of the contrite ones.'

What is referred to here, it need scarcely be said, is not that 'voluntary humility' condemned by the apostle, which is little else than veiled pride and self-righteousness, but the true, genuine, evangelical humility which ever disclaims all merit, magnifies grace, and bows lovingly and trustfully at the feet of Jesus. All who have this spirit in them are very dear to the Lord; like Abraham, they are his choice friends, enjoy intimate fellowship, and are constantly receiving from his bountiful hand. As the showers flow down from the mountains and rest upon the lowly vales, so the Lord giveth grace to the lowly, yea, and more grace, till his work in them is fully perfected. It is not by proud but by lowly instruments that God ever does his greatest things in the church and world.

'If we desire to be used by the Lord,' says George Müller of Bristol, 'a lowly mind must be in us, and a desire to be but an axe or sword in the hand of the Lord. From the very heart we must say, "Lord, if thou wilt condescend to use me, I will give thee all the honour and glory."'

And what is true of usefulness is true of comfort: the more humble we are, the more peaceful; 'the nearer the dust, the nearer heaven.'

This was finely exemplified by Thomas Jackson, the patriarch of Methodism, who, when within two years of eighty, said at a meeting of Conference: 'I am happy in God, and have been so for sixty years; and the Saviour's love is as sweet to me in old age as it was when I was converted in my teens. And now, at the close of a long life, as the result of all, my language is, "God be merciful to me a sinner. I trust to go to heaven a sinner saved by grace."'

> Humble yourselves in the sight of the Lord, and he shall lift you up.—JAMES 4:10.

> Let nothing be done through strife or vainglory; but in lowliness of mind let each esteem other better than themselves.—PHIL. 2:3.

AUGUST 21

THE JEWS WHO BELIEVED.

THE apostasy of Israel eighteen centuries ago was so widespread and bitter, that the springing up of any Christian church in Judaea must have seemed, to human eye, the most unlikely of things. Nevertheless there was 'a remnant according to the election of grace,' a spiritual seed of Abraham within the natural, an Israel within Israel, who in the end lovingly bowed the knee to Jesus. It was of them the apostle spoke when, in writing to the Thessalonians, he said: 'For ye, brethren, became followers of churches of God which in Judaea are in Christ Jesus: for ye also have suffered like things of your own countrymen, even as they have of the Jews.'

These churches evidently were true and living, for, like all the faithful, they were of God the Father and in Christ Jesus the Son. They not only came out from Judaism, with all its false confidences, but, at the risk of everything dear to them, openly avowed themselves to be Christ's disciples, and counted it all joy to suffer for his sake. This they did with such faith and holy courage as powerfully to influence other churches, and especially the believers in Thessalonica.

Referring to this interesting fact, a good old bishop once said: 'Who would become their followers, and willingly learn to be so persecuted and made gazing-stocks to all the world?' And then added: 'Yet this discouraged not the Thessalonians from becoming their followers. They were a thousand miles distant from Judaea, but were joined to the believers there in the fellowship of the gospel and in brotherly love. Hearing of their mildness and constancy, they were stirred up by their example.'—This was a great fact, and the best of all proofs of the spiritual vitality and loving energy of the churches of Judaea. Many come far short of this. They live, it may be, but never influence, never stimulate; they possess the truth, but do nothing to diffuse it.

> We are the circumcision, which worship God in the spirit, and rejoice in Christ Jesus, and have no confidence in the flesh.—PHIL. 3:3.

> He is not a Jew, which is one outwardly; neither is that circumcision, which is outward in the flesh: but he is a Jew, which is one inwardly; and circumcision is that of the heart, in the spirit, and not in the letter; whose praise is not of men, but of God.—ROM. 2:28, 29.

AUGUST 22

THE JEWS WHO BELIEVED NOT.

IT is thus written of the unbelieving Jews: 'Who both killed the Lord Jesus, and their own prophets, and have persecuted us; and they please not God, and are contrary to all men: forbidding us to speak to the Gentiles that they might be saved, to fill up their sins alway: for the wrath is come upon them to the uttermost.'

What sadder or more awful words than these could have been written of any people; yet they were true to the very letter. They not only rejected the Son of God, but they slew him; for when Pilate would have acquitted him, they sternly said, 'If thou let this man go, thou art not Caesar's friend'; and then, assuming the whole responsibility of the murderous deed, they cried with one accord, 'His blood be upon us and upon our children.' And the woe did come, and soon. Indeed the tribulation that thereafter befell them, alike in severity and duration, has been altogether without parallel in the annals of mankind. But, thanks be to God, it is not to be so always with the seed of Abraham. They are not as a people to be forever scattered, peeled, exiled, and hardened in unbelief; nor is their land to be a perpetual desolation: for both their conversion to the Lord and their restoration to the land are fully and clearly predicted.

In the year 1808, the generous Lewis Way, when riding with a friend in Devonshire, had his attention drawn by a companion to some stately trees in a park they were passing. 'Do you know,' said his friend, 'the singular condition that is attached to these oaks? A lady who formerly owned this park, stipulated in her will that they should not be cut down until Jerusalem should again be in possession of Israel; and they are growing still.' Mr Way's heart was deeply moved by this incident. The idea of the restoration of the Jews took possession of his mind. In the following year he succeeded in forming the London Society of the Jews. The labours of this and other kindred societies have since been so graciously owned, that in England and on the Continent there are now, we are told, at the lowest estimate, between twenty and thirty thousand Jewish converts, of whom four hundred are ministers of the gospel, some of them preachers and students whose names have become almost household words in the church of Christ.

There exists not a little at present to encourage the hope that the time to favour Zion is at hand. It is somewhat remarkable that not long ago a Jew of note said openly, and with great earnestness, to his brethren of the house of Israel, 'How is it that we have been waiting for the coming of our Messiah, and still he does not come? Let us search after the reason why God has forsaken us. What dreadful crime have we committed, that nearly for two thousand years God will not listen to us?' Even Jewish children have been taught in some quarters to sing,—

> *See in yon East the glowing gleam!*
> *Faith is not false, nor hope a dream—*
> *Messiah come! Rejoice our eyes,*
> *And lo, in yonder Eastern skies*
> *The Sun of righteousness shall rise,*
> *And on its healing pinions bear*
> *Love, peace, and joy, for all the world to share.*

Facts like these may well inspire us with fresh vigour and hopefulness in labouring and praying for the conversion of Israel.

Jerusalem shall be trodden down of the Gentiles, until the times of the Gentiles be fulfilled.—LUKE 21:24.

Afterward shall the children of Israel return, and seek the Lord their God, and David their king; and shall fear the Lord and his goodness in the latter days.—HOS. 3:5.

Behold, I will gather them out of all countries, whither I have driven them in mine anger, and in my fury, and in great wrath; and I will bring them again unto this place, and I will cause them to dwell safely: and they shall be my people, and I will be their God: and I will give them one heart, and one way, that they may fear me for ever, for the good of them, and of their children after them: and I will make an everlasting covenant with them, that I will not turn away from them, to do them good; but I will put my fear in their hearts, that they shall not depart from me. Yea, I will rejoice over them to do them good, and I will plant them in this land assuredly with my whole heart and with my whole soul.—JER. 32:37-41.

AUGUST 23

STERLING FIDELITY.

OUR blessed Lord and Master demands and expects that his people be, above all things, faithful alike in the little and in the great. 'Be thou faithful unto death,' he said to some of them, 'and I will give thee a crown of life.' This required fidelity must be an individual thing: 'Be *thou* faithful.' There is intense individuality in Christ's love and faithfulness to his people. 'He loved *me*,' said Paul, 'and gave himself for *me*.' And so must it be also with their loving faithfulness to him. It must be a personal, individual thing, and each must be ready to follow the Lamb whithersoever he goeth.

Very precious is such fidelity in the sight of the Lord. This is touchingly brought out in his letter to the church in Pergamos, when he says, 'Even in those days wherein Antipas was my faithful martyr, who was slain among you, where Satan dwelleth.' What a different world would this have been if all in every age who have borne the Master's name had been worthy of a commendation as special and loving as this. But, alas! like the Galatians, there are some who, to all appearance, begin well, love warmly, and work zealously, but long before the close of life they faithlessly turn back, and are never seen more with the Lord or his people. In spite of the early blossom, when autumn comes, there is nothing but leaves; when the end comes, nothing but words; and when the Bridegroom comes, there are only lamps that go out when most they are needed. Their fidelity always gives way when the suffering point is reached, and sacrifices have to be made for righteousness' sake.

When more is demanded than mere profession or fair words, they are ready to exclaim, 'This is a hard saying; who can hear it?' Not so the truly faithful; they deem nothing too hard to do or suffer for him who laid down his very life for us.

When, in early times, the aged Polycarp was promised life if he would but reproach Christ, 'No,' he said; 'eighty and six years I have served him, and he hath never wronged me; and how can I blaspheme my King, who hath saved me?' And when he was about to be put to death, he exclaimed, 'O God of all principalities, and Father of thy beloved and blessed Son Jesus Christ, I bless thee that thou hast counted me worthy of this day and this hour, to receive my portion in the number of the martyrs in the cup of Christ.'

> From that time many of his disciples went back, and walked no more with him.—JOHN 6:66.

> Take heed, brethren, lest there be in any of you an evil heart of unbelief, in departing from the living God.—HEB. 3:12.

AUGUST 24

LOVE IN FULLEST REVELATION.

NOTHING so unfolds the perfection of divine love as the mode of its manifestation. 'In this,' says the apostle, 'was manifested the love of God toward us, because that God sent his only begotten Son into the world, that we might live through him.' Doubtless, in other ways also the Lord unfolds his love to us; for his tender mercies are over all his works, and every divinely opened eye takes joyous note of them. Paul reminded the heathen men of Lycaonia of this when he said, 'Nevertheless God left not himself without witness, in that he did good, and gave us rain from heaven, and fruitful seasons, filling our hearts with food and gladness.'

With all this, however, there are often in providence so many things dark and perplexing that it is only dimly and imperfectly that we can see therein the love of God. But it is otherwise with redemption; for in it the manifestation of divine love is so clear, full, and undoubted, that it virtually unlocks every mystery, and sheds cheering light even on the very darkest of dispensations. Had God sent even one of the meanest of his servants to sympathise with us in our forlorn state, it would have been an act of great condescension; and still more, had he in addition commissioned the very chief of angels to minister partial relief in our need and extremity. But he went far beyond this; for it was his Son he sent—the Son only begotten and infinitely beloved—and at the very time of our deepest unworthiness. 'Is there love in nothing else?' says an old divine. 'Yes: to have a being among rational creatures is love; to have our life for years carried like a taper in the midst of winds and storms, and not be blown out, is love; but the love of loves is the gift of his Son for our redemption.'

When Jesus appeared among us, it was not simply to be a gospel herald bringing good tidings, but to be a Saviour and Substitute, expressly to bear our sins and make atonement for our guilt. For this end he not only gave his all, but gave himself, for it was as the God-man he hung upon the cross: he 'his own self bare our sins in his own body on the tree.' This was love indeed.

> Love strong as death; nay, stronger—
>   Love mightier than the grave,
> Broad as the earth, and longer
>   Than ocean's widest wave:
> This is the love that sought us,
> This is the love that bought us,—
> To gladdest day from saddest night,
> From deepest shame to glory bright.

God so loved the world that he gave his only begotten Son, that whosoever believeth in him should not perish, but have everlasting life.—JOHN 3:16.

Herein is love, not that we loved God, but that he loved us, and sent his Son to be the propitiation for our sins.—1 JOHN 4:10.

AUGUST 25

LOVE MASTERING FEAR, AND EXPELLING IT.

THERE is more than one kind of fear referred to in the word, and therefore we may be said to fear God and yet not be afraid of him. Indeed, the fear of God in the Bible sense is a main part of true religion, and includes in it regard and reverence for his name, and thorough loyalty to his authority and government. 'Holy fear,' said an old saint, 'is a searching of the camp that there be no enemy within our bosom to betray, and a seeing that all be fast and sure.' Now, perfect love never casts out this fear; it rather cherishes and strengthens it day by day.

But to be afraid of God is a very different thing. This arises from guilt, alienated feeling, and dark suspicions. Such fear hath torment, and never can there be rest or peace in the soul till it is cast out; and one thing only can do this, namely, the perfect love of God in Christ believed and realised.

The jailer of Philippi had this fear when he fell trembling at the feet of Paul and Silas, saying, 'Sirs, what must I do to be saved?' And what mastered this fear? Not any sense of his own worthiness or sufficiency, for he had none. That which cast it out was faith in the Lord Jesus; for the very moment he truly believed in him, fear went out of his soul, and peace and joy went into it. So was it also on the day of Pentecost, when awakened thousands, in fear and trembling, cried out with one accord, 'Men and brethren, what shall we do?' What calmed them? It was the joyful sound of redeeming love, and of full remission of sins through Jesus Christ. The moment they believed and realised the love, they lost the fear.

Obviously, then, the reason why many Christians have so much fear when they might have none, is that they look too much within at their own hearts, and too little without at the infinite love and finished work of Jesus Christ. 'Do not say thy wound is incurable,' said Andrew Gray, two hundred years ago; 'but comfort thyself with this, that there is balm in Gilead and a Physician there. Let thy case be never so broken, bring it to Christ, and he will heal it. Commit it to the Advocate that never lost a cause.'

Alike in the beginning, the middle, and the end of life, therefore, divine love must be our meditation and our delight. An old soldier of the 92nd, when dying, after signing to Major Malan to put his ear close to his lips, whispered, ''Tis naething, sir, but the love of Jesus can burst the gate of a sinner's heart.'

> There is no fear in love; but perfect love casteth out fear: because fear hath torment. He that feareth is not made perfect in love.—
> 1 JOHN 4:18.

> Ye have not received the spirit of bondage again to fear; but ye have received the Spirit of adoption, whereby we cry, Abba, Father.—
> ROM. 8:15.

AUGUST 26

PRECIOUS AS THE WORD IS, HOW FEW PROFIT BY IT!

THE very possession of the word of God involves a weighty responsibility; and just as we deal with it will it prove to us either a savour of life unto life, or a savour of death unto death. If it fails to make us better, it will assuredly leave us worse. When referring to this, James directs us 'to receive with meekness the engrafted word which is able to save your souls.' In like manner Peter says, 'As new born babes, desire the sincere milk of the word, that ye may grow thereby.' And John adds, 'Whoso keepeth his word, in him verily is the love of God perfected.' But read the word as often as we may, it will avail us nothing, unless we read it believingly; for it is written, 'The word preached did not profit them, not being mixed with faith in them that heard it.'

This unprofitable possession of the word was mournfully exemplified in the Jews at the time of our Lord. 'Believing the Bible,' says Adolph Saphir, 'and rejecting Jesus; glorying in the written word, and casting Jesus out of the beloved city; holding the Bible in one hand, and crucifying Jesus with the other. So the Bible now is to many among us, as it was to the Jews, not the voice of the living God, but *instead* of that voice; so that while they believe it contains the truth, they do not believe the truth it contains.'

The salutary operation of the Bible is confined to the believing soul. There only the incorruptible seed of the word takes root, and brings forth the peaceable fruits of righteousness. To profit thoroughly by it, therefore, we must receive it with reverence, deepest gratitude, and unreplying submission alike of the understanding and of the will. It is only as we so receive it that we will be able to stand in the evil day.

He who is convinced, not by divine testimony, but by mere human reasoning, may have his faith shaken by opposite artful reasoning, and may let it go entirely when the popular current fully sets in in a different direction; whereas he who embraces religion as the truth of God, and with love of that truth, will have a faith that, to his own salvation and the glory of God, will firmly and abidingly endure every trial. 'We are generally,' one says, 'desirous to have fair and well-printed Bibles, but the fairest and finest impression of the Bible is to have it well printed in the reader's heart.'

> When ye received the word of God which ye heard of us, ye received it not as the word of men, but as it is in truth, the word of God, which effectually worketh also in you that believe.—1 Thess. 2:13.
>
> Let the word of Christ dwell in you richly in all wisdom.—Col. 3:16.

August 27

WHATEVER THE CLOUDINGS NOW, THERE WILL BE LIGHT UNDIMMED HEREAFTER.

ON all vital matters, the views of unconverted men are often very dark. They misunderstand God's character, they misinterpret his ways, they misread his word, and the future is an impenetrable mystery to them. With the renewed it is otherwise; for the darkness of nature is past with them, and the true light now shineth.

Old Testament saints, it is true, saw but dimly; for they, so to speak, had only starlight to guide them,—the Sun of righteousness had not yet fully risen. They had beautiful types of the coming salvation, but not yet the visible fulfilment. When in the fulness of time, however, the Word was made flesh and dwelt among us, the day broke and the shadows flew away. The perception of this led old Simeon to say, 'Lord, now lettest thou thy servant depart in peace, according to thy word: for mine eyes have seen thy salvation, which thou hast prepared before the face of all people; a light to lighten the Gentiles, and the glory of thy people Israel.' And Peter could add, 'Ye are a chosen generation, a royal priesthood, an holy nation, a peculiar people; that ye should shew forth the praises of him who hath called you out of darkness into his marvellous light.'

With all this, however, even those who have most light now have frequently such cloudings in their experience, through manifold temptations that, compared with what is coming, their present state is still a dark one. It is only afterwards that they will be saints in light, absolutely and entirely, and have in fullest measure brightness without obscurity, holiness without defect, and happiness without alloy.

'This is the last July evening,' said one, 'I shall probably ever see; but be it so. If I never again welcome this smiling month, never again breathe this balmy air, nor view the radiance of these sunlit skies—I go to the unfailing Source of light, the lovelier scenes of paradise, the brighter glories of heaven; but more than all, I go to Jesus, and the very thought is more than enough to make all sadness fly away.'

> *Reveal thyself before my closing eyes;*
> *Shine through the gloom and point me to the skies:*
> *Heaven's morning breaks, and earth's vain shadows flee;*
> *In life, in death, O Lord abide with me!*

And the city had no need of the sun, neither of the moon, to shine in it: for the glory of God did lighten it, and the Lamb is the light thereof. And the nations of them which are saved shall walk in the light of it.—REV. 21:23, 24.

The Lord shall be thine everlasting light, and the days of thy mourning shall be ended.—Isa. 60:20.

AUGUST 28

THERE IS BUT ONE HIGH PRIEST, AND NO OTHER IS NEEDED.

IN Old Testament times there were not only many priests, but many offerings; and they were constantly repeated, because, being more typical than real, they had no inherent efficacy in taking away sin. But now it is otherwise; for it is the privilege of all true believers to have a great High Priest that is passed into the heavens—Jesus, the Son of God. A greater, indeed, there could not be; for in nature, character, sacrifice, and sympathy, he has pre-eminence over all.

When, eighteen centuries ago, he went to the altar, he laid but one sacrificial offering upon it; but it was an offering so marvellous and so divinely sufficient, that nothing had ever to be added. It was *himself* he presented; even as it is written: 'Who his own self bare our sins in his own body on the tree.' And he did so expressly that he might 'finish the transgression, make an end of sins, and bring in everlasting righteousness.' Or, as it is put elsewhere, 'Now once in the end of the world hath he appeared to put away sin by the sacrifice of himself.' And, as if to mark the completeness of the atonement then made, never since among the Jews has there been anywhere sacrifice or oblation.

Moreover, we have in our Lord Jesus Christ not only a complete but an abiding High Priest. All other priests, no matter what their character or the service rendered by them, died like other men, and were buried, and to this hour their dust mingles with kindred dust. But our High Priest, though he died and was buried, yet, ere three days had run their course, he came forth from the grave and ascended into heaven; and there, at the right hand of the Father, he ever liveth to make intercession for his people, and an intercession, moreover, that never fails in any case.

More cheering still: amid all his present glory he is never unmindful of his parting promise to come again. We know that when the high priest entered within the veil to present the blood and make intercession, he did not remain there, but, after a brief interval, came forth again to bless the people. So will it be with our great High Priest. Though now within the veil, he will in the fulness of time come forth again to bless his redeemed. Of all the hopes we are permitted to cherish, this may well be called the very brightest; for at that glad era exiles get home, the weary get rest, and the struggling get final and triumphant victory.

Remembering all this, it is not strange that St Bernard should have said, 'The name of Jesus, to a believer, is as honey in the mouth, music in the ear, and a jubilee in the heart.'

Holy brethren, partakers of the heavenly calling, consider the Apostle and High Priest of our profession, Christ Jesus.—HEB. 3:1.

We have not an high priest which cannot be touched with the feeling of our infirmities; but was in all points tempted like as we are, yet without sin. Let us therefore come boldly unto the throne of grace, that we may obtain mercy, and find grace to help in time of need.—HEB. 4:15, 16.

AUGUST 29

NONE ARE EXCLUDED FROM THE REFUGE WHO SEEK TO ENTER IN.

IN ancient times only some could enter a city of refuge and find safety. There were conditions of entrance; and one of them was, if not the absence of sin in the entrant, yet at least little sin, and a clear establishment of the fact that there was neither purpose nor malice in his manslaying, but accident only and lamented mistake. The kind of involuntary murder for which refuge was provided is thus detailed: 'Whoso killeth his neighbour ignorantly, whom he hated not in time past; as when a man goeth into the wood with his neighbour to hew wood, and his hand fetcheth a stroke with the axe to cut down the tree, and the head slippeth from the helve, and lighteth upon his neighbour, that he die; he shall flee unto one of those cities, and live.' All others were excluded, and especially those who smote their fellows in cherished enmity. Even if a deliberate murderer could pass through the gate into the city, it would be no defence to him. He could be followed and seized, and at once dragged out again and slain on the spot.

But, blessed be God, it is not so with the true Refuge, the Lord Jesus Christ. Before coming to him, and sheltering in him, we have not first to prove a comparative innocence on our part, or that our sins are venial only, and not mortal. On the contrary, let our sins be the worst and vilest that ever burdened this earth with their guilt, we have but to come as we are to the real Refuge, and mercy's gate will swing open to let us go in.

Some time ago, it is said, an Englishman visited some Italian brigands whom the law had laid hold of. In one room there were a hundred and twenty of them, nearly every man a murderer in purpose, at least, if not in act. Now, of old not one of these men could have got within a city of refuge, even though, Esau-like, he had carefully sought the privilege with tears. But with the great gospel Refuge it is wholly otherwise; for such is the grace of Christ and the infinite efficacy of his atoning blood, that not even the vilest of them would be rejected, if he came in faith, saying, with the publican, 'God be merciful to me a sinner.' Such chief of sinners, when made monuments of grace, will, on entering heaven, be the very chief of singers in praise of the Lamb that was slain.

Where sin abounded, grace did much more abound.—ROM. 5:20.

In whom we have redemption through his blood, the forgiveness of sins, according to the riches of his grace.—EPH. 1:7.

AUGUST 30

SHALL THE DEAD LIVE AGAIN?

WHEN the question is put, 'If a man die, shall he live again?' not a few in our times reply, 'No, never; death is a sleep from which there is no awaking, and every cherished hope of immortality is but a delusion—a dream. How can the mouldering dust of past generations,' they ask, 'ever again be refashioned and spring up living, thinking, rejoicing men?' It could not be, doubtless, if it depended on the creature; but is anything too hard for the Almighty Creator?

In so judging of possibilities, men err like the Sadducees of old, and for a like reason—'not knowing the Scriptures,' as our Lord tells us, 'nor the power of God.' When the grain is put into the earth it dies and rots, but from the decomposed kernel there spring up the blade, the ear, and the ripe and yellow corn, beautifying the field and filling the reaper's heart with joy. Why may it not be so also when the dead are laid in the grave? But in this matter we are not left to mere conjecture, or probability, or beautiful emblem; beyond all this we have the sure and unerring testimony of the word of God on which to rest our hopes. More cheering still, we have in addition the grand and undeniable fact of Christ, our resurrection. After his passion, he showed himself alive to his disciples by many infallible proofs—being seen of them forty days, in all variety of place and circumstance; for they sat with him, and walked with him, and conversed with him, and ate with him, and touched the very print of the nails. Ever after, accordingly, they bore clear, harmonious, and joyous testimony to Christ's resurrection, not as an opinion or conscientious belief firmly held by them, but as a fact which their own eyes had fully and unmistakably witnessed. And this they continued resolutely to do till their dying hour, in spite of all the obloquy and scourging it brought upon them.

We have thus the very amplest evidence to prove that the apostles were neither deceived nor deceivers when witnessing to the resurrection of our blessed Lord. Their testimony, therefore, is worthy of all acceptance, and may well be rejoiced in with joy unspeakable; for his resurrection is the grand earnest and pledge of the resurrection of all his people. When Henry Otto, one of the Bohemian martyrs, was condemned to die, he said, 'Kill my body, disperse my members whither you please, yet do I believe that my Saviour will gather them together again, so that with these eyes I shall see him, with these ears I shall hear him, with this tongue I shall praise him, and rejoice with this heart forever.'

Take comfort, then, bereaved saints. The loved ones in the Lord ye mourn are not lost, but only gone home a little earlier, nor is the time of separation from them long; they are in the happy harbour of God's saints, on the sweet and pleasant soil.

> *You laid them down to sleep,*
> *But not in hope forlorn;*
> *You laid them but to ripen there,*
> *Till the last glorious morn.*

Marvel not at this: for the hour is coming, in the which all that are in the graves shall hear his voice, and shall come forth; they that have done good, unto the resurrection of life; and they that have done evil, unto the resurrection of damnation.—JOHN 5:28, 29.

The dead in Christ shall rise first: then we which are alive and remain shall be caught up together with them in the clouds, to meet the Lord in the air: and so shall we ever be with the Lord. Wherefore comfort one another with these words.—1 THESS. 4:16-18.

AUGUST 31

HOWEVER SLOW IN COMING, DELIVERANCE WILL BE
MARVELLOUSLY COMPLETE WHEN IT COMES.

IN spite of diversity of sphere and social position, there is in the experience of all God's children in relation to their heavenly Father a remarkable similarity. Having manifold wants and trials, they all alike need his sympathy and aid. To this there is no exception. Saints that never have a sorrow nor shed a tear shall everywhere be found in heaven, but assuredly never are they seen anywhere on earth.

And as they all alike need his help, so they all alike seek it. There are no dumb children in God's family. Even the feeblest of them can say, 'Abba, Father,' and open their lips in prayer. In measure, too, all of them receive as well as ask—little at one time, it may be, more at another, but with overflowing fulness in the end. We have sweet and varied exemplification of this in the Psalms, and very specially and fully in the thirty-fourth. It is there written, 'I sought the Lord, and he heard me, and delivered me from all my fears'—'The righteous cry, and the Lord heareth, and delivereth them out of all their troubles'—'Many are the afflictions of the righteous, but the Lord delivereth him out of them all.' In the way of deliverance nothing could be more complete than this,—from all fears, from all troubles, and from all afflictions.

Meanwhile, it is true, the deliverance is only partial. Sunshine is soon followed by cloud, smiles by tears, the rest of today by the toil of tomorrow. Nevertheless, partial though it be, it is a sure earnest of the complete, joyous, and everlasting deliverance yet to be experienced by all the saints. But even here and now, to help them on their homeward way, the assurance is given, that as their day so shall their strength be. 'He,' says an old writer, 'that freely opens the upper, will never wholly close the nether springs. There shall be no silver lacking in Benjamin's sack when Joseph has it to throw in. When the best of Beings is adored, the best of blessings are enjoyed.' We may well then say, 'How excellent is thy lovingkindness, O God; therefore the children of men put their trust under the shadow of thy wings.' Would that all knew the excellency of this shelter and nestled beneath it.

> *When the clouds around thee gather,*
> *Doubt him not;*
> *Always hath the daylight broken;*
> *Always hath the comfort spoken;*

Better hath he been for years
Than thy fears.

And I was delivered out of the mouth of the lion. And the Lord shall deliver me from every evil work, and will preserve me unto his heavenly kingdom: to whom be glory for ever and ever. Amen.—2 TIM. 4:17, 18.

What persecutions I endured: but out of them all the Lord delivered me.—2 TIM. 3:11.

The Lord God is a sun and shield: the Lord will give grace and glory: no good thing will he withhold from them that walk uprightly.— PSA. 84:11.

SEPTEMBER I

NONE CAN OVERVALUE THE SON, BUT MANY UNDERVALUE THE SPIRIT.

MANY who would not say, like the men at Ephesus, 'We have not so much as heard whether there be any Holy Ghost,' yet greatly need to be taught that the Spirit is no mere principle, attribute, or influence, but a distinct Person of the blessed Trinity, and possessed to the full of every divine perfection. As the Father planned redemption, and the Son purchased it, so the Holy Spirit makes gracious application of it to the children of men; and all, therefore, that can be said of the love of Father and Son, can be said with equal truth of the love of the Spirit. It is free, infinite, everlasting. Indeed all believers, from personal experience, can testify that but for the teaching, guiding, upholding, and comforting of the Holy Spirit, they would never have known aright the way of life, or the power and preciousness of redeeming love.

We are dependent on the Spirit, not at the first only, but all through life. Even at a throne of grace there are seasons with us when we scarcely know how to pray, or what to pray for, and sometimes even lack the heart to pray at all; but in our time of need the Holy Spirit lovingly helps our infirmities, and maketh intercession for us with groanings that cannot be uttered. We may well, therefore, feel greatly encouraged in prayer; for while Christ intercedes on our behalf in heaven, the Spirit intercedes on earth. The one pleads without us, the other pleads within us, and both plead for us; nor is there anywhere a comforter like him in the tenderness of his helpful sympathy.

'It does seem a marvel,' says one, 'that the Holy Ghost should be a comforter. To teach, to preach, to command with authority,—how many are willing to do this, because it is honourable work! But to sit down and bear with the infirmities of the creature, to enter into all the stratagems of unbelief, to find the soul a way of peace in the midst of seas of trouble,—this is compassion like a God.'

Robert M'Cheyne tells us that when little Jamie Laing was nearing the valley of the shadow of death, he said—'God the Father made and preserves me; God the Son came into the world and died for me; God the Holy Spirit came into my heart and *made me love God* and *hate sin*.' Sweet testimony from the lips of a child!

> The God of hope fill you with all joy and peace in believing, that ye may abound in hope, through the power of the Holy Ghost.—Rom. 15:13.

> The love of God is shed abroad in our hearts by the Holy Ghost which is given unto us.—Rom. 5:5.

SEPTEMBER 2

TRUE RELIGION IS A CHOICE, NOT A CONSTRAINT.

WHEN speaking of Mary of Bethany, the Lord graciously said, 'Mary hath chosen the good part.' It was not forced upon her as a thing unwelcome and distasteful; or taken up merely by accident, without serious thought of any kind. On the contrary, out of the many things within her reach, she through the Spirit made free, deliberate, and hearty choice of the 'good part which shall not be taken away.'

It should be so with all. But with too many, alas! religion is more a thing of tradition than of conviction, of old custom than of felt life, of respect for ancestry than of reverence for God; and so it becomes easily shaken, especially in perilous and testing times. With others, again, religion is more real, for there is somewhat of conviction in it; nevertheless, it is essentially defective, because the thing that mainly operates with them is the constraint of fear, and not free choice and trustful love. Sooner or later, therefore, it begins to be a weariness to them; and then springs up the sore temptation to dispense with it altogether.

Even in the worst of times, however, there are always not a few noble exceptions to this: Ruths and Marys, Joshuas and Calebs, who not only make hearty choice of the good part, but resolutely adhere to it. It may be that the first thing that moves them to it is its indispensable necessity and divine fitness; but by-and-by, through fuller light and felt experience, it becomes a delight and joy to them—yea, dearer than life itself. And often, in looking back, that which seems the brightest spot in all their past experience is the time when first they closed with Christ, and were enabled to say, 'He is all my salvation and all my desire.'

> O happy day! that fixed my choice
> On thee, my Saviour and my God.

There must be no indecisiveness or halting where God and mammon are concerned, but immediate, resolute, and final choice. 'The world,' says an old divine, 'gives no certificate to saints, and saints give no certificate to the world. He that gets a certificate from both—Lord, what is he? a saint, or a worldling?'

> God crowneth no divided heart;
> Oh, hallow to him all thy life!
> Who loveth Jesus but in part,
> He works himself much pain and strife.

One thing have I desired of the Lord, that will I seek after; that I may dwell in the house of the Lord all the days of my life, to behold the beauty of the Lord, and to enquire in his temple.—PSA. 27:4.

Whom have I in heaven but thee? and there is none upon earth that I desire beside thee.—Psa. 73:25.

I count all things but loss for the excellency of the knowledge of Christ Jesus my Lord: for whom I have suffered the loss of all things, and do count them but dung, that I may win Christ.— Phil. 3:8.

September 3

THOSE WHO SEEM LIKELIEST TO COME FIRST TO CHRIST OFTEN NEVER COME AT ALL.

IN the parable of the Great Supper—designed to set forth the fulness of redemption and the generous freeness with which it is offered—those to whom the servant was first sent might have been thought the worthiest to get the invitation, and the likeliest to accept it. They were the respectable, the industrious, the well-to-do—men who had ground of their own, and oxen of their own. But not one of them would come. Though civil to the servant and respectful, yet with one consent they began to make excuse. Thus the likeliest to come first never came at all, and entirely missed the feast with all its joys.

Not succeeding in his first attempt, and with the first class, the servant had to go out a second time,—not an easy thing to do after such previous failure. Fishermen have little heart to cast in the net again, if all the night before has been one of weary and fruitless toil. So this servant, after such discouragements in the beginning, would have but little heart for renewed message-bearing, especially to another and seemingly outcast class, in the streets and lanes, the highways and hedges. Nevertheless, at his master's command, he went forth and did as he was enjoined, with cheering results.

Now, in like manner, Christ's servants still go forth with the invitations of grace, commissioned to tell that all things are ready; and in particular, that in and through Christ, forgiveness, acceptance, adoption, and peace, yea, and all redemption blessings, are provided in richest fulness, and yet without price. Nevertheless, how often is it that those who were expected to be the first to welcome this salvation are the very last to do so, if ever they do so at all! And why? Simply this: they are too busy with other pursuits; the farm and the family take up all their time and thoughts. In all such cases, 'I cannot come' is the alleged reason, but 'I will not come' is the real one; for when the heart is true the duties of the farm never interfere with the privileges of the feast, nor is it ever found that there is any necessary antagonism between family joys and the joy of the Lord.

A dying child, urging his father to repentance, said, 'Father, I am going to heaven; what shall I tell Jesus is the reason why you won't love him?' Such a question might well startle any rejecter or neglecter of the great salvation.

How shall we escape, if we neglect so great salvation?—HEB. 2:3.

And ye will not come to me, that ye might have life.—JOHN 5:40.

SEPTEMBER 4

FAITH, EVEN IN EVIL TIMES, CAN THINK BRIGHTLY AND SPEAK CHEERILY.

WHEN Joshua and Caleb testified to the goodness of the land, they did not conceal the difficulties and dangers in the way; but instead of hinting discouragement on this account, they boldly and unhesitatingly declared, 'Let us go up at once, and possess it; for we are well able to overcome it': 'God is with us, and who can stand against us?' This utterance was both manly and true, and being in thorough harmony alike with the command and the promise of God, should at once have inspirited the people and moved them forward.

Their companions in the search, however, were not so minded; for sense alone guided them, and not faith. 'We be not able,' they said, 'to go up against the people; for they are stronger than we. The sons of Anak are there, which come of the giants: and we were in our own sight as grasshoppers, and so we were in their sight.' Verily nothing makes such cowards of men as unbelief. 'The wicked flee when no man pursueth: but the righteous are bold as a lion.' By such an utterance these unfaithful men so discouraged the people that with one accord they cried out, 'Were it not better for us to return into Egypt?'

It is so, more or less, still; for in like circumstances history often strangely repeats itself. There are always some who, when difficulties arise, take dark and gloomy views of things, and speak discouraging words, thereby turning many aside from the heaven-ward way, or grievously hindering their progress. Like Timorous and Mistrust, in the 'Pilgrim's Progress,' they cry, 'The lions! the lions!' and never advert to the fact that the lions are chained. They always take the dreary side of the question, bringing up an ill report of the land.

But, blessed be God! if there are still old desponders like these, full of fears and doubtings, there are still also old Calebs, full of faith and love, who never fail to bring up a good report of the land and of the Lord of it; and right heartily they say, 'Come thou with us, and we will do thee good: for the Lord hath spoken good concerning Israel.'

> Come, brothers, let us onward,
> Night comes without delay,
> And in this howling desert
> It is not good to stay.
> Take courage and be strong,
> We are hasting on to heaven;
> Strength for warfare will be given,
> And glory won ere long.

God is our refuge and strength, a very present help in trouble. Therefore will not we fear, though the earth be removed, and though the mountains be carried into the midst of the sea.—PSA. 46:1, 2.

Though he slay me, yet will I trust in him.—JOB 13:15.

Rejoice not against me, O mine enemy: when I fall, I shall arise; when I sit in darkness, the Lord shall be a light unto me.—MICAH 7:8.

SEPTEMBER 5

*THERE CAN BE NO STEADY WALKING WITHOUT
DIVINE UPHOLDING.*

A S we begin the Christian life by coming to the Lord, so we
continue in it by abiding in him, and walking with loving
consistency in all his commandments.

The references in the word to such a walk are very frequent. It
is longed for: 'Oh that my people had hearkened unto me, and
Israel had walked in my ways.' It is commended: 'And they were
both righteous before God, walking in all the commandments and
ordinances of the Lord blameless.' It is delighted in: 'I have no
greater joy than to hear that my children walk in truth.' And it is
expressly enjoined: 'We beseech you, brethren, and exhort you by
the Lord Jesus, that as ye have received of us how ye ought to walk,
and to please God, so ye would abound more and more'—'See
then that ye walk circumspectly, not as fools, but as wise.'

Such a walk needs constant care and caution. Indeed, such is
the feebleness and inconstancy of our nature, and such the number
and subtilty of our spiritual enemies, that a walk like this, so holy
and blessed, is only possible by ever remembering our own weakness, and pleading for needed and promised strength. 'Let him,'
says the apostle, 'that thinketh he standeth take heed lest he fall.'

Had Peter remembered this better, he might have been spared
his sad stumbling and bitter weeping. With some, apparently,
there is so much of self-confidence, that it needs repeated falls
thoroughly to humble them and bring them to their right mind.
Only then are they heard to say, 'Hold up my goings in thy paths,
that my footsteps slip not,' and thereafter they are seen to walk
humbly and softly with their God.

There may be a wise love in occasionally permitting such things,
painful though they be in themselves. When her child is learning
to walk, a loving mother sees it is getting over-confident: it may
come to a dangerous place, and if possessed of all this confidence,

may fall and destroy itself. 'And so,' as one says, 'she permits it to fall at such a place, and in such a way, as that it may be wholesomely hurt, but not dangerously so. It has now lost its confidence, and clings all the more fondly and trustingly to the strong hand that is able to keep it from falling.' In a like way, and for a like end, the Lord still deals with his children when such dealing is needful.

Restore unto me the joy of thy salvation; and uphold me with thy free spirit.—Psa. 51:12.

Hold thou me up, and I shall be safe: and I will have respect unto thy statutes continually.—Psa. 119:117.

SEPTEMBER 6

STRANGE REQUESTS SOMETIMES COME FROM WICKED LIPS.

IN one of the parables of our Lord we find these words: 'I pray thee, father Abraham, that thou wouldest send Lazarus to my father's house: for I have five brethren; that he may testify unto them, lest they also come into this place of torment.' Apart altogether from the reply given, the very fact of such a prayer, in such a place, coming from the lips of such a castaway, is itself so great a mystery, that the question naturally arises, What could have prompted it? Was it compassion or unselfish regard for his brethren's good? It might have been so, if anything in the narrative had indicated that while yet on earth there had been any thoughtful and generous tendencies in him. Of this, however, there is no evidence. We are simply informed that he was a rich man, who fared sumptuously every day; and that from time to time a certain beggar was laid at his gate, full of sores, and desiring to be fed with the crumbs which fell from his table. In all likelihood, therefore, kindly as the request seemed, the real motive that prompted it may have been entirely a selfish one. Death does not obliterate the master passion in men. If hard and unfeeling before it, they will be hard and unfeeling after it. This man in his lifetime had probably done much both by word and example to corrupt his five brethren and confirm them in unbelief, and he might well fear that in coming thither they would load him with bitterest reproaches as the real author of their ruin. Companions in sin are never comforters in sorrow when the day of reckoning finally comes. In spite of the old adage, therefore, that 'misery loves company,' wicked tempters to evil would rather suffer in solitude than suffer with their victims.

As the joy of the righteous will be increased by every sinner whom they have helped to save, so in the end will the woe of the wicked be intensified by every sinner whom they have helped to ruin. Yet with what readiness is this evil work done by not a few. How often do they hint to their fellows that to get real freedom of thought and enjoy life to the full, they must discard all old beliefs and religious scruples, and eat, drink, and be merry. Should their counselling unhappily prevail with any, and issue in their ruin, the day is assuredly coming when those who gave it would fain, like the rich man in the parable, send a messenger to unsay what they had said, and unwrite what they had written, and undo what they had done.

It is said that, when dying, Thomas Paine, referring to one of his works, deeply deplored that ever he had published it, and advised those around him not to read it. His regrets, however, came all too late; for though the author died, his book lives on, misleading, corrupting, and ruining souls.

> Wisdom is better than weapons of war: but one sinner destroyeth much good.—ECCLES. 9:18.

> As a mad man who casteth firebrands, arrows, and death, so is the man that deceiveth his neighbour, and saith, Am not I in sport?—PROV. 26:18, 19.

> Be not deceived; God is not mocked: for whatsoever a man soweth, that shall he also reap.—GAL. 6:7.

September 7

*SALT MUST BE IN THE RIGHT PLACE, AND HAVE THE
TRUE SAVOUR.*

THE true salt of the earth are the believers who are in it; for they are the best preservatives of society, and its richest blessings. To be such, however, they must be in their right place. While not of the world, in spirit or aim, they must yet be in it, each following his appointed calling, and faithfully discharging every social duty, alike to those within the fold and those without.

In some of the early centuries, many thought that they could keep themselves spiritual only by keeping themselves wholly apart; and so they made the desert their home, and themselves useless. In our own time, there is with some a tendency to fall into the same error. Their thought seems to be that there is such corruption in the world, and such defectiveness in the church, that the only remedy is entire separation from all the usual fellowship of the Christian sanctuary. This, however, is neither more nor less than an utter misplacement of the salt, and a forbidden separation of it from the sphere of its holiest influence on the hearts and lives of men.

But, besides the right place, there must also be a maintaining of the holy savour. As there is so little true salt in the world, though it needs it so much, nothing should satisfy believers but grace in amplest fulness. When they walk worthy of their high vocation and of the name they bear, they not only preserve society, but also sweeten its breath and mellow its tone. Like Elisha at the well of Jericho, they cast healing salt into the world's bitter springs, and thereby not only make the poisoned healthful and the bitter sweet, but clothe the desert fields around with verdure and beauty. It was not without reason, therefore, that a noted Jewish writer once said, 'Let us pray that the righteous may remain with us for a preservative, as a pillar in the house, as the salt of the earth.'

Ye are the salt of the earth: but if the salt have lost his savour, wherewith shall it be salted? it is thenceforth good for nothing, but to
be cast out, and to be trodden under foot of men.—MATT. 5:13.

Let your speech be alway with grace, seasoned with salt, that ye may
know how ye ought to answer every man.—COL. 4:6.

Salt is good: but if the salt have lost his saltness, wherewith will ye
season it? Have salt in yourselves, and have peace one with another.
—MARK 9:50.

SEPTEMBER 8

THE VERY HOLINESS OF JESUS IS THE HOPE OF THE UNHOLY.

TYPICALLY and symbolically the priests of old were all holy.
The garments of the high priest were to be holy garments, the
crown to be worn a holy crown, the oil for anointing to be holy
oil, and all the service to which he was set apart was to be holy
service. But personally the priests were sinful even as others, and
consequently could do nothing for sinning men beyond typifying
the real redemption needed.

How different with the true High Priest! He was so unmistakably the Holy One that even devils knew the fact, and openly
acknowledged it: 'What have we to do with thee, thou Jesus of
Nazareth? I know thee who thou art, the Holy One of God.'
He was 'holy, harmless, and undefiled,' a Lamb without blemish
and without spot; and though daily going out and in among the
diseased and the dying, he ever remained the Undefiled One, and
could ask without fear, 'Which of you convinceth me of sin?' This
fact is largely dwelt on in the word, just because, had he not been
thus sinless, he could not have been the Sin-bearer, the sinner's
Substitute, the true Paschal Lamb; and so to this hour we would
have been still in our sins, without help or hope of any kind.

'No sunbeam,' says one, 'is more clear from darkness than Jesus
from sin's shade. If it could have been otherwise, how could he
have atoned for us? Sin's touch would have made him amenable to

justice. Death would have been due for his own faults. But now he gives his soul, his body, without one blemish,—a pure, fit, all-sufficient sacrifice, for all the sins of his most sinful flock.'—Thus the very holiness of Jesus is the hope of the unholy.

I lay my sins on Jesus,
The spotless Lamb of God;
He bears them all, and frees us
From sin's accursed load.

All thus saved through faith in Jesus should daily strive to be like him; all the more, as it is invariably the likest to the blessed Master who are the most used by him in all service, most filled by him with all peace, and the most ripe and meet for the glory to be revealed.

The next day John seeth Jesus coming unto him, and saith, Behold the Lamb of God, which taketh away the sin of the world.— JOHN 1:29.

He was manifested to take away our sins; and in him is no sin.— 1 JOHN 3:5.

Christ also hath once suffered for sins, the just for the unjust, that he might bring us to God.—1 PET. 3:18.

SEPTEMBER 9

THOSE WHO WASTE TIME FORGET ITS BREVITY AND HOW
MUCH DEPENDS ON IT.

IT is interesting to note how thoroughly the saints of old realised the brevity of their lifetime on earth: 'Behold, thou hast made my days as an handbreadth; and mine age is as nothing before thee: verily every man at his best state is altogether vanity'—'I am a stranger before thee, and a sojourner, as all our fathers were'—'My days are like a shadow, that declineth'—'My days are swifter than a weaver's shuttle,' yea, 'swifter than a post: they flee away, they see no good. They are passed away as the swift ships: as the eagle that hasteth to the prey.' So short indeed is even the longest life here, that when it is over it is 'like a tale that is told,' or 'like a dream of the night.'

Yet, with all its brevity, what is more precious? It is a God-given season for saving ends, the seed-time for eternity—yea, the only seed-time; for if this brief day of grace is finally wasted, there is no other to follow. We may lose money, yet find it again, and lose influence, yet by steady rectitude recover it again, and lose friendships, yet enjoy their sweetness again; but when time is lost, it is irrecoverable. All that can be done is to turn to good account any little remnant of it that may still be ours. What the Lord said of the loaves and fishes we should say of time: 'Gather up the fragments that remain, that nothing be lost'; all the more, as very much may depend on the right use even of a single day or an hour.

The dying thief on the cross had little more than one hour left him, yet how thoroughly did he turn it to saving account. In that fragment of time he not only found forgiveness through faith in the Saviour, but found also the way to paradise, and joyously entered in.

> 'Tis not for man to trifle. Life is brief,
>   And sin is here;
> Our age is but the falling of a leaf,
>   A dropping tear.
> We have no time to sport away the hours—
> All must be earnest in a world like ours.
>
> Not many lives, but only one have we—
>   One—only one;
> How sacred should that one life ever be—
>   That narrow span!
> Day after day, filled up with blessed toil;
> Hour after hour, still bringing in new spoil.

This I say, brethren, the time is short.—1 COR. 7:29.

What is your life? It is even a vapour, that appeareth for a little time, and then vanisheth away.—JAMES 4:14.

Boast not thyself of to morrow; for thou knowest not what a day may bring forth.—PROV. 27:1.

SEPTEMBER 10

THOUGH IT IS WELL TO PRAISE THE LORD EVEN WITHOUT
SONG, IT IS BETTER STILL TO PRAISE HIM WITH IT.

IT has in all time been the delight of good men to praise the Lord in joyous song. When in the full fervour of their souls they engage in this blessed exercise, they feel for the time lifted above the world, brought near to their Lord, and enjoy the very liveliest foretastes of heaven.

Should there ever be failure with us in this sacred duty, it cannot be from any lack of psalms and hymns and spiritual songs; for these have been accumulating from age to age, and they are not only sweet to the ear, but precious to the heart, because full of Christ and richest spiritual experience.

Nor are examples wanting. Our blessed Lord went not out to the Mount of Olives till he had sung an hymn. Paul and Silas, even in prison and at midnight, sang praises to the Lord. Job teaches the sorrowful inquirer, 'Where is God my Maker, who giveth songs in the night?' And James says, 'Is any merry? let him sing psalms.' 'Sense,' says one, 'sings only now and then, but faith is an eternal songster.'

All should try to engage in this duty, however feeble in voice or defective in skill. Doubtless it is easier for some than for others, but few need be altogether silent. Old Thomas Fuller, who was as noted for his quaintness as for the wisdom of his remarks, had a defective voice; but he did not refuse to praise on this account. 'Lord,' he said, 'my voice by nature is harsh and untunable, and it is vain to lavish any art to better it. Can my singing of psalms be pleasing to thine ears, which is unpleasant to my own? Yet, though I cannot chant with the nightingale, or chirp with the blackbird, I had rather chatter with the swallow than be altogether silent. Now what my music wants in sweetness, let it have in sense. Yea, Lord, create in me a new heart, therein to make melody, and I will be contented with my old voice, until in due time, being admitted into the choir of heaven, I shall have another voice more harmonious bestowed upon me.'

So let it be with us. Let us ever sing in the same spirit and in the same joy and hope.

> *Since better is thy love than life,*
> *My lips thee praise shall give.*

Whoso offereth praise glorifieth me.—Psa. 50:23.

O sing unto the Lord a new song; for he hath done marvellous things: his right hand, and his holy arm, hath gotten him the victory.—Psa. 98:1.

Speaking to yourselves in psalms and hymns and spiritual songs, singing and making melody in your heart to the Lord.—Eph. 5:19.

September 11

REJECTING THE WORD BEFORE READING IT.

THE Bible professes to have a divine Author, to set forth God's mind and will, to announce good tidings, to make known the only way of salvation, and to bring life and immortality to light; and in every age thousands of the greatest and best of men have openly acknowledged its claims, bowed to its authority, and rejoiced in its utterances. Moreover, it invites, yea, earnestly urges, the most thorough examination. It says, 'Search the scriptures'—'Prove all things,' and, 'Hold fast that which is good.'

Such being its character, and such, too, the scrutiny it demands, we might well be justified in expecting men would give it a fair and candid perusal. Nevertheless, it is a startling fact that of those who reject the Bible the vast majority have never *even once* read it through from beginning to end, nor any part of it otherwise than with hasty and thoughtless glance. It is not thus they deal with other books widely approved and professedly of value. They do not read a few pages here and there hurriedly one week, and afterwards at random a few pages more another week. On the contrary, with patience and care they read them through and through, and it may be again and again, before they venture to pronounce a final and authoritative judgment. If men would but so deal with the word of God, humbly praying at the same time for promised help and guidance, avowed unbelievers would be hard to find.

'I have spent most of my life,' said one, 'in reading and expounding the Bible, but every time I read it through it seems as if I had never seen it before; it is so new, so rich, so varied—the truth flashing from a thousand unexpected and undiscovered points above the brightness of the sun. If any one does not believe the Bible, he has never read it through; he may have read a little here and there, with general commentaries and criticisms between, but he has not read the whole. Once two men said, "We will disprove the conversion of Paul." They read it through, and wrote a book in proof of it.'

> *He alone who hath*
> *The Bible need not stray;*
> *But he who hath and will not give*
> *That light of life to all who live,*
> *Himself shall lose the way.*

Every word of God is pure: he is a shield unto them that put their trust in him.—PROV. 30:5.

The entrance of thy words giveth light; it giveth understanding unto the simple.—PSA. 119:130.

SEPTEMBER 12

THE TROUBLERS AND THE TROUBLED.

WHEREVER God has a people to serve him, there will always be some inclined and stirred up to trouble and afflict them; for it is plainly made known beforehand that 'all that will live godly in Christ Jesus shall suffer persecution.' It has been so in the past, and it will continue to be so till the kingdoms of this world have become the kingdoms of our Lord, and of his Christ.

Such times are both trying and perilous, for they sorely test faith as well as patience. This is especially the case when believers not only see truth and righteousness openly trodden underfoot, but evil men in full prosperity and ease. Instead, however, of allowing themselves to doubt a present providence on this account, they should only thereby be made the more fully assured of a future and righteous judgment. Accordingly, an old divine says: 'The saints' sufferings are an ocular demonstration of a future judgment, wherein all their wrongs shall be redressed, and all their labours of love recompensed. This held John's head above water, when else he had been overwhelmed with his flood of affliction.' In the end it shall go hard with the wicked; and as certainly in the end also it shall go infinitely well with the righteous. For their comfort it is expressly written, 'To you who are troubled *rest with us*, when the Lord Jesus shall be revealed from heaven with his mighty angels.'

The rest of Canaan was only a shadow of good things to come—a dim type of a grand reality. The real rest—sure, perfect, and abiding—is yet in the future, and will only be experienced in its fulness at the coming of the Lord. And when he comes it will be a rest shared in by all the redeemed, and be all the sweeter on that very account. They do not rest apart, but together. It is 'rest with us,' says the apostle.

'Christ and his cross,' said the saintly Rutherford, 'are not separable in this life; howbeit, Christ and his cross part at heaven's door, for there is no room for crosses in heaven. One tear, one sigh, one sad heart, one fear, one loss or thought of trouble cannot find lodgings there; they are but marks of our Lord down in this wide inn and stormy country on this side of death.'

Arise ye, and depart; for this is not your rest: because it is polluted.— MICAH 2:10.

Let us therefore fear, lest, a promise being left us of entering into his rest, any of you should seem to come short of it.—HEB 4:1.

SEPTEMBER 13

THE SAD ALIKENESS OF MEN.

IN the third chapter of the Epistle to the Romans it is the express design of the apostle to prove that not only the lawless Gentile, but the law-breaking Jew, is guilty before God. 'What then?' he asks; 'are we better than they? No, in no wise: for we have before proved both Jews and Gentiles, that they are all under sin.'—'There is *no difference*: for all have sinned, and come short of the glory of God.'

It is not said that all have equally transgressed, and are equally guilty. There are degrees in sin, and the Bible recognises the fact; for while it represents some as owing but fifty pence, it speaks of others as owing five hundred. And as there are degrees in the guilt, so in the end will there be degrees in the punishment. This fact, too, Scripture recognises; for it speaks of a beating with few stripes in the case of some, and a beating with many in that of others.

But whatever the difference in these respects, all are alike in this,—in being convicted offenders, proved violators of the divine law. From the absolute perfection of his nature, God could not give other than a perfect law. And so perfect is it, that, as one says, 'It stands on earth a pillar of light and glory, a specimen of God, to tell us that he himself is holy, just, and good. And nothing short of a complete fulfilment can meet its requirements; for thus it is written, "Whosoever shall keep the whole law, and yet offend in one point, he is guilty of all."' Obviously, therefore, any failure, great or small, in heart or life, involves us in guilt, and brings us under condemnation. And as, more or less, such failure is universal, salvation by the law is utterly impossible. But, through the riches of divine grace, what the law could not do, in that it was weak through the flesh, God has done by sending his own Son in the likeness of sinful flesh, and 'for sin condemned sin in the flesh, that the righteousness of the law might be fulfilled in us, who walk not after the flesh, but after the Spirit.'

Thy pains, not mine, O Christ,
Upon the shameless tree,
Have paid the law's full price,
And purchased peace for me.

Some time ago, a valued Christian friend was visiting a poor sickly widow woman. After conversing for a little she asked her if she had found salvation yet. 'No,' she replied; 'but *I am working hard for it.*' 'Ah, you will never get it in that way,' my friend said. 'Christ did all the working when he suffered and died for us, and made complete atonement for our sins. You must take salvation solely as a gift of free, unmerited grace, else you can never have it at all.' The poor woman was at first amazed beyond measure at this, and felt for the moment as if all hope had been taken from her; but very soon the enlightenment came, and she was enabled to rest joyously on Christ alone. When speaking afterwards of the friend who had been so helpful, she said, 'Oh how I will welcome her into heaven, for she guided me to the Saviour.'

God sent forth his Son, made of a woman, made under the law … that we might receive the adoption of sons.—GAL. 4:4, 5.

By him all that believe are justified from all things, from which ye could not be justified by the law of Moses.—ACTS 13:39.

SEPTEMBER 14

TRUE CLEANSING.

IT has often been said that the whitest thing in nature is snow just dropped from heaven. Yet there is one thing that can be made whiter still, as it were, and that is the sinner's heart washed in the blood of the Lamb; for the Psalmist says, 'Purge me with hyssop, and I shall be clean: wash me, and I shall be whiter than snow.' And it is not merely for one here or there it can do this, and in slow succession. No; it can do it for the many as well as for the few, and do it at once, as on the memorable day of Pentecost, when three thousand souls were savingly added to the Lord. Nor is its efficacy confined to one age or century. Bethesda healed and cleansed many in apostolic times; but it heals none now, and never will heal again. It is not so with the blood of the Lamb. Hence, when referring to it, John did not use the past tense and say, 'It cleansed'; for then the fear might arise that though it had efficacy at an early era, it might have no efficacy now. Neither did he use the future tense and say, 'It will cleanse'; for there might be the fear that the time for cleansing had not yet come. What the apostle says is, 'It cleanseth'; as if to intimate that it has continuous efficacy, to the very end of time.

> *Dear dying Lamb, thy precious blood*
> *Shall never lose its power,*
> *Till all the ransomed church of God*
> *Be saved, to sin no more.*

Verily, then, there is salvation for all who will but look where the dying thief looked, and trust as he trusted.

When Mr Balfour said to Brownlow North, 'I have often thought that the verse on which I would like to die is, "The blood of Jesus Christ his Son cleanseth us from all sin,"' he replied, 'That is the very verse on which I am now dying. One wants no more.' He then added, 'I have now peace—perfect peace.' Precious possession; may it be ours.

Unto him that loved us, and washed us from our sins in his own blood.—Rev. 1:5.

These are they which came out of great tribulation, and have washed their robes, and made them white in the blood of the Lamb.—Rev. 7:14.

September 15

WE SHOULD FEAR DISSENSIONS, AND TRY TO HEAL THEM.

THE strife that arose between the herdmen of Abram's cattle and the herdmen of Lot's was a grief of mind to the patriarch for two reasons; namely, the unsafety of it, on the one hand, for 'the Canaanite and the Perizzite dwelt then in the land'; and the unseemliness of it, on the other, from the closeness of the relationship between himself and Lot. This led him with gracious forbearance to say, and his words will ever be memorable, 'Let there be no strife, I pray thee, between me and thee, and between my herdmen and thy herdmen; for we be brethren. Is not the whole land before thee? separate thyself, I pray thee, from me: if thou wilt take the left hand, then I will go to the right; or if thou depart to the right hand, then I will go to the left.'

Even in apostolic times like differences arose where least we might have expected them. Paul and Barnabas, than whom two better and nobler men never existed, had yet on one occasion their hot contention. Euodias and Syntyche, too, were both excellent Christians, and eminently helpful to the apostles in the service of the Lord, yet, through some unhappy misunderstanding, their friendship for a time seems to have been cooled. We are not told what led to this. Probably, indeed, it may have been nothing more, as one suggests, than some little question about priority, or privilege, in carrying on the good work in which both were so heartily engaged; nevertheless it necessitated the apostle to say, 'I beseech Euodias, and beseech Syntyche, that they be of the same mind in the Lord.'

In all such cases, when opportunity is given, it is ever a blessed and Christ-like thing kindly and prudently to interpose our good offices, and pour oil on the troubled waters. There are always peace-disturbers enough, but peace-makers are often rare, and it should ever be our aim, therefore, to add to their number.

'In most quarrels,' says one, 'there is fault on both sides. A quarrel may be compared to a spark which cannot be produced without a flint as well as a steel; either of them may hammer on wood for ever, no fire will follow.'

Be of one mind, live in peace; and the God of love and peace shall be with you.—2 Cor. 13:11.

If it be possible, as much as lieth in you, live peaceably with all men.—Rom. 12:18.

September 16

WHEN WE STAND NEAR THE LORD, WE ARE BEST ABLE TO STAND FAST.

TO stand fast in the Lord, is neither to wander nor waver in our relationship to him; or, as one puts it, it is 'to love him without rival, and serve him without compromise.' Few may reach an attainment like this, but it is the duty of all resolutely to aim at it.

Stedfastness is constantly enjoined in the word: 'Stand fast in the faith, my dearly beloved'—'Stand fast in one spirit, with one mind striving together for the faith of the gospel'—'Stand fast in the liberty wherewith Christ hath made us free.' And, finally, 'Now we live, if ye stand fast in the Lord.'

So to stand fast in the Lord is no easy thing; nevertheless it is not impossible, as many in every age, through grace, have cheeringly evidenced. The time has been when both the many and the mighty have been against the saints, and they had to face both; yet, as this did not alter their duty, neither did it change their practice. Daniel stood fast in the Lord, though the lions' den was before him. Shadrach, Meshach, and Abednego stood fast, though the fiery furnace, seven times heated, awaited them. The Protestant Reformers stood fast, though priests and rulers alike poured forth their threatenings and thirsted for their blood.

Fidelity like this is difficult at any time, but never so much so as when desertion and failure begin to be witnessed on every side. Yet even in such circumstances faithful witnesses have not been wanting. Christopher Chober, when about to suffer, said to his fellow-martyrs, 'We are God's corn sown in the field of the church; and that we may be for our Master's use, we are now to suffer death. But be of good cheer, God is able to raise up a thousand worshippers of himself out of every drop of our blood; for though truth now suffers violence, yet Christ reigns, and no man shall cast him down from his throne.'

> Ye therefore, beloved, seeing ye know these things before, beware lest ye also, being led away with the error of the wicked, fall from your own stedfastness.—2 PET. 3:17.

> Little children, abide in him; that, when he shall appear, we may have confidence, and not be ashamed before him at his coming.—1 JOHN 2:28.

SEPTEMBER 17

WE MUST PUT ON CHARITY.

AS no grace of the Spirit is more highly commended than charity,—for it is expressly said, 'Now abideth faith, hope, charity, these three; but the greatest of these is charity,'—so no grace is more earnestly enjoined. 'Above all these things,' says the apostle, 'put on charity, which is the bond of perfectness.'

In so speaking, he, as it were, represents it as an outer robe to be thrown over the rest of the attire, and to be girded closely about us: and of all the adornments of Christian character, it is the fairest and most attractive; for 'it suffereth long, and is kind; it envieth not; it vaunteth not itself; is not easily provoked; thinketh no evil.'

But charity is not a garment only, but a girdle—'a bond of perfectness,' by which the other graces, as it were, are held together for gracious ends. Indeed, unless through the Spirit we possess this love in some fulness, we can neither rightly bear testimony to Christ as the Saviour, nor rightly evidence that we are his disciples.

'It is a great mistake,' said John Owen, 'to believe that grace subdues only our carnal corruption, and doth not change our natural temper. It does both: it makes the leopard to lie down with the kid, and the bear to eat straw with the ox, as it is promised; it makes the forward meek, the passionate patient, and the morose benignant and kind.' And then he added: 'I had rather a thousand times see a church filled with love, than filled with the best and highest and most glorious of gifts that any men in this world may be made partakers of.' Yes, it is even so; for a church full of love is a church full of beauty and full of strength, and God will do great things by it.

John Howe, when chaplain to Cromwell, had so much of this beautiful spirit, and was in those eventful times so helpful to men of all parties, that on one occasion the Protector said to him, 'Mr Howe, you have asked favours for everybody but yourself; pray, when does your turn come?' 'My turn, my Lord Protector,' he replied, 'is always come when I can serve another.'

> Seeing ye have purified your souls in obeying the truth through the Spirit unto unfeigned love of the brethren, see that ye love one another with a pure heart fervently.—1 PET. 1:22.

> Be kindly affectioned one to another with brotherly love.—ROM. 12:10.

SEPTEMBER 18

OUR LORD'S TIMELY CAUTION.

AFTER intimating that as iniquity abounded in the days of Noah, so will it be when the Son of man cometh, our Lord uttered these memorable words: 'Take heed to yourselves, lest at any time your hearts be overcharged with surfeiting, and *drunkenness*, and cares of this life, and so that day come upon you unawares.'

This timely 'Take heed' has not only saved many from over-engrossment with earthly things, but from the intemperance so prevalent in our time, and which so surely debases man's nature and excludes from the kingdom. Indeed, so thorough is the wreck it makes of character, affection, and means, that there is not a more wretched spectacle on earth than a drunkard's home. This sin is singularly deceitful in its working, and we cannot, therefore, be too prayerfully on our guard against it. It comes in with our joys, as if to increase them, and often wins in festive seasons its greatest triumphs. It comes in also with our griefs, as if to lessen them, but in reality it adds woe to woe.

Men sometimes speak lightly of this sin, but God puts it side by side with the vilest enormities: 'Envyings, murders, *drunkenness*, revellings, and such like; of the which I tell you before, as I have also told you in time past, that they which do such things shall not inherit the kingdom of God.'

Yet, vile as this sin is, and terrible in its grasp, and to be ever abhorred and shunned, even the righteous have at unguarded moments been temporarily mastered by it. 'Who would look,' says Bishop Hall, in his striking way, 'to have found righteous Noah, the father of the new world, lying drunken in his tent; that wine should overthrow him that was preserved from the waters; that he who could not be tainted with the sinful examples of the old world should begin the example of a new sin of his own? What are we men if we are but left to ourselves! While God upholds us, no temptation can move us; when he leaves us, no temptation is too weak to overthrow us.'

How forcibly does all this say, 'Be distrustful of yourselves!' The man who says most confidently, 'There is no fear of me,' is the very man who has most of all reason to fear. How impressively, too, does it say, 'Shun every usage that might prove a snare, and every companionship, however genial or gifted, that would tempt you aside!' In this matter no man is beyond peril of stumbling who stops at mere reformation. We are only safe when the Spirit of God is dwelling within us; for he alone can impart the divine grace without which we can do nothing; and therefore the apostle says, 'Be not drunk with wine, wherein is excess; but *be ye filled with the Spirit.*'

In the spring of the year 372 a young man, we are told, in the thirty-first year of his age, in evident distress of mind, entered his garden near Milan. The sins of his youth—a youth spent in sensuality and impiety—weighed heavily on his soul. Lying under a fig tree, moaning and pouring out abundant tears, he heard from a neighbouring house a young voice saying, and repeating in rapid succession, 'Take and read! take and read!' Receiving this as a divine admonition, he procured the roll of Paul's epistles. Describing the scene, he says: 'I opened it, and read in silence the chapter on which my eyes first lighted (it was the thirteenth of Romans): "Let us walk honestly, as in the day; not in rioting and drunkenness, not in chambering and wantonness, not in strife and envying. But put ye on the Lord Jesus Christ, and make no provision for the flesh, to fulfil the lusts thereof."' All was decided by a word. He did not desire to read any more; nor was there any need—every doubt had vanished, and the Day Star had risen in his heart. 'Jesus has conquered,' as one beautifully adds, 'and the grand career of Augustine, the holiest of the Fathers, then commenced. A passage of God's word kindled that glorious luminary which was to enlighten the church for ten centuries, and whose beams gladden her even in the present day.'

What grace did for Augustine, it can do for all who put themselves into Christ's hands, and let his word dwell richly in them in all wisdom.

> Walk in the Spirit, and ye shall not fulfil the lust of the flesh. And they that are Christ's have crucified the flesh, with the affections and lusts.—Gal. 5:16, 24.

> Wine is a mocker, strong drink is raging: and whosoever is deceived thereby is not wise.—Prov. 20:1.

> Wherefore let him that thinketh he standeth take heed lest he fall.—1 Cor. 10:12.

September 19

REAL CONTENTMENT IS RARE.

FEW men have had severer trials of faith and patience than Paul. He was in journeyings oft, in perils of waters, in perils of robbers, in perils of his own countrymen, in perils of the heathen, in perils in the city, in perils in the wilderness, in perils in the sea, in perils of false brethren; in weariness and painfulness and watchings often; in hunger and thirst and fastings often. Yet, in spite of every such varying experience, he could truthfully say, 'I have learned, in whatsoever state I am, therewith to be content.'

This contentment, on his part, did not spring from indifference or apathy, nor was it mere sullen submission to hard fate. He felt what want was, and felt it keenly, and when obtainable he gladly accepted relief. Nevertheless, in every condition, and whether relieved or straitened, he ever sweetly bowed to the will of God. Contentment like this is manifestly not a flower that grows in nature's garden, a thing born with us; nor is it one of the immediate results of imparted grace. Even Paul, after his conversion, did not at first possess it to the full. He had to learn it; and where? Not among the Jewish doctors, but at the feet of Jesus, and in the school of sore yet gracious discipline. Gold is not refined at once, neither are saints.

When at any time tempted to discontent, we should remember that, let our state be what it may, it is always better than we deserve. Being sinners, both by nature and by wicked works, we have so forfeited every claim to God's favour and lovingkindness, that it is purely of his rich mercies we are not consumed. Instead of ever opening our lips, therefore, in discontented murmurs, we should rather exclaim, with adoring wonder and gratitude, 'Who is a God like unto thee, that pardoneth iniquity and passeth by transgression?' 'I would give little for your piety,' said one, 'if you did not sometimes creep into a corner with the poor publican and say, "God be merciful to me a sinner."'

The grand and only remedy for discontent is a thorough acceptance of Christ, and keeping ever in remembrance that, whatever the wants and sorrows of earth, there are none in heaven.

> Godliness with contentment is great gain. And having food and raiment let us be therewith content.—1 Tim. 6:6, 8.

Let your conversation be without covetousness; and be content with such things as ye have: for he hath said, I will never leave thee, nor forsake thee.—HEB. 13:5.

SEPTEMBER 20

FORGIVENESS IS NEVER A SOLITARY GIFT.

INDISPENSABLE and precious as forgiveness is, it is yet but the first in order of gospel blessings, and never stands alone. Those privileged to get pardon, sooner or later get purity also; indeed, the sure possession of the one may be taken as a sweet earnest and pledge of the ultimate possession of the other,—yea, and of every other promised blessing. 'Such were some of you,' says the apostle; 'but ye are washed, but ye are sanctified, but ye are justified, in the name of the Lord Jesus and by the Spirit of our God.'

It is true that, even with believers, owing to the corruption still lingering within, the spiritual conflict is sometimes so severe as not only to evoke the cry, 'O wretched man that I am! who shall deliver me from the body of this death?' but almost, for the moment, to strip them of all hope. Becoming, however, humble in their weakness, and distrustful of self, and leaning anew and more simply on the Lord alone, they gather fresh strength for the struggle, and resolutely exclaim, 'Rejoice not against me, O mine enemy: when I fall, I shall arise; when I sit in darkness, the Lord shall be a light unto me.' Their course thereafter, through grace, is steadily onward, till at length, made fully meet for the inheritance of the saints in light, they joyously enter on its eternal possession.

Whatever the Lord does in forgiving and subduing sin, he does without constraint; for he delighteth in mercy, and it is his joy to dispense it. As the father in the parable *ran* to meet the returning prodigal, so the Lord, while slow to condemn, makes haste to forgive.

Some time ago, a devoted Christian worker in Edinburgh, finding a young woman—one of the fallen—in rapid decline, earnestly entreated her to go back to her home. 'No,' she said, 'I cannot; my parents would never receive me.' Her Christian friend knew what a mother's heart was, so she sat her down and wrote a letter to the mother, telling her that she had met her daughter, who was deeply grieved, and wanted to return. The next post brought an answer back, and money along with it for the journey, and on the envelope was written, *'Immediately! immediately!'* That was a mother's heart; she fully forgave, and desired the earliest possible return.

This is what the great and loving God is saying to every wandering sinner: 'Come immediately.' Yes, backsliders, you cannot come home too soon; for he will forgive you graciously and love you freely, and in heaven there will be joy unspeakable over your return.

The Lord is merciful and gracious, slow to anger, and plenteous in mercy.—Psa. 103:8.

There is forgiveness with thee, that thou mayest be feared. Let Israel hope in the Lord: for with the Lord there is mercy, and with him is plenteous redemption.—Psa. 130:4, 7.

SEPTEMBER 21

THE PROMISED PRESENCE OF THE GOD OF PEACE.

IN a troubled, weeping world like ours, where peace is one of the most needed of blessings, no title could well be sweeter than the one embodied in the brief but precious utterance, 'The God of peace shall be with you.' It is not, however, with every peace that God is associated. A truly pacified conscience is sometimes confounded with a merely stupified one, though the difference between them is marked and essential. The one is a peace of ignorance only, and not of knowledge; a peace without God, not with God; a peace so temporary and uncertain that every wind that blows ruffles it, and in the end it vanishes wholly, like a mist on the mountains: whereas the other, coming directly from God as the source, through Christ as the channel, is genuine and abiding. 'Let us ask this peace,' said Thomas Watson. 'The stars cannot make day without the sun; and in a deserted soul none can make day but the Sun of righteousness. The wilderness cannot water itself, but remains dry and parched till the clouds drop down moisture; so our hearts cannot have peace till the Lord in mercy impart it by his Holy Spirit.'

Happily, the Lord is never with his people as the God of peace without being with them also as the God of power, guiding and shielding in every danger. Moreover, what he is to the individual believer, he is ever at the same time to the church at large. This fact is peculiarly precious, especially in those times when great and good men are removed from the midst of us, and we instinctively say, 'Help, Lord, for the godly man ceaseth.'

'I am greatly saddened,' said Dr Robert Buchanan, in a letter to Mr Dickson, 'by our beloved friend Candlish's death. It gives me an increasing sense of loneliness. Our life-long friendship and close association, both in public and private, makes this event very trying. The world holds me, in consequence, by sensibly more slender ties. I spent nearly an hour at his bedside last week, and never shall I forget the inimitable tenderness of his affection as he held my hand in his and poured out his feelings. He was calm and peaceful, and trustful as regards his own great change, which was then drawing on, and spoke of it with perfect freedom. Alas, that we shall see him no more! Help, Lord.'

Yes, verily, he who is the God of peace, and comforteth us in all our tribulation, will help; for, come what may, and depart who may, he abidingly remains with his church and people.

> Be thy loved presence felt,
>   Blissful and near;
> By thine own Spirit's power
> Strength give in evil hour;
> When clouds of sorrow lower,
>   Comfort and cheer.

Lo, I am with you alway, even unto the end of the world. Amen.— Matt. 28:20.

At my first answer no man stood with me, but all men forsook me
... Notwithstanding the Lord stood with me, and strengthened
me.—2 Tim. 4:16, 17.

And the very God of peace sanctify you wholly.—1 Thess. 5:23.

September 22

*ESSENTIALS IN RELIGION ARE EVER FIRST WITH THE LORD,
AND SHOULD BE WITH US.*

CIRCUMCISION, in ancient times, had its own appointed place, and served important ends; but the moment men began to make an essential of it, especially after Christ's coming, the apostle gave stern resistance, that the truth of the gospel might continue among them: 'Behold I say unto you, that if ye be circumcised, Christ shall profit you nothing. For I testify again to every man that is circumcised, that he is a debtor to do the whole law. Christ is become of no effect unto you, whosoever of you are justified by the law; ye are fallen from grace.'

It is even so with baptism. As an ordinance it is most important, because expressly enjoined by our Lord and Master. 'Go ye therefore,' he said, 'and teach all nations, baptizing them in the name of the Father, and of the Son, and of the Holy Ghost'; and every true disciple, therefore, will give due heed to it. It would, however, be a fatal mistake to put it in the room of faith, or to make it indispensable to salvation. Ordinarily there should be both, yet not in the same rank and in the same order of necessity. The teaching and the believing are more fundamental things than the baptizing, else Paul would never have said, 'I thank God that I baptized none of you, but Crispus and Gaius. For Christ sent me not to baptize, but to preach the gospel.' There might be salvation without baptism, but not salvation without believing, among such as are capable of it.

'A man,' says Mr Moody, 'might be dead and buried without either having been baptized or taken the Lord's supper, and yet be saved. Did they want a proof? Look at the last man that Christ saved before he died on the cross. He had an idea that Christ just saved that man to establish this glorious truth. The man could not work for salvation; his hands and feet were nailed to the cross. He received it as a free gift. They could not nail his mind or his heart, and his heart laid hold on Christ, as he cried, "Lord, remember me when thou comest into thy kingdom." Did Christ say that when he was baptized he would save him? or that when he had taken the Lord's supper he would save him? There he was hanging between heaven and earth;—it was impossible. The gracious answer came at once; "This day shalt thou be with me in paradise." In the morning, a felon; in the evening, he was in the paradise of God with the Saviour. There was no baptism in the case, and no Lord's supper, and neither was necessary to salvation.'

Evidently, then, to the great question, 'What must I do to be saved?' the grand and only answer still is, 'Believe on the Lord Jesus Christ, and thou shalt be saved.' None who look to him in faith can miss salvation, and none who turn away from him can find it. Those so saved ever strive to keep all the enjoined ordinances of the Lord.

> In Christ Jesus neither circumcision availeth any thing, nor uncircumcision, but a new creature.—GAL. 6:15.

> For we are the circumcision, which worship God in the spirit, and rejoice in Christ Jesus, and have no confidence in the flesh.—PHIL. 3:3.

SEPTEMBER 23

MIGHTY AND WILLING TO SAVE.

HOWEVER willing to save their fellows, men entirely lack the power. This is true even of the most gifted and gracious among them. But what is too hard for them is never too hard for their loving Lord; for he has a name above very name, and, being invested with a power that knows no limits, he can save to the very uttermost. Even when on earth he gave full evidence of this; for though thousands on thousands applied to him in all variety of circumstances and need, yet at no time was any trustful applicant ever put to shame. Nor is it otherwise now. Men may have gone to the utmost distance from God in estrangement of soul, or have sunk so low as to come visibly the very vilest of the vile, yet even then he can rescue.

Perhaps there are no two men in all history whose conversion would have been pronounced beforehand more certainly impossible than Manasseh and Saul of Tarsus; for the one was a man of blood and crime, and multiplied abomination, and the other a daring blasphemer, who persecuted to the death the saints of God. Nevertheless, aggravated as their guilt was, both became blessed monuments of redeeming mercy and power. Verily we should be slow to lose hope even in the worst of cases.

Dr Krapf speaks of having on one occasion, when much cast down and wearied with the sottish blindness and dullness of the Wanica people, gone out by night and looked up to the starry heavens; and finding all his misgivings scattered by the flashing upon his mind of that text, 'Who is gone into heaven, and is on the right hand of God; angels, and authorities, and powers being made subject unto him'—'What!' he said to himself, 'is this true, and I in doubt of his power to touch the hearts of the poor Wanica? Was not my heart as blind and unimpressed as theirs? and cannot the same divine power which wrought the saving change in my heart convert them also?'

> Thou spakest in vision to thy holy one, and saidst, I have laid help upon one that is mighty.—Psa. 89:19.

> Who is this that cometh from Edom, with dyed garments from Bozrah? this that is glorious in his apparel, travelling in the greatness of his strength? I that speak in righteousness, mighty to save.—Isa. 63:1.

> Wherefore he is able also to save them to the uttermost that come unto God by him, seeing he ever liveth to make intercession for them.—Heb. 7:25.

SEPTEMBER 24

SUPPLIANTS ENCOURAGED.

IN many cases, even when the form of prayer is maintained, its spirit, life, and quickening energy are wholly wanting. One main reason for this is simply the lack of faith in its prevailing efficiency. To meet this unhappy state of mind, our Lord does not only say, 'Ask, and it shall be given; seek, and ye shall find; knock, and it shall be opened unto you'; but adds the further cheering word, 'If ye then, being evil, know how to give good gifts unto your children, how much more shall your heavenly Father give the Holy Spirit to them that ask him?' He appeals in these words to the fact that depraved as men's fallen nature is, the father spirit is yet strong within them. Indeed, very rarely, even in the vilest of our race, does love for their offspring completely die out; and in times of need their children instinctively rely on it. They feel sure, in making request, that they will not get a stone for bread, or for an egg a scorpion. Now if it is so even with sinful earthly parents, what may we not expect from our heavenly Father, if we only come to him in loving trustfulness; all the more as we are expressly told that he is not merely as willing as earthly parents, but infinitely more so, for thus runs the promise: '*How much more* shall your heavenly Father give the Holy Spirit to them that ask him?'

Whatever the defects in earthly parents, there are none in him. He is good, and only good; yea, so lovingly generous, that it is his very joy to be ever dispensing with large and ungrudging hand. But the grandest of all manifestations of his goodness is the gift of his only begotten Son for our redemption. After a gift like this, what may his trusting children not expect? Verily, 'He that spared not his own Son, but delivered him up for us all, how shall he not with him also freely give us all things?' Having so freely parted with the greater, how can he withhold the less?

What things soever ye desire, when ye pray, believe that ye receive them, and ye shall have them.—MARK 11:24.

If thou knewest the gift of God, and who it is that saith to thee, Give me to drink; thou wouldest have asked of him, and he would have given thee living water.—JOHN 4:10.

SEPTEMBER 25

A MYSTERY SOLVED.

WHEN the disciples, in trying to heal, fully realised their utter helplessness, doubtless they communed much, both with themselves and one another, regarding it. As no light, however, was thereby thrown on the mystery that perplexed them, what could they do but just turn to the blessed Master himself and say, 'Lord, why could not we cast him out?' It was well they did so—well for themselves, well for us, and well for the whole church of God in every age; for their question drew from the lips of Jesus one of the most precious of his manifold utterances. 'Ye could not,' he said, 'because of your unbelief; for verily I say unto you, If ye have faith as a grain of mustard seed, ye shall say unto this mountain, Remove hence to yonder place; and it shall remove; and nothing shall be impossible unto you. Howbeit this kind goeth not out but by prayer and fasting.'

Now, in connection with the disciples two things must be noted as accounting for the failure here related—the one a special sin to which they yielded, the other a special duty in which they came short.

The special sin was unbelief. Not that they had no faith, for, with the exception of Judas, they were all true and living believers, and knew savingly the grace of God; but though they had faith, unbelief so largely mingled with it that, instead of being able to move a mountain, they could scarcely lift a little stone from their path. In the very nature of things, where there is little faith there must be little power for any good work.

But besides coming short in faith, they came short also in prayer; for this is clearly implied in the added words of our Lord,

'Howbeit this kind goeth not forth but by prayer and fasting.' The word 'kind' here used may mean the entire species of evil spirits, or it may mean the special kind of evil spirit which infested this child. The latter is the more probable meaning, and we may safely conclude that our Lord designed to indicate that for the expulsion of this sort more than usual spiritual vigour was required.

Now, whatever may be the nature of the fasting here spoken of in connection with prayer, whether literal or spiritual, or partly both, the great general lesson to be drawn is, that when there is any special case of evil to be dealt with, any marked conversion to be sought, or any great and peculiar temptation to be resisted and overcome, then mere ordinary supplication will not suffice. The speciality in the case demands speciality in the watchfulness and prayer, and an abstaining from everything that might in any degree lessen the fervour of our desires or the firmness of our expectancy. One quaintly but truly says in connection with this: 'If you want to be a giant, keep your head out of the lap of indulgences, which would soon put a pair of shears through your locks.'

> Jesus said unto him, If thou canst believe, all things are possible to him that believeth. And straightway the father of the child cried out, and said with tears, Lord, I believe; help thou mine unbelief.—MARK 9:23, 24.

> And Jehoshaphat feared, and set himself to seek the Lord, and proclaimed a fast throughout all Judah.—2 CHRON. 20:3.

SEPTEMBER 26

THE TRUE SWEETENER OF EVERY BITTER.

WHEN of old the people found that the waters of Marah were bitter, their murmurings became more bitter still, and with wrathful impatience they said to Moses, 'What shall we drink?' He at once cried unto the Lord; and the Lord showed him a tree which, when cast into the waters, at once sweetened them.

Judging by the mere seeming fitness of things, and apart from the divine power accompanying it, there was nothing less likely to accomplish the end designed than so strange an instrumentality. Some travellers, it is true, have tried hard to find out in the desert some tree or shrub possessing the natural quality of healing such unwholesome waters, but every such effort has been vain. 'As well,' says one, 'might they have looked near Jericho for the kind of salt with which Elisha healed the waters of the fountain there. No, the tree never existed the mere immersion of whose branches could naturally correct the bad qualities of water needed by so mighty a host.' Verily, if God had not spoken, Moses might have cut down every tree in the wilderness and have cast them into the waters, but they would have remained bitter still. It was not in the tree the virtue lay, but in the word, power, and blessing of the Lord.

Now, what God, in an answer to prayer, did for Moses and Israel, he is still able and willing to do for us. He has many ways of sweetening Marahs into Elims; indeed, even when our cup is bitterest, and we are sorely tempted to dash it to the ground in rebelliousness of spirit, he has but in the riches of his grace to cast in some sweet word of promise and it is bitter no more.

There may be nothing directly typical in this tree of Moses, but yet we can scarcely fail to be reminded by it of the words of Peter: 'He who his own self bare our sins in his own body on the tree'; for that tree, the cross of Christ, is the only effectual healer of all the bitter waters and woes of fallen humanity.

'The Jews have a tradition,' says Matthew Henry, 'that this tree of Moses was itself bitter, yet it sweetened the waters of Marah; so the bitterness of Christ's suffering alters the properties of ours. Whoever, therefore, would have his bitter sweetened must come to Christ and look steadily to the cross.'

> For the preaching of the cross is to them that perish foolishness; but unto us which are saved it is the power of God.—1 COR. 1:18.
>
> The full soul loatheth an honeycomb; but to the hungry soul every bitter thing is sweet.—PROV. 27:7.

For I reckon that the sufferings of this present time are not worthy
to be compared with the glory which shall be revealed in us.—
ROM. 8:18.

SEPTEMBER 27

RESURRECTION AND LIGHT.

WHILE the apostle never failed to give peculiar prominence
to the atoning death of Christ, he yet never failed to testify
in addition to the grand and all-important fact of his resurrection.
In our times, however, some, in their tenderness to unbelief and in
deference to it, would fain make even the resurrection of Christ an
open question among Christian men. If men believe it, it is well;
if they believe it not, it is also well;—thereby clearly implying that
whether it is fact or fiction matters very little. But is it really so?
No, verily; for if there is no resurrection there is no redemption, no
atonement, and no hope. 'If Christ be not risen,' says the apostle,
'then is our preaching vain, and your faith is also vain. Yea, and we
are found false witnesses of God; because we have testified of God
that he raised up Christ: whom he raised not up, if so be that the
dead rise not. For if the dead rise not, then is not Christ raised: and
if Christ be not raised, your faith is vain; ye are yet in your sins.'
Everything, therefore, depends on the resurrection of Christ; and,
blessed be his name, this is not only emphatically declared, but
the testimony borne to it by witnesses who could not be deceived
themselves, and could have no motive for deceiving others, was so
ample, consistent, and continuously resolute, even unto death, as
to make Christ's resurrection the most assured and reliable of all
facts.

But besides, when our Lord, through his resurrection, becomes
the life of his people, he also, the apostle tells us, becomes their
light. Wherever there is sin there is darkness; and the more intense
the one, the more intense and dismal is the other; and but for
Christ this darkness in our fallen world would have been hopelessly

perpetuated. His coming in the fulness of time, however, changed all this; for it revealed the Father, and the riches of grace, and the way of salvation, and brought life and immortality to light: and bright as this light is now, it will be brighter far one day.

Judging by the fact that the creatures brought up from the greatest depths below the surface of the sea are singularly phosphorescent, it has been thought by some that, instead of the unfathomed caves of ocean being black with outer darkness, they are ablaze with golden splendour. This thought is full of interest; but however it may be with the hidden depths of ocean, we know assuredly that, when the fulness of time has come, it will be absolutely true of the hidden depths of providence and grace. Perhaps, indeed, the very darkest and saddest of our experiences meanwhile, may yet in their ultimate issues be found to be the brightest and most blessed of them all.

> Jesus said unto her, I am the resurrection, and the life: he that believeth in me, though he were dead, yet shall he live.—John 11:25.

> In him was life; and the life was the light of men.—John 1:4.

September 28

THE HIGHEST CITIZENSHIP.

THOUGH an alien and a citizen may be found dwelling for a time within the same walls, the difference between them is great; for it is the latter only who enjoys the full freedom of the city, and all the rights and privileges connected with it.

Now, so far as this world in its worldliness is concerned, true believers have no proper citizenship at all. They are in the world, but not of it; and so vital is this distinction that it never goes well with them when practically they lose sight of it. It is thus their Lord speaks of them: 'I have given them thy word; and the world hath hated them, because they are not of the world, even as I am not of the world. I pray not that thou shouldest take them out of the world, but that thou shouldest keep them from the evil.'

But though believers have no citizenship here, like those who live for the world only, blessed be the Lord, they have it elsewhere. 'Our conversation,' says the apostle (or, as the word should rather be rendered, 'our citizenship'), 'is in heaven.' Yes, their names are inscribed in heaven, in the roll of its citizens, and in the Lamb's book of life, by the Lord himself; and once there, they are there forever. There may be erasures from other records, but never can there be any from those he keeps.

Moreover, the authority they own is in heaven. Meanwhile it is the usurper that gets most and heartiest homage in this fallen and disloyal world; but never does he get it from the genuine saints of the Lord. Their daily prayer, on the contrary, is, '*Thy* kingdom come, *thy* will be done in earth, as it is done in heaven'; and never is their joy so great as when he alone is not only ruling over them, but reigning within them.

Besides, their warmest affections are in heaven. All that they most prize is there;—their home, their inheritance, their eternal rest; above all, their God and Father, and the Lord Jesus, their adorable Redeemer.

'It is,' said Merle d'Aubigné, 'the great misfortune of man that he cannot separate himself from this world and become a citizen of the world to come. The cross performs this miracle: it crucifies him to the world, and crucifies the world to him.'

> Now they desire a better country, that is, an heavenly: wherefore God is not ashamed to be called their God: for he hath prepared for them a city.—HEB. 11:16.

> Ye are come unto mount Sion, and unto the city of the living God, the heavenly Jerusalem, and to an innumerable company of angels, to the general assembly and church of the firstborn, which are written in heaven.—HEB. 12:22, 23.

September 29

THERE IS NO GRATITUDE LIKE THAT WHICH IS
HEAVEN-KINDLED.

WITH the great apostle of the Gentiles, gratitude was not a mere feeling or sentiment, but a moral obligation—a binding duty, from which he could not possibly get free, and would not if he could. 'We are *bound*,' he said, 'to thank God always for you, brethren, as it is meet, because that your faith groweth exceedingly, and the charity of every one of you all toward each other aboundeth.' It is in this light that all divinely-taught and experienced Christians look upon the grace of gratitude. It is at once a duty and a privilege in their eyes; for they are daily recipients of God's bounty, and entirely dependent on him for all they possess.

Moreover, however much they may be bound to God in requirement, he is in no degree bound to them in benefaction. Whatever rights they might have had as creatures pure and unfallen, assuredly they have none whatever now. Indeed, not a crumb from his table or one drop from his spring can they claim as a right; and far less the gifts and benefits innumerable so freely conferred on them. The knowledge of this intensifies their gratitude, and often fills them with wonder at the marvellous grace of the Lord. If others murmuringly say, 'So little is not worthy of thanks,' they rather say, 'So much is beyond all praise.' They become like the poor but Christian cottager of whom we read. She was but meanly lodged, and on her hard and scanty board nothing was visible save a crust of bread and a little water. Yet never was king at royal feast more grateful than she; for with wondering eye and uplifted hand she said, 'Have I all this, and Christ too?' So should it ever be. Gratitude should be no mere fitful thing with us, but rather the constant and all-prevailing feeling of our heart.

If there are times when we can see nothing bright in our own experience, let us note, like Paul, whatever is bright and blessed in the experience of others, and give our hearty thanksgiving on account of it. 'This of itself,' as one says, 'would often brighten the dark shadows that occasionally fall upon our path, and help them the sooner to flit one by one away.'

> O give thanks unto the Lord; call upon his name: make known his deeds among the people.—PSA. 105:1.

> In every thing give thanks: for this is the will of God in Christ Jesus concerning you.—1 THESS. 5:18.

SEPTEMBER 30

AFTER THE PARTINGS WILL COME MEETINGS AGAIN.

IN this vale of tears, through the blighting influence of sin, there is meanwhile such a ceaseless emptying of houses and filling of graves that a day never comes in which there are not sad partings somewhere. True, there are favoured homes that remain longer without them than others; but sooner or later they too become darkened by grief. This has been the case in all generations; and there is scarcely a page of history that does not record such sorrowful scenes. Scripture affords manifold illustrations of this. We see it at Jerusalem, when 'devout men carried Stephen to his burial, and made great lamentation over him'; we see it, too, at Nain, when a dead man laid on his bier was carried out—the only son of his mother, and she was a widow; and we see it yet again at Bethany, when, amid the manifold tears of sisters and friends, an only and beloved brother was committed to the tomb. We may truly, then, say,—

> *Brethren, arise,*
> *Let us go hence!*
> *Death and the grave are here—*
> *The sick-bed and the bier!*
> *The children of the tomb*
> *May love this kindred gloom;*
> *But we, the deathless band,*
> *Must seek the deathless land:*

> *The mortal here may rove—*
> *The immortal dwell above.*
> *Here we can only die:*
> *Let us ascend on high!*

A few years ago an aged mother—well known to me—who had lost many children, said to her dying son, 'O Andrew, how can I live without you?' 'Be of good comfort, mother,' he replied; 'you will not be long behind. And what a meeting we will have then!'

Without such reunions the divine purpose would lack fulfilment, redemption would prove a failure, and our every bright hope for the future be eternally quenched. But why speak we thus, when the regathering in heaven is a very certainty of certainties, resting on facts the most assured and on promises that cannot fail?

The saintly Alfred Cookman, on the death of his brother George, when referring to the certainty of such reunion, said: 'Blessed be God, our life has a future as well as a past. We knelt at the same mother's knee; and we shall kneel with that same mother and our glorified father in the presence of the enthroned Jesus. We sported on the same lawn; ay, and we shall, in our immortal youth, roam together the

> *Blest fields on the banks of life's river,*
> *And sing of redemption forever and ever.*

Our present separation is only a parenthesis in our fraternal intercourse.' Yes! thanks be to God, though the partings are sad now, yet nothing is surer than the sweet meetings again.

And if I go and prepare a place for you, I will come again, and receive you unto myself; that where I am, there ye may be also.—JOHN 14:3.

Then we which are alive and remain shall be caught up together with them in the clouds, to meet the Lord in the air: and so shall we ever be with the Lord. Wherefore comfort one another with these words.—1 THESS. 4:17, 18.

October 1

WHAT WE CAN WORK OUT, AND WHAT WE CANNOT.

FEW words have been more misunderstood and misapplied than those of the apostle, 'Work out your own salvation with fear and trembling.' Taken by themselves and apart from the context, they would seem strangely legal and self-righteous in their aspect, and the inference might readily be drawn that, after all, it is not through believing but through working we can gain acceptance with the Lord. Rightly interpreted, however, they have no such meaning, but are in entire harmony with his uniform teaching, that 'Not by works of righteousness which we have done, but according to his mercy he saved us, by the washing of regeneration, and renewing of the Holy Ghost.' We can readily do much to secure death, but never by any amount of working can we possibly secure its opposite; for life eternal is a pure unmerited gift of God through Jesus Christ.

Many entirely overlook the fact that the apostle's words were addressed not to unsaved men who stood in need of forgiving mercy, but to believers—men already in Christ, forgiven and saved, whose special need was fuller sanctifying grace. Accordingly, what they were urged to do was not to labour *for* acceptance, but to labour *from* it and to make it their starting point in pressing on to higher attainments in the divine life. Evidently, therefore, the term 'salvation' in this passage refers rather to the development of salvation than to its first reception. So far as the unsaved are concerned, their first and grand duty is not to work but to believe, and to take the Lord at his word when he says, 'Him that cometh to me I will in no wise cast out.'

A few years ago, at the close of one of the free breakfasts for the poor in Edinburgh, a man was observed pacing slowly up and down, his face indicating that he was uneasy and anxious. A Christian lady went up to him and asked if he was a Christian. 'No,' he said; 'but I am going to be, though not yet, for I am not just ready.' 'But now is the accepted time,' she replied; 'and the very first thing you are asked to do is to receive Christ.' 'Don't tell me,' he said, 'that I can be saved without doing anything.' As he was saying this, a little boy, of about eleven years of age who had been looking out a passage in his Bible, touched the lady, and, holding the Bible open, said, 'Please read that to him.' It was Romans 4:5: 'But to him that worketh not, but believeth on him that justifieth the ungodly, his faith is counted for righteousness.' The lady read it. The man listened most attentively, and after a little exclaimed, 'It's a fact! God says it "*to him that worketh not*."' The word to all appearance entered his soul with saving power, and then in the warmth of his gratitude, grasping the lady's hand, he said, 'I'll thank you all the days of my life!'

> What shall we do, that we might work the works of God? Jesus answered and said unto them, This is the work of God, that ye believe on him whom he hath sent.—JOHN 6:28, 29.

> Let us cleanse ourselves from all filthiness of the flesh and spirit, perfecting holiness in the fear of God.—2 COR. 7:1.

OCTOBER 2

GREAT INIQUITY NEEDS A GREAT FORGIVENESS, AND GOD GIVES IT.

WHEN, long centuries ago, these awful words were heard in the streets of Nineveh, 'Yet forty days, and Nineveh shall be overthrown,' there was not only dismay on every side, but the people, believing the warning, proclaimed a fast, and put on sackcloth, from the greatest of them even to the least, and began to cry mightily unto God. As to the result, however, the utmost they could venture to say was, 'Who can tell if God will turn and repent, and turn away from his fierce anger, that we perish not?'

How widely different is our case. We have certainty where they had but conjecture; and therefore, while they could only cry, '*Who can tell?*' we can unhesitatingly declare 'that there is forgiveness with God, that he may be feared.'

This forgiveness is the grand blessing of the gospel, and is attainable only through the precious blood of God's dear Son. The death of Christ was not a mere example of patient suffering, but a true expiation, and apart from it never could a holy God clear and justify a guilty sinner. He might without it be just, and let the sinner perish, or, on the other hand, be merciful, and let truth and righteousness be darkened; but he could not be both. Happily, however, in Christ he can be at once a just God and a Saviour; and so ample is his forgiving mercy, that there is absolutely nothing between the sinner and immediate salvation but unbelief.

'As every sin,' says Caryl, 'has the more need of pardon by how much the greater it is, so God will have the more glory in pardoning by how much the greater it is.' And he adds, 'Mercy covereth those iniquities which we confess, and those which we conceal shall be discovered by justice.'

> For thy name's sake, O Lord, pardon mine iniquity; for it is great.— Psa. 25:11.

> In whom we have redemption through his blood, the forgiveness of sins, according to the riches of his grace.—Eph. 1:7.

> The blood of Jesus Christ his Son cleanseth us from all sin.—1 John 1:7.

October 3

IT IS POOR HEARING THAT IS NOT FOLLOWED BY HEARTY DOING.

THE man who published so zealously in Decapolis how great things Jesus had done for him, was no mere hearer of the word, but a doer as well; and what he did was so evidently done with his whole heart that all men did marvel.

When Christ is revealed to us, we should immediately seek to reveal him to others. Indeed, a holy evangelistic activity is the only thing that will keep our own religion healthful. While the stream keeps running, it keeps pure; but let it cease to flow, and it will speedily become stagnant, and breed corruption and death.

In the fulfilment of this duty there must be no loitering, for many whose claims were pressing have already gone where our voice cannot reach them, nor our prayers profit; and at no distant day we too must pass hence, and therefore the urgently-needed work now left undone by us may never be done at all. 'Are there not some of you,' one asks, 'who can enjoy being a Christian while your dearest friend is not? What were you hired for, if it was not to work; what were you saved for, if it was not to spread salvation?'

On one occasion, when Mr Spurgeon was urging the same duty, he was led to say from the pulpit that perhaps there was a mother present who had been intending to speak to her daughter Jane about her soul, but she had not done so; and then entreated her, the moment she reached home, to put her arms around her child's neck, and invite her to come to Christ. A few days after, he received a letter from a woman who had been present, saying that he had exactly described her case. She had a daughter named Jane; she had intended to speak to her, but had not done so. 'But I went home,' she said, 'after hearing you, put my arms round her neck, and entreated her to come to Jesus. She did so; is now, I trust, converted; and is coming to speak with you about joining the church.' 'God knows,' Mr Spurgeon added, 'the names of your daughters, and can tell his ministers their names also.'

> But be ye doers of the word, and not hearers only, deceiving your own selves.—JAMES 1:22.
>
> If ye know these things, happy are ye if ye do them.—JOHN 13:17.
>
> Not every one that saith unto me, Lord, Lord, shall enter into the kingdom of heaven; but he that doeth the will of my Father which is in heaven.—MATT. 7:21.

October 4

THERE IS NO TRAINING LIKE BIBLE TRAINING.

MUCH may be learned from what Moses said to Israel in the name of the Lord: 'Hear, O Israel, the statutes and judgments which I speak in your ears this day, that ye may learn them, and keep, and do them'; and, 'These words, which I command thee this day, shall be in thine heart: and thou shalt teach them diligently unto thy children.' It is Bible training that is here enjoined; and no training is like it, because it comes with all the weight of divine authority—'Thou shalt teach the words which I command thee.'

This of itself is an all-important element, especially for practical purposes. Even when instruction is seemingly wise and excellent, and in every way appropriate, it may yet be utterly impotent for good simply from lack of authority. It is only man dealing with man; and considering the moral obstacles to be overcome, this is never of itself enough. Nothing has the power or majesty of a 'Thus saith the Lord'; and when prayerfully used in faith, it imparts to parental counsellings a marvellous efficacy.

Moreover, all Bible training is linked with promised blessing; for it is written, 'Train up a child in the way he should go, and when he is old, he will not depart from it.' 'Two ways lie before every child—the way in which he *would* go, headlong to ruin, and the way in which he *should* go, the pathway to heaven.' Now, in endeavouring to train up children in the latter way, and as God directs, this promise gives great encouragement. Even the child of many prayers, it is true, and of many efforts, may for long bitterly disappoint the fondest hopes by the grievousness of his departure from the right way; yet if faith hold out, whatever he may do in the beginning, sooner or later, through grace, smothered convictions will revive, and, like the prodigal of old, he will return penitent and loving to his Father's house. Let Christian parents, even in darkest hours, only believe like Abraham, and hope against hope, and they shall never be put to shame.

The promise is unto you, and to your children, and to all that are afar off, even as many as the Lord our God shall call.—Acts 2:39.

Fear not, O Jacob, my servant; and thou, Jesurun, whom I have chosen. For I will pour water upon him that is thirsty, and floods upon the dry ground: I will pour my spirit upon thy seed, and my blessing upon thine offspring.—Isa. 44:2, 3.

OCTOBER 5

IT NEEDS BOTH CARE AND PRAYER TO KEEP HOPE BRIGHT.

WHEN seeking to make their election sure to a seat in Parliament, what amazing energy men display; yet what is any seat there, which may be gained one year and lost the next, compared with a place forever among the redeemed in the City of the Great King? To obtain an assured hope of this, and preserve it in its brightness, is worthy of any effort.

As little foxes can spoil the vines, so even little sins of heart or life deliberately cherished can grieve away the Spirit and cloud our hopes; nor will light and comfort be again restored till the idols that offended have been utterly cast out.

Colour of skin, we are told, corresponds very closely in intensity to latitude, elevation, and the nature of the soil. Accordingly it is mentioned as a striking fact that among the tribes inhabiting the southern slopes of the Himalaya there is little colour on the hill-tops, more on the hill-sides, but most of all in the swampy bottoms and low jungles. Now, so is it with doubtings and fears: they are rare high up on the hills of holiness, but greatly abound in the low swamps of worldliness and unbelief. The more watchful and spiritual we are, therefore, the brighter does our hope become.

This is often made sweetly manifest in the closing hours of believers. The veil is lifted then, the glory is revealed, and they are heard to say, as did that martyr of blessed memory, Hugh McKail, when on the scaffold in Edinburgh: 'Farewell the world and all its delights! Welcome God and Father; welcome sweet Lord Jesus; welcome Spirit of all grace; welcome glory; welcome eternal life!'

> Although my house be not so with God; yet he hath made with me an everlasting covenant, ordered in all things, and sure: for this is all my salvation, and all my desire.—2 SAM. 23:5.

> Wherefore, beloved, seeing that ye look for such things, be diligent that ye may be found of him in peace, without spot, and blameless.—2 PET. 3:14.

OCTOBER 6

A HOPEFUL BEGINNING MAY HAVE A SORROWFUL ENDING.

CONSIDERING the wealth and social position of the young man so specially referred to in the Gospel, it is an agreeable surprise to find him in contact with Christ at all. We become the more hopeful of him when we find that he knelt before him; that his very first utterance was, 'Good Master'; and his first inquiry, 'What good thing shall I do that I may have eternal life?' The very putting of such a question showed that in some faint measure, at least, he did feel the power of the world to come. There was in him, besides, an amiability of disposition and outward purity of character peculiarly attractive.

With all this, however, he was but a beautiful specimen of the natural and unrenewed man,—'one of the rare wildflowers,' as one expresses it, 'that occasionally adorn this desolate wilderness.' The law of God deals with the heart as well as with the life, with thoughts as well as words, with hidden motives as well as outward actions. But of all this seemingly he was entirely ignorant, else he never would have said, 'All these things have I kept from my youth up.' Evidently he knew nothing aright of divine requirement or human weakness, of his own sin or of God's grace. Moreover, he knew nothing of the Saviour's true character; and therefore, though he gave him all outward homage, he would commit neither himself nor his interests to his eternal keeping, but, loving mammon more than Christ, he went away sorrowful.

How many like him still cleave to the world as a portion, and when they cannot purchase salvation, refuse to accept it as a gift of grace. Dining one day with Bishop Porteus, one of his clergy noticed with contempt the line of a hymn—'A sinner saved by grace alone'—expecting that the bishop would join in condemning it; but instead of this, he looked very solemnly at the clergyman, and said, 'Pray, sir, can you tell me of any other way by which a sinner can be saved?'

> Children, how hard is it for them that trust in riches to enter into the kingdom of God!—MARK 10:24.

> If any man serve me, let him follow me; and where I am, there shall also my servant be: if any man serve me, him will my Father honour.—JOHN 12:26.

OCTOBER 7

TO BE STRONG, WE MUST BE TRUE.

THERE is no sin more expressly forbidden in the word of God than untruthfulness. Every reader of it is familiar with utterances like these: 'Wherefore putting away lying, speak every man truth with his neighbour.'—'The lip of truth shall be established for ever: but a lying tongue is but for a moment.' A sin so condemned cannot be too sternly resisted; all the more, as sincerity, or a perfect conformity between word and intention, is the primary character of the new creature in Christ Jesus.

The Bible rule is to put away all lying without exception; but it is one often sadly overlooked. Some, while condemning falsehood in general, would fain palliate certain falsehoods in particular, and call them by gentle names. No change of name, however, can change its nature; for even the whitest lie that is in man's eyes is so black in the Lord's that it needs the blood of Jesus Christ to wash it away, and what have been sometimes called pious frauds are the most offensive frauds of all. We must adopt no crooked methods in serving the Lord. Jacob would have got the blessing without cheating his father; and but for his sin in doing so, he might never himself have been so grievously cheated in turn by his father-in-law.

One reputed to be among the wisest of ancient teachers, while enjoining all others to abstain from falsehood, yet allowed princes to lie. This is nowhere the teaching of the sacred volume; on the contrary, to prince and peasant alike it says emphatically, 'Lying lips are an abomination to the Lord: but they that deal truly are his delight.'

'Trust,' said William Arnot, 'is a lovely thing; but it cannot stand unless it get Truth to lean upon. When its tender hand has been often pierced by a broken reed of falsehood, it pines away and dies of grief. A man would find it easier to be trustful if his neighbours were trustworthy.' How sweet to know that the Lord we trust in keepeth truth forever!

Behold, thou desirest truth in the inward parts.—Psa. 51:6.

Our rejoicing is this, the testimony of our conscience, that in simplicity and godly sincerity, not with fleshly wisdom, but by the grace of God, we have had our conversation in the world.— 2 Cor. 1:12.

October 8

THERE MAY BE GREAT LOVE IN GRANTING RECOVERY, BUT SOMETIMES LOVE GREATER STILL IN WITHHOLDING IT.

THERE were times, apparently, when Paul, though an apostle of the Lord, could neither relieve himself nor others. Painful as was the thorn in his own flesh, he was powerless to pluck it out; and equally so to deliver his son Timothy from special bodily ailment and often infirmity.

It was the same in the case of Epaphroditus. Much as Paul loved him and needed his help, he could not raise him up from his bed of sickness. What he could not himself do, however, the

Lord graciously did for him, and raised up his afflicted friend. 'The Lord,' as an old writer says, 'commonly reserves his hand for a dead lift'; thereby the faith of his people is not only better exercised, but their gratitude is deepened.

Here, perhaps, the thought may arise in some, How would matters have stood had there been no recovery? Would this necessarily have been an unkindness on the Lord's part to Epaphroditus? Far from it, for often to his saints death is a most welcome messenger. It ends their sorrows, it terminates the weary pilgrimage, it sets the captive spirit free, and they depart to be with Christ, which is far better.

Nor is the Lord's kindness less to those who are left behind; for how often has their salvation been instrumentally brought about by the death of those they most fondly loved! How many can testify to this from their own experience! The death of a parent, a child, or other loved one, has not unfrequently been the means, in the Spirit's hand, of gathering in a whole family to the Lord.

When mourning an early removal, we should remember that God sometimes shows his kindness to his own by taking them away from the evil to come. 'God takes them soonest whom he loveth best.' There is rich comfort in this to bereaved mourners. True, to the eye of sense, the sickness of their loved ones was unto death; but to faith, how different! Instead of being unto death, it was unto life; yea, a richer, fuller life than ever before enjoyed.

> *A voice is heard on earth of kinsmen weeping*
> *The loss of one they love;*
> *But he is gone where the redeemed are keeping*
> *A festival above.*

For to me to live is Christ, and to die is gain. But if I live in the flesh, this is the fruit of my labour: yet what I shall choose I wot not. For I am in a strait betwixt two, having a desire to depart, and to be with Christ; which is far better.—PHIL. 1:21-23.

OCTOBER 9

*SOMETIMES THE MOST HOPEFUL OF SYMPTOMS IS
A CLOSED LIP.*

S O long as they are callous and impenitent, men usually are very
free in their utterance and self-justifying. When grace, however,
begins to operate, it is very different. They then become still before
the Lord, and open not their mouth. Not a word of self-defence, or
of artful palliation, or of murmuring complaint, is ever whispered
by them. If they open their lips at all, it is to say, with Ezra of old,
'O my God, I am ashamed, and blush to lift up my face unto thee';
or, with the publican, 'God be merciful to me a sinner.'

Now, a closing of the lip like this is always a hopeful token, yea,
a sure sign of awakened thought and begun contrition, and when
witnessed in saints it is not unfrequently a blessed mark of ripening
grace. When the son of Jesse was under the chastening hand of
God, much as he felt the stroke, yet he neither excused himself
nor accused the Lord, but bowed before him in sweet submission
and holy silence. 'I was dumb,' he said, 'I opened not my mouth;
because thou didst it.' So, too, was it with Aaron, the high priest,
when his two sons, Nadab and Abihu, were struck down at the
altar, because of their sin in offering strange fire before the Lord.
We cannot well conceive a sorer or more crushing affliction, owing
to the closeness of the relationship and the solemnity of the event.
Yet such was his holy, unmurmuring submission that, even in the
depth of his sorrow, 'he held his peace.'

Such an attainment is rare. Many, it is true, hold their peace
in affliction, but it is rather in amazement and sullenness than in
true and sweet submission. Though the tongue is silent, the heart
is clamorous, and 'there is no voice louder than a speechless repin-
ing of the soul.' But in true submission, the heart is silent as well
as the lip. It owns God's sovereignty, feels its deep unworthiness,
and longs rather to have the chastening sanctified than removed;
anything rather than to be let alone in sin.

Be still, and know that I am God: I will be exalted among the heathen, I will be exalted in the earth.—Psa. 46:10.

I was dumb, I opened not my mouth; because thou didst it.—Psa. 39:9.

It is the Lord: let him do what seemeth him good.—1 Sam. 3:18.

October 10

A TRUE GOSPEL MINISTRY IS A CHOICE HEAVENLY GIFT.

IF men do not destroy the wheat to get rid of the tares, so neither should they set aside the true in spiritual service in order to get rid of the false. It should not be forgotten that if, on the one hand, there is no greater curse than a dead ministry, who neither preach the gospel nor live it, there is, on the other hand, no greater or richer blessing than a living ministry orderly set up, Spirit-quickened and Spirit-owned. Indeed, it is one of Heaven's choicest gifts to men; for thousands and tens of thousands in every age have thereby been savingly brought to the Lord; yea, and sweetly sustained in their pilgrimage heavenward.

It is true, in themselves ministers are but earthen vessels, easily broken, and with many a chip and flaw; nevertheless, it is golden treasure they carry and saving work they do. It is on this account that the apostle says so earnestly, 'Know them which labour among you, and are over you in the Lord, and esteem them very highly in love for their work's sake.' 'The great Head of the church,' says one, 'has ordained three grand repositories of his truth: in the Scriptures he has preserved it by his providence against all hostile attacks; in the hearts of Christians he has maintained it by the almighty energy of his Spirit, even under every outward token of general apostasy; and in the Christian ministry he has deposited the treasure in earthen vessels, for the edification and enriching of the church in successive ages.'

But as even the most gifted of labourers can do nothing of themselves without the constant presence and power of the Spirit of God,—for, 'Who then is Paul, and who is Apollos, but ministers by whom ye believed, even as the Lord gave to every man?'—they should ever be specifically remembered at a throne of grace. 'Pray for your ministers,' said a saintly man, 'that they may be made faithful and wise stewards. Whether they plant or water, learn not to despise any of the true servants of God. Are all apostles? are all prophets? He hath appointed some to stand at the door, and some to break the children's bread: despise neither.'

> And he gave some, apostles; and some, prophets; and some, evangelists; and some, pastors and teachers; for the perfecting of the saints, for the work of the ministry, for the edifying of the body of Christ.—Eph. 4:11, 12.

> Let the elders that rule well be counted worthy of double honour, especially they who labour in the word and doctrine.—1 Tim. 5:17.

OCTOBER 11

BEWARE OF UNCERTAIN THINGS.

USUALLY riches are least true to those who trust in them most: hence Paul's words to Timothy, 'Charge them that are rich in this world, that they be not high-minded, nor trust in uncertain riches, but in the living God, who giveth us richly all things to enjoy'; and the no less striking words of Solomon, 'Riches certainly make themselves wings; they fly away as an eagle toward heaven.' Who is not familiar with examples of this among all classes, and in every variety of circumstances? 'Can any man,' says an old writer, 'say that the wild-fowl in his grounds are his, which suddenly take wing and fly away and for a while make a stay in another man's field, and thereby give a little property to the second, as they did to the first? No more can any man call riches truly his which, like winged birds, are ever shifting their owners.'

But riches are not more fleeting than unsatisfying. We are told of the wise king of Israel that he withheld not his heart from any joy that riches could yield; yet he emphatically declared in the end that all was 'vanity and vexation of spirit.' Indeed, outward things never yield less than when we press them most; and this is wisely ordered, for otherwise riches would often fatally ensnare. Very solemn are our Lord's words, 'How hardly shall they that have riches enter into the kingdom of God!' Doubtless it is possible,—for, like Abraham, some of the saintliest of believers have been among the richest; but it is difficult, for great wealth from its very nature strongly tempts us to minister to the flesh rather than to the Spirit, and to foster earthliness and unbelief, to the serious peril of the soul.

It is a startling fact that eighteen centuries ago, when the Son of God was on the earth, while the common people heard him gladly, the rich and the mighty, with rare exceptions, turned to him a deaf ear. The very thought of this might well moderate the eagerness with which all are so apt to seek higher social position and greater wealth.

> Lo, this is the man that made not God his strength; but trusted in the abundance of his riches, and strengthened himself in his wickedness.—Psa. 52:7.

> But seek ye first the kingdom of God, and his righteousness; and all these things shall be added unto you.—Matt. 6:33.

OCTOBER 12

ENRICHMENT WITH BETTER THAN GOLD.

THE poor cripple who day by day was laid at the Beautiful Gate of the temple thought of alms only when he made his application to Peter. It was but little help of this kind the apostle could impart, for silver and gold he had none; but, through the grace of his Lord, he bestowed something greater far, even a cure so immediate and thorough that never again did he need stay or crutch of any kind. Nor was this all, for he got spiritual healing besides. We may reasonably infer this, not merely from the gratitude expressed by him, but also from the fact that it was not Peter and John he warmly praised, but the Lord himself.

Knowing how long this poor cripple lay at the Beautiful Gate of the temple, the question naturally arises, How came he to miss a cure from Christ, whom he must so often have seen as he was entering the temple? Probably his cure was kept purposely in reserve by our Lord, to grace the mission of his apostles, and to prove that he himself, though now in heaven, both could and would still carry on the work he had begun on earth. Others may lay foundations, yet fail to build on them, but he never does.

It is told of Thomas Aquinas that, when he came to Rome, and was looking with great amazement at the mass of plate and treasure on every side, the Pope said to him, 'You see, Thomas, we cannot say, as St Peter did of old, "Silver and gold have I none."' 'No,' said Aquinas; 'nor can you command, as he did, the lame man to rise and walk.'

What though there be no lack of gold in a church, if there is a lack of faith and of soul-healing?

I am sought of them that asked not for me; I am found of them that sought me not.—Isa. 65:1.

And they went forth, and preached every where, the Lord working with them, and confirming the word with signs following.—Mark 16:20.

OCTOBER 13

THE LOVE IN GOD, AND THE ENMITY IN MAN.

WHILE readily acknowledging a measure of sinfulness in men, many will not admit the existence, in any degree, of inherent alienation. Nevertheless, the uniform teaching of Scripture is, that our moral condition, by nature, is one of entire estrangement from God and the things that please him. 'I know you,' said our Lord, 'that ye have not the love of God in you.'

Though nothing can be more reasonable than the law of God,— for the sum and substance of it is, that we love the Lord our God with all our heart, and our neighbour as ourselves,—yet, such is the enmity of the carnal mind that it is not subject to this law, 'neither, indeed, can be.' It is constantly warring with the will, and way, and purposes of God. Where there should be harmony there is discord, and where there should be sweet submission there are fretting murmurs.

Besides, as in all cases of marked estrangement, there is intense unwillingness to have any indebtedness. Usually it is only hard necessity that will make men either ask favours or accept them from those they dislike. It is too often just so with many in their dealings with God. Even when they take the gifts, they ignore the Giver; and the greatest one of all, the unspeakable gift of his Son, they deliberately put away from them.

Men may love an ideal god of their own creation, but the God of the gospel stirs up opposition: his holiness alarms them; and his very scheme of salvation offends them, because it presses on them, as ruined and helpless sinners, a gratuitous pardon which they could never win.

'Children of God,' said one, 'this was once your state; eat bitter herbs with your Passover this day.' But he might have added: 'As this is not now your state, eat it also with gladness and singleness of heart, praising God.'

> And you, that were sometime alienated and enemies in your mind by wicked works, yet now hath he reconciled.—COL. 1:21.

> For if, when we were enemies, we were reconciled to God by the death of his Son, much more, being reconciled, we shall be saved by his life.—ROM. 5:10.

OCTOBER 14

TREASURE IN EARTHEN VESSELS.

THE Lord's messengers, even at their best, are mere earthen vessels; but the message they are commissioned to bring is a very treasure of treasures, for its sum and substance is the Lord Jesus Christ. 'I determined,' says the apostle, 'not to know anything among you, save Jesus Christ and him crucified.' And this purpose was equally manifest in his writings. All his epistles are full of Christ, and overflow with references to his nature and offices, his grace and glory. In him only could he find the grand essentials wherewith to enlighten the minds of men, and pacify their consciences, and purify their hearts. Nor should it be otherwise now, either with the ministers or the members of the church of Christ. What was his chief theme should ever also be theirs.

It never goes well with any church when Christ begins to be a mere subordinate or occasional theme with its preachers. Men cannot live without food; and if Christ is not preached, the bread of life, by which alone the soul can be nourished, is wholly wanting. Nor, if the expression may be used, will it do to present only a half Christ—his doctrine, but not himself; or his person, but not his work; or his life, but not his death; or his sympathy, but not his atonement. However eloquent, no preaching can be savingly fruitful in which the incarnation is dwelt on, but never the cross. 'Some,' it has been forcibly said, 'preach Christ, but they do not preach him crucified—the firm, strong, decisive side of our Lord's character, which reveals the majesty of law, and the glory of righteousness, and the terribleness of transgression; which shows no tenderness for sin, though a mighty mercy to the sinner; and their preaching lacking this, lacks power and backbone.'

> But we have this treasure in earthen vessels, that the excellency of the power may be of God, and not of us.—2 COR. 4:7.

> I count all things but loss for the excellency of the knowledge of Christ Jesus my Lord.—PHIL. 3:8.

OCTOBER 15

THE RECEIVING OF CHRIST AND SALVATION.

IT being the fixed idea of many that before obtaining anything from Christ they must bring something to him, they go on toiling for years in the vain hope of thereby meriting the Lord's favour and blessing. Alas! what can a poor, empty sinner bring to the mercy-seat but his sin and misery? As salvation is wholly a gift and never a purchase, those coming to the Redeemer must bring nothing in their hand, and offer nothing as a price, but just come as they are; in so doing, even the most worthless will get welcome and the weariest rest.

Saints must be receivers to the very end, for, as one says, 'they are not wells, but cisterns into which the living waters flow. They are but the empty vessel; sovereign mercy puts them under the conduit pipe, and they receive grace upon grace, till they are filled to the brim.'

In accepting Christ, it is not mere impersonal abstraction they receive, but a true and living Saviour, human yet divine, who is their life and safety, their pattern and power. He is as real to them as their own flesh and bones, and infinitely dearer than brother or friend. And just because he saves them from their sins, the name Jesus is the name of names to them, and ever sounds sweetly in their ear. 'It is the music with which the bells of heaven ring,' George Herbert says; 'a song in a word, an ocean for comprehension, a gathering up of the hallelujahs of eternity in five letters.'

As ye have therefore received Christ Jesus the Lord, so walk ye in him.—Col. 2:6.

But as many as received him, to them gave he power to become the sons of God, even to them that believe on his name.—John 1:12.

October 16

LOVE REFUSING.

WHEN the man out of whom the devils were cast prayed that he might be with him, Jesus suffered him not. At first such a refusal takes us by surprise, for in the circumstances the request was a most natural one. As the woman loved much because much had been forgiven her, so this man loved much because he had just been the recipient of so great a deliverance, and in the warmth of his gratitude he would fain have companied with Jesus wherever he went.

But besides being natural in the man, the request could scarcely fail to be agreeable to Christ, not merely from the pure unselfish love that prompted it, which is always to him like the odour of a sweet smell, but from the fact that what was the man's desire was in a manner his Lord's also. He, too, longs for abiding fellowship with his people: witness his prayer—'Father, I will that they also whom thou hast given me be with me where I am, that they may behold my glory.'

In spite of all this, however, the request was denied. 'He suffered him not.' And why? Not because it was wrong in itself, but simply because it was premature and wrongly timed. The granting of it would have involved a double loss—a loss to the man himself of needful training and healthful discipline, and a serious loss to Gadara, for the one and only witness for the truth in it would have been taken away. In mercy, therefore, to the man's kindred and friends, to whom he might prove a light and a blessing, the Lord suffered him not to go with him. It was thus love that refused, not anger; and doubtless he himself saw this afterwards, and praised the Lord for it.

> O Lord, my best desire fulfil,
> And help me to resign
> Life, health, and comfort to thy will,
> And make thy pleasure mine.

Jesus answered and said unto him, What I do thou knowest not now; but thou shalt know hereafter.—JOHN 13:7.

For this thing I besought the Lord thrice, that it might depart from me. And he said unto me, My grace is sufficient for thee: for my strength is made perfect in weakness.—2 COR. 12:8, 9.

OCTOBER 17

CONTINUANCE IN THE FAITH.

'THEY,' says Matthew Henry, 'who are continually surrounded by temptations to apostasy, have need to be continually attended by exhortations to perseverance.' It was on this account that Paul earnestly exhorted the disciples in Lystra and Iconium 'to continue in the faith.'

This was an advice which was not easy for them to follow, for their circumstances were peculiar. They had heathenism all round them, dark, bigoted, and persecuting, and therefore, in continuing to be Christians, they did not only risk their property, position, and dearest friendships, but hazarded their very lives. The stones were yet lying on the ground that had nearly killed Paul, and might next be gathered up by murderous hands to cast at any one of themselves.

There is no open persecution meanwhile, but even in these quiet times it is neither an easy thing to come to the faith, nor an easy thing to continue in it in holy simplicity and firmness.

Owing to the inherent corruption in us, we are all to a greater or less extent wrongly biased, and all our natural sympathies draw us to sin rather than to righteousness, and to error rather than to truth; and unless we take this deep undercurrent of our nature into account, we may insensibly get upon the rocks and make utter shipwreck of our faith.

But besides this general danger common to all, there is a peculiar one forcibly presented in these words of inspiration: 'The time will come, *when they will not endure sound doctrine*, and they shall turn away their ears from the truth.' In our own time these words seem getting not a little of startling fulfilment. There is with many a growing intolerance of the revealed and supernatural in every form; nay, as if in fulfilment of John's words, 'He is antichrist, that *denieth the Father and the Son*,' not a few now speak as if the very acme of scientific progress would be to prove that there is neither Creator nor Redeemer, but that man himself is all in all.

Were it to come to this, not merely with the few but with the many, the measure of iniquity and unbelief would be well-nigh filled to the brim, and transgressors be as ripe for their doom as the men before the Flood, or the guilty Cities of the Plain. Jude tells us that when the Lord cometh to execute judgment upon all, he will decisively mark not only ungodly deeds, but '*all the hard speeches* which ungodly sinners have spoken against him.' To be safe, therefore, we must resolutely continue in the faith; and this we can best do by receiving the truth in the love of it, and practically carrying it out in daily life.

He that shall endure unto the end, the same shall be saved.—MATT. 24:13.

Rooted and built up in him, and stablished in the faith, as ye have been taught, abounding therein with thanksgiving.—COL. 2:7.

If a man abide not in me, he is cast forth as a branch, and is withered.—JOHN 15:6.

OCTOBER 18

CONFLICT HAS NO CESSATION HERE.

WHEN, after the great overthrow of the Midianites, fifteen thousand escaped, and were in full flight, there would, from very weariness, be a natural tendency to let the fugitives alone. They are now, it would be said, not only so few in number, but so weakened and full of fear, that they will never again be able to trouble us. But Gideon did not so reason. He was thankful, indeed, for what had been done, and gladly praised the Lord; yet no victory short of one thorough and complete in every sense could satisfy him. On this account, what he had begun, through the help of his God, he determined to finish; for he knew well that, unless crushingly pursued, a fleeing Midianite might soon again become a fighting one.

Now, a like spirit should ever animate all believers; for they, too, have a conflict, and the enemies they have to contend with are no ordinary ones. They must beware of whispering to themselves, True, there are still sins unsubdued and corruptions unmortified; but they are so few in number, and you are so weary, that they may be safely let alone. In thus speaking, they forget that, though they tire and slumber, their great adversary never does; and they forget, moreover, that sin, from its very nature, unless persistently resisted and watched, will ever be taking deeper root and gaining increased power.

Every sin so tolerated now will not only mar the peace of believers, but lessen their ultimate reward. There must therefore be no truce with our spiritual enemies, and no cessation of the conflict. When urging on to perfected holiness, Robert M'Cheyne once said: 'Oh, it is sweet to give up oneself to God, to be filled with his Spirit, to be ruled by his word, and to be a little vessel full of him, to bear his name!'

Fight the good fight of faith, lay hold on eternal life.—1 TIM. 6:12.

I press toward the mark for the prize of the high calling of God in Christ Jesus.—PHIL. 3:14.

OCTOBER 19

THE CHASTENING OF THE LORD IS RARELY WELCOMED, HOWEVER NEEDED.

THOSE who are so regardless that they neither mark the wrong in their children nor care to correct it, not only do them grievous injury, but plant many a thorn in their own pillow. With our great Father in heaven how different is it! In the training of his children, authority and love, instruction and discipline, are invariably combined. Not one of them, therefore, escapes chastening, just because in one or other of its manifold forms it is an absolutely needed and gracious privilege. There may be unchastened sons in the families of men, but there are none in the family of God. To be otherwise dealt with would be markedly ominous of coming evil; for when God refuses to correct, it is because he intends to destroy.

But while chastening is thus a privilege of adoption, it is one that most men would willingly forego. Nay, even the holiest have instinctive shrinkings when it is approaching them; for 'no chastening for the present seemeth to be joyous, but grievous.' Nevertheless, the Lord's chastenings are always wisely timed and tenderly administered. He has no pleasure in afflicting his children, but would rather, were it possible, break the rod than use it. Moreover, if he smites with the one hand, he heals with the other, and into all our bitter he drops many a sweet. He never forgets his own promise, 'As thy days, so shall thy strength be.'

> *Child of my love, lean hard,*
> *And let me feel the pressure of thy care.*
> *I know thy burden, child; I shaped it—*
> *Poised it in my hand—made no proportion*
> *Of its weight to thine unaided strength;*
> *For even as I laid it on, I said,*
> *I shall be near, and while she leans on me*
> *This burden shall be mine, not hers.*

Whom the Lord loveth he correcteth; even as a father the son in whom he delighteth.—PROV. 3:12.

As many as I love, I rebuke and chasten: be zealous therefore, and repent.—REV. 3:19.

Blessed is the man whom thou chastenest, O Lord, and teachest him out of thy law.—PSA. 94:12.

OCTOBER 20

THE GREAT FAITH WHICH HONOURED GOD, AND THAT GOD HONOURED.

WHILE the father of the faithful possessed in sweetest harmony not the true and the just only, but the lovely and gracious as well, yet the grace for which he was most of all distinguished was faith. Its great and pre-eminent strength in him was manifested in a twofold way.

First of all, it could patiently wait. The Lord's promise of a son, in whom so many bright hopes centred, came to him at a comparatively early period, and probably he expected an early fulfilment. But instead of this, year after year, yea, and decade after decade passed wearily away, without any sign of the longed-for blessing. This was more than Sarah could bear; for she fretted and murmured at the delay, and took forbidden courses that only added to her sorrow.

But though her faith failed, Abraham's did not; and while it patiently waited for the promised fulfilment, it could at the same time resolutely ignore every difficulty in the way. When in his nine-tieth year, and while the son of promise was yet unborn, the Lord appeared to him and said, 'Thou shalt be a father of many nations; and I will make thee exceeding fruitful, and kings shall come out of thee,'—he did not say, as multitudes would have done, 'The thing is inconceivable; it cannot be.' On the contrary, ignoring all the strangeness and unlikelihood and even seeming impossibility of such a thing, he proved strong in faith, and 'against hope believed in hope.' 'It is enough to Abraham,' one says, 'that God hath said it. He sees not the means, he sees the promise; and he feels assured that God would rather raise him a seed from the stones that he trod on than himself should want a large and happy issue.'

So it always is when faith is strong; nothing staggers it. Beholding the promise,—

> *It looks to that alone,*
> *Laughs at impossibilities,*
> *And says, 'It shall be done!'*

'May I walk,' said Thomas Chalmers, 'in the footsteps of faithful Abraham, and, like him, believe the word of God in the face of the strongest unlikelihoods of nature and experience; and though against hope, in the hope that all which God hath said he will infallibly make good. It is a strong unlikelihood that I, a worthless creature, should be taken into gracious acceptance by a God who is of purer eyes than to behold iniquity. Yet let me do homage to God's faithfulness by believing in his word that it is even so. It is another strange unlikelihood in the eye of nature that this carnal and earthly heart of mine should give up its rooted ungodliness, and that I, divinely quickened, should, by the power of a new birth, become a new creature in Jesus Christ my Lord; nevertheless, like the father of the faithful, let me do homage to the truth of God, and pray without wavering for that holy impregnation which is the chief of all those promises that are Yea and Amen in Christ.'

> He staggered not at the promise of God through unbelief; but was strong in faith, giving glory to God; and being fully persuaded that, what he had promised, he was able also to perform.—ROM. 4:20, 21.

> With God nothing shall be impossible ... Blessed is she that believed: for there shall be a performance of those things which were told her from the Lord.—LUKE 1:37, 45.

OCTOBER 21

THE SURE AND THE DEFINITE.

IT is strange that definiteness and certainty should be so greatly prized in scientific research and commercial transactions, and yet be so little valued in what pertains to the very highest interests of men. Mere appearances and plausibilities will not be accepted as sufficient securities where property is concerned; but anything seems to satisfy in connection with Godward relationships and the world to come. While quite ready to hear in a general way of the Redeemer and his work, they will yet take no real interest in the *definite teachings* of Scripture regarding him.

Very different, however, is it with them when, through the Spirit, they become convinced of sin, and realise danger, and the great question becomes a personal one,—'What must I do to be saved?' Mere generalities will not satisfy them now; nor will they intrust the keeping of their soul to anyone that offers, but must have a Redeemer who can save to the uttermost, and to whom, like Thomas, they can say, 'My Lord and my God.' Verily, then, when guilt and danger are so real and definite, and the day of grace so brief, nothing should ever satisfy us but the salvation in Jesus Christ so definitely set forth in the word.

Dr Bonar tells us of a friend getting into conversation with a workman, whom she found to be a happy Christian. 'How long have you been thus rejoicing?' she asked. 'Six months ago,' he said, 'I heard an address on the words, "Whosoever believeth hath everlasting life." I would not take it to myself,' he said; 'but when I went home that night, I dreamed that "whosoever" meant *me*. I got bang out of bed, and got the Bible to see the words, and there was "whosoever."' 'But you knew it was in the Bible, didn't you?' 'Yes; but I wanted *to see it with my own eyes*, and I have been happy ever since.'

> We believe and are sure that thou art that Christ, the Son of the living God.—JOHN 6:69.

> I know whom I have believed, and am persuaded that he is able to keep that which I have committed unto him against that day.— 2 TIM. 1:12.

OCTOBER 22

THE PRAYER OFFERED ON THE NIGHT OF NIGHTS.

NOTHING so intensifies prayer as deep trouble, and never was this more strikingly illustrated than in the garden of Gethsemane. The prayer of our Lord there came, as it were, from his whole being. It is thus written: 'He went a little further, and fell on his face, and prayed, saying, O my Father, if it be possible, let this cup pass from me.' Again the second time, and then a little after, the third time, 'he prayed the same words.' Nothing is here said of his weeping, but the Epistle to the Hebrews makes it very evident that his prayers were mingled with strong crying and tears. As an old divine affectingly puts it,—'He filled the silent night with his crying, and watered the cold earth with his tears, more precious than the dew of Hermon, or any moisture next to his own blood that ever fell on God's earth since the creation.'

But never, even in the darkest moment, did he lose filial confidence or let go his hold. To the last he could still look up from earth to heaven, and trustfully say, 'Abba, Father.' At first, indeed, the words, 'O my Father, let this cup pass from me,' would seem to indicate that the greatness of the agony in Gethsemane brought about a faltering in purpose with him, a begun regret that he had ever undertaken to be the sinner's Substitute, and to purchase redemption for the perishing at such a cost. But it was not so, as two words in the heart of the petition itself clearly show,—namely, the 'if' and the 'nevertheless'—'O my Father, if it be possible, let this cup pass from me! nevertheless, not as I will, but as thou wilt.'

Beyond question, the passing of that cup of woe and death from his lips would have been the eternal passing of the cup of life and salvation from ours. Knowing this, Jesus no sooner said, 'Father, save me from this hour,' than he added, 'but for this cause came I unto this hour. Father, glorify thy name.' 'The victory,' as one says, 'has now been won, on the theatre of an invincible will, to give his life a ransom for many. He shall win it next in the arena of the cross, where it is to become an accomplished fact. "I will suffer," is the result of Gethsemane; "It is finished," bursts from Calvary.'

What, then, do we owe to Christ?—nay, rather, what do we not owe to him? Verily, if we had each a thousand hearts instead of one, and a thousand tongues as well, it would be but fitting to love and praise him with them all.

I came down from heaven, not to do mine own will, but the will of him that sent me.—JOHN 6:38.

Though he were a Son, yet learned he obedience by the things which he suffered.—HEB. 5:8.

OCTOBER 23

*THOUGH WE CAN DESTROY GOD'S IMAGE, WE CANNOT
RESTORE IT AGAIN.*

WHEN a coin is fresh from the mint, so perfect often is the impress the die leaves on it, that as soon as men see it they exclaim, 'It is the king's very image!' But were it through carelessness to drop from its owner's hand, and fall beneath treading feet or on grinding wheel, soon scarcely one feature could be recognised.

It has been even so with man. When fresh from his Maker's hands, he bore to the full his Maker's image—in intelligence, holiness, and true blessedness. But when through sin he fell from the divine keeping, all became changed. Where formerly love, purity, and peace reigned, defilement and enmity are now found. Thus God's image has not only been defaced, but well-nigh obliterated.

But though the destruction is man's work, the salvation never is; hence the well-known words: 'O Israel, thou hast destroyed thyself; but in *me* is thine help.' Yes! from him alone can we obtain the great and needed renewal. It was the knowledge of this that led the apostle, when seeking for himself and others a closer likeness to the Lord, to say so earnestly, '*The very God of peace* sanctify you wholly; and I pray God your whole spirit and soul and body be preserved blameless unto the coming of our Lord Jesus Christ.'

When fulfilling such a petition, it is ever as the God of peace, as God reconciled in Christ, that the Lord does it, and not for any merit in us. Yet in their blindness not a few would fain make their purity, not a blessed fruit of pardon, but the price wherewith they would purchase it; the inevitable result of which has again and again been the utter failure of every attempt to get the lost image of God restored.

Nothing less than a complete spiritual restoration should ever satisfy believers. 'Let every lineament of the earthly Adam be erased,' Dr Bonar says, 'and let every feature of the heavenly Adam be engraven upon thee. The day of perfection, and restoration, and dominion is coming, but it has not yet arrived. Live looking for it; live as men who believe it; walk worthy of it.'

Create in me a clean heart, O God; and renew a right spirit within me.—Psa. 51:10.

If any man be in Christ, he is a new creature: old things are passed away; behold, all things are become new.—2 Cor. 5:17.

OCTOBER 24

IT IS A SNARE TO DWELL RATHER ON THE LITTLE ATTAINABLE IN SANCTIFICATION, THAN ON THE MUCH.

WHAT others have really attained in the divine life may be safely held to be attainable by us. If, in spite of surrounding evil, Enoch could maintain a close and holy walk with God; and Jacob could wrestle for the blessing, and as a prince have power with God and prevail; and Stephen could be full of the Holy Ghost and of faith; and Paul could advance so far as to say, 'Ye are witnesses, and God also, how holily and justly and unblameably we have behaved ourselves among you that believe,'—why may not we reach to like attainments?—all the more when we remember that naturally they were of like passions and like infirmities with ourselves, and had at first the same condemnation over them and the same corruption in them that we have. What grace did for them it can certainly do for us, provided we do not hinder by unbelief.

Great is the present need-be with all for a sanctification more marked and elevated; for how manifold still are the defects and shortcomings of not a few of those who bear the name of Christ! How weak their faith! how cold their love! how mingled their motives! and in unwatchful hours how prone are they to backslide! 'I am persuaded,' one says, 'that when at last we meet our Lord, and see him as he is, we shall be utterly ashamed and confounded at the feebleness of our love. We shall see it was the merest spark, and not a flame at all.' We should ever, therefore, through grace, be pressing onward and upward.

To encourage us in so doing, not only is it said, 'Return unto the Lord thy God,' but the Lord adds such cheering words as these: 'I will heal thy backsliding, I will love thee freely. I will be as the dew unto Israel: he shall grow as the lily, and cast forth his roots as Lebanon.'

> *Come, drink, and be at rest!*
> *On Him who died for thee believe;*
> *The Spirit's quickening grace receive;*
> *No more the God who seeks thee grieve:*
> *Be holy, and be blest.*

Having therefore these promises, dearly beloved, let us cleanse ourselves from all filthiness of the flesh and spirit, perfecting holiness in the fear of God.—2 Cor. 7:1.

Every man that hath this hope in him purifieth himself, even as he is pure.—1 John 3:3.

October 25

GUILT THE GREATEST AND GRACE THE RICHEST MET ON THE CROSS.

NOTHING so startles or arrests men as a great crime committed by unlikely hands, in unlikely circumstances; and there have been many such in this world's dark history. But in all the annals of crime, never was there a deed of infamy like that of Calvary. It was not simply a taking of life, or a preferring of the worst of criminals to the best of benefactors; but it was a killing of the Prince of life, a crucifying the Lord of glory at the very time that unspeakable love was glowing in his heart. What added to the awfulness of this crime were the numbers who joined hand in hand in committing it. Herod and Pilate took part in it, and the priests and the people; and in the end the whole nation virtually assumed the responsibility, and joined in the awful cry, 'His blood be upon us and upon our children.'

But while thus on the cross we see guilt the most appalling, we also see there love altogether unparalleled. 'I can understand many things,' said a good old man, 'but the love of Christ I cannot understand; it is above all my thinking, and it is only when I reach the better country, and see him as he is, that I expect the veil to be fully lifted up.' It may, doubtless, admit of illustration from rare instances of self-sacrifice for country or kindred or friend; but 'every such comparison,' as one says, 'is at the same time a contrast, and acts only as a foil, to set off the love of God to men in the death of his Son'; for 'God commendeth his love toward us, in that, while we were yet sinners, Christ died for us.'—'If when we were enemies, we were reconciled to God by the death of his Son, much more, being reconciled, we shall be saved by his life.' If peradventure for a good man some would even dare to die, yet who but Jesus would die for the vilest of enemies, and let his grace be richest at the very moment their guilt was greatest?

> More of thyself, oh, show me hour by hour,
> More of thy glory, O my God and Lord;
> More of thyself in all thy grace and power,
> More of thy love and truth, Incarnate Word.

Who his own self bare our sins in his own body on the tree, that we, being dead to sins, should live unto righteousness: by whose stripes ye were healed.—1 PET. 2:24.

Ye know that he was manifested to take away our sins; and in him is no sin.—1 JOHN 3:5.

OCTOBER 26

THERE IS NO PROMISE-KEEPER LIKE THE LORD.

MANY are the things which prevent the fulfilment of human promises. Men often promise hastily, simply to get rid of an importunate applicant, and with no sincerity of purpose to perform. At other times they give their promise deliberately, but in deceit; for they so frame it as to be able to keep it to the ear, while they break it to the sense. But there is no such unrighteousness with God. He cannot lie; even if we believe not, he abideth faithful. He ever means what he says, and does what he means, and therefore his every promise may be confidently relied on. And as he gives no promise that he does not intend to keep, so neither does he ever give one beyond his power to fulfil.

In a changeable world like this, events and circumstances often vary so rapidly that what may be easily done one day cannot be done the next. The will may remain, but there is no longer the power. But never is it so with the Lord. Nothing can at any time interpose between him and his promises to make them void. 'Hath he said, and shall he not do it? or hath he spoken, and shall he not make it good?' Nay, more: it is so truly his delight to fulfil as well as to give promises, that he is ever presenting them to our view, impressing them on our memory, and letting us know that it is, as it were, a grief of heart to him when unbelief on our part comes to stay his generous hand. Many have little comfort, because, though they possess the promises, they fail to use them.

When Giant Despair had put his victims into the castle, Bunyan tells he was wont to beat them with a crab-tree cudgel. Lying in that dungeon, Christian began to think whether it were not better to destroy himself. Yet, foolish man, all the while the key of promise was in his bosom, and he needed not to have been rotting in that dungeon for a single hour. Let every desponding soul take note of this.

There hath not failed one word of all his good promise, which he promised by the hand of Moses his servant.—1 KINGS 8:56.

For all the promises of God in him are yea, and in him Amen, unto the glory of God by us.—2 COR. 1:20.

OCTOBER 27

THE HUMBLING FAILURE OF ONE DISCIPLE AND THE LOVING
FIDELITY OF ANOTHER.

PETER, though a genuine and warm-hearted disciple of his
Master, was at times so strangely unstable that at Antioch Paul
found him so much to be blamed that he withstood him to the
face. At first he asserted boldly the right of believing Gentiles to
all the privileges of the gospel, and freely mingled with them in
spiritual fellowship. But when certain Jews made their appearance,
whom he did not wish to offend, he withdrew from the Gentiles,
and deliberately resumed his Jewish exclusiveness. By so doing he
virtually built again the wall that had been thrown down, made
circumcision essential to salvation, and thereby grievously darkened the gospel of the grace of God.

This was Peter's sin; and, unhappily, he did not sin alone. An
old writer says, 'The sins of teachers are the teachers of sins.' It
was so here; for when Peter dissembled, the other Jews dissembled
with him, insomuch that Barnabas also was carried away with their
dissimulation.

But Paul stood firm; nay more, when he saw that they walked
not uprightly according to the truth of the gospel, he said reprov-
ingly to Peter, before them all, 'If thou, being a Jew, livest after the
manner of Gentiles, and not as do the Jews, why compellest thou
the Gentiles to live as do the Jews?'

It is not easy at any time to administer reproof to a friend.
Doubtless, the precept is clear and express: 'Thou shalt in any
wise rebuke thy neighbour, and not suffer sin upon him.' Still the
duty is one from which all naturally shrink. It is painful to wound
one we love, and run the risk of breaking the friendship of years.
Nevertheless, Paul proved faithful; and he was all the more resolute
in his remonstrance, because by Peter's conduct the whole church
was in danger of being led away from the truth as it is in Jesus.
On the most vital of points—the way of a sinner's acceptance

with God—and through Paul's single instrumentality, the Lord preserved the church and the gospel at that critical era.

How much may even one Christian man be honoured to accomplish for truth and righteousness, if only strong in faith and lowly in spirit. It was to Peter's honour that, instead of loving Paul less thereafter, he loved him more.

> O Israel, return unto the Lord thy God; for thou hast fallen by thine iniquity. I will heal their backsliding, I will love them freely.—Hos. 14:14.
>
> Rebuke a wise man, and he will love thee.—Prov. 9:8.
>
> Thou shalt in any wise rebuke thy neighbour, and not suffer sin upon him.—Lev. 19:17.

October 28

THE DISCIPLES' CENSURE OF MARY.

WHEN at Bethany, six days before the passover, Mary took a pound of ointment of spikenard and anointed the feet of Jesus, there was indignation, and they said, 'To what purpose is this waste?' Had such words come from the lips of Judas only, we could not have wondered; but for a time, at least, even such true-hearted disciples as John, James, and Peter joined in the rebuking murmurs. Seemingly, as yet, they had scarcely grace enough rightly to appreciate a spirituality so intense and a love so ardent as that of Mary's, and therefore, instead of commending, they keenly censured her.

We often see similar misjudgments in our time among those who cannot appreciate grace in its highest manifestations. When Henry Martyn laid all his university honours and brightest earthly prospects at the feet of Jesus, and gave himself up to be a despised missionary of the cross to the perishing heathen, he was looked upon by many as a misguided enthusiast, who was throwing himself away. 'What waste,' they said, 'of fine talents and rare opportunities!' They should rather have said, What moral grandeur, what Christ-like love and service!

Those who know their Lord, and truly love him, count it sweet to make sacrifices for his sake, and never feel able to praise him enough. 'If I had as many angels' tongues to praise,' said Samuel Rutherford, 'as there have fallen drops of rain since the creation, or as there are leaves of trees in all the forests of the earth, or stars in the heaven, yet my Lord Jesus would ever be behind with me.'

> *Naught, naught I count as treasure*
> *Compared, O Christ, with thee!*
> *Thy sorrow without measure*
> *Earned peace and joy for me.*

I count all things but loss for the excellency of the knowledge of Christ Jesus my Lord: for whom I have suffered the loss of all things, and do count them but dung, that I may win Christ.—PHIL. 3:8.

But grow in grace, and in the knowledge of our Lord and Saviour Jesus Christ.—2 PET. 3:18.

OCTOBER 29

CONFIRMATION NEEDFUL.

SOME are bent so exclusively on securing the conversion of souls, that they take comparatively little thought about after spiritual growth and development. With Paul and Barnabas, however, it was otherwise; accordingly, after labouring for a time at Derbe with great success, they resolved to return once more to Lystra and Iconium, that they might confirm the souls of the disciples. While at Derbe, Paul was not far from the well-known pass which leads down from the central table-land to Cilicia and Tarsus; but his thoughts did not centre on an earthly home, or if he had any desires at this time to revisit the city of his birth, they were all quenched by higher longings and more pressing claims. Yes, even Lystra, where he was so cruelly handled and fiercely stoned, and into which it might well be thought he would never enter again, had far greater attractions to him than Tarsus itself. And why? Just because, through the Spirit of the Lord, there were fruits of his ministry there, recovered jewels, the Lord's little ones, dear brethren in Christ, whom he could cheer and sustain in their day of need. Indeed, his renewed presence among them in such perilous circumstances would itself be a mighty confirmation to them. The very courage of such an act, with the faith and quenchless love it evinced, could scarcely fail to give a firmer rooting to their every grace.

He would strengthen them, also, by further instruction, and especially by a fuller exposition of the word; for it is generally found that the surest and most effective way of confirming souls is scripturally to enlighten and impress them. When thereby graciously confirmed, they would, 'though troubled, not be distressed; and though perplexed, not be in despair.' In the great emergencies of life, and especially in the dying hour, believers often require to fall back upon their stored-up knowledge of God's ways and word. Some years ago, when an aged Christian, who greatly delighted in the word, was on his dying bed, his minister said to him, 'Well, my friend, how do you feel today?' 'Very weel, sir,' was the answer, 'very weel, *but just a wee confused wi' the flittin'.*' If he had had less of the needful confirmation, such calmness would have been impossible at such an hour.

I will put my fear in their hearts, that they shall not depart from me.—Jer. 32:40.

If children, then heirs; heirs of God, and joint-heirs with Christ; if so be that we suffer with him, that we may be also glorified together.—Rom. 8:17.

October 30

THE FULNESS THAT DWELLS IN CHRIST WARRANTS ANY AMOUNT OF FREENESS IN DRAWING FROM IT.

WHEN the French, by means of deep Artesian wells, brought up in the desert of Algeria gushing streams of water, the

Arabs from all quarters flocked to behold and enjoy. They laved themselves in the welcome abundance; mothers dipped their babes in the running stream; while the old sheikh, we are told, fell on his knees and wept, and returned thanks to Allah and the French.

This is but a feeble picture of the fulness of the water of life we find in Christ. When we believe in him and receive his Spirit, we get within us a well of water, springing up into everlasting life; and out of us begin to flow rivers of living water for the refreshment of others. On this account Jesus said to the woman of Samaria, 'If thou knewest the gift of God, and who it is that saith to thee, Give me to drink; thou wouldest have asked of him, and he would have given thee living water.' And again, to the multitude he also said: 'If any man thirst, let him come unto me and drink.'

Few responded to that invitation then, and few, alas! respond to it even now; but such is the fulness that dwells in him of enriching grace, and helpful power, and every conceivable blessing, that even if all of every kindred, tongue, and people crowded to him to drink, not one would have to mourn his thirst unquenched from failing supply. Whatever is needed to save a fallen world, or to sustain and cheer and comfort his people, is treasured up in him in inexhaustible fulness; and nothing honours and delights him more than a thorough realisation of this on our part, and an open, trustful, and loving application to him in our every time of need.

It should never be forgotten that all this fulness dwells in him, just because he is God manifest in the flesh: 'The Word—God heard; the Light—God seen; and the Life—God felt'; the same yesterday, today, and forever. Many an image has been employed to illustrate this fulness, but so infinite is it that nothing can adequately set it forth. Who can utter the unutterable? 'When I have watched,' said Dr Guthrie, 'the rise of the sun as he shot above the crest of the mountain, or into a sky draped with golden curtains sprang up from his ocean bed, I have wondered to think that he has melted the snows of so many winters, and renewed the verdure of so many springs, and painted the flowers of so many summers, and ripened the golden harvests of so many autumns, and yet shines as brilliant as ever; his eye not dim, nor his natural force abated, nor his floods of light less full for centuries of boundless profusion: yet what is this but an image of the fulness that is in Christ! Blessed Saviour, divine Redeemer, in thy presence is fulness of joy, at thy right hand are pleasures for evermore.'

In him dwelleth all the fulness of the Godhead bodily.—COL. 2:9.

For it pleased the Father that in him should all fulness dwell.—COL. 1:19.

And of his fulness have all we received, and grace for grace.—JOHN 1:16.

OCTOBER 31

WHEN THE TIMES ARE EVENTFUL, WE CANNOT BE TOO WATCHFUL.

I T is in Scripture, doubtless, we ever find the clearest and most impressive teaching of the Lord's will. But events also have a voice; and therefore, for practical ends, it is always needful to study providences. Indeed, not to regard the operation of God's hands in the varied events of daily life is a serious dereliction of duty. This was a severely rebuked sin of the Jews at the first coming of the Lord. There were then signs innumerable to indicate the approach of a new era, and of the true Messiah; but so completely did the Jews fail to discern them, that when the long-expected Seed of promise came, they received him not.

It will be very similar with many at the second coming of the Lord. There will be no lack of signs preceding and heralding the great event, but there will be a sad lack of eyes to discern them. So immersed in worldliness will multitudes be then, and so bent on business or pleasure, that no signs, however plain and visible they may be, will make the least impression on them.

It is beyond question that the times we live in are so remarkable that many of all classes and of all lands, cultured and uncultured alike, are now given free and open expression to their deep-felt convictions with regard to them. 'The signs of the times,' says Lord Shaftesbury, 'are really unparalleled and most wonderful; and I think it does not proceed from any spirit of fanaticism if we say that we are tending to some great consummation.' Another says: 'All the lines of prophecy are fast converging, and we seem to be approaching a universal change.'

Such views are not stated as conjectures merely, but are professedly founded on not a few prophetic passages of the word bearing on what Scripture calls 'the fulfilment of the times of the Gentiles,' or 'the time of the end.' It is predicted that immediately before that great era there is to be an unprecedented increase of discovery and locomotion,—it is thus written: 'Shut up the words, and seal the book, even to the time of the end: many shall run to and fro, and knowledge shall be increased' (Dan. 12:4);—and that then, also, there is to be a season of missionary and evangelistic effort so world-wide that there will scarcely be a land unvisited or a language in which the gospel has not been preached. 'This gospel of the kingdom,' said our Lord, 'shall be preached in all the world *for a witness* unto all nations; and then shall the end come' (Matt. 24:14). And further, it is foretold that, after centuries of neglect, Palestine will again so draw to it every eye, that everything about it—its hills and valleys, its pools and streamlets, its every stone, yea, its very dust—will suddenly become invested with a new and peculiar interest. These are the striking words of the Psalmist: 'Thou shalt arise, and have mercy upon Zion: for the time to favour her, yea, the set time, is come. For thy servants take pleasure in her stones, and favour the dust thereof. So the heathen shall fear the name of the Lord, and all the kings of the earth thy glory. When the Lord shall build up Zion, he shall appear in his glory' (Psa. 102:13-16).

But, strange as it may seem, it is predicted that almost simultaneously with these things, or closely upon them, there will be a development of worldliness and wickedness and unbelief so great, that the very worst of former days of evil will repeat themselves. It is thus written: 'As it was in the days of Noe, so shall it be also in the days of the Son of man. They did eat, they drank, they married wives, they were given in marriage, until the day that Noe entered into the ark, and the flood came, and destroyed them all' (Luke 17:26, 27). 'This know also, that *in the last days* perilous times shall come. For men shall be lovers of their own selves, covetous, boasters, proud, blasphemers, disobedient to parents, unthankful, unholy, without natural affection, trucebreakers, false accusers, incontinent, fierce, despisers of those that are good, traitors, heady, highminded, lovers of pleasure more than lovers of God; having a form of godliness, but denying the power thereof … Evil men and seducers shall wax worse and worse, deceiving, and being deceived' (2 Tim. 3:1-5, 13). 'Now the Spirit speaketh expressly, that in the latter times men shall depart from the faith, giving heed to seducing spirits' (1 Tim. 4:1). These varied passages seem to intimate that, towards the end, the Christian and the Antichristian, the true and the false, the evil and the good, shall not only be found in energetic action at one and the same time, but the Antichristian element may, for a brief season at least, prove itself the master power.

There is not a little in this, doubtless, to depress and sadden; nevertheless, if we are true and watchful believers, there is much also in it to sustain and cheer. Things such as these may be dark as *events*, and yet be very bright as *signs*. Our Lord, accordingly, expressly says, 'When ye see these things begin to come to pass, look up, lift up your heads, *for your redemption draweth nigh.*'

'The bursting glories of spring,' one says, 'come directly out of the bleak winter; the darkest hour is said to be that which immediately precedes the day: and the Scriptures teach that so it will be in the ushering in of the great consummation. The sun must darken, and the moon withhold her light; and then shall the Sun of righteousness arise with healing in his wings.'

Ye can discern the face of the sky; but can ye not discern the signs of the times?—MATT. 16:3.

The children of Issachar … were men that had understanding of the times, to know what Israel ought to do.—1 CHRON. 12:32.

NOVEMBER 1

THE VEIL RENT, AND THE WAY OPENED.

AS soon as Jesus cried with a loud voice and gave up the ghost, 'the veil of the temple,' we are told, 'was rent in twain from the top to the bottom.' The veil was the thick and gorgeously wrought curtain which was hung between the holy place and the holiest of all, shutting out all access to the presence of God as manifested above the mercy-seat and between the cherubim. Into this holiest of all none might enter; not even the high priest, save once a year, and then only with the blood of atonement in his hands, which he sprinkled on and before the mercy-seat, to signify that access for sinners to a holy God is through atoning blood alone.

So it continued to be with the veil so long as the only blood-shed and sprinkled was that of bulls and goats; it debarred only, and prevented access. But all became changed the very moment the reality of sacrifice took the place of the shadow, and the great Victim so long prefigured expired on Calvary. The veil of the temple was then without hands mysteriously rent in twain from the top to the bottom. The rending began at the top, as if to inti-mate that unless the Lord himself had rent it, in rich grace and by his own hand, it could never have been rent at all. Yes! salvation is wholly of the Lord. When the river of life begins to flow, it is never from any mere earthly source, but always from the throne of God and of the Lamb.

So complete and thorough was the tearing asunder of the veil, that straightway the whole mercy-seat stood open to the gaze of every eye, as if to tell us that now there was freest access for all through the blood of the Lamb. How marvellous the change! for while formerly it was death to any sinner to go in, now it is death for any sinner to stay out.

Happily for us, what was rent then remains rent still. The veil has never been rehung; and never shall be, because Christ's work was a finished one, and has such infinite sufficiency that it needs no repetition. If any, therefore, miss salvation, it will not be because there is no open way, but because there is in themselves a shut heart and a shut will: 'Ye will not come unto me, that ye might have life.'

He is our peace, who hath made both one, and hath broken down the middle wall of partition between us.—Eph. 2:14.

I am the door: by me if any man enter in, he shall be saved, and shall go in and out, and find pasture.—John 10:9.

November 2

THOSE OFT IN JOURNEYINGS SHOULD BE OFT IN PRAYER.

IN these days much has been said and written about the place and power of prayer, and the things that may or may not be presented at a throne of grace. Paul had no difficulties regarding this matter, but ever carried out to the full the blessed command, 'Be careful for nothing; but in every thing by prayer and supplication with thanksgiving let your requests be made known unto God.' He prayed for things spiritual as few before or since have ever done. But if they were needed, he equally prayed for things temporal. In sore hungering, he prayed for bread; in cold and nakedness, he prayed for shelter; in perilous storms, he prayed for safety; in bonds and imprisonment, he prayed for escape and liberty; and very markedly, too, in hindered journeyings he prayed for providential guidance, as when he said, 'Now, God himself, and our Father, and our Lord Jesus Christ, direct our way unto you.'

So should it be with us. In all our ways, and specially in all our journeyings, the Lord should be acknowledged by us, and with full expectancy that he will direct our steps. This should be done not merely in connection with all movements and outgoings of a directly missionary nature, like those of the apostle, but also in connection with the ordinary visits and journeyings of daily life, even though business and friendship may be the main end of them. All the more should this be done considering how much often depends on a single journey, and that none assuredly know when may be the going out from which there is to be no return; yet, even in such a case, it is always well with those who are the Lord's.

When once comforting a deeply sorrowing father, who had lost a son far from home, Samuel Rutherford said, 'Dying in another land, where his mother could not close his eyes, is not much. Who closed Moses' eyes, and who put on his winding-sheet? For aught I know, neither father nor mother nor friend, but God only. And there is as fair and easy a way between Scotland and Heaven as if he had died in the very bed in which he was born. The whole earth is the Father's, and any corner of our Father's home is good enough to die in.'

> *Thy way, not mine, O Lord,*
> *However dark it be;*
> *Lead me by thine own hand,*
> *Choose out the path for me.*
> *Smooth let it be or rough,*
> *It will be still the best;*
> *Winding or straight, it matters not,*
> *It leads me to thy rest.*

Trust in the Lord with all thine heart; and lean not unto thine own understanding. In all thy ways acknowledge him, and he shall direct thy paths.—PROV. 3:5, 6.

Thine ears shall hear a word behind thee, saying, This is the way, walk ye in it, when ye turn to the right hand, and when ye turn to the left.—ISA. 30:21.

NOVEMBER 3

IT IS NOT LITTLE BUT LARGE PETITIONING THAT THE LORD MOST DELIGHTS IN.

IT may not always be safe to ask very largely at the hands of men, for human resources are limited; or to ask too often, for human generosity is more limited still. In pleading with them, therefore, under-asking in the beginning usually succeeds better than over-asking. But at the throne of grace the rule is otherwise. Those best succeed there who are large in their asking, provided they are humble and expectant as well. It is even as one of the most familiar of the Olney hymns puts it:—

> *Thou art coming to a King,*
> *Large petitions with thee bring;*
> *For his love and power are such,*
> *None can ever ask too much.*

The Apostle Paul was never afraid to open his mouth wide and ask great things. 'We desire,' he said, 'that ye may be strengthened with all might, according to his glorious power, unto all patience and longsuffering with joyfulness.' Here was large petitioning: it was asking that not one, but every kind and degree of *inward strength*, might be imparted to the Colossian believers, to meet all and every requirement of the Christian life.

Divine power has always a peculiar glory when seen in the operations of grace. While the heavens declare the greatness and glory of God, yet, as one says, 'it is in the internal victories which he enables the weakest saints to achieve over the mightiest adversaries that God makes known most illustriously the glory of his power, wisdom, and love.' Occasionally, in times of need, when there is unusual faith in his people, the Lord does for them most unusual things.

When Myconius lay apparently dying, he wrote a letter to his friend Luther, who, after reading it, fell on his knees and began to pray with great earnestness and faith; he concluded by saying, 'O Lord, my God, thou must not yet take our brother Myconius to thyself; thy cause will not prosper without him. Amen.' He then rose up and wrote to his sick brother: 'There is no cause for fear, dear Myconius; the Lord will not let me hear that thou art dead. You shall not, and must not die. Amen.' These words made the most powerful impression on the heart of Myconius, and aroused him in such a manner that he recovered.

If ye abide in me, and my words abide in you, ye shall ask what ye will, and it shall be done unto you.—JOHN 15:7.

Go, and say to Hezekiah, Thus saith the Lord, the God of David thy
father, I have heard thy prayer, I have seen thy tears: behold, I will
add unto thy days fifteen years.—Isa. 38:5.

Hitherto have ye asked nothing in my name: ask, and ye shall
receive, that your joy may be full.—John 16:24.

November 4

*WHEN SPOKEN IN THE SPIRIT, EVEN A SINGLE WORD IS OFTEN
SAVINGLY EFFECTUAL.*

SOLOMON says, 'A word spoken in due season, how good is
it!' Nor does it need to be uttered by learned lips. When the
little captive maid said, in the love of her heart, 'Would God my
lord were with the prophet that is in Samaria! for he would recover
him of his leprosy,' little did she dream of all that would flow from
her simple utterance. It not only resulted at the time in the cure
and conversion of Naaman, but all down the ages its influence for
good has been felt.

It is a frequent complaint of some that their lot is too humble
and their position too obscure to admit of any usefulness in it;
but by this interesting case the Lord has taught us that even the
humblest may be used, if only they are living in the fear of the Lord.
Mark the simplicity of the means—it was but a simple remark, yet
being prayerful in its spirit it was powerfully influential. So will it
ever be when love and faith are on the outlook for opportunities
of usefulness.

'What awakened you?' said a Christian minister on one occasion
to a young friend. 'It was what you said to me one evening coming
out of the lecture-room. As you took me by the hand you said,
"Mary, one thing is needful." You said nothing else, and passed on;
but I could not forget it.' It was a word spoken in the Spirit, and
the Lord accompanied it with saving power.

It was once said by another, wise in winning souls, 'My old
friend, suppose that you and I begin this New Year with the

determination to be better men; let us turn over a new leaf.' The man thus addressed on a New Year's Eve was fifty years old, and had never given one hour to his Lord. He left with a thoughtful look on his countenance. That evening, for the first time, he was in the prayer meeting. Within a month he had set up his family altar and been admitted to the church of Christ. It touched the man just at the impressible moment, and did what a thousand sermons had failed to do. After narrating this interesting case, Dr Cuyler adds: 'We never can tell when the tinder will catch and flame up. It is ours to touch the torch of truth; the Divine Spirit may be in the torch, and we know it not.' There are few who know the Lord who have not many sad memories of golden opportunities of this nature entirely and forever lost.

> Lost for want of a word,
>   A word that you might have spoken;
> Who knows what eyes may be dim,
>   Or what hearts may be aching and broken!
> Go scatter beside all waters,
>   Nor sicken at hope deferred;
> Let never a soul by thy dumbness
>   Be lost for want of a word.

The Lord God hath given me the tongue of the learned, that I should know how to speak a word in season to him that is weary.—Isa. 50:4.

Let your speech be alway with grace, seasoned with salt, that ye may know how ye ought to answer every man.—Col. 4:6.

November 5

WE MUST TEST AS WELL AS LISTEN.

CHRISTIANITY does not require men to ignore facts, or to accept without scrutiny whatever may be presented. It says, on the contrary, 'Believe not every spirit, but try the spirits whether they are of God: because many false prophets are gone out into the world.'—'Prove all things; hold fast that which is good.' The 'all things' to be thus proved are obviously not all things in a wide and general sense, but simply all things belonging to religious truth, and that claim a divine origin and authority. We are not required, however, to read and study everything that can be said for every kind of error before rejecting it. It is enough to read or hear sufficiently to judge. 'Where error,' says Mr Spurgeon, 'is manifest on the surface, to expose our minds to its pernicious influence is as great a madness as to test the strength of a fever by lying in its lair. Against the siren's song the only safety was deaf ears. Only a gross simpleton would leap into a pit full of rattlesnakes to see if they would do him any harm. A wise man is content to leave the experiment untried.'

In carrying out this enjoined testing, Scripture everywhere insists on a right state of the heart and life towards God as an indispensable condition of all right and safe judging of the things of God. 'If any man will do his will, he shall know of the doctrine whether it be of God.'—'Unto the upright light ariseth in the darkness.' Conduct and opinion constantly act and react, the one upon the other. Every wrongness in the heart ever tends to produce more or less of darkness in the mind.

> *Faults in the life breed errors in the brain,*
> *And these reciprocally those again.*

In all cases the one grand standard, to which everything must be referred, is the word of God. 'To the law and to the testimony: if they speak not according to this word, it is because there is no light in them.' Paul commended the Bereans because they searched the Scriptures daily whether these things were so. Seeing, then, that even the apostles desired to be so tested, we may unhesitatingly prove all things, by whomsoever delivered; yea, even if an angel from heaven were to come to teach us, our duty still would be, as God has given us a perfect standard, to refer everything to it and to try everything by it. In doing this, however, we must ever seek the help and guidance of the Holy Spirit; for thereby only can we get *the humble mind* that will bend and bow with all readiness to every utterance of the Lord. 'In every age people have gone astray,' says Dr James Alexander, 'by going away from the Bible. The statements of Scripture are positive truths, given on divine authority; and faith is as necessary as obedience, for it is as much our duty *to believe what God says* as to do what he commands.'

> Jesus answered and said unto them, Ye do err, not knowing the scriptures, nor the power of God.—MATT. 22:29.
>
> They have Moses and the prophets; let them hear them.—LUKE 16:29.
>
> All scripture is given by inspiration of God, and is profitable for doctrine, for reproof, for correction, for instruction in righteousness: that the man of God may be perfect, thoroughly furnished unto all good works.—2 TIM. 3:16, 17.

NOVEMBER 6

WE CAN NEITHER TOO EARLY NOR TOO EARNESTLY SOW THE GOOD SEED OF THE KINGDOM.

WHEN restoring Peter after his fall to office as well as to honour, our Lord said, 'Feed my lambs,' as well as, 'Feed my sheep.' Though at first addressed to but one disciple, these words in the spirit of them are equally applicable to all disciples. They must remember the little ones, the young, the lambs of the flock, and seek their saving good always; and seek not earnestly only, but expectantly.

Perhaps no kind of Christian effort has been more richly and abundantly blessed than labours of love among the young. Faithful ministers and teachers in every land have found it so; and the countless jewels they have been privileged to gather in Bible classes and Sabbath schools have been a joy unspeakable to them. In a peculiar degree, however, the duty referred to is binding on parents; hence the impressive counsels given in Old Testament times: 'These words, which I command thee this day, shall be in thine heart: and thou shalt teach them diligently unto thy children, and shalt talk of them when thou sittest in thine house, and when thou walkest by the way, and when thou liest down, and when thou risest up. And thou shalt bind them for a sign upon thine hand, and they shall be as frontlets between thine eyes. And thou shalt write them upon the posts of thy house, and on thy gates.'

None can be too early in the discharge of this all-important duty. It is related of Ben Syra that when a child he begged his preceptor to instruct him in the law of God; but he declined, saying that he was yet too young to be taught these sacred mysteries. 'But, master,' said the boy, 'I have been in the burial ground, and measured the graves, and find some of them shorter than myself. Now, if I should die before I have learned the word of God, what will become of me then, master?' Ben Syra's question is one that all parents should earnestly ponder. They may be too late in teaching their children the way of life, but they cannot be too early.

A few years ago, one earnestly said, 'Father, where is your child tonight?—Mother, where is your son? Are they on the way to glory? Have they been gathered into the fold of Christ? Are their names written in the Lamb's book of life. Depend upon it, so long as the church is living so much like the world, we cannot expect our children to be brought into the fold. Come, O Lord, and wake us up to feel the worth of our children's souls! May they never bring our grey hairs with sorrow to the grave, but may they become a blessing to the church and to the world.'

> He appointed a law in Israel, which he commanded our fathers, that they should make them known to their children: that the generation to come might know them, even the children which should be born; who should arise and declare them to their children: that they might set their hope in God.—Psa. 78:5-7.

> Train up a child in the way he should go: and when he is old, he will not depart from it.—Prov. 22:6.

NOVEMBER 7

TRUE GRATITUDE EVER PANTS FOR EXPRESSION.

WHEN the Lord healed the ten lepers, possibly all of them felt for the moment a measure of thankfulness; but so feeble was it, that by nine of them no outward expression of it was ever given. The Samaritan, the one exception, not only turned back and with a loud voice glorified God, but, falling down at the feet of Jesus, poured out to him his warmest thanks. On seeing this, our Lord said, 'Were there not ten cleansed? but where are the nine? There are not found that returned to give glory to God, save this stranger.'

Were it with us as it ought to be, the Lord's gracious dealings and generous bestowments, which none can number, instead of being allowed to drop from our memory, would be ceaselessly constraining us to say with the Psalmist, 'Bless the Lord, O my soul, and forget not all his benefits.' Nay, we would be frequently striving to bring back to remembrance forgotten mercies, just that we might anew express our grateful emotions. 'Let us read our diaries,' one says, 'and see if there be not choice favours recorded there, for which we have rendered no grateful return. Remember how the Persian king, when he could not sleep, read the chronicles of the empire, and discovered that one who had saved his life had never been rewarded. How quickly did he do him honour! The Lord has saved us with a great salvation; shall we render him no recompense, and yield him no praise, when so infinitely and eternally worthy of it?'

It is sometimes well, when special mercies are obtained, to give, not thanks, but *thank-offerings*. A very singular and interesting example of this is mentioned by Dr James Hamilton. 'When coming downstairs on Monday morning, I met Miss Fector coming in. She had come with £50 for the schemes of the church—a thank-offering from her mother. It seems that Mrs Fector had a cataract in her eye, and was intending to undergo the usual operation for its removal; but she did not like the idea of the operation any more than the prospect of losing the eye, and she prayed earnestly that, if it were the Lord's will, he would remove it himself. Three weeks ago, to her amazement the cataract was gone. She sent for Alexander the oculist, who was to have extracted it; and he said it was a case almost unprecedented, but had been done by a very peculiar action of the muscles of the eye. So the good old lady, in the fulness of her heart, sent this acknowledgment.'

> O Lord ... thou hast loosed my bonds. I will offer to thee the sacrifice of thanksgiving, and will call upon the name of the Lord.—Psa. 116:16, 17.

> By him ... let us offer the sacrifice of praise to God continually, that is, the fruit of our lips giving thanks to his name.—Heb. 13:15.

> And whatsoever ye do in word or deed, do all in the name of the Lord Jesus, giving thanks to God and the Father by him.—Col. 3:17.

November 8

OBEDIENCE HAS BUT LITTLE VALUE IF UNLINKED WITH THE NAME OF JESUS.

THEY utterly mistake Christianity who suppose that its aim is merely to make a man do certain specified things, at certain specified times and places, and then have done with him. It claims, on the contrary, to regulate and control his whole nature and practice, including thought and feeling, will and way; and not in the sanctuary only, but in all the affairs of everyday life. It requires him to be guided and governed in everything by the will of Christ. 'Whatsoever ye do in word or deed, do all *in the name of the Lord Jesus*, giving thanks to God and the Father by him.'

When the apostles were asked by the high priest, 'By what power, or by what name, have ye done these things?' their reply was ready—'By the name of Jesus.' So must it be with us. We must strive to regulate our every action by his law, and conform our whole lives to his will. 'Christ,' says one, 'has shown his love in trusting his cause to us, and lent us as volumes of his library for the perusal of the world.' At times such obedience is simple and easy; at other times it is so hard and difficult, as to be like the cutting off of a right hand or the plucking out of a right eye. Yet we must cheerfully bear the very worst of evils, rather than wilfully and deliberately violate the very least of the Lord's commands. It may be terrible to suffer, but it is ever infinitely more terrible to sin. Besides, whatever we suffer for righteousness' sake and for Christ is never in the end a loss, but a gain—never a sorrow, but a joy; and therefore in early times believers rejoiced that they were counted worthy to suffer shame for his name.

'As you see,' said an old author, 'that those servants of a prince who have been peculiarly favoured set up his arms through all their houses, and adorn their halls and chambers with his picture, and have his praises always in their mouth, and fill up their whole life with his name and glory; so should we do to Jesus, and with so much the more zeal, as he is infinitely more rich, more clement, more liberal, more beneficent, than any monarch of the earth.'

For to me to live is Christ, and to die is gain.—PHIL. 1:21.

If any man speak, let him speak as the oracles of God; if any man minister, let him do it as of the ability which God giveth: that God in all things may be glorified through Jesus Christ.—1 PET. 4:11.

None of us liveth to himself, and no man dieth to himself. For whether we live, we live unto the Lord; and whether we die, we die unto the Lord: whether we live therefore, or die, we are the Lord's.—ROM. 14:7, 8.

NOVEMBER 9

THE LORD'S JEWELS ARE WIDELY GATHERED.

THE time was when the Lord's redeemed seem to have been gathered mainly from one land and people; for as yet the middle wall of partition between Jew and Gentile had not been broken down. It became entirely otherwise at the coming of our Lord; for then the apostles, by divine command, went forth to all the world to preach the gospel to every creature. Ever since, the ransomed of the Lord have, through the same divine power and saving grace, been gathered from all lands, and with heart and soul have joined in showing forth the praises of him who called them out of darkness into his marvellous light. Their song, however oft repeated through coming ages, will ever be new, because ever sung with fresh gratitude and joy: 'Thou art worthy ... for thou wast slain, and hast redeemed us to God by thy blood out of every kindred, and tongue, and people, and nation; and hast made us unto our God kings and priests.'

Meanwhile, those gathered out from year to year may seem few in number—a little band, with little influence; but the day is hastening on when they shall be a multitude which no man can number: and the certainty of this may well cheer and sustain us amid all the conflicts and discouragements of present times.

But it is not only out of every tribe and tongue the redeemed are gathered, but also out of every rank and class. Men of every variety of occupation and profession have been converted by the gospel and savingly won to Christ. Cornelius was a soldier, Dionysius a senator, Luke a physician, Zenas a lawyer, Lydia a merchant, Matthew a tax-gatherer, Peter a fisherman, Aquila a tent-maker; yet all alike were brought lovingly to the feet of Jesus.

Great practical ends are served by such variety of sphere, social position, and mode of life among the Lord's disciples; and therefore young converts should beware of changing their calling in rash and inconsiderate haste. In the ardour of their first love they sometimes forget that it is not Christian ministers only the church and the world need, but Christian physicians, lawyers, merchants, and tradesmen as well, and that, however situated, it should be their constant aim to glorify the Lord in their calling, and to let their calling glorify the Lord. Indeed, the Christian ministry is never so powerful for good as when surrounded and supported by consistent witnesses for the truth belonging to every class in the community. Though the Redeemer alone could purchase the jewels—for nothing less than his own precious blood could avail for this—yet all his people may share in the joy and honour of helping to gather them. And the more they succeed in this, through faith and prayer and loving self-sacrifice, the brighter will their own crown be, and the nearer will they themselves be to him who is dearer to them than life itself.

> I saw another angel fly in the midst of heaven, having the everlasting gospel to preach unto them that dwell on the earth, and to every nation, and kindred, and tongue, and people.—REV. 14:6.

> And he shall send his angels with a great sound of a trumpet, and they shall gather together his elect from the four winds, from one end of heaven to the other.—MATT. 24:31.

> After this I beheld, and, lo, a great multitude, which no man could number, of all nations, and kindreds, and people, and tongues, stood before the throne, and before the Lamb, clothed with white robes, and palms in their hands.—REV. 7:9.

NOVEMBER 10

NEEDFUL FIXITY.

IT would have been but a little thing to the men of Judah to be brought out of Babylon, if they had not, in addition, been brought unto Zion, and seen their Temple restored, with all its attendant service and privilege. Everything needful, however, they fully obtained; for in rich mercy the Lord enabled them to set up anew the house of their God, and repair, in part at least, the desolations thereof: and therefore they said, 'Now for a little space grace hath been shewed from the Lord our God, to leave us a remnant to escape, and to give us a nail in his holy place.'

We are never in the true Holy Place till we are in Christ Jesus, through whom we have access by one Spirit to the Father; and if so privileged, it must be our constant aim to bring our whole spirit and conduct into entire conformity with the divine will, whether as revealed in God's law or embodied in Christ's life. 'I want to be like Christ,' said the saintly Judson; 'I want to follow him only, drink in his spirit, place my feet in his footprints, and measure my shortcomings by these alone.'

When Ezra speaks, not only of a holy place, but of a nail in it, his words suggest the thought that, besides holy fervour, there must be fixedness in our religion, as if by a sure nail securely driven. There is no greater blemish in Christian character than instability; yet of how many might it be said, as of Reuben, 'Unstable as water, thou shalt not excel.' They are always unsettled, and more or less inclined to take out the nails and loosen the fastenings of life, and turn liberty into license.

Whoever may so act, let our resolute purpose be to have fixed principles and fixed afflictions, and to say as the Psalmist did, even in the midst of enemies, 'My heart is fixed, O God, my heart is fixed; I will sing and give praise.' 'One would have thought,' says Mr Spurgeon, 'he would have said, "My heart is fluttered." But no; he is calm, resolute, established. When the axle is secure, the whole wheel is right. If our great bower anchor holds, the ship cannot drive. "O God, my heart is fixed"; I am resolved to trust thee, to serve thee, and to praise thee. Blessed are they whose once roving hearts become firmly fixed on God.'

> I have set the Lord always before me: because he is at my right hand, I shall not be moved.—PSA. 16:8.

> Then Paul answered, What mean ye to weep and to break mine heart? for I am ready not to be bound only, but also to die at Jerusalem for the name of the Lord Jesus.—ACTS 21:13.

NOVEMBER 11

THE DAY THAT NONE CAN KNOW.

WHAT was said by Isaac may be said by all: 'I know not the day of my death.' There have been rare occasions, indeed, when the time of their departure has been known by men beforehand. This was the case with King Hezekiah; for not only, in answer to prayer, was his life spared, but a definite number of years was added to it. 'I have heard thy prayer,' the Lord said to him, 'I have seen thy tears: behold, I will add unto thy days fifteen years … And this shall be a sign unto thee that the Lord will do this thing that he hath spoken; behold, I will bring again the shadow of the degrees, which is gone down in the sun-dial of Ahaz, ten degrees backward. So the sun returned ten degrees, by which degrees it was gone down.' Hezekiah had thus a secret conveyed to him of a very remarkable kind, for he was told the exact measure of his time—that fifteen years more would be given him. But in all other cases such knowledge is withheld.

This fact is a practically suggestive one. First of all, it should awaken thankfulness. Sometimes the wish springs up in us that we could lift the veil from the future, and know all that awaits us in our after-pilgrimage; forgetting that if such a wish were granted, instead of ministering to our comfort, it would only intensify our grief. One says,—'It is a righteous and tender hand which keeps the next day's page safely folded down.' It is even so; for meanwhile we could not bear a full revelation of the earthly future before us in all its manifold details. It would wholly unfit us for duty. Better far is it for us to get the knowledge little by little as each day comes; all the more, as it is thus the promise runs: 'Thy shoes shall be iron and brass; and as thy days, so shall thy strength be.' It is day by day, just as it is needed, that sustaining grace is given.

But, again, this fact should hasten preparedness. No man in his natural state is prepared to die; for being an alien from God, and still in his sins, he is necessarily under condemnation. The express words of our Lord himself are: 'He that believeth on him is not condemned: but he that believeth not is condemned already, because he hath not believed in the name of the only begotten Son of God.' To believe in the Lord Jesus, therefore, is a first and pressing duty. We may be too late in it, but it is impossible to be too early. When, however, we know the Lord, to be found working for him is as good a preparation for meeting him as to be found waiting and praying. A lady once said to John Wesley, 'Suppose you knew you were to die at twelve o'clock tomorrow night, how would you employ the intervening time?' 'Why, just as I intend to spend it now. I would preach this evening at Gloucester, and again at five tomorrow morning. After that, I should ride to Tewkesbury; preach in the afternoon; meet the societies in the evening; then repair to friend Martin's, who expects to entertain me; converse and pray with the family as usual; retire to my room at ten o'clock; commend myself to my heavenly Father; lie down to rest; wake up in glory!'

> Boast not thyself of to morrow; for thou knowest not what a day may bring forth.—PROV. 27:1.

> Go to now, ye that say, To day or to morrow we will go into such a city, and continue there a year, and buy and sell, and get gain: Whereas ye know not what shall be on the morrow. For what is your life? It is even a vapour, that appeareth for a little time, and then vanisheth away.—JAMES 4:13, 14.

> The world passeth away, and the lust thereof: but he that doeth the will of God abideth for ever.—1 JOHN 2:17.

NOVEMBER 12

TWO CLASSES CONTRASTED.

AFTER commending the unjust steward because he had done wisely, our Lord added,—'For the children of this world are in their generation wiser than the children of light.' There are here two great and distinctly marked classes set before us—the children of this world, and the children of light: the former being the unrenewed, who forget God, and live only for time; and the latter, the divinely quickened, who were sometimes darkness, but are now light in the Lord.

The difference between them is great and vital. Other distinctions are merely outward, and in no degree interfere with present peace or eternal safety, for, happily, neither wealth nor poverty are ever allowed to make any saving difference. A man may be poor, uncultured, or dark as the tents of Kedar, and yet be a very gem of grace; or, on the other hand, be rich and cultured, and yet be a very slave of sin: or the reverse—the rich may welcome the Saviour, and the poor reject him. But one thing is certain—we cannot continue to be children of this world and enter the kingdom, or be children of light and be excluded from it.

This distinction has existed more or less from the very beginning. As one says: 'All along through history you see the two seeds in contention: if there is Abel, there is Cain who slays him; if there is Noah, there is an ungodly world all around him; if there is an Isaac, so also is there an Ishmael, who will mock him. There cannot be an Israel without Pharaoh, or Amalek, or Edom, or Babylon to oppose.'

Most of the present distinctions among men are temporary only—ephemeral things that have no tomorrow; but the one referred to here between the righteous and the wicked, the God-fearing and the godless, is one abiding, as these words of inspiration clearly intimate: 'He that is unjust, let him be unjust still: and he which is filthy, let him be filthy still: and he that is righteous, let him be righteous still: and he that is holy, let him be holy still.'

So long, however, as the day of grace lasts, there may be a blessed transition from the one class to the other.

As long as life its term extends,
Hope's blest dominion never ends;
For while the lamp holds on to burn,
The greatest sinner may return.

'The depths of misery,' says an old divine, 'are never beyond the depths of mercy.' But as the term of life is altogether uncertain, the seeking of this mercy should be immediate.

Ye were sometimes darkness, but now are ye light in the Lord: walk as children of light.—EPH. 5:8.

Ye are all the children of light, and the children of the day: we are not of the night, nor of darkness. Therefore let us not sleep, as do others; but let us watch and be sober.—1 Thess. 5:5, 6.

NOVEMBER 13

THE SUPERIORITY DECLARED.

WISDOM has been said to consist in choosing the best end, and the most suitable means for securing it. Now, insofar as the grand end of life is concerned, believers have the superiority in every way over mere men of the world. But in choosing the best means for attaining the object aimed at, and energetically using them, they have not even equality with them; hence the memorable words of our Lord: 'The children of this world are wiser in this generation than the children of light.' They are wiser in this respect, that they keep more constantly in view their chosen end, whether it be business success, honourable distinction, or pleasurable ease. It never gets a mere secondary place with them. With the children of light it is often otherwise. Though they have chosen the right end, they do not always keep it in view as they ought, and set their heart on it, and diligently use every means for its attainment. Too often they cleave to the dust, instead of pressing onward and mounting heavenward like the lark, of which it has been so beautifully said,—

> *Higher, still higher*
> *From the earth thou springest,*
> *Like a cloud of fire*
> *The blue deep thou wingest,*
> *And singing still dost soar,*
> *And soaring ever singest.*

Besides, they are inferior, too, in courage; for while the children of this world openly avow their aims and hopes, the children of light, on the contrary, often act as if they were ashamed of the Master they serve, the name they bear, and the hopes they cherish.

There are always, however, noble exceptions—believers so true and loyal that even in the worst of times they fearlessly follow the Lamb whithersoever he goeth. A few years ago an Irish convert, when urged on his death-bed to receive the priest, firmly replied, 'I wish no sinful saviour while Jesus is with me'; and on the threat being held out that none of the relatives would attend his funeral, he calmly replied, 'Well, I shall have the burial of Moses; God and angels will see me laid in my quiet grave.'

> Thou hast a few names even in Sardis which have not defiled their garments; and they shall walk with me in white: for they are worthy.—REV. 3:4.

> Whosoever therefore shall confess me before men, him will I confess also before my Father which is in heaven.—MATT. 10:32.

NOVEMBER 14

TRUSTFUL RELIANCE.

THOSE who have true faith in lively exercise, not only rightly turn, but rightly trust, and on all fitting occasions give full and open expression to the confidence they feel. When a traveller who has become weak and weary has a strong and loving friend by his side, he leans on him; and the more he leans, the better he proves the reality of his trust. Now this is a faint type of believers in their journey homeward. Many a time they are, as it were, dusty, footsore, and sadly discouraged because of the way. Yet there is no hopeless despondency with them. Just because having the Lord by their side, they not only lean on him once and again, but all the desert through; and, happily, lean as they may, they can never over-lean. When faith is in exercise, it is always a direct and personal thing.

There are many things that one can do for another, but to exercise faith is not one of them. None can believe for another, either for the saving of his soul, or the refreshment of his spirit. No; faith is an individual thing, a personal act; and each believer for himself must exercise it, just as the Psalmist did when he said, 'In the Lord put *I my* trust.' When the wounded Israelites were perishing in the wilderness, and the brazen serpent was lifted up for their healing, however willing he might be, one wounded Israelite could not look for another. He might point the place to him, or wisely counsel him, or kindly lift his drooping head; but not unless his own individual eye rested on the uplifted serpent could healing come and life be preserved.

It is even so still. If ever we are to be truly saved, there must on our side be individual looking to an uplifted Saviour, and individual trust. Even now the Lord is graciously saying, 'Look unto me, all ye ends of the earth, and be ye saved.' Speaking of looking and leaning on Christ, the saintly Rutherford says: 'What could we do without him? It is good for us that ever Christ took the cumber of us. It is our heaven to lay many weights and burdens upon him, and to make him root and top, beginning and ending of our salvation. Lord hold us here.'

> What time I am afraid, I will trust in thee. In God I will praise his word, in God I have put my trust; I will not fear what flesh can do unto me.—PSA. 56:3, 4.

> David was greatly distressed; for the people spake of stoning him … but David encouraged himself in the Lord his God.—1 SAM. 30:6.

NOVEMBER 15

BEFORE WE CAN ABIDE WE MUST COME.

THERE are in Scripture two words distinct in meaning, yet closely allied, and both so precious that, like sweet melody, we can scarcely hear them too often. These are 'Come' and 'Abide.' They are both uttered by the same divine lips, and with the same warmth of affection; and though at times it is the latter only that is spoken of, yet it presupposes the former, for we cannot possibly abide in Christ till first we come to him.

In mounting a ladder, if we expect to reach the summit we must begin by putting our foot on its lowest round. Even so, in aspiring to a pure and lofty communion with him who alone is our life and salvation, we must begin by a lowly drawing near to him in simple faith. Accordingly, the very first invitations we have to do with are such as these,—and they are familiar as household words,—'Come unto me, all ye that labour and are heavy laden, and I will give you rest.'—'Him that cometh to me I will in no wise cast out.'

But here, alas! many sadly stumble. They cannot believe that a salvation so precious can be acquired so simply, and so, making that difficult which the Lord has made easy, they would first throw off their burden, then come to the Burden-bearer; first get rid of their debt, then come to the Surety; first wipe off their defilement, then enter the fountain opened for sin and uncleanness.

What could be more hopelessly unwise than this? An old divine says: 'Sin gives you your first title to the Friend of sinners; and a simple, naked faith the second. Do not, then, puzzle yourself about contrition, love, joy, and a thousand such things, which the tempter will persuade you you must bring to Christ. He will receive you gladly even with a mountain of sin, and the smallest grain of faith at Christ's feet will remove that mountain.' What the Lord asks of you is simply to come as you are, and leave yourself in his loving hands.

When I come with troubled heart,
Jesus bids me not depart
* Till he stills it;*
When I come with empty urn,
Jesus bids me not return
* Till he fills it.*
Once I came in tattered dress,
And the God of holiness
* Did not loathe me;*
Bringing nothing for the payment,
When I came for change of raiment
* He did clothe me.*

In the last day, that great day of the feast, Jesus stood and cried, saying, If any man thirst, let him come unto me, and drink.—JOHN 7:37.

The Spirit and the bride say, Come. And let him that heareth say, Come. And let him that is athirst come. And whosoever will, let him take the water of life freely.—REV. 22:17.

Ye will not come to me, that ye might have life.—JOHN 5:40.

NOVEMBER 16

AFTER COMING WE MUST ABIDE.

TO come to Christ is invariably the first thing to be done: but, having come, we must then abide; for it is not merely our peace that depends on this abiding, but our very salvation. When the mariners, in the time of Paul, were about to desert the ship, and were in the very act of letting down the boat into the stormy sea, he said, with resolute earnestness, 'Except these abide in the ship, ye cannot be saved.' So is it in this case. Except we abide in Christ we perish. Apart from him we have no blood to cleanse us, no righteousness to justify, no Spirit to sanctify, nor strength to sustain, nor hope to cheer. It is only, therefore, as we now abide with him in grace that we can hereafter abide with him in glory.

We are not from this to suppose that there can be any final falling away of true saints, or that they will ever be abandoned by the Lord. There may, indeed, be occasional and even humiliating backsliding, and on this very account severe and bitter chastenings, but there will be no final desertion. His own blessed promise makes this sweetly sure to us: 'If his children forsake my law, and walk not in my judgments; if they break my statutes and keep not my commandments; then will I visit their transgression with the rod, and their iniquity with stripes. Nevertheless my lovingkindness will I not utterly take from him, nor suffer my faithfulness to fail. My covenant will I not break, nor alter the thing that is gone out of my lips.' However it may be with mere human affection, which is often so fitful and transient, it is never so with the love of the Redeemer. Like his own nature, it is immutable: having loved his own from the beginning, he loves them to the end. Still, through unwatchfulness on the part of his people, while they may have saving union with their Lord, they may have very little intimate and sweet communion.

> *I need thy presence every passing hour:*
> *What but thy grace can foil the tempter's power?*
> *Who like thyself my guide and stay can be?*
> *Through cloud and sunshine, O abide with me!*

Many would fain come to God as refuge who fail to abide in him as a home.

> I am crucified with Christ: nevertheless I live; yet not I, but Christ liveth in me: and the life which I now live in the flesh I live by the faith of the Son of God, who loved me, and gave himself for me.—GAL. 2:20.

> Abide in me, and I in you. As the branch cannot bear fruit of itself, except it abide in the vine; no more can ye, except ye abide in me.—JOHN 15:4.

> Little children, abide in him; that, when he shall appear, we may have confidence, and not be ashamed before him at his coming.— 1 JOHN 2:28.

NOVEMBER 17

ABRAHAM GOD'S FRIEND.

IT was one of the high distinctions of Abraham to be known as the friend of God. 'Art not thou our God,' said Jehoshaphat, 'who didst drive out the inhabitants of this land before thy people Israel, and gavest it to the seed of Abraham *thy friend*?' To be so related to God, and so spoken of, was one of the very richest of privileges. Many friendships are merely nominal; they are hastily formed, and, being without either vitality or warmth, they are often just as hastily dissolved. But not so the sacred intimacy enjoyed by the patriarch. It was the friendship of friendships, pure, elevated, and enriching. All through life God guarded and blessed him, opening up his way, directing his steps, showing him favour, and supplying his need. Nay, more: in infinite condescension he communed and talked with him as a man with his friend. And in times when special sin demanded special judgment, he confided to him his secret purpose, saying, 'Shall I hide from Abraham that thing which I do?'

And what he did then he is ever ready to do still, in fulfilment of the promise: 'The secret of the Lord is with them that fear him, and he will shew them his covenant'; and in fulfilment, too, of these words of the Redeemer: 'Ye are my friends, if ye do whatsoever I command you. Henceforth I call you not servants; for the servant knoweth not what his Lord doeth: but I have called you friends; for all things that I have heard of my Father I have made known unto you.' True, the disciples, as well as all Christians, continue to be the servants of Christ, but not in the sense in which the *servant* excludes the friend, but in that sense in which the servant is the *chosen friend* as well. 'They are,' says one, 'no longer servants, but *children*, and heirs, and *friends*; because they have been redeemed from the bondage of the law, and have received the spirit of adoption, and abide forever in the house with the Son, and are admitted into the secrets of their Lord through the unction of the Holy Ghost.'

When we read such promises as these,—'Fear not, Abram: I am thy shield, and thy exceeding great reward'—'Arise, walk through the land in the length of it and in the breadth of it; for I will give it to thee,'—it is well to remember that it is not Abraham only who has an interest in these and like promises, but all his spiritual seed, the faithful in Christ Jesus. They too shall inherit the earth, even as it is written: 'The kingdom and the dominion, and greatness of the kingdom under the whole heaven, shall be given to the people of the saints of the most High, whose kingdom is an everlasting kingdom, and all dominions shall serve and obey him.'

The God of Abraham praise!
Whose all-sufficient grace
Shall safely guide me all my days,
In all his ways:
He calls a worm his friend!
He calls himself my God!
And he shall save me to the end,
Through Jesu's blood.

Then they that feared the Lord spake often one to another: and the Lord hearkened, and heard it, and a book of remembrance was written before him for them that feared the Lord, and that thought upon his name. And they shall be mine, saith the Lord of hosts, in that day when I make up my jewels.—MAL. 3:16, 17.

Blessed be the Lord, who daily loadeth us with benefits, even the God of our salvation.—PSA. 68:19.

NOVEMBER 18

MIGHT ALONE COULD NOT HAVE DELIVERED US.

TO deliver needed love on Christ's part as well as power,—a love that could not merely teach and serve for the objects of it, but suffer and die. It bodes ill for the future of any church or people when they begin to ignore such loving substitution, and to speak contemptuously of blood and atonement; for if there be one thing on earth surer than another, it is that without shedding of blood there is no remission of sin, nor any hope of needed salvation. No utterances could be more express than these: 'Christ hath redeemed us from the curse of the law, being made a curse for us.'—'Christ hath once suffered for sins, the just for the unjust, that he might bring us to God.'

These precious words, as clearly revealing the divine method of redemption, may well yield the richest comfort to every sin-burdened and anxious soul. 'When the iniquities of us,' says an old writer, 'are by the Lord laid upon Christ, they cannot be upon us and upon Christ too: if they be reckoned to Christ, they are not reckoned to him that doth receive Christ.' When the chief captain learned that Paul was a Roman, he said, 'With a great sum obtained I this freedom.' But the redeemed obtain theirs with an infinitely greater price,—not with silver or gold, but with the precious blood of God's own Son.

This blood has had a marvellously redeeming efficacy in every age, and shall never lose its cleansing power till the very last of the countless multitude of the redeemed has been savingly washed in it. Our case may be seemingly the most hopeless imaginable,—

> Yet not the less that blood avails
> To cleanse away my sin;
> And not the less that cross prevails
> To give me peace within.

The history of the church of Christ abounds with striking exemplifications of this. In his 'Fulfilling of Scripture,' Mr Fleming relates the case of a man who, after a career of appalling wickedness, was condemned to death in the town of Ayr. He had been so dull and brutish that all who knew him thought him entirely beyond the reach of all ordinary means of grace. But while the man was in prison the Lord wonderfully wrought on his heart, and in such a measure discovered to him his sinfulness, that, after much serious exercise and sore wrestling, a most kindly work of repentance followed, with great assurance of mercy; insomuch that, when he came to the place of execution, he astonished all the onlookers, for he could not cease crying out, under the sense of pardon, 'Oh, he is a forgiver,—a great forgiver; and perfect love hath cast out fear. Nothing now can be laid against me, for Jesus Christ hath paid all; and those are free whom the Son makes free.'

Deliver him from going down to the pit: I have found a ransom.—JOB 33:24.

The Son of man came not to be ministered unto, but to minister, and to give his life a ransom for many.—MATT. 20:28.

And the ransomed of the Lord shall return, and come to Zion with songs and everlasting joy upon their heads: they shall obtain joy and gladness, and sorrow and sighing shall flee away.—ISA. 35:10.

[469]

NOVEMBER 19

THE FRUIT OF CHASTENING.

THOUGH affliction's rod is often heavy and hard to bear, yet, to those who are exercised by it, it becomes like that of Aaron, and buds and blossoms and brings forth fruit, not abundant only, but most precious—even 'the peaceable fruits of righteousness.' In itself it has not this tendency, but rather the very opposite; for in fallen man the natural fruit of affliction is not righteousness and peace, but increased rebellion and deeper misery. When lovingly controlled by God, however, the very thing that would naturally sour and harden men is made to minister to their highest life and spiritual growth. When, therefore, they are brought to kiss the hand that smites, there is cheering evidence that not nature only, but grace, has been efficaciously operating.

Though the rod of affliction, however, is fruitful, it is not always so at once. The rod of Aaron in a single night not only bloomed blossoms, but yielded almonds. It is otherwise with the fruits that spring from the chastening of the Lord; for the apostle tells us that it is not immediately, but *afterwards* they appear.

One of the most precious fruits of sanctified affliction is a growing submission to the will of God, and a cheerful saying from day to day, 'Not my will, but thine be done.' But for our alienated nature, this should not be difficult; for the Lord's will is not more sovereign in its nature than loving and wise. 'The will of God,' it has been said, 'is a perpetual calm; for there are no cross tides nor contrary winds in it; and the tempest-tossed soul that puts into it, as into a harbour, becomes both safe and blessed.'

Other fruits of chastening are, a growing tenderness of conscience, delight in the word, deepening sympathy with the sorrowful, and a fuller energy in every work of faith and labour of love.

Sanctified afflictions may well, therefore, be viewed as an evidence of adoption; for we do not prune dead trees to make them fruitful, nor those which are planted in the desert, but such as belong to the garden and possess life.

> *I do not ask, O Lord, that life may be a pleasant road;*
> *I do not ask that thou wouldst take from me aught of its load;*
> *I do not ask that flowers may always spring beneath my feet—*
> *I know too well the poison and the sting of things too sweet;—*
> *For one thing only, Lord, dear Lord, I plead,—lead me aright,*
> *Though strength should falter, and though heart should bleed,*
> *Through peace to light.*

Before I was afflicted I went astray: but now have I kept thy word.—PSA. 119:67.

No chastening for the present seemeth to be joyous, but grievous: nevertheless afterward it yieldeth the peaceable fruit of righteousness unto them which are exercised thereby.—HEB. 12:11.

NOVEMBER 20

RIGHT GLORYING AND WRONG.

THE church in Thessalonica was poor, persecuted, and despised; yet the apostle, so far from being ashamed of it on this account, only prized and loved it the more. 'We ourselves,' he said, '*glory in you* in the churches of God for your patience and faith in all your persecutions and tribulations that ye endure.' The patience they showed was not the stubbornness of mere natural courage, but a blessed fruit of faith. They were patient, because, in spite of all their trials, they believed that God loved them, and would preserve them, and make all things work together for good. 'Faith,' says an old commentator, 'patienteth the heart by putting the head into heaven beforehand. It says to a suffering saint, "Be of good courage and of good carriage under the cross." It wraps itself in the promises, lays the soul upon Christ, and maketh the weak to become strong. Whatsoever cross cometh upon it, faith is either a wreath betwixt the burden and the shoulder, that it wring not, or else a remover of it, by virtue of that writ, "Cast thy burden upon the Lord."'

When Paul beheld such grace in them, he could not restrain his joy and gracious encouragement. 'We ourselves,' he said, 'glory in you in the churches of God.' Such words, from such lips, accompanied as they were with such warm, loving sympathy, not only sweetly sustained them, but mightily stimulated and quickened others. Would that all believers among us were possessed of a Christianity as warm and thorough as theirs. An Irish gentleman, pointing to a young man, once said, 'Is he an O. O.?'—'What do you mean by O. O.?'—'I mean,' was the reply, 'is he out and out for Christ?' This is what all ought to be who bear Christ's name.

'When all who belong to the Lord,' one says, 'are willing to speak for him, willing to work for him, willing to die for him, then Christianity will advance, and we shall see the work of the Lord prosper.'

> In nothing terrified by your adversaries: which is to them an evident token of perdition, but to you of salvation, and that of God.—PHIL. 1:28.

> Blessed are they which are persecuted for righteousness' sake: for theirs is the kingdom of heaven.—MATT. 5:10.

> Beloved, think it not strange concerning the fiery trial which is to try you, as though some strange thing happened unto you: but rejoice, inasmuch as ye are partakers of Christ's sufferings; that, when his glory shall be revealed, ye may be glad also with exceeding joy.—1 PET. 4:12, 13.

NOVEMBER 21

THE THIRSTING WELCOMED.

'I F any man thirst,' said our Lord, 'let him come unto me and drink.' Were these precious words now made known to us for the first time, apart altogether from their context, we could scarcely fail to see that if they were really words of truth, he could be no mere man that uttered them. Coming even from the greatest of our race, they would have been but a profane egotism, a cruel mockery; for we might as well attempt to illuminate the universe with a taper as to supply a perishing world with the water of life from mere creature sources. The words of this invitation possess such combined simplicity and majesty, that they befit no lips but those of the Master himself, in whom dwelt all the fulness of the Godhead bodily.

So ample and generous is his invitation, that it is *all-inclusive*. There is not a word in it either about peculiar lineage, or place of birth, or previous worthiness, to make any limitation. Coming is all that is needed: and when we really come, what the Lord mainly considers is, not our demerits, but our pressing wants; and not our guilt, but his own rich grace and promise.

When a generous offer is made by men, they are sometimes rather pleased than offended when it finds no acceptance; but it is never so with the Lord. When he brings men to the wells of salvation, it is not merely to look at them, or analyse them, but that by drinking from them they may have life and joy everlasting.

The evangelist, when referring to the words that follow, 'He that believeth on me, as the scripture hath said, out of his belly shall flow rivers of living water,' says, 'This spake he of the Spirit, which they that believe on him should receive.' Hence the continuance of their joy. Others have but wells without them, and when these dry up they are helpless; but believers possessing the fulness of the Spirit have a well within whose living waters are ever springing up to refresh and gladden them.

Now it is God's design that all who are thus receivers of blessing should also be dispensers of it. The Holy Spirit, one beautifully says, is not like those rivers we read of which flow through barren sand till they sink in the earth and disappear. It is an imperishable stream, and when it flows from Jesus into any barren heart it is never lost there—it appears again, and flows forth to the world in rivers of life and refreshing; for the scripture must be fulfilled: 'Out of his belly shall flow rivers of living water.' Wherever, therefore, a true Christian dwells, he should be a living well in it—a fountain of blessing to all around.

Ho, every one that thirsteth, come ye to the waters, and he that hath no money; come ye, buy, and eat; yea, come, buy wine and milk without money and without price.—Isa. 55:1.

I am Alpha and Omega, the beginning and the end. I will give unto him that is athirst of the fountain of the water of life freely.— Rev. 21:6.

November 22

WE CANNOT SAVE, BUT WE MAY VARIOUSLY HELP.

WHATEVER their wisdom or grace, none can by any means redeem his brother, or give to God a ransom for him; nevertheless, if only believing and compassionate enough, all may do much for the deliverance of those who are drawn unto death.

It is in the power of all to warn. This of itself may have mighty efficacy; indeed, it often needs but a word seasonably and earnestly spoken to make the erring shrink back and regain their hold of truth and righteousness ere the tide of evil has swept them away. Years ago, when a young man on a Sabbath day was hastening to the fields for mere amusement, he was unexpectedly met by a friend, who spoke to him so wisely and lovingly of his sin and danger that he changed his purpose. The result was, that on that very night, in God's house, the intending Sabbath-breaker was savingly converted, and afterwards became one of the most distinguished missionaries of modern times. A word in season, how good is it! Yet how many fail to speak it even when opportunity is given.

Further: it is in the power of all to supplicate. This is a method of blessing within every one's reach; for the poor can pray as well as the rich, the sickly as well as the strong, the prisoner in his cell as well as the free and unfettered, and with like prevailing efficacy. To forbear so to plead, therefore, is to forbear to deliver. A good man once said, 'If you only pray for yourself, you have never yet prayed aright.'

Again: it is in the power of all to be helpful by heartily support-ing the varied Christian agencies around us. Thereby we cannot merely aid the poor and needy at our own door, but can also, as it were, stretch out a helping hand even to the outcast and perishing in far-off lands. Thousands and tens of thousands have thereby been savingly gathered into the fold of Christ. Doubtless the first and chief concern of every one must be his own personal salvation, for till this is secured he can do little or nothing effectually for the saving good of others. The man who is himself swimming for his life, and struggling hard among the breakers, is little able to rescue others in similar peril. But too often those who are themselves in Christ fail to help others as they might. If ever we are tempted self-ishly to say, like Cain, 'Am I my brother's keeper?' we should call to mind the solemn words: 'If thou forbear to deliver them that are drawn unto death, and those that are ready to be slain; if thou sayest, Behold, we knew it not; doth not he that pondereth the heart consider it? and he that keepeth thy soul, doth not he know it? and shall not he render to every man according to his works?'

> Rescue the perishing, care for the dying—
>   Snatch them in pity from sin and the grave;
> Weep o'er the erring one, lift up the fallen—
>   Tell them of Jesus, the mighty to save.

As we have therefore opportunity, let us do good unto all men, espe-cially unto them who are of the household of faith.—GAL. 6:10.

We are journeying unto the place of which the Lord said, I will give it you: come thou with us, and we will do thee good: for the Lord hath spoken good concerning Israel.—NUM. 10:29.

Brethren, if any of you do err from the truth, and one convert him; let him know, that he which converteth the sinner from the error of his way shall save a soul from death, and shall hide a multitude of sins.—JAMES 5:19, 20.

November 23

WE MUST NOT LIGHTLY LEAVE OUR SPHERES.

LIKE many a saint in Scripture times, believers are still occasionally strongly tempted to desert their appropriate sphere or appointed work. Perhaps it is the very one designed for them, and where their usefulness can be greatest; but simply because thorns unexpectedly spring up, and difficulties present themselves, they become hopelessly despondent. Then come the whisperings of the tempter: You have mistaken your calling—you are not in the right place; and therefore, toil as you may, you can never succeed. Some of the best of men have occasionally been so sorely buffeted in this very way, that they have been on the point of finally leaving spheres where afterwards they have been most abundantly blessed.

When so tempted, it might be well to remember what is sweetly told of a good mother. 'She had a little room of her own, where on a stand always stood open the great family Bible; and when work pressed hard and children were untoward, or when sickness threatened—when the skeins of life were all crossways and tangled—she went quietly to that room, and through faith and prayer took hold of a warm, healing, invisible hand, that made the crooked straight, and rough places plain.' Were this oftener done, the tempted would find such light in darkness and strength in weakness, that they would abide hopefully where the Lord had placed them.

In all these cases we should only pray the more and then work the harder, fully assured that whatever of grace or strength is lacking, the Lord himself will bountifully supply. The Lord's all-sufficiency is ours for constant use, and he never forgets us.

> *How often a gleam of glory, sent*
> *Straight through the deepest, darkest night,*
> *Has filled the soul with heavenly light—*
> *With holy peace and sweet content:*
> *Content to wait the will of God;*
> *To cast on him the heavy load;*

To walk with him the weary road,—
With patience leaning on the Lord!

They thought to do me mischief. And I sent messengers unto them, saying, I am doing a great work, so that I cannot come down: why should the work cease, whilst I leave it, and come down to you?—Neh. 6:2, 3.

And he called his ten servants, and delivered them ten pounds, and said unto them, Occupy till I come.—Luke 19:13.

November 24

FAITH OVERCOMING.

THOUGH David evidently felt the pressure of temptation when he said, 'How are they increased that trouble me! Many there be which say of my soul, There is no hope for him in God,' yet he did not yield to it. On the contrary, he boldly faced every foe, and dared every danger, rather than show any distrust of the Lord his God. He was strengthened in all this, not only by many a blessed promise of the word, but also by many a bright memory in his own experience. In a very peculiar and critical era of Israel's history, and while David was yet in his youth, Saul said to him: 'Thou art not able to go against this Philistine to fight with him: for thou art but a youth, and he a man of war.' He replied: 'Thy servant kept his father's sheep, and there came a lion, and a bear, and took a lamb out of the flock: and I went out after him, and smote him, and delivered it out of his mouth: and when he arose against me, I caught him by his beard, and smote him, and slew him.' And then he added—'The Lord that delivered me out of the paw of the lion, and out of the paw of the bear, he will deliver me out of the hand of this Philistine.' His faith made him fearless. Nor was it put to shame; for, as one says, 'In the language of faith there is no such word as impossibility; that martial grace knows how to fight, but she knows not how to flee.'

Now, as it was with him, so is it with all who make the Lord their trust. They resist and overcome. They do not, however, always overcome at once. In great national conflicts one battle is sometimes so decisive and crushing, that for a whole generation to come there is never any need for another; and it is sometimes thought that it might also be even so in the great Christian conflict. Young believers especially are very apt to indulge in such hopes and expectations; and when they are disappointed in this, and find that, in spite of victory today, the battle has to be renewed on the morrow, they are often greatly discouraged and cast down. But it should not be so; for we are always told in the word that the whole Christian life is more or less a warfare, and that it is not an easy one. True, it is a good fight the Christian is engaged in—the very noblest on earth; and it is a peculiar honour to be engaged in it. Nevertheless, it is a hard one; and not unfrequently hardest of all just at the very moment that final and triumphant victory is nearest. A year or two ago a saintly man, when nearing his end, said: 'It is a hard battle, but I know the victory is sure; and, thank God, though I have many conflicts, I have no fears.' And then, in very homely phrase, he added: 'I am just like a package that is all ready to go by train: packed, corded, labelled, paid for—waiting for the Express to take me to glory.' A homely expression, truly, but expressing much.

> *Beyond the parting and the meeting,*
> *I shall be soon;*
> *Beyond the farewell and the greeting,*
> *Beyond the pulse's fitful beating,*
> *I shall be soon.*
> *Love, rest, and home,—*
> *Sweet hope!*
> *Lord, tarry not, but come.*

Thanks be to God, which giveth us the victory through our Lord Jesus Christ.—1 COR. 15:57.

For whatsoever is born of God overcometh the world: and this is the victory that overcometh the world, even our faith. Who is he that overcometh the world, but he that believeth that Jesus is the Son of God?—I JOHN 5:4, 5.

By faith Moses, when he was come to years, refused to be called the son of Pharaoh's daughter; choosing rather to suffer affliction with the people of God, than to enjoy the pleasures of sin for a season; esteeming the reproach of Christ greater riches than the treasures in Egypt.—HEB. 11:24-26.

NOVEMBER 25

GOD IS OUR FATHER.

THE apostle says, in one of his many epistles, 'Now unto God our Father.' This precious appellation, especially in its fulness, is peculiar to the Christian dispensation. Till Christ became incarnate, finished his work, and opened up a new and living way of access, there was always somewhat of veil and felt distance between God and his children. But now, in their conscious experience, he is everything to them that the sweet name of Father implies. He provides for them, educates them, guides them, and when burdens press he lovingly sustains and cheers them; and therefore, even in their most desolate times, they need never be afraid to say, 'When father and mother forsake me, the Lord will take me up.'

Our Lord, when guarding his disciples against overcarefulness and anxious distrust in connection with daily supplies, gave the sweet assurance, 'Your heavenly Father *knoweth* that ye have need of all these things.'

> *What can these anxious cares avail,*
> *These never-ceasing moans and sighs?*
> *What can it help us, to bewail*
> *Each painful moment as it flies?*
> *Our cross and trials do but press*
> *The heavier for our bitterness.*
>
> *Only your restless heart keep still,*
> *And wait in cheerful hope, content*

To take whate'er his gracious will,
  His all-discerning love, hath sent.
No doubt our inmost wants are known
To him who chose us for his own.

Many years ago, when in my country charge, I returned one afternoon from a funeral, fatigued with the day's work. After a long ride, I had accompanied the mourners to the churchyard. As I neared my stable door, I felt a strange prompting to visit a poor widow who, with her invalid daughter, lived in a lonely cottage in an outlying part of the parish. My natural reluctance to make another visit was overcome by a feeling which I could not resist, and I turned my horse's head towards the cottage. I was thinking only of the poor widow's spiritual needs; but when I reached her little house, I was struck with its look of unwonted bareness and poverty. After putting a little money into her hand, I began to inquire into their circumstances, and found that their supplies had been utterly exhausted since the night before. I asked them what they had done. 'I just spread it out before the Lord!' 'Did you not tell your case to any friend?' 'Oh no, sir; naebody kens but himsel' and me! I kent he wadna forget, but I didna ken hoo he wad help me till I saw you come riding ower the brae, and then I said, There's the Lord's answer!' Many a time has the recollection of this incident encouraged me to trust in the loving care of my heavenly Father.

I ascend unto my Father, and your Father; and to my God, and your God.—JOHN 20:17.

Ye have not received the spirit of bondage again to fear; but ye have received the Spirit of adoption, whereby we cry, Abba, Father. The Spirit itself beareth witness with our spirit, that we are the children of God.—ROM. 8:15, 16.

When ye pray, say, Our Father.—LUKE 11:2.

NOVEMBER 26

TROUBLE, YET PEACE.

THE present experience of believers is a mingled and often also a seemingly mysterious one, for they are represented as at once troubled and in peace. 'Christ's children,' says Samuel Rutherford, 'must not expect always to lean upon his bosom. He sometimes sets them down on the cold, frosty side of the hill, and makes them walk barefooted upon thorns. Yet does he keep his eye of love upon them all the while.'

In the world, Christ says, ye shall have tribulation; but in me ye shall have peace. These words reveal the interesting fact that in Christian experience the state of tribulation and the state of peace are not consecutive, but contemporaneous; and, strange to say, very frequently the intenser the tribulation the deeper is the peace, just because at such times believers feel most their need of Christ, and draw nearest to him. Indeed, apart from Christ there is no real peace of any kind, nor any possibility of finding it.

And as it is in Christ through faith this peace is found, so it is through him also it is graciously preserved. It is a fruit of his purchase, a gift of his love; yea, a blessed legacy bequeathed to his church and people throughout all time. 'Peace,' he says, 'I leave with you, my peace I give unto you: not as the world giveth, give I unto you. Let not your heart be troubled, neither let it be afraid.' There is, even in experienced believers, so much of lingering sin and infirmity that, but for the ceaseless intercession and power of their loving Lord, they could not maintain their peace a moment; hence the firmness with which they grasp the gracious promise, 'Thou wilt keep him in perfect peace whose mind is stayed on thee, because he trusteth in thee.'

So divine and blessed is this peace, that it is entirely independent of mere outward circumstances, and often exists in all its sweetness in the very midst of trouble and when the night is darkest. 'Even when a believer sees no light,' says an old divine, 'he may feel some hope; when he cannot close with a promise, he may lay hold on an attribute, and say, "Though flesh and heart fail, yet divine compassion and faithfulness fail not. Though I can hardly discern at present either sun, moon, or stars, yet will I cast anchor in the dark, and ride it out until the day break, and the shadows flee away."'

Very different is it with mere men of the world.

But however precious even on earth, it is in heaven only this peace is perfect. On one occasion, when a little Irish boy was sitting on the doorstep, and singing,—

> *There will be no sorrow there,*
> *There will be no sorrow there,*

a doubting and downcast stranger who was passing said, 'What place, my boy, can that be, in which there is no sorrow?' He at once replied,—

> *In heaven above,*
> *Where all is love.*

The words were simple, but they were used by the Spirit to calm his troubled heart and fill it with peace.

For he is our peace ... And came and preached peace to you which were afar off, and to them that were nigh.—EPH. 2:14, 17.

Therefore being justified by faith, we have peace with God through our Lord Jesus Christ.—ROM. 5:1.

Be careful for nothing; but in every thing by prayer and supplication with thanksgiving let your requests be made known unto God. And the peace of God, which passeth all understanding, shall keep your hearts and minds through Christ Jesus.—PHIL. 4:6, 7.

NOVEMBER 27

WE CANNOT OVER-HOPE IN GOD'S MERCY.

FROM his very nature God delights in those whose wills are ever in sweet accord with his own. Being himself love, he cannot but love the lovable; and being himself pure, he cannot but delight in the undefiled. But this, though cheering to some, is to others a sore discouragement. They are ready to say, Were we saints like Enoch or Caleb, ever walking closely with the Lord and following him fully, he might take pleasure in us; but seeing that we are sinners, at once worthless and weak, how can he do so?

They forget, in so speaking, these express and blessed words, 'The Lord taketh pleasure in them *that hope in his mercy.*' There is surely comfort here for the most bruised reed that is; for those indicated in the promise are not the far advanced in the divine life, but rather those who, like the publican, are just entering on it, and saying, 'God be merciful to me a sinner.'

They forget, too, that the mercy they are called to hope in is divine. It is God's mercy, not man's—mercy, therefore, at once so rich and free that it can meet to the full every necessity of the very worst of cases, without in one tittle staining a single perfection of the divine nature. On this account it is not ordinary sinners only we find in heaven, but the very chief. Saul of Tarsus is there, and the crucified thief; blood-stained Manasseh, and some of the very murderers of the Son of God. Truly, if even they found mercy, who need despair?

This forgiving mercy is not offered merely, but lovingly pressed on the acceptance of all: 'Let the wicked forsake his way, and the unrighteous man his thoughts: and let him return unto the Lord, and he will have mercy upon him; and to our God, for he will abundantly pardon.'

> *Come, ye sinners, lost and wretched,*
> *Weak and wounded, sick and sore;*
> *Jesus ready stands to save you,*
> *Full of pity, full of power:*
>   *He is able,*
>   *He is willing; doubt no more.*

'Go to Christ,' said Thomas Wilcox, 'with all thy impenitence and unbelief; get faith and repentance from him.' And he added: 'When a sense of guilt is raised up, take heed of getting it allayed in any way but by Christ's blood; all other ways tend to harden the conscience. Make Christ thy peace; not thy duties, or thy tears.' Look to him only. To see grace and salvation in Christ is the greatest sight in the world.

Where sin abounded, grace did much more abound.—ROM. 5:20.

I, even I, am he that blotteth out thy transgressions for mine own sake, and will not remember thy sins.—ISA. 43:25.

Who is a God like unto thee, that pardoneth iniquity, and passeth by the transgression of the remnant of his heritage? he retaineth not his anger for ever, because he delighteth in mercy. He will turn again, he will have compassion upon us; he will subdue our iniquities; and thou wilt cast all their sins into the depths of the sea.—MICAH 7:18, 19.

NOVEMBER 28

NOT MAN'S OPINION, BUT THE LORD'S, SHOULD EVER BE
SUPREME WITH US.

IN critical times public opinion has often been, in the providence of God, a power for good. It has exposed the wrong, sided with the right, and proved a powerful shield in many a noble struggle. Nevertheless, in matters of truth and righteousness, where most of all it should be stable, it has again and again proved variable as the wind.

The world's history all down the ages affords mournful illustrations of this. When Paul and Barnabas were at Lystra, the people at first could not honour them enough. 'The gods,' they cried, 'are come down among us in the likeness of men'; and they were about to worship them. But not long thereafter, rising up against the apostle, they stoned him, and drew him out of the city, supposing he had been dead. Such is the world, fickle as a wayward child. First it brings garlands, then stones. 'Is there no mean,' says an old writer, 'betwixt deifying and stoning? How soon turns the wind into a contrary corner.'

Happily, to be so judged was a small thing with the apostle, for the supreme thing with him was not public opinion, but divine; and having a good conscience, a good cause, and a good Master, in spite of every trial he was ever in peace.

This Lystra experience has been no rare one in the history of the world. On many a sad occasion the multitude, instead of being on the side of right, has fiercely voted it down. In the days of Noah the wicked were everywhere, and did wickedly, and he alone and his household feared the Lord. In the days of Elijah so complete was Israel's apostasy, that in the desolateness of his spirit he exclaimed, 'They have thrown down thine altars, and slain thy prophets with the sword; and I, even I only, am left, and they seek my life to take it away.' There was a like universality of corruption in the time of the Captivity. As soon as the sound was heard of cornet, flute, harp, sackbut and psaltery, all the people, the nations, and the languages, fell down and worshipped the golden image that Nebuchadnezzar had set up, save Shadrach, Meshach, and Abednego. They alone, at peril of their lives, refused to bow the knee and worship. And apparently it is to be so again for a season, when the last Antichrist shall be fully realised; for in the thirteenth chapter of the Book of Revelation it is thus written: '*All that dwell upon the earth* shall worship him, whose names are not written in the book of life of the Lamb slain from the foundation of the world.'

In all these instances we see public opinion and divine in open and deadly antagonism, and the redeemed alone proving faithful and true. 'Christianity was designed,' says Vinet, 'to produce a race of men who should believe *in truth*, not in numbers, nor in years, nor in force—men, consequently, who should be ready to pass for fools'; and, it may be added, ready also not only to be bound, but to die for the name of the Lord Jesus. Let none of God's children, however, be discouraged because of these things: for if such a conflict is coming, it is to be the last, and is to be brief, and all helpful grace shall be given; and better than all, joy and glory unspeakable are immediately to follow.

What a world, when all its sorrow
Shall forever pass away!
What an earth, when each tomorrow
Shall be fairer than today!

As the Lord liveth, what the Lord saith unto me, that will I speak.—
1 Kings 22:14.

Then Peter and the other apostles answered and said, We ought to obey God rather than men.—ACTS 5:29.

When Daniel knew that the writing was signed, he went into his house; and his windows being open in his chamber toward Jerusalem, he kneeled upon his knees three times a day, and prayed, and gave thanks before his God, as he did aforetime.—DAN. 6:10.

Thy shoes shall be iron and brass; and as thy days, so shall thy strength be.—DEUT. 33:25.

When thou passest through the waters, I will be with thee; and through the rivers, they shall not overflow thee: when thou walkest through the fire, thou shalt not be burned; neither shall the flame kindle upon thee.—ISA. 43:2.

NOVEMBER 29

SILENCED FOR A MOMENT, TRIUMPHANT FOREVER.

AT the beginning of our Lord's public ministry eager crowds followed him, and it was the common utterance on every side, 'Never man spake like this man'—'He doeth all things well.' It was widely different towards the close of it. Many then went wholly back; friends grew feeble; enemies grew bold; till at length, with combined and resolute malignity, they hurried him off to ignominy and death. It was the hour and power of darkness, and every cherished hope of his disciples now lay buried in his grave. Brief was the victory, however; for on the third day Jesus rose again as the Prince of Life, the Lord of Glory, the Hope of Israel and the world.

It is thought that, like her Lord, the church also, knowing 'the fellowship of his sufferings,' will have her dark passion-week followed by a bright resurrection morning. In the eleventh chapter of Revelation we are told that when the faithful witnesses, the true and living church of Jesus Christ, 'shall have finished their testimony, *the beast* that ascendeth *out of the bottomless pit* shall make war against them, and shall overcome them, and kill them'; and that 'they that dwell upon the earth shall rejoice over them, and make mercy, and shall send gifts one to another.'

If it is to be so, then also will be the hour and power of darkness, and sorely will the saints of God be tried. Their trial, however, if severe, is to be short; for we read that '*after three days and a half* the Spirit of life from God entered into them, and they stood upon their feet and great fear fell upon them which saw them. And they heard a great voice from heaven saying unto them, Come up hither. And they ascended up to heaven in a cloud; and their enemies beheld them.'

Hitherto the view generally entertained has been that this chapter refers to past events exclusively; but with many earnest students of the word the growing conviction now is, that this prophecy, at once dark and bright, has never yet been fulfilled. Several things lead them to this conclusion. First of all, *the time specified* in the prophecy for the silencing of the witnesses is 'when they shall have *finished* their testimony'; but this they have not yet done in any sense that clearly and unmistakably fulfils the prediction, for they are still testifying in an evil world for truth and righteousness. Still further, the peculiar persecuting power specified as the one destined to prevail in the end,—namely, *the beast* from *the bottomless pit*—a power seemingly hellish in its origin, and full of atheistic blasphemy, has not yet arisen. The Church of Rome, though all along, doubtless, a great and persecuting Apostasy, has yet never been avowedly infidel, or openly denied the Father and the Son, as it is emphatically predicted the Antichrist will do. Moreover, final, permanent triumph, has never yet come. To this very hour we see symbols, not of victory, but of humiliation, in the reproach, obloquy, and suffering still borne by so many of the faithful for Christ's sake. Necessarily, therefore, as there has never yet been the predicted triumph of the witnesses, so neither has there been the complete silencing of them that is to precede it. Both are still future.

When referring to this symbolic prediction, Thomas Scott the commentator said, 'I cannot but think that this prophecy relates to events yet future; and it is of vast importance that Christians should be aware of it, and act accordingly.' Later still, Dr Lillie stated it as his solemn belief, 'that the last, the subtlest, and the most depraved of all the Antichrists is still to appear in Christendom, and draw the whole world wondering after him.'

This to all will be a dark and trying era, yet believers have no need to yield to despondency. Come what may, the Lord, in the riches of his grace, will sustain and strengthen them, and gladden them also; for what will be fearful to others will be to them sure and joyous tokens that their redemption draweth nigh. 'Don't fear,' said a good man; 'Antichrist is indeed coming, but Christ also comes behind him.' Better comfort could not have been given, for Christ can cheer even in the darkest hour. When the tidings were brought to John Bradford in prison that next day he was to be burned in Smithfield, and that already the chain that was to bind him was bought, putting off his cap, and lifting up his eyes to heaven, he said, 'I thank God for it; I have looked for the same a long time, and therefore it cometh not to me suddenly, but as a thing waited for every day and hour. The Lord make me worthy thereof!' Then turning to his companion he said, 'Be of good comfort, brother; we shall have a joyful supper with the Lord this night.'

> Because thou hast kept the word of my patience, I also will keep thee from the hour of temptation, which shall come upon all the world, to try them that dwell upon the earth.—Rev. 3:10.

> Fear none of those things which thou shalt suffer: behold, the devil shall cast some of you into prison, that ye may be tried; and ye shall have tribulation ten days: be thou faithful unto death, and I will give thee a crown of life.—Rev. 2:10.

> If we suffer, we shall also reign with him: if we deny him, he also will deny us.—2 Tim. 2:12.

And then shall that Wicked be revealed, whom the Lord shall consume with the spirit of his mouth, and shall destroy with the brightness of his coming.—2 THESS. 2:8.

NOVEMBER 30

THE LORD'S COMMENDATION OF MARY.

IT would have gone hard with Mary when severely censured, had the judgment of men been final. But happily for her the Lord himself was near, and instead of condemning, approved with emphatic fulness and love: 'Why trouble ye the woman? she hath wrought a good work upon me ... for she hath come aforehand, to anoint my body to the burying.'

Here the question naturally arises, Did Mary understand and design this? It may be that she did not, and that our Lord simply ascribes his own thoughts to her, and interprets and glorifies her good work of affectionate love into a prophetic act, so that, like the word of Caiaphas, it was nothing more than an unconscious prophecy. Nevertheless, there is much that might well lead one to believe that in what she did Mary had conscious intention. The usual rule in interpretation is to take the obvious and literal meaning of words, unless there are strong reasons to the contrary. But there seem to be no such reasons in this case. Our Lord, it should be remembered, did not conceal from his disciples that he was to suffer and die. On the contrary, he made frequent and open reference to his death; more vaguely in the beginning, when he said, 'The Son of man came not to be ministered unto, but to minister, and to give his life a ransom for many'; but more clearly and expressly afterwards, as when he said to the twelve, 'Behold, we go up to Jerusalem; and the Son of man shall be delivered unto the chief priests, and unto the scribes; and they shall condemn him to death, and shall deliver him unto the Gentiles: and they shall mock him, and *shall scourge him*, and *shall spit upon him*, and *shall kill him*: and *the third day he shall rise again*.' These utterances were not symbolical, but plain and unmistakable; yet we are told that the disciples understood none of these things. Why? Simply because though they had warm love they had weak faith, and therefore could not receive these words as true, even though uttered by their blessed Lord and Master. Now, was it so also with Mary? We think not. Our conviction is that Mary, who lived very near her Lord—who fed on his truth and drank deeply of his spirit—had faith enough to take in these predictive words. What strengthens this conviction is the marked peculiarity of the commendation bestowed on her. As all through his ministry nothing so called forth the admiration of Jesus as great faith, we feel persuaded that it was just because, in addition to her warm love, Mary had such faith that she received from her lord this extraordinary commendation, 'Verily I say unto you, Wheresoever this gospel shall be preached in the whole world, there shall also this, that this woman hath done, be told for a memorial of her.' This is the more noticeable, as nothing of this kind is said of the other woman, referred to by Luke, though she also brought precious ointment. It would seem, therefore, as if Mary alone really comprehended our Lord's humiliation, looked for his death, and made loving preparation for his burial; hence the great commendation and the predicted fame. 'So clearly,' says one, 'was our Lord master of the great future, that while great deeds have been done and yet forgotten in all the world, this simple act of tender premonition is to be told through the world, yea, and the very name of Mary to be forever sweet in the ears of mankind.'

The righteous shall be had in everlasting remembrance; and verily, if we remember Mary, much more should we remember Mary's Lord, and all his grace and mercy and dying love.

The memory of the just is blessed: but the name of the wicked shall rot.—Prov. 10:7.

For ye have the poor with you always, and whensoever ye will ye may do them good: but me ye have not always. She hath done what she could: she is come aforehand to anoint my body to the burying.—Mark 14:7, 8.

What shall I render unto the Lord for all his benefits toward me?—Psa. 116:12.

DECEMBER 1

WORTHLESS, YET WELCOME.

E ASY as it is to speak of salvation by grace, it is the hardest of things to believe it; and usually with every increase in the knowledge and sense of sin the difficulty intensifies. This arises from the fact that, till enlightened by the Spirit of God, men imagine that it is impossible to get grace without first deserving it; and that therefore, though there may be hope for the good and righteous, there can be none whatever for the guilty and depraved. They are confirmed in this fear when they find that the law holds out no hope whatever for the worthless. It commands, it threatens, it condemns, but never does it forgive. Nor is it otherwise with conscience. It too condemns, and in proportion to its enlightenment are the keenness and severity with which it accuses. Nevertheless, nowhere is it the teaching of the word, and at no time has it been the rule of the kingdom, that the worthy only can enter in. On the contrary, it is expressly written that Christ Jesus came into the world to save sinners, even the chief.

No matter, then, how weak, or weary, or wicked any poor sinner may be, if he but come in simple faith to Jesus, he will be lovingly welcomed, yea, and be everlastingly saved. That promise is as true today as when first it was uttered: 'Him that cometh unto me I will in no wise cast out.' Mark the words: it is not said, 'him that doeth,' or 'him that giveth,' or 'him that deserveth,' but simply, 'him that cometh,' whatever his past or present. 'Faith,' says Ebenezer Erskine, 'is the beggar's hand which comes, not to give, but to get Christ and all with him *for nothing.*' Perhaps, indeed, no text in the word has been more frequently quoted or more signally blessed than this one. 'For all I have preached or written,' said the venerable James Durham in his last illness, 'there is but one scripture I can remember and dare grip to. Tell me if I dare lay the weight of my salvation upon it: "Him that cometh to me I will in no wise cast out."' His friend replied, 'You may indeed depend upon it, though you had a thousand salvations at hazard.' It was a sweet word in season, for it lighted up a gleam of joy in the soul of the dying saint which never left him.

> Come unto me, all ye that labour and are heavy laden, and I will give you rest.—MATT. 11:28.

> Come now, and let us reason together, saith the Lord: though your sins be as scarlet, they shall be as white as snow; though they be red like crimson, they shall be as wool.—ISA. 1:18.

> Let the wicked forsake his way, and the unrighteous man his thoughts: and let him return unto the Lord, and he will have mercy upon him; and to our God, for he will abundantly pardon.—ISA. 55:7.

DECEMBER 2

SEEK FIRST THINGS FIRST.

ONE of the memorable sayings of our blessed Lord is, 'Seek ye first the kingdom of God and his righteousness, and all these things shall be added unto you.' The great principle embodied here is, that we should seek first things first; and by first things are meant things that beyond all question are pre-eminent in importance and value.

Wealth, honour, and the varied comforts of life, may be freely enjoyed, but they cannot be called *first things*; because a man may have them all, and yet finally perish; or a man may lose them all for conscience' sake, and yet have peace unspeakable, be a child of God and an heir of glory. The rich man in the Gospel who said, 'Soul, take thine ease, eat, drink, and be merry,' had such fulness that he had to pull down his barns and build greater, for he had no room where to bestow his fruits; but that did not delay the fatal message: 'Thou fool, this night thy soul shall be required of thee.' On the other hand, the poor man in the parable was in such straits that he would gladly have accepted the crumbs which fell from the rich man's table, yet neither did that prevent his happy homegoing; for the moment he died, angels carried him at once with joy to Abraham's bosom.

But while it is so with mere earthly things, those of the kingdom, on the contrary—things spiritual and heavenly—are not desirable merely, but absolutely indispensable. We cannot do without them, and must therefore seek them first and above all.

> *Lean not on Egypt's reeds; slake not thy thirst*
> *At earthly cisterns; seek the kingdom first.*
> *Though man and Satan fright thee with their worst,*
> *Have faith in God.*

Verily, then, the duty of seeking first things first is as reasonable as it is urgent.

Some years ago a wealthy merchant in London said, with inexpressible sadness, when dying,—'Alas! I have done everything for my body, but I have done nothing whatever for my soul.' An utterance like this can scarcely fail to remind us of the homely but telling words of John Flavel. 'Two things,' he said, 'a master commits to his servant's care—the child, and the child's clothes. It will be a poor excuse for the servant to say at his master's return, "Sir, here are all the child's clothes neat and clean, but the child is lost." Much so with the account that many will give to God of their souls and bodies at the great day.'

What shall it profit a man, if he shall gain the whole world, and lose his own soul?—MARK 8:36.

Godliness is profitable unto all things, having promise of the life that now is, and of that which is to come.—1 TIM. 4:8.

There is no man that hath left house, or brethren, or sisters, or father, or mother, or wife, or children, or lands, for my sake, and the gospel's, but he shall receive an hundredfold now in this time, houses, and brethren, and sisters, and mothers, and children, and lands, with persecutions; and in the world to come eternal life.—MARK 10:29, 30.

DECEMBER 3

THE SICKNESS OF PAUL'S FRIEND.

T HESE are touching words of the apostle: 'For indeed he was sick nigh unto death: but God had mercy on him; and not on him only, but on me also, lest I should have sorrow upon sorrow.' Of the immediate secondary cause of this illness of Epaphroditus we know nothing. Nor are we told whether it was a first sickness with him, or one of several from time to time experienced. A first severe sickness, like a first disappointment in life, or a first loss in business, is frequently a thing very hard to bear, and requiring no little effort submissively to say, 'Thy will be done.' But whether it was his first sickness or not, it was at least very nearly becoming his last; for it is expressly said of him, 'He was sick nigh unto death.'

This sore sickness of his friend not only saddened Paul, but it greatly grieved the whole Philippian church, the more so as it was for the work of Christ his life was imperilled. All felt that were he removed it would be a helpful friend away, a bright light extinguished, a rich blessing lost; and doubtless many a fervent prayer ascended for his recovery. And not in vain; for the Lord, who is ever a present help in trouble and a cheerer of saddened hearts, raised him up for further service.

Of those whom God sees meet to remove, they are blessed who have so lived as to be missed when they die. Our sadness is their gladness, our loss their gain; for though absent from us, they are present with the Lord and the days of their mourning are forever ended.

When we think of the countless numbers of such now gathered in heaven, it should be easier for us to be heavenly-minded, and to set our affection on things above. Some time ago, speaking of a departed friend, one beautifully said, 'I found him tender as a woman, yet fearless as a lion, and true as steel. He was valiant for the truth, and hated every false way. The death of such men,' he added, 'has a real power in making us willing to die. The society of which he is now a member is composed of the *elite* of the universe. Every choice spirit that has passed away belongs to that blessed company who worship before the throne in a world where the wicked cease from troubling and the weary are at rest.'

> *I saw thee in thy narrow rest,*
> *The clods upon thy coffin pressed;*
> *The clouds dropped tears, yet in my breast*
> *God said, 'We'll meet again.'*

Blessed are the dead which die in the Lord from henceforth: Yea, saith the Spirit, that they may rest from their labours; and their works do follow them.—Rev. 14:13.

Precious in the sight of the Lord is the death of his saints.—Psa. 116:15.

Go thou thy way till the end be: for thou shalt rest, and stand in thy lot at the end of the days.—Dan. 12:13.

December 4

NOTHING GIVES SUCH EFFICACY TO PRAYER AS ABIDING INTIMACY WITH THE LORD.

WHEN men are not in communion with the Lord, prayer is usually a cold, burdensome, heartless task, in which there is neither faith nor expectancy; but when there is loving intimacy with him, prayer becomes sweetly natural, and has life and power in it. Men always feel more or less restraint in the presence of strangers, and it is with difficulty they can bring themselves to ask any favour at their hands. With intimate friends, however, they have no such hesitancy or reserve, but feel as free and ready to ask a kindness as they would be to grant it. It is just so in Christian experience. The nearer we come to the Lord, and the more intimate our fellowship, the easier it always is to pour out our hearts in fervent supplication. Prayer then becomes an absolute necessity with us, an essential of our being, a vital breath, and we cannot do without it. It was somewhat scoffingly said to a good old Christian woman, 'I will give you half a sovereign if you will not offer up another prayer all this day.' 'No,' she replied; 'not for all the worlds this side of heaven. It is the very joy of my heart; and if you but knew the Lord, it would be your joy also.'

But further: such intimacy makes prayer wisely appropriate. In daily life there is a great deal of what Scripture calls asking amiss; and in very mercy to the suppliants, asking of this kind is not followed by any receiving. Though a needful, this is often at the time a very bitter, experience. Now, in such a case abiding communion would be an effectual remedy; for by its very nature it tends to assimilate the will of the believer to the will of the Lord, and to control and wisely regulate the manifold desires that may arise in the heart. Many things are earnestly sought by young and inexperienced Christians, that veteran saints would never dream of asking; and why? just because, from their greater intimacy with the Lord, their judgments are more enlightened, and their desires more sanctified, and they can ever better discriminate between the shadowy and the real. Thereby they know better not only how to pray, but what to pray for; and they rarely pray in vain. 'I no more believe,' says one, 'that God leaves a right prayer, offered in the right spirit, to pass unnoticed, than I believe he will let this whole summer pass without a drop of rain or dew to refresh a parched earth.' 'O prayer, prayer,' said George Whitefield, 'it raises up man to God, and brings down God to man, and keeps them sweetly together.'

> If ye abide in me, and my words abide in you, ye shall ask what ye will, and it shall be done unto you.—JOHN 15:7.

> Whatsoever ye shall ask in my name, that will I do, that the Father may be glorified in the Son. If ye shall ask any thing in my name, I will do it.—JOHN 14:13, 14.

> He that keepeth his commandments dwelleth in him, and he in him. And hereby we know that he abideth in us, by the Spirit which he hath given us.—I JOHN 3:24.

DECEMBER 5

MEN MAY BE HEAVY LOSERS WITHOUT KNOWING IT.

THOUGH God never finally forsakes his own,—for this would be to leave unfinished what he himself had begun,—yet there are seasons when he withholds for a time the wonted gifts and tokens of his divine lovingkindness. It is never, however, in mere arbitrariness that the Lord does this, or because he has any pleasure in afflicting; but simply because he will not tolerate cherished sin, in whomsoever found, and least of all in those who bear his name and are his professed disciples.

We see this exemplified in the case of Samson, in whom there mingled so strangely strength and weakness, wisdom and folly. Sword and shield were powerless against him, but not the wiles of an artful woman. He could carry away the gates of Gaza; but a Delilah could thoroughly enslave him, and hold him fast. While yielding to such influences, he was neither unwarned nor uncorrected; but in spite of every remonstrance, he made light of danger, till at length, the long-coveted secret of his strength being artfully drawn out of him, his locks were shorn, and he became weak as other men. Nevertheless, 'he wist not that the Lord was departed from him,' and vainly dreamed of a still unbroken strength. Bitter experience, however, soon taught him that what the Philistines never could do before, they could easily do now. They bound him, mocked him, smote him, and with torturing malice burned out his very eyes with a hot iron. What a fall was here! 'We might well,' says one, 'stand and weep over poor, blind Samson. That he should have lost his eyes was terrible; that he should have lost his strength was worse; but that he should have lost for a while the favour of his God, and become the sport of God's enemies, was the worst of all.'

As seen in Satan's promises, backsliding from God is more a good than an evil: it is freedom from unmanly scruples; a being neighbour-like; a pleasurable indulgence; and the only sure pathway to wished-for happiness. This is his picture. See now the Lord's: 'Thine own wickedness shall correct thee, and thy backslidings shall reprove thee: know therefore and see that it is an evil thing and bitter, that thou hast forsaken the Lord thy God, and that my fear is not in thee, saith the Lord God of hosts.' From its very nature, every sin is at once a step backward from God and a step downward from peace; and unless God in sovereign mercy interpose, it will issue finally in everlasting ruin. 'Let the weary, wandering soul bethink itself, and return to God,' said John Howe: 'he will not mock thee with shadows, as the world hath done.'

> Ask for the old paths, where is the good way, and walk therein, and ye shall find rest for your souls.—JER. 6:16.

> Return unto thy rest, O my soul; for the Lord hath dealt bountifully with thee.—PSA. 116:7.

> O Israel, return unto the Lord thy God; for thou hast fallen by thine iniquity … I will heal their backsliding, I will love them freely: for mine anger is turned away from him. I will be as the dew unto Israel.—HOSEA 14:1, 4, 5.

DECEMBER 6

THERE ARE ALWAYS WISE REASONS FOR STRANGE COMMANDS.

WHEN the brook Cherith dried up, the Lord said to Elijah: 'Arise, get thee to Zarephath, which belongeth to Zidon, and dwell there: behold, I have commanded a widow woman there to sustain thee.' The command was a somewhat trying one; for the land of Zidon was beyond the borders of Israel, among a heathen and debased people, and the native country of Jezebel, his bitterest enemy: yet he yielded obedience. But how great must have been his surprise when the first sight that met his eye in Zarephath was a poor woman gathering sticks for her last meal, and the first words heard were—'As the Lord thy God liveth, I have not a cake, but an handful of meal in a barrel, and a little oil in a cruse: and, behold, I am gathering two sticks, that I may go in and dress it for me and my son, that we may eat it, and die.'

Had the prophet been following the devices of his own heart, and not the leadings of God's providence, such an answer might have sorely perplexed him; but strong in faith, and recalling to mind his wonderful preservation at Cherith, he encouragingly said unto her: 'Fear not; go and do as thou hast said: but make me thereof a little cake first, and bring it unto me, and after make for thee and for thy son. For thus saith the Lord God of Israel, The barrel of meal shall not waste, neither shall the cruse of oil fail, until the day that the Lord sendeth rain upon the earth.'

But whatever may have been the thought of Elijah, it was a time of peculiar trial to the widow—perhaps the darkest and saddest hour of all her life. Yet her extremity was God's opportunity; for, as an old divine says, 'It is his glory to help at a pinch, to begin where we have given over, that our relief might be so much the more welcome by how much it is less looked for.' The remarkable promise, so graciously given her, was fulfilled to the very letter. There was daily supply for daily need; the barrel of meal did not waste, nor the cruse of oil fail, until the day that the Lord sent rain upon the earth.

And so is it still in the Lord's dealings with his people. He may give but little at a time, but always enough. It is daily bread and daily grace that are promised, but never stores laid up for many years. There is wise love in this arrangement; for thereby is our faith better exercised and our dependence deepened. 'I find,' says one, 'that when I have a little extra stock of gifts or grace, that the worm of pride is sure to breed in the meal. It becomes like the manna of old, which always bred worms when men vainly tried to hoard it up. Besides, even if it did keep, how much better it would be to have the bread of heaven new every day, and water from the rock fresh every moment!'

Thus to his poor he still will give
Just for the present hour;

But for tomorrow they must live
Upon his word and power.

Take therefore no thought for the morrow: for the morrow shall take thought for the things of itself. Sufficient unto the day is the evil thereof.—MATT. 6:34.

O fear the Lord, ye his saints: for there is no want to them that fear him. The young lions do lack, and suffer hunger: but they that seek the Lord shall not want any good thing.—PSA. 34:9, 10.

But my God shall supply all your need according to his riches in glory by Christ Jesus.—PHIL. 4:19.

DECEMBER 7

THOSE WITHIN SHOULD THINK OF THOSE WITHOUT.

CONSIDERING the infinite sufficiency there is in Christ, the warmth of his invitations, and the widely open door, it is saddening to think how many refuse to enter in. It is all the more so, because, until there is such entrance, men have no interest in the promises of God, and are without hope in the world. But so blind are many to their true condition, and so resistant, that they not only refuse to enter, but bid those be silent and depart who lovingly seek their good.

Nevertheless, even then they must not be dealt with as castaways, for whom we need no more care. It is true, believers are told to come out from the world and be separate, and to have no fellowship with the unfruitful works of darkness; yet, remembering what was once their own condition, and would have been still but for the riches of sovereign grace, they must, while so separating, never lose interest in those without, or cease to pray for them.

Besides, the command is express, 'Walk in wisdom *toward them that are without*'; and doubtless one great end to be had in view in so doing is to win and save them. To accomplish this we must see well to our own ways, for nothing is more certainly destructive of influence for good than any glaring inconsistency of walk. If this does not always shut the mouth of the teacher, which it ought to do, it will at least be sure to shut the ear of the listener. In the early days of the church it was no unusual thing for a heathen to say of a disciple of Christ, 'Truly he is a good man, and there is nothing to be blamed in him but that he is a Christian.' This was a noble testimony; and if the same could only be said now of all who bear the name of Christ, what a widely different world would meet our eye, and how many who are now repelled from the Redeemer's fold might be happily won to it. To do all aright in such well-doing needs wisdom as well as earnestness. If our zeal is without knowledge, or our energy without discretion, it will be in its effects more like the heavy and destructive thunder-shower than the noiseless, gentle rain which softens and fertilises.

> *Give me a faithful heart,*
> *Likeness to thee;*
> *That each departing day*
> *Henceforth may see*
> *Some work of love begun,*
> *Some deed of kindness done,*
> *Some wanderer sought and won,*
> *Something for thee.*

Walk in wisdom toward them that are without, redeeming the time.—Col. 4:5.

See then that ye walk circumspectly, not as fools, but as wise.—Eph. 5:15.

Be gentle unto all men, apt to teach, patient, in meekness instructing those that oppose themselves; if God peradventure will give them repentance to the acknowledging of the truth; and that they may recover themselves out of the snare of the devil, who are taken captive by him at his will.—2 Tim. 2:24-26.

December 8

*THE MORE SPONTANEOUS OUR BENEFICENCE THE
MORE PRECIOUS.*

THE most striking feature of the liberality of the Macedonian believers was its warm spontaneousness. They needed no pressing to give, no impassioned appeal, as is too generally the case. The pressure, on the contrary, was all the other way; for so heartily and overflowingly generous were they, that when the apostle, knowing their circumstances, hesitated to accept, 'they were willing of themselves,' he said, 'praying us *with much entreaty that we would receive the gift.*' It was thus rather restraint than incitement they needed—to be held back than to be urged forward—a rare peculiarity truly with most professors of Christianity.

We are clearly taught by the words of our Lord, 'It is more blessed to give than to receive,' that giving is not a duty simply, but a peculiar privilege. But so little is this realised by many, that no matter what the interest, or moral grandeur, or indispensableness of the object, it is only after manifold persuasion and pressure they contribute of their means. Manifestly, giving in such a spirit, however large the amount, has little or no acceptability; for it is expressly written, 'Every man according as he purposeth in his heart, so let him give; not grudgingly, or of necessity: for God loveth a cheerful giver.' This in a pre-eminent degree is his own character; hence the reasoning of the Apostle: 'He that spared not his own Son, but delivered him up for us all, how shall he not with him also freely give us all things?'

In this, it should be our constant aim to be lowly and grateful imitators of our Father in heaven. As he gives ungrudgingly and largely, so should we, insofar as our creature nature admits, and as the Lord prospers.

> *Largely thou givest, gracious Lord;*
> *Largely thy gifts should be restored.*
> *Freely thou givest, and thy word*
> *Is 'Freely give';*

He only who forgets to hoard
Has learned to live.

It is told of the excellent Mrs Graham of New York, that when on one occasion £1000 came unexpectedly into her possession, she immediately said, 'Quick! quick! let me appropriate the tenth before my heart grows hard.' And forthwith the money was sent to Mr Mason, in aid of the fund he was collecting for the establishment of a theological seminary.

> Speak unto the children of Israel, that they bring me an offering: of every man that giveth it willingly with his heart ye shall take my offering.—EXOD. 25:2.

> He that hath a bountiful eye shall be blessed; for he giveth of his bread to the poor.—PROV. 22:9.

> There is that scattereth, and yet increaseth; and there is that withholdeth more than is meet, but it tendeth to poverty. The liberal soul shall be made fat: and he that watereth shall be watered also himself.—PROV. 11:24, 25.

DECEMBER 9

THE INCURABLE CURED.

WE read in the Gospels of a woman who had been so long and to all appearance so hopelessly ill, that she was deemed by every one to be utterly incurable. Probably this was also her own view; for though for twelve long years she had consulted every physician and tried every remedy, she was yet nothing bettered, but rather grew worse. Hearing, however, of Jesus of Nazareth, and of all the wonderful cures he had wrought, she felt convinced that though all others had failed, he could heal her. Nor was her trustful confidence put to shame.

While her faith, however, in one aspect of it, was so strong that she felt sure that even the very slightest touch would draw forth healing virtue, yet in another it was extremely weak. It was so, because it rested only on one part of our Lord's perfections.

She had no misgivings about the power of Christ, but was slow of heart to believe in his love and grace. Accordingly, as if Christ might grudge the needed blessing, and so frown her away, she tried to come secretly, and with stealthy touch obtain a cure. Yet so gracious is the Lord that, imperfect as her faith was, it proved effectually operative, and brought healing at once to body and soul. How strange that any should doubt the Saviour's willingness, after all the marvellous proofs he has given of forgiving mercy and unchanging love! Where is the penitent he ever rejected, or the returning prodigal he ever repelled?

It is a blessed thing to know that when once healed we are healed forever, and united indissolubly to the divine Healer himself. A hope like this not only sweetens life, but can flood with light and gladness even the dark valley itself. Some years ago a visitor said to a poor wounded soldier, who lay dying in the hospital, 'What church are you of?' 'Of the church of Christ,' he replied. 'I mean, what persuasion are you of?' 'Persuasion,' said the dying man, as he looked heavenward, beaming with love to the Saviour; 'I am persuaded that neither death, nor life, nor angels, nor principalities, nor powers, nor things present, nor things to come, shall separate me from the love of God, which is in Christ Jesus.' None should rest contented with any hope less sure or bright.

> Jesus seeing their faith said unto the sick of the palsy; Son, be of good cheer; thy sins be forgiven thee.—MATT. 9:2.
>
> The blind men came to him: and Jesus saith unto them, Believe ye that I am able to do this? They said unto him, Yea, Lord. Then touched he their eyes, saying, According to your faith be it unto you.—MATT. 9:28, 29.
>
> Jesus said unto him, If thou canst believe, all things are possible to him that believeth. And straightway the father of the child cried out, and said with tears, Lord, I believe; help thou mine unbelief.—MARK 9:23, 24.
>
> He said to the woman, Thy faith hath saved thee; go in peace.— LUKE 7:50.

DECEMBER 10

SOME BELIEVE, BUT FAIL TO CONFESS.

ON the occasion when our Lord looked round and said, 'Who touched me?' it could not possibly have been for mere information that the question was put; for nothing either of the outward history of the woman who touched, or of her inward conflict, was hid from him. Why, then, was the inquiry made? It was just because, though he knew all that was passing in her mind, and rejoiced in it, none else knew, not even the disciples: indeed, so little were they aware of what had taken place, that in all likelihood their eye never once lighted on the woman, and of her disease and healing alike they were wholly ignorant. The inquiry, however, brought all to light; for though at first almost speechless through fear, the woman at length, falling down before him, told all the truth.

This was the very thing the Lord designed to bring about. She would have been satisfied with mere secret discipleship; but the Lord demanded open confession, not merely for her own sake, but specially for the benefit of others. Doubtless among the afflicted in the crowd that gathered round Jesus, there were some longing for healing, yet afraid of a repulse; others desiring a cure, but doubtful as to his ability. If so, what could be more encouraging to them than the blessed and declared experience of that healed, saved, and joyous woman. Might they not well say, If she has found healing, why may not we?

A still further reason for the Lord's inquiry was to bring grace to maturity. Though the woman had real grace when she touched Christ, yet it was feeble and undeveloped. She was imperfectly acquainted with Christ's real character and her own duty; but this questioning tended to correct all this. It enabled her to see what she had never clearly seen before, the goodness as well as the greatness of Christ, and to cast off her false shame, and openly and lovingly confess the Lord. They are blessed, indeed, who not only get grace, but year by year grow in grace.

Some time ago a saintly old man was carried out from a dark alley where there had been a great fire, his hands severely scorched and his clothes terribly torn. A sweet expression of satisfaction was on his countenance. He rested a minute, and then lifting up his burned hands, and with eyes upturned to heaven, he exclaimed, 'I thank God that I have something up yonder that cannot burn.' Soon after, he breathed his last on earth, and departed to be with Christ, which is far better.

> Go home to thy friends, and tell them how great things the Lord hath done for thee, and hath had compassion on thee. And he departed, and began to publish in Decapolis how great things Jesus had done for him: and all men did marvel.—MARK 5:19, 20.

> Restore unto me the joy of thy salvation; and uphold me with thy free spirit. Then will I teach transgressors thy ways; and sinners shall be converted unto thee.—PSA. 51:12, 13.

> Come and hear, all ye that fear God, and I will declare what he hath done for my soul.—PSA. 66:16.

DECEMBER 11

TRUE HOLINESS IS A THING OF DETAIL AS WELL AS OF GENERALITY.

WHEN men are thoroughly under the mastery of evil, sin shows itself in endless detail—in thought, in desire, in purpose, in action—and in all the varied relationships of life. And so must it be with all who come under the influence of grace. Holiness must be a thing of particulars with them as well as of general principles, and be seen not in worship only, or in emotion, or in utterance, but also in action, and in all the ordinary business of everyday life. To be complete in their Christian profession they must attend to all the virtues of it, and keep resolutely in view whatsoever things in their present relations are true, honest, just, and lovely, as well as those things which more immediately relate to God and their interests for eternity.

In the word, accordingly, gracious privileges are never dissociated from corresponding duties; indeed, the latter are usually introduced by way of natural and necessary inference from the former. 'Having therefore these promises, dearly beloved,' says the apostle, 'let us cleanse ourselves from *all filthiness of the flesh and spirit*, perfecting holiness in the fear of the Lord.' In like manner, after speaking of the exceeding great and precious promises, Peter immediately makes use of them for practical ends, and urges a careful cultivation, not of one merely, but of all the Christian graces. 'Give diligence,' he says; 'add to your faith virtue; and to virtue knowledge; and to knowledge temperance; and to temperance patience; and to patience godliness; and to godliness brotherly kindness; and to brotherly kindness charity. For if these things be in you, and abound, they make you that ye shall neither be barren nor unfruitful in the knowledge of our Lord Jesus Christ.'

These various graces are not indeed equally developed in all the children of God, nor even in the same individual; but it is nonetheless true that all the fruits of the Spirit hang on the same stem, and draw their life and nourishment from one and the same root. Even if imperfect in *attainment*, therefore, we must nevertheless ever be perfect in *aim*, otherwise we cannot have any sure and satisfactory token of adoption, and that in very deed we are true and loyal servants of Christ. One has truly said: 'No man can have any evidence that he obeys the will of Christ in one particular, unless he sincerely and strenuously *aims* to obey it in every particular; for the will of Christ is one.'

Adorn the doctrine of God our Saviour in all things.—Titus 2:10.

Abstain from all appearance of evil.—1 Thess. 5:22.

Let your conversation be as it becometh the gospel of Christ.—Phil. 1:27.

Be thou an example of the believers, in word, in conversation, in charity, in spirit, in faith, in purity.—1 Tim. 4:12.

DECEMBER 12

IT IS PRESSURE THAT TESTS MEN.

ONE of the striking characteristics of the Psalms is their marvellous adaptation to all the ever-changing circumstances and experiences of believers. No matter what they may be feeling or fearing, needing or desiring, they are sure to find in one or other of them some precious words as directly suitable as if they had been written expressly for their own individual case. It may be that it is his own experience the Psalmist is delineating, his own difficulties or deliverances. Nevertheless, in telling these, and the workings of his own heart in connection with them, he is virtually telling ours also.

On one memorable occasion, when Saul was seeking the Psalmist's life, his timid friends, alarmed for his safety, urged upon him immediate flight to some distant hiding-place, where he might securely shelter himself from his relentless foe. All such counselling, however, at the time he rejected, and resolutely said, 'In the Lord put I my trust: how say ye to my soul, Flee as a bird to your mountain?' Here was faith in lively exercise; and it was not put to shame. In peaceful times it is sometimes difficult to distinguish between a Christian and a worldling, because then there is little or nothing to call out very visibly the faith of the one or the unbelief of the other; but when pressure or affliction comes, it is very different. As the same sun that melts the wax hardens the clay, so the same trial that drives the worldling to the mountain, drives the believer nearer to his God in loving trustfulness.

When backsliding had begun in the days of our Lord, and many forsook him and went back to the world, he said sorrowfully to his disciples, 'Will ye also go away?' To which they at once and unhesitatingly replied, 'Lord, to whom shall we go but unto thee? for thou hast the words of eternal life.' So it ever is with the truly loyal. As surely as the needle turns to the pole, so do they in all times of difficulty and temptation turn at once to the Lord, yea, and cleave to him also, saying, 'Whom have I in heaven but thee? and there is none upon the earth that I desire beside thee.' 'In my early days,' said an old Christian, 'when trouble came upon me, and I longed for sympathy and help, I used always to go first to friends and neighbours, and especially to fellow-believers, to pour into their ears my varied anxieties. But now,' he said, 'I take a shorter way and a better; for I go straight to the Lord at once, and never fail to get the help and blessing needed.'

> Commit thy way unto the Lord; trust also in him; and he shall bring it to pass ... He shall deliver them from the wicked, and save them, because they trust in him.—Psa. 37:5, 40.

> The Lord is my strength and my shield; my heart trusted in him, and I am helped.—Psa. 28:7.

> Oh how great is thy goodness, which thou hast laid up for them that fear thee; which thou hast wrought for them that trust in thee before the sons of men!—Psa. 31:19.

December 13

A PLEASING PERPLEXITY.

FEW, if any, pass through life without experiencing seasons of perplexity, in which they find it extremely difficult to come to a decision. Such a season had the old patriarch Jacob when there was famine in Canaan, and corn could only be found in the land of Egypt. He was then so placed that he must either perish for want or risk the liberty and life of his beloved Benjamin. Such a season, too, had David after he offended the Lord by the numbering of the people. It was a fearful choice that was set before him: 'Go and say unto David, Thus saith the Lord, I offer thee three things; choose thee one of them, that I may do it unto thee ... Shall seven years of famine come unto thee in thy land? or wilt thou flee three months before thine enemies, while they pursue thee? or that there be three days' pestilence in thy land?' No wonder that he exclaimed, on hearing these words, 'I am in a great strait.' But he wisely decided when he said, 'Let us fall now into the hand of the Lord; for his mercies are great: and let me not fall into the hand of man.' And such a season, too, had Paul, the great apostle of the Gentiles, when he said, 'I am in a strait betwixt two, having a desire to depart and be with Christ; which is far better.' In his case, however, the perplexity in which he found himself had this marked peculiarity, that it was not a painful, but a pleasing one; for his difficulty lay not in choosing between two things that were evil, but between two things that were good—namely, between remaining on earth to serve the Master he loved, or departing to be forever in his beatific presence.

Doubtless, had Paul considered only his own personal and immediate enjoyment, he would have been in little or no strait, but would at once have said, 'To depart and be with Christ is far better.' Believers, it is true, when they die, do not enter on their full inheritance; for while in their disembodied state this is impossible. Till the coming of the Lord the crown promised them is laid up, but not actually worn: witness the memorable words of the apostle, 'I have fought a good fight, I have finished my course, I have kept the faith: henceforth there is laid up for me a crown of righteousness, which the Lord, the righteous judge, shall give me at that day: and not to me only, but unto all them also that love his appearing.' But though the full glory is deferred till then, not so the stainless purity and perfect blessedness. These are enjoyed the very moment they are absent from the body and present with the Lord.

Why, then, did the apostle hesitate? It was simply because, though to depart and be with Christ would be far better for himself, yet to abide in the flesh was more needful for others; and the latter accordingly was what he preferred. This was a Christlike spirit, and were it more common what a widely different church and world would we soon have! 'If you labour to be seen of men,' says one, 'the spirit of your work will have little rallying power. If you do all things heartily as to the Lord, the contagion of your patience and enthusiasm may spread in many hearts, even though your Master wisely keeps you ignorant of it.'

We are confident, I say, and willing rather to be absent from the body, and to be present with the Lord.—2 Cor. 5:8.

And having this confidence, I know that I shall abide and continue with you all for your furtherance and joy of faith.—Phil. 1:25.

In whom, though now ye see him not, yet believing, ye rejoice with joy unspeakable and full of glory.—1 Pet. 1:8.

December 14

THE LEADER DIVINELY GIVEN.

IN the prophetic volume it is thus written of Christ: 'Behold, I have given him for a witness to the people, a leader and commander to the people.' This was a great gift, bestowed by the Father in great love and for a great end, even the eternal redemption of a lost world. Nor was the Father more willing to give than the Son to accept so blessed a commission; for he said, 'Lo, I come: in the volume of the book it is written of me, I delight to do thy will, O my God.'

In the passage referred to it is as a divinely-appointed Leader our Lord is presented to us. And in the fulfilling of this mission it is interesting to note that it is not to the few he addresses himself, but to the unlimited many; for with loving entreaty he invites all men everywhere to follow him. It is worthy of note also that, to secure a following, it is never his way, like other leaders, merely to present the inducements, and conceal the difficulties. On the contrary, he is as frank and explicit in speaking of the cross as of the crown. 'If any man,' he says, 'will come after me, let him deny himself, and take up his cross, and follow me. For whosoever will save his life shall lose it; and whosoever will lose his life for my sake shall find it.' As one puts it, 'The devil flatters men into his way,—he lets them see the bait, but not the hook; but Christ holds the crown in the one hand and the cross in the other, and the cross nearest to the sinner, as first to be taken up. His counsel is, Either build not, or first count the cost; venture not to sea, or else be resolute to ride out the storm.'

Notwithstanding the cross-bearing, however, very blessed is it to be permitted to follow the Lord. In a world like this, surrounded as we are by so many enemies, and with snares and temptations on every side, we would utterly fail were we left to our own guidance; but with such a Divine Leader, all-wise and almighty, we are absolutely safe. No foe can overcome, nor real evil ever befall us. When leading the Israelites through the wilderness, Moses had ever and again to cry to the Lord for direction and help; but Jesus himself is to his people the pillar of cloud by day and of fire by night. He needeth not, as Moses, to strike the flinty rock that the streams may flow; for he himself is the smitten Rock, whence gush rivers of living water to cheer and satisfy every longing soul. Nor needeth he to cry for flesh; he is the true Manna, the Bread of Life, whereof if a man eat he shall hunger no more. Thus his people are led safely on from strength to strength; and when at last they come to Jordan's cold and sullen waters, he bears them safely through into the bright land of promise.

> *Jesus, I my cross have taken,*
> *All to leave, and follow thee;*
> *Destitute, despised, forsaken,*
> *Thou from hence my all shalt be.*
>
> *Man may trouble and distress me,*
> *'Twill but drive me to thy breast;*
> *Life with trials hard may press me,*
> *Heaven will bring me sweeter rest.*

These are they which came out of great tribulation, and have washed their robes, and made them white in the blood of the Lamb.— Rev. 7:14.

No man should be moved by these afflictions: for yourselves know that we are appointed thereunto.—1 Thess. 3:3.

Remember the word that I said unto you, The servant is not greater than his lord. If they have persecuted me, they will also persecute you; if they have kept my saying, they will keep yours also.— John 15:20.

DECEMBER 15

THE UNLIKELY BRINGERS OF OUR BEST THINGS.

WHEN the Lord laid disease upon Naaman, and that one of the very worst that flesh is heir to, it seemed the utter blighting of his every hope. Yet, strange to say, that very leprosy was, as it were, the first imparted medicine for his eternal healing,—a marked proof of unmerited and saving kindness, and an early token of intended adoption; for 'whom the Lord loveth he chasteneth, and scourgeth every son whom he receiveth.' But for that very disease he might never have been effectually humbled or taught his own nothingness, or have been made to realise his need of help mightier far than any that creature hand could impart. And doubtless, on many an after-day in his life he himself, when reviewing the past and all the marvellous way in which he had been led, would often be ready to say, with grateful heart, 'It is good for me that I have been afflicted.'

It is thus the Lord deals more or less with all his people. He chastens and afflicts them for their good. As without the furnace the gold would never get rid of its dross, so without trials sin would retain its mastery over our corrupt nature. Unbroken prosperity might be more pleasing to us, but adversity, and even storm and tempest, are often more profitable.

Keen students of nature, and especially of marine life in all its forms, often welcome the tempest, because after it they frequently get their choicest specimens. In the journal of the late Dr Coldstream it is thus written: 'This morning, as the storm had subsided, I determined to go down to the sands of Leith, that I might revel in the riches that might have been cast up by the deep after the terrible storm.' So is it with believers; their very richest experiences and the choicest tokens of the divine favour are often got in and after their stormiest trials.

This was remarkably exemplified in the dying experience of Dr Payson. Though his bodily sufferings were intense, yet the peace and joy of his soul completely outweighed them all. It seemed as if he were dwelling in the land of Beulah. 'If God had told me,' he said, 'that he was about to make me as happy as I could be in this world, and then said that he would begin by crippling me in all my limbs, and removing me from all my usual sources of enjoyment, I should have thought it a very strange mode of accomplishing his purpose. Yet how is his wisdom manifest even in this! for if you should see a man at midday shut up in a close and stifling room, idolizing a set of lamps and rejoicing in their light, and you wished to make him truly happy, you would begin by blowing out his lamps, and throwing open the shutters and letting in the light and air of heaven.'—It is even so, believers; and if you cannot always realise this on earth, you will at least most certainly do so in heaven, and thank the Lord with heart and soul for every affliction sent you.

> We glory in tribulations also: knowing that tribulation worketh patience; and patience, experience; and experience, hope: and hope maketh not ashamed; because the love of God is shed abroad in our hearts by the Holy Ghost which is given unto us.—Rom. 5:3-5.

> It is good for me that I have been afflicted; that I might learn thy statutes.—Psa. 119:71.

> Blessed is the man whom thou chastenest, O Lord, and teachest him out of thy law.—Psa. 94:12.

December 16

A HASTY DELIVERANCE IS APT TO BE AN
IMPERFECT ONE.

WHILE the removal of the Israelites from Egypt to Canaan was a great event, it was also, in the mode of its accomplishment, a gradual one. There was wise and gracious design in this. A sudden translation, however seemingly desirable, would not have been safe; for it would have brought them prematurely into Canaan, before either in spirit or character they were fully prepared for it. It needed the long and sore discipline of the wilderness to purge and cleanse them from their manifold corruptions, and make them sweetly ready for all the duties and privileges of the land of promise.

And so is it with the great spiritual translation so often referred to in the word. True, the moment we believe in Christ we are brought into the kingdom of grace; but frequently there is, so to speak, a long and weary wilderness to traverse ere we get into the kingdom of glory. Even after conversion, what continued discipline we need, to refine and purify us, and to make us fully meet for the inheritance of the saints in light.

We are, meanwhile, like children getting our education; and one school is not enough for this end, nor one lesson. We need line upon line, and precept upon precept; here a little, and there a little, day by day; and sooner or later it will be the testimony of every true child of God, that their Divine Teacher hath done all things well, and that no part of their training could have been spared.

At last, in my heavy sorrow,
I looked from the cross;
I saw the Master watching,
With a look of tender love.
He turned to the cross before me,
And I thought I heard him say,—
'My child, thou must bear thy burden,
And learn thy task today.'
And thus I learned my lesson,
Taught by the Master alone;
He only knows the tears I shed,
For he has wept his own.
But from them came a brightness
Straight from the home above,
Where the school of life will be ended,
And the cross will show the love.

It has been said of John Evangelist Gossner: 'He was long in the school, learning and unlearning. It was the time of an ordinary life; but he left it ready for his calling, and such a teacher never dies. The tediousness of pupilage is no waste when the workman needeth not to be ashamed. From humble little Hausea and the unnoticed struggles of a country priest to the Father Gossner of a reverent, religious Germany, from Feneberg's little parlour to the farthest ends of heathendom, and a name that is lovingly spoken on every continent of the globe, is a mighty stride. Neither brilliant talents nor the tide of fortune helped him. Whoever seeks the way to it will find it to be that plain, old-fashioned one of faith and prayer.'

But let patience have her perfect work, that ye may be perfect and entire, wanting nothing.—JAMES 1:4.

The Lord will perfect that which concerneth me: thy mercy, O Lord, endureth for ever: forsake not the works of thine own hands.— PSA. 138:8.

But the God of all grace, who hath called us unto his eternal glory by Christ Jesus, after that ye have suffered a while, make you perfect, stablish, strengthen, settle you.—I PET. 5:10.

DECEMBER 17

THE FULFILMENT THAT MUST BE.

ON a memorable occasion the Lord Jesus said to his disciples, 'All things *must be fulfilled* which were written in the law of Moses, and in the prophets, and in the psalms, concerning me.' This clearly shows that it is not the Law and the Prophets only that are full of Christ, but the Psalms likewise; and it is only as we bear this fact in mind that we can rightly understand and appreciate them. Of those of them that refer to his sufferings, perhaps the most remarkable is the twenty-second. Beyond all others it is the Psalm of the Cross. 'I know not,' says Martin Luther, 'whether any psalm throughout the whole book contains matter more weighty, or from which the godly can so truly perceive those sighs and groans which their Lord and head uttered when conflicting for us in the midst of death, and in the midst of "the pains and terrors of hell."'

To realise this, little more is needed than simply to read such verses as these: 'I am poured out like water, and all my bones are out of joint: my heart is like wax; it is melted in the midst of my bowels. My strength is dried up like a potsherd; and my tongue cleaveth to my jaws; and thou hast brought me into the dust of death.' And yet again: 'They pierced my hands and my feet ... They part my garments among them, and cast lots upon my vesture.' More mournful still, in his desolate loneliness and desertion, he exclaimed: 'My God, my God, why hast thou forsaken me?' Now, when we remember that all this was written long centuries before the things described in it occurred, the exactness of correspondence between the predictions and the facts is all the more remarkable. Indeed, the harmony between them is so complete, that the whole psalm reads more like history than prophecy.

If thus in the Psalms we have such clear revealings of all that our Redeemer was to endure, and if, in minutest detail, all have been fulfilled, not less surely do the Psalms unfold the glory and triumph that are to follow, when as King he shall come to judge the world in righteousness: 'In his days shall the righteous flourish; and abundance of peace so long as the moon endureth.'—'His name shall endure for ever: his name shall be continued as long as the sun: and men shall be blessed in him: all nations shall call him blessed.'

Well may we long and pray for this glorious coming. Come, Lord Jesus, come quickly.

> *We wait for thee, All-glorious One,*
> *We look for thine appearing;*
> *We bear thy name, and on the throne*
> *We see thy presence cheering.*
> *Faith even now*
> *Uplifts its brow,*
> *And sees the Lord descending,*
> *And with him bliss unending.*

O fools, and slow of heart to believe all that the prophets have spoken: ought not Christ to have suffered these things, and to enter into his glory? And beginning at Moses and all the prophets, he expounded unto them in all the scriptures the things concerning himself.—LUKE 24:25-27.

Thinkest thou that I cannot now pray to my Father, and he shall presently give me more than twelve legions of angels? But how then shall the scriptures be fulfilled, that thus it must be?—MATT. 26:53, 54.

The scripture cannot be broken.—JOHN 10:35.

DECEMBER 18

PRAYERFUL MENTION.

FROM some lips the words, 'Money we cannot give, but you may count upon our prayers,' would awaken nothing but suspicion. But there are thousands of others in humble life so true-hearted that we would have no misgivings, no matter how often they might say, like Peter, 'Silver and gold have I none; but such as I have give I unto thee.' When they supplicate, it is ever with such hearty reality and true faith that their prayers become the very best and choicest of gifts, and infinitely more operative for good than any amount of money they could possibly bestow; just because we are assured, 'The effectual fervent prayer of a righteous man availeth much.'

Doubtless, when Onesiphorus was taking note of his blessings, he would count among the very chief of them the fact that he had found a place in the prayers of so great and good a man as Paul. We can readily imagine him again and again with wonder and gratitude reading to himself and to his children these precious words: 'The Lord give mercy unto the house of Onesiphorus; for he oft refreshed me, and was not ashamed of my chain: but, when he was in Rome, he sought me out very diligently, and found me. The Lord grant unto him that he may find mercy of the Lord in that day: and in how many things he ministered unto me at Ephesus, thou knowest very well.'

Our prayerful mention should as much as possible resemble this, and be specific as well as earnest and believing. When prayers are so vague and general that no one thing in particular is singled out and specially pleaded for, it is scarcely possible to have either intense desire or true expectancy. But it is very different when in our prayers particular mention is made of persons, places, and things alike. This at once imparts a reality and interest to them which otherwise they would not have. We then expect, as well as ask; and so, when the sought-for blessing comes, instead of calling it a striking coincidence, we say at once, What a gracious answer! and give the Lord the glory that is due.

In private parental pleadings, it is well to mention each child by name, and to ask, so far as may be, the very thing each specially needs. Nor should we ever do this hesitatingly; for if anything in this world is sure of success, it is believing prayer. Trade fails oftentimes, crops perish, and property wastes; but never is prayer a failure, for the Lord liveth, and no promise of his ever lacks fulfilment. The more we so pray in faith and fervour, the more will we find from blessed experience the truth of what an old writer says: 'Prayer delights God's ear; it melts his heart, it opens his hand. Plead with him earnestly, and either he will remove the affliction or remove the impatience.'

Even mental prayer is not unheard. Hannah spake in her heart, and she testified, 'The Lord hath given me my petition which I asked of him.' When the heart is so full that it can only groan in prayer, yet God writes that down: 'My groanings are not hid from thee.'

> Epaphras, who is one of you, a servant of Christ, saluteth you, always labouring fervently for you in prayers, that ye may stand perfect and complete in all the will of God.—COL. 4:12.
>
> The effectual fervent prayer of a righteous man availeth much.— JAMES 5:16.
>
> But we will give ourselves continually to prayer, and to the ministry of the word.—ACTS 6:4.

DECEMBER 19

INVITING TO DINE.

IN ordinary circumstances, when men are laid on their dying pillow, and utter what are called their *last words*, there come no other words thereafter; for the death of men brings to a final close their recorded history. Nor will it ever be otherwise till the grave reopens on the great resurrection morn. The living may speak and help, but never the dead.

In an Arab legend it is written that Akrimah, the Yemenite chief, when once upon a time passing a cairn, said to his companion: 'Men report that Hatim when alive never sent a guest away empty. Now, here we are at his tomb: our provisions have run short, and there is no village near; let us see whether after death he will do anything for us.' With this he halted, and called out: 'O Hatim, here we stand at your door—I, Akrimah of Yemen, and my followers—all of us hungry and weary; what can you do for us?'

Alas! Hatim could do nothing; for death had closed his eyes, and extinguished his power forever. But it was not so with our blessed Redeemer. His tomb was not like Hatim's. It is true, he died and was buried, and a mighty stone was rolled to the door of the sepulchre. Nevertheless, ere three brief days had run their course, he who for our sakes laid down his life, once more took it up again; and it was as the Risen One he lovingly said to his disciples at the Sea of Galilee, 'Come and dine.'

Nothing could have been simpler than the repast. It was only bread and fish that were set before them. But if the provision was ordinary, not so the love that provided it, or the blessing that accompanied it, or the guests that sat at it; for they were all redeemed men, with the risen Redeemer himself in the midst.

We, too, may feast and commune with our Lord. 'If any man hear my voice,' he says, 'and open the door, I will come in to him, and will sup with him, and he with me.' This is especially the case at the Supper of the Lord. On the table he then spreads for us in the wilderness, bread and wine alone are visible to the eye of sense: nevertheless, to the eye of faith it is the most wondrous table of all; for the heavenly Manna is on it—the Bread of life—and the wine of the kingdom; and the Lord we love is saying, 'Eat, O friends; drink, yea, drink abundantly, O beloved.'

> *We taste thee, O thou living Bread,*
> *And long to feast upon thee still;*
> *We drink of thee, the Fountain-head,*
> *And thirst our souls from thee to fill.*

Any feast now, however, can give us but little idea of the feast that shall be; for these are our Lord's own words: 'Blessed are those servants, whom the lord when he cometh shall find watching: verily I say unto you, that he shall gird himself, and make them to sit down to meat, and will come forth and serve them.' The joy of that great feast shall have a wondrous beginning, and it shall never have an end.

Ho, every one that thirsteth, come ye to the waters, and he that hath no money; come ye, buy, and eat; yea, come, buy wine and milk without money and without price.—Isa. 55:1.

Tell them which are bidden, Behold, I have prepared my dinner: my oxen and my fatlings are killed, and all things are ready: come unto the marriage.—Matt. 22:4.

December 20

THE ONLY FOUNTAIN OPENED FOR SIN AND FOR UNCLEANNESS.

TILL truly awakened, sin in ordinary circumstances gives men little or no concern. They think lightly of it, and usually imagine that at any time, by a little effort, they can themselves do all that is needful in the way of moral cleansing. When, however, they begin to realise in some degree sin's real nature, they are apt to turn to the opposite extreme, and give way to the fear that nothing whatever can save them from its guilt and power. More especially is this the case with those who, in their own strength, have been long and laboriously going about to establish their own righteousness. They cherish hope for a time, it may be; but when they find at length that their every effort ends in failure, and that instead of getting better they daily grow worse, they are ready to fold their hands in the idleness of despair. The great enemy strives to intensify this feeling by many a dark suggestion, just that he may the more effectually hinder their final salvation.

Happily, however, what we cannot do, the Lord can. Yes! in the riches of his marvellous grace he has opened a fountain for sin and for uncleanness, where the very vilest may wash and be made clean.

> *The dying thief rejoiced to see*
> *That Fountain in his day;*
> *And there may I, as vile as he,*
> *Wash all my sins away.*

So infinite is the cleansing efficacy of the blood of Jesus when believingly applied, that by means of it, though our sins be as scarlet, they shall be white as snow; though they be red like crimson, they shall be as wool. In Jeremiah's day the Lord said: 'O Jerusalem! wilt thou not be made clean? when shall it once be?' And to all who hear the word he virtually puts the same question now. May it never be said of us—'I would,' but 'ye would not.'

During an illness, that illustrious scholar, Bengel, sent for a student in the Theological Institution, and requested him to impart a word of consolation. The youth replied: 'Sir, I am but a pupil, a mere learner; I don't know what to say to a teacher like you.' 'What!' said Bengel; 'a divinity student, and not able to communicate a word of scriptural comfort!' The student, abashed, contrived to utter the text, 'The blood of Jesus Christ his Son cleanseth us from all sin.' 'That is the very word I want,' said Bengel—'it is quite enough'; and taking him affectionately by the hand, dismissed him.

> But ye are washed, but ye are sanctified, but ye are justified in the name of the Lord Jesus, and by the Spirit of our God.—1 Cor. 6:11.

In whom we have redemption through his blood, the forgiveness of sins, according to the riches of his grace.—EPH. 1:7.

Unto him that loved us, and washed us from our sins in his own blood, and hath made us kings and priests unto God and his Father; to him be glory and dominion for ever and ever. Amen.— REV. 1:5, 6.

DECEMBER 21

THE OUTCOME OF GRACE.

WHILE in their natural state, the only outcome we are led to expect from men is that referred to by our Lord when he says, 'Out of the heart proceed evil thoughts, murders, adulteries, fornications, thefts, false witness, blasphemies.' But when renewal comes through the Spirit of God, the outcome that before was only evil is now good, and makes itself manifest in sanctified thought, expression, and continuous well-doing. Hence these words of the apostle, 'The fruit of the Spirit is love, joy, peace, longsuffering, gentleness, goodness, faith, meekness, temperance.'

These and other graces are so mutually dependent, that what is true of the members of Christ's mystical body is also true of them. If one grace suffers, all the graces suffer with it; or if one grace be honoured, all the graces rejoice with it.

From its very nature, true grace is a seed that never rots, but in due time develops in blossom and fruit. 'Ye shall know them by their fruits,' says our Lord. 'Every good tree bringeth forth good fruit; but a corrupt tree bringeth forth evil fruit. A good tree cannot bring forth evil fruit, neither can a corrupt tree bring forth good fruit.' Wherever, therefore, there is the real root of the matter in the soul, there will also sooner or later be, so to speak, the fruit of the matter in the life; and if the latter is wanting, we may well fear that the former is lacking also.

One sweetly says: 'In a window this summer there was a flowerpot, containing a plant whose use it was to be odorous and beautiful. The leaves were just beginning to curl up. I poured a cupful of water into the saucer in which the flowerpot stood; and a child looking on asked, "Why did you not rather pour water on the leaves?" It was a child that asked, and I explained the reason; adding, that when God would bring beauty and fragrance and healthfulness into our lives, he waters us at the root.'

It is even so; and yet how many are there who are just like that child. The leaf is everything to them, the root nothing. 'Why dwell so much on the love of Christ,' they say, 'and on faith in him, and on atonement and conversion, and other doctrines of grace, when, after all, it is better morality we need, and better living and acting?' They forget that there is nothing more practical for all kinds of true work than the letting the love of Christ 'get in about the roots of our being.' They forget also that, as we cannot gather grapes from thorns and figs from thistles, so neither can we get the graces of the Spirit and the fruits of righteousness from natures wholly unrenewed. Till the tree is made good, it is vain to expect to have the fruit good; so, till man's nature is renewed through saving grace, it is utterly vain to dream of elevated aims and an ennobled life. Obviously, then, we cannot too earnestly pray for the Spirit of all grace, provided our aim in doing so is the fullest outcome of the fruits of righteousness to the glory of the Lord.

> A good man out of the good treasure of his heart bringeth forth that which is good; and an evil man out of the evil treasure of his heart bringeth forth that which is evil.—LUKE 6:45.
>
> In this the children of God are manifest, and the children of the devil: whosoever doeth not righteousness is not of God, neither he that loveth not his brother.—1 JOHN 3:10.
>
> Being made free from sin, and become servants to God, ye have your fruit unto holiness.—ROM. 6:22.

DECEMBER 22

OUT OF THE KINGDOM, AND IN IT.

THE kingdom of God, alike in its grace now and in its glory hereafter, is frequently set before us in the sacred volume. We are urged to seek it: 'Seek ye first the kingdom of God and his righteousness.' We are cheered by the hope of it: 'Fear not, little flock; for it is your Father's good pleasure to give you the kingdom.' We are moved by the nearness of it: 'The kingdom of God is at hand: repent ye therefore, and believe the gospel.' And in the Gospel of Luke we are told this interesting fact in connection with it, that since this time (the time of John) 'the kingdom of God is preached, and every man presseth into it.'

With regard to our relation to this kingdom, it is all-important to note that no man is in this kingdom by nature. Being sinners, fallen, guilty, lost, we are all of us, without exception, outside the kingdom, not in it. This is the teaching of Scripture in every page of it, and all history confirms its truth; but, alas! it is a teaching that very few believe and realise. The common thought is, that the morally sunken of our race may be outside the kingdom, but never the outwardly moral and amiable. But no; there is no difference. So long as we are out of Christ we are out of the kingdom, and are without God and without hope in the world.

Though no man, however, is in the kingdom by nature, happily any man may get into it through grace. There is a way into it, a way divinely opened, and graciously wide—even Christ, 'the way, the truth, and the life.' 'By me,' he says, 'if any man enter in, he shall be saved, and shall go in and out, and find pasture.'

Now, if it be really so that no man is in this kingdom by nature, and that yet any man may get into it by grace, should not every man just do as they did in John's time—at once press into it, and be saved? What real pressers into the kingdom ever mainly ask about the way is not, Is it rough or smooth, gloomy or lightsome, long or short? but simply, Is it the right way, the appointed way, the way that all the saints have travelled, and is heaven at the end of it? When assured of this, they straightway press resolutely onward.

> *I can but perish if I go;*
> *I am resolved to try:*
> *If I stay away, I know*
> *I must forever die.*

If the kingdom is won, everything is won; for the kingdom includes in it every blessing that a faithful God has promised or a sanctified heart can desire—forgiveness, acceptance, adoption, joy, and glory everlasting.

> From the days of John the Baptist until now the kingdom of heaven suffereth violence, and the violent take it by force.—MATT. 11:12.
>
> Strive to enter in at the strait gate: for many, I say unto you, will seek to enter in, and shall not be able. When once the master of the house is risen up, and hath shut to the door, and ye begin to stand without, and to knock at the door, saying, Lord, Lord, open unto us; and he shall answer and say unto you, I know you not whence ye are.—LUKE 13:24, 25.

DECEMBER 23

THE SHUTTING OF THE DOOR.

IN the days of Noah, in spite of appalling wickedness, the Lord gave a long respite to men, even a hundred and twenty years. Instead, however, of profiting by it, they only became day by day more and more hardened. If they had some fear in the beginning, on hearing the first warning that came from Noah's lips, they had none whatever in the end, but were bold, reckless, and openly defiant. Doubtless, many a time they said to Noah, 'Are you still at your old folly, putting fancy for fact, and preparing for dangers that can never come?'

Such mockery was hard to bear; yet never for one moment did it shake his faith in the truth of God's warning word, or stay his preparation. He still gathered his materials, studied his plans, put beam to beam, and plank to plank, and never let the sound of hammer cease till the last needed nail had been driven in. Then when at length the fated hour had come, and Noah had entered, *the Lord shut him in.*

Come what may, he at least was now safe. There might be waters from above, and waters from below, and wild rolling waters on every side; but this mattered not to him, for he was within the ark, and its door was securely shut by God's own hand. There was, however, judgment as well as mercy in the shutting of that door; for while it was salvation to all within, it was utter destruction to all without.

'What a sound was that,' said Mr Stewart of Cromarty, 'when in the listening ominous hush of Earth's last evening God shut the door. There have been sounds as well as sights to make the boldest hearts quail and the flintiest hearts melt,—the cry has gone up from cities given over to fire and sword, or the shuddering throe of earthquakes which hurries myriads to death; but except the cry on Calvary which corresponded to it, no more solemn or melancholy sound has been heard by human ears than that which passed into the evening stillness when the broad green earth was left to be the grave of mankind, and God shut the door of the ark.'

Once again God will shut the door. Man will not do it, angels will not do it. But oh, what a sigh and shudder will pass through the listening universe when God will shut the door of the heavenly ark upon the lost! This last-named event is still in the future: nevertheless, the shutting of the first door is not more certain than the final shutting of the second; and the fact that it is to be sudden and unexpected should powerfully urge every unsaved soul to an immediate repentance and closing with offered mercy in Christ.

> Strive to enter in at the strait gate: for many, I say unto you, will seek to enter in, and shall not be able, ... when once the master of the house is risen up, and hath shut to the door.—LUKE 13:24, 25.
>
> Afterward came also the other virgins, saying, Lord, Lord, open to us. But he answered and said, Verily I say unto you, I know you not.—MATT. 25:11, 12.

For the Lord knoweth the way of the righteous: but the way of the ungodly shall perish.—Psa. 1:6.

December 24

THE DAY THAT FOLLOWS THE NIGHT.

FREQUENT reference is made in Scripture to a coming day. All are familiar with expressions like these: 'The day is at hand.'—'The day shall declare it.'—'May he find mercy of the Lord in that day.'—'Sealed unto the day of redemption.'—'Hasting unto the coming of the day of God.' Very plainly, a day so spoken of can be no ordinary one. To those who reject the Son of God it can only be a day of terror and dismay, while to his believing people it will be the completion of all they have ever hoped or longed for.

There are many darkening mists meanwhile, through latent worldliness and lingering unbelief; but as soon as that promised day breaks every cloud and shadow shall vanish away. There will be no more dark mysteries in God's providence, or sore hidings of his face, or seeing through a glass, darkly. Such things shall all have passed away forever.

Besides being a day of brightness, it will also be one of unbroken peace. Whatever the wars, tumults, and commotions beforehand, there will be none after. Instead of tempest there will be calm, and instead of discord, harmony. 'Ephraim shall not envy Judah, and Judah shall not vex Ephraim.' 'And they shall beat their swords into plowshares, and their spears into pruninghooks: nation shall not lift up sword against nation, neither shall they learn war anymore.'

Moreover, it will in every sense be a day of gladness and joy, for it will be the harvest-day, when those who have sown in tears shall reap in joy; and the resting-day, when work is done and home is reached; and the marriage day, with all its joyous feasting and gladsome song. And it will be a rewarding day—the day when the cross shall be exchanged for the crown; for if we suffer with our Lord, we shall also reign with him.

Best of all, it will be a day followed by no night. Here the brightest and longest day has always its ending; it closes in night. But this day of days is not merely a bright day and a happy day; it is an eternal day. When the weeping of the night is over, a joy cometh in the morning; and that morning never has an evening again. With all its blessedness and glory, it abideth ever. It is written, 'Our light affliction, which is but for a moment, worketh out for us a far more exceeding and *eternal* weight of glory.'

Now, to all appearance, this is a day not far off. Even were long ages to elapse before it came, it would be well worth waiting for, just because it brings such blessings in its train. But it is not thus distant; for the apostle, in speaking of it, does not say, 'The night is just beginning, and the day is far off,' but, on the contrary, 'The night is far spent, and the day is at hand.' 'It is certain,' said Samuel Rutherford, 'that there is not much sand to run now in our Lord's sand-glass. The fair morning is at hand; the day-star is near its rising; and we are not many miles from home. What matters, then, the ill entertainment in the smoky inns of this miserable earth? We are not to stay here, and we shall be dearly welcome to him to whom we go.' Meanwhile, till that glad day come, let us be daily found praying with more faith, and loving with more ardour, and working with more energy, than ever we have done before.

Until the day break, and the shadows flee away, turn, my beloved, and be thou like a roe or a young hart upon the mountains of Bether.—SONG OF SOL. 2:17.

Of the times and the seasons, brethren, ye have no need that I write unto you. For yourselves know perfectly that the day of the Lord so cometh as a thief in the night. But ye, brethren, are not in darkness, that that day should overtake you as a thief. Ye are all the children of light, and the children of the day: we are not of the night, nor of darkness. Therefore let us not sleep, as do others; but let us watch and be sober.—1 THESS. 5:1, 2, 4-6.

DECEMBER 25

THE MARRIAGE FEAST, AND JESUS THERE.

IT is sweet to think that not in our sorrows only can we count on the sympathy of Jesus, deep and tender, but also in all our joys. While he ever readily enters the house of mourning to impart peace and comfort to troubled hearts, he enters just as willingly the house of gladness to bless it with his smile. This was touchingly exemplified at the marriage feast in Cana of Galilee. There was no declinature on his part of the invitation sent; no staying away because it was to be a marriage feast. On the contrary, he gave not his presence only, but his blessing also—yea, and a bounteous supply besides.

This is a fact of peculiar interest; for in these days of growing lawlessness there are many who not merely ignore marriage as a divine institution, but resist and resent it as an undue interference with human freedom. With socialistic license, they would have all men free to form unions, and as absolutely free to dissolve them at pleasure. There are others who, while in words admitting marriage to be a divine institution, yet in reality degrade it by representing it as not pure enough for the saintly, and altogether incompatible with a sacred calling and a consecrated life. In opposition to all this our blessed Lord, by his presence at the feast, not only gave his solemn sanction to the ordinance of marriage, but imparted to it an honour and dignity even higher far than it before possessed; so that now, more than ever, it stands out as a choice gift of Heaven to men, 'a safeguard of society, a nurse of charities and the holy home of all the virtues.' When comparing it with its opposite, an old divine says: 'It hath more care, but less danger; it is more merry and more sad; it is fuller of sorrows and fuller of joys; it lies under more burdens, but is supported by all the strength of love and charity.'

In its holiest and happiest form marriage is again and again referred to in Scripture as a blessed type of the union between the church and her Lord. He is the bridegroom, and his people are the bride; and their completed hopes and joys will be made gloriously visible at the second advent and the marriage supper of the Lamb.

> 'Tis thy church's voice that cries,—
> Rend those long unrended skies;
> Bridegroom of the church, arise!
> Take to thee thy power and reign,
> Purify this earth again,
> Cleanse it from each curse and stain.

And the Lord God said, It is not good that the man should be alone; I will make him an help meet for him ... Therefore shall a man leave his father and his mother, and shall cleave unto his wife: and they shall be one flesh.—GEN. 2:18, 24.

Marriage is honourable in all, and the bed undefiled: but whore-mongers and adulterers God will judge.—HEB. 13:4.

Let us be glad and rejoice, and give honour to him: for the marriage of the Lamb is come, and his wife hath made herself ready. And to her was granted that she should be arrayed in fine linen, clean and white: for the fine linen is the righteousness of saints. And he saith unto me, Write, Blessed are they which are called unto the marriage supper of the Lamb ... These are the true sayings of God.—REV. 19:7-9.

DECEMBER 26

WORDS TO CHEER FROM KINGLY LIPS.

IN ordinary circumstances, it is joy and not fear that is awakened by the sight of a friend; yet in referring to the Redeemer, John said, 'When I saw him, I fell at his feet as dead.' The brightness of his unveiled glory was more than feeble nature could bear, and he sank beneath it. This did not long continue, however; for in loving tenderness the Lord perfected strength in weakness, and laying his right hand upon him, he graciously said to the trembling disciple, 'Fear not; I am the first and the last: I am he that liveth, and was dead; and, behold, I am alive for evermore.' The gentle pressure of that hand could scarcely fail to relieve him, especially accompanied as it was by so gracious a 'fear not.' From mere human lips such 'fear nots' are often but idle breath; but from the lips of the Saviour-King they are not so much words as deeds, and have unfailing efficacy.

Brief as was the utterance, 'I am he that liveth, and was dead; and, behold, I am alive for evermore,' yet what tongue can tell all that is included in it. We have here the mystery of mysteries—the Lord of life not only assuming our nature, but dying in our stead. If this does not comfort, what can?—for in dying, he not only atoned for sin, but destroyed death, and secured for all his people life and immortality as an eternal possession. To John, in particular, these words, and especially the last clause, 'Behold, I am alive for evermore,' must have been peculiarly comforting, because at the very time they were uttered a fierce persecution was raging, and many Christians had perished, and many more were in exile, and of the original Twelve almost all save John himself had gone to their rest. In these circumstances, to the eye of sense, it would appear as if all hope were cut off. But no, all was safe, just because die who may, Jesus is alive for evermore. In the time of the Indian Mutiny, a native Christian martyr said to his wife, who was standing by his side, weeping and comfortless, 'I feel confident, if our missionaries live you will be taken care of; and should they all perish, yet Christ lives forever.' This was a noble utterance, and, coming as it did from such a quarter, it has the cheering quality of good news from a far country.

> Then said I, Woe is me! for I am undone; because I am a man of unclean lips, and I dwell in the midst of a people of unclean lips: for mine eyes have seen the King, the Lord of hosts.—Isa. 6:5.

> He that is our God is the God of salvation; and unto God the Lord belong the issues from death.—Psa. 68:20.

> The Lord appeared unto him the same night, and said, I am the God of Abraham thy father: fear not, for I am with thee, and will bless thee.—Gen. 26:24.

DECEMBER 27

THE FAME THAT WILL BE EVER EXTENDING.

IN the early days of David how little was there to betoken the great future that awaited him. He was in humble life, a mere shepherd, the youngest of seven sons, and utterly unknown beyond the circle of his own family and friends; and yet, almost before manhood had been fully reached, there was not a greater name in Israel.

It was even so with him who was at once David's Son and David's Lord. For full thirty years his home was in the little town of Nazareth, and he dwelt there in such lowliness and obscurity that he was never regarded as more than a poor carpenter's son; yet all of a sudden thereafter there was such a lifting of the veil, such a revealing of the glory, that he became everyone's wonder, and 'his fame went throughout all Syria.' He had fame as a teacher, for never man spake like him; he had fame as a physician, for 'he healed all manner of sickness and all manner of disease among the people'; and he had fame as the great Prophet of promise, for the people said of him, 'This is of a truth that prophet that should come into the world.'

Nor was his fame like that of so many—a mere evanescent thing. It was once said: 'A great deed, a striking book, a noble speech, sets a man up high before the eyes of all the land, and he deems his fame made. It is made; but that very hour it begins to be unmade: in a month, in a year, it is gone.' Such precisely, in the end, was the expectation of the Jews regarding Christ. When they condemned him, and scourged him, and crucified him, and buried him, they never for a moment doubted that his name and fame were forever extinguished; but instead of this, after Gethsemane and Calvary, he became more than ever known and magnified, not in Syria alone, but throughout the wide world.

In our own time, as among the unbelieving Jews of that era, there exists in many not a little of the same spirit of hostility to the Son of God; and the hope is not merely cherished by them, but openly expressed, that his religion and his following have had their day, and will soon be forever among the forgotten things of the past.

Many of God's children are not simply saddened by such things, but almost staggered. But they need not; for let such opposers combine as they may, and do their utmost, yet in the end 'every knee shall bow to him, and every tongue confess that Jesus Christ is Lord, to the glory of God the Father.' It is expressly written, 'The Lord shall be king over *all the earth*.' 'He shall have dominion from sea to sea, and from the river to the ends of the earth. All kings shall fall down before him; all nations shall serve him.' This may be but prophecy meanwhile, but the day is fast hastening on when it shall become veritable history visible to every eye. 'Hath the Lord said, and shall he not do it? or hath he spoken, and shall he not make it good?'

Sometimes subjects say to their monarchs, 'O king, live forever!' But in spite of this they flit away like shadows, and their empires with them. But in response to such an utterance from his subjects, our King replies: 'I am he that liveth, and was dead; and, behold, I am alive for evermore'; and, 'To him that overcometh will I grant to sit with me in my throne, even as I also overcame, and am set down with my Father in his throne.'

> His name shall endure for ever: his name shall be continued as long as the sun: and men shall be blessed in him: all nations shall call him blessed. And blessed be his glorious name for ever: and let the whole earth be filled with his glory; Amen, and Amen.—PSA. 72:17, 19.
>
> In thee shall all families of the earth be blessed.—GEN. 12:3.
>
> The earth shall be filled with the knowledge of the glory of the Lord, as the waters cover the sea.—HAB. 2:14.

DECEMBER 28

WEARY NOT.

WHEN writing to the Galatians, the apostle said: 'Let us not be weary in well-doing; for in due season we shall reap, if we faint not.' These words were not unneeded then, neither are they unneeded now; for even with the best it needs constant watchfulness to resist and overcome the weariness here forbidden. There is a weariness which invites no censure, such as that felt even by our blessed Lord himself, of whom it is written: 'Now Jacob's well was there. Jesus therefore, being wearied with his journey, sat thus on the well; and it was about the sixth hour.' So, too, has it often been with his faithful servants. 'In journeyings often,' says Paul, 'in *weariness* and painfulness.' In later times it has been just the same. Accordingly, Whitefield was repeatedly heard to say, 'I am often weary *in* my Master's work, but I am never weary *of* it.' The weariness, therefore, against which we are solemnly cautioned in the word, is never the weariness that springs from mere feebleness of frame, or advancing years, or fulness of loving work.

Censurable weariness is something wholly different from this. It springs from sloth, and love of ease, and chilled affection, and over-engrossment with the world. Even in ordinary life, nothing is grudged when affection is ardent. So is it with believers when their love to Christ is warm. It not only keeps weariness away, but it so sweetens all labour and service, and even sorest sacrifice, for his sake, that, like the apostle, they can say, 'None of these things move me; neither count I my life dear unto myself, that I may finish my course with joy.' The Christian who, though neither enfeebled by work nor by years, yields to weariness, and ceases to labour, is sure, sooner or later, to find thorns in his pillow. Will no voice ever say to him, What doest thou here, Elijah? 'Looking at his means, powers, and opportunities,' as one says, 'will he not be ashamed to have them, and will they not reproach him with the use he might make of them, especially when workers are few and the activity of evil is great. If he have conscience and generous feeling left, his must be a restless state.'

In doing work for Christ, we have always much to encourage us. It is never lost labour, for we are expressly assured that 'in due season we shall reap, if we faint not.' But though true sowing will always be followed by sure reaping, yet we must not limit the Lord as to the time of it. There is 'a due season,' and of this it is he only, and not we, that can rightly judge. Till this due season come, therefore, we must unweariedly wait and work, knowing assuredly that the longer and heartier the toil, the richer will be the harvest. A true and hearty labourer for Christ said not long ago to his flock, in his own way, 'I do not want to go just yet. But I believe,' he added, 'that if we could but realise what God has in reserve for us, we would everyone be eager to go tonight, stepping right out from the sanctuary into the glories of the skies.'

> Therefore, my beloved brethren, be ye stedfast, unmoveable, always abounding in the work of the Lord, forasmuch as ye know that your labour is not in vain in the Lord.—1 Cor. 15:58.

> For ye have need of patience, that, after ye have done the will of God, ye might receive the promise.—Heb. 10:36.

> He that goeth forth and weepeth, bearing precious seed, shall doubtless come again with rejoicing, bringing his sheaves with him.—Psa. 126:6.

DECEMBER 29

THE LORD'S PROMISE OF THE SPIRIT.

ALIKE in the Old Testament and in the New, there are many references to the Holy Spirit; and we clearly learn from some of them that this most needed of blessings is in the end to come, not merely in scattered drops, but in plenteous showers, and not on one land only, but to be far-reaching as the wide earth itself. It is thus written: 'It shall come to pass afterward, that I will pour out my spirit upon all flesh; and your sons and your daughters shall prophesy, your old men shall dream dreams, your young men shall see visions: and also upon the servants and upon handmaids in those days will I pour out my spirit.'

What promise could well be larger or richer than this. True, it may not necessarily include every individual of our race, but manifestly it includes the race in general, and individuals throughout it of every tribe and tongue, whether Jew or Gentile, Greek or Barbarian, bond or free. It implies, moreover, that in that predicted day alike the lofty and the lowly in position shall not only be taught and blessed of God themselves, but shall also be made helpful blessings to others. 'Your sons and your daughters shall prophesy'—'Your servants and handmaids' as well,—that is, enlightened and quickened by the Spirit, they shall be able to speak of Jesus and his love for the saving and edifying of others. Indeed, so wide and all-embracing is this promise in Joel, that Peter, when referring to it, said: 'The promise is unto you and to your children, and to all that are afar off, even as many as the Lord our God shall call.'

In connection with this, it is somewhat remarkable that in Joel, immediately after the promise, 'I will pour out my spirit upon all flesh,' there follow these striking words: 'And I will shew wonders in the heavens and in the earth, blood, and fire, and pillars of smoke. The sun shall be turned into darkness, and the moon into blood, before the great and the terrible day of the Lord come.' From such words it may be inferred that, as eighteen centuries ago there was a remarkable outpouring of the Spirit before the terrible day to Jerusalem for its guilty unbelief, so in all likelihood, towards the close of this dispensation, there will be another remarkable outpouring of the Spirit before the great and terrible day of which Joel speaks. And possibly, as not a few earnest students of the word think, the marvellous times of blessing which churches and believers in so many lands have been during the last few years enjoying through the outpoured Spirit, are precursors of those times to which our Lord refers when he says: 'There shall be signs in the sun, and in the moon, and in the stars; and upon the earth distress of nations, with perplexity; the sea and the waves roaring; men's hearts failing them for fear, and for looking after those things which are coming on the earth.'

In his concluding address as Moderator of the Free Church of Scotland, Dr Andrew Bonar lately said: 'Times of trial may be very near: the mystery of iniquity is at work with all skill. We may soon see political convulsions, not in the East only, but over the kingdoms. But all the more let us raise the cry, "Come from the four winds, O Breath, and breathe upon the slain." Some of us look for the speedy advent of the Lord Jesus, often remembering that it is when the three unclean spirits, like croaking frogs, are going forth to gather the nations to the battle of Armageddon, that the cry from the throne startles the Earth, "Behold, I come quickly!" All the more, on this account, do we labour and earnestly pray for the fuller outpouring of the Spirit before "that great and terrible day of the Lord."'—Should such a day be near, the true followers of the Lamb at least, who make his all-atoning blood their trust, have no reason for dismay: no plague can come nigh their dwelling; for, like Rahab, they hang out, as it were, the scarlet thread in the sight of the Lord, and like her shall be delivered.

> If ye then, being evil, know how to give good gifts unto your children: how much more shall your heavenly Father give the Holy Spirit to them that ask him?—LUKE 11:13.

> For I will pour water upon him that is thirsty, and floods upon the dry ground: I will pour my spirit upon thy seed, and my blessing upon thine offspring.—ISA. 44:3.

DECEMBER 30

THE HOME OF HOMES.

WHEN, in obedience to the injunction given him, the healed demoniac was going home to this friends, there was more of sadness in his heart than gladness, because for the time at least, every step he took homeward was a step away from him who was dearer to him than life. Besides, the home he was going to was but an earthly one, and in earthly homes there are often sad minglings of those who love the Lord and of those who love him not; and sad changes, for sickness enters them, and death, causing joyful voices to become dumb through sorrow, and harps that were once melodious to hang idly on the willows. But it will not lie so with the last and greatest home-going of all; for then every step believers take will be at once Christ-ward and heavenward, and that will leave sorrow and sighing forever behind.

The eye and ear have seen and heard many things, but for purity and beauty, love and peace, brightness and glory, never hath eye seen or mind conceived a home like the promised heavenly one. In it there will be happy reunions, but no after-partings—joys, but no griefs—and sweet converse and song, as day by day there is revealed some new wonder of providence or some fresh glory of grace. But the joy of joys in it to believers will be, to be forever with the Lord in endearing fellowship. It will thus be the very home of homes; and Augustine truly said, 'Who would not yearn for that city out of which no friend departs, and into which no enemy enters?'

This is set forth by Bunyan in his matchless Allegory with touching simplicity and beauty: 'Now I saw in my dream that these two men went in at the gate; and, lo! as they entered, they were transfigured, and they had raiment put on that shone like gold. There were also those that met them with harps and crowns, and gave them to them; the harps to praise withal, and the crowns in token of honour. Then I heard in my dream that all the bells in the city rang again for joy, and that it was said unto them, "Enter ye into the joy of your Lord." I also heard the men themselves, that they sang with a loud voice, saying, "Blessing, and honour, and glory, and power, be unto him that sitteth upon the throne, and unto the Lamb, for ever and ever." Now, just as the gates were opened to let in the men, I looked in after them, and, behold, the city shone like the sun; the streets also were paved with gold; and in them walked many men, with crowns on their heads, palms in their hands, and golden harps to sing praises withal. There were also of them that had wings, and they answered one another without intermission, saying, "Holy, holy, holy is the Lord!" And after that they shut up the gates; which when I had seen, I wished myself among them.'

> *What no human eye hath seen,*
> *What no mortal ear hath heard,*
> *What on thought hath never been*
> *In its noblest flight conferred,*
> *This hath God prepared in store*
> *For his people evermore.*

Glorious things are spoken of thee, O city of God.—Psa. 87:3.

And the city had no need of the sun, neither of the moon, to shine in it: for the glory of God did lighten it, and the Lamb is the light thereof.—Rev. 21:23.

And God shall wipe away all tears from their eyes; and there shall be no more death, neither sorrow, nor crying, neither shall there be any more pain: for the former things are passed away.—Rev. 21:4.

December 31

THE LAST PROMISE IN THE WORD,
AND THE GRANDEST.

WHEN a valued friend sets out for a distant land, nothing relieves the sorrow of the parting like an early and loving letter in his own hand. The very sight of it revives us, and makes us feel as old Jacob did when he saw the wagons sent from Egypt: 'It is enough,' he said, 'it is enough: Joseph my son is yet alive; I will go and see him before I die.' Now, the blessed announcement of our Lord, 'Behold, I come quickly,' coming as it did from heaven, serves a similar end: it gives us the sweet assurance that our Joseph, the Brother of brothers, yea, the Saviour-King, is yet alive, and will surely come again at no distant day.

Frequently in Scripture, when special attention is called to any great fact or truth, the word 'Behold' is prefixed, as in passages like these: 'Behold the Lamb of God, which taketh away the sin of the world.'—'Behold, what manner of love the Father hath bestowed upon us.'—'Behold, the bridegroom cometh.'—'Behold, I come as a thief.'—'Behold, he cometh with clouds.' So in like manner this last announcement of the advent, in the Bible's last chapter, gets emphatic repetition. We have it in the seventh verse: 'Behold, I come quickly: blessed is he that keepeth the sayings of the prophecy of this book.' We have it again in the twelfth verse: 'Behold, I come quickly; and my reward is with me'; and, finally, we have the promise in the twentieth verse: 'He which testifieth these things saith, Surely I come quickly.'

Now, why such frequency of announcement? Was it because our Lord knew that, as years and centuries rolled on, and the cry of the scoffer grew louder, 'Where is the promise of his coming?' even his own people would be in danger of letting 'the blessed hope' drop from their memory and from their faith, and of being found thereby with their loins ungirt and their lamps untrimmed when at last the cry shall be heard, 'Behold the Bridegroom cometh'?

The coming of the Lord will ever remain, not only one of the grandest and most joyous of Christian verities, but also one of the most stimulating and practical. And verily if ever there was a time when believers should watch and work as never before, it is in perilous times like these; yet to them not more perilous than bright, for their sure issue will be the consummation of their every hope. To this our Lord refers when he says: 'When ye see these things begin to come to pass, look up, lift up your heads, for your redemption draweth nigh.'

When conversing some years ago with a very poor and sorely-afflicted believer in Dublin, a Christian visitor sought to comfort him in parting with the text: 'In my Father's house are many mansions.' 'Stop a minute,' said the dying but happy sufferer; 'that is a beautiful text, but there is one sweeter than it in the next verse: "I will come again and receive you unto myself."' Might we not add, the sweetest thing of all is that both promises are ours by sure and blessed heritage?

The whole creation groans,
And waits to hear that voice
That shall restore her comeliness,
And make her wastes rejoices.

Come, Lord, and wipe away
The curse, the sin, the stain;
And make this blighted world of ours
Thine own fair world again.

Behold, I come quickly: hold that fast which thou hast, that no man take thy crown.—REV. 3:11.

So Christ was once offered to bear the sins of many; and unto them that look for him shall he appear the second time without sin unto salvation.—HEB. 9:28.

For our conversation is in heaven; from whence also we look for the Saviour, the Lord Jesus Christ: Who shall change our vile body, that it may be fashioned like unto his glorious body, according to the working whereby he is able even to subdue all things unto himself.—PHIL. 3:20, 21.

THE END.

BANNER *of* TRUTH

The Banner of Truth Trust originated in 1957 in London. The founders believed that much of the best literature of historic Christianity had been allowed to fall into oblivion and that, under God, its recovery could well lead not only to a strengthening of the church, but to true revival.

Interdenominational in vision, this publishing work is now international, and our lists include a number of contemporary authors, together with classics from the past. The translation of these books into many languages is encouraged.

A monthly magazine, *The Banner of Truth*, is also published, and further information about this, and all our other publications, may be found on our website, banneroftruth.org, or by contacting the offices below:

Head Office:
3 Murrayfield Road
Edinburgh
EH12 6EL
United Kingdom
Email: info@banneroftruth.co.uk

North America Office:
610 Alexander Spring Road
Carlisle, PA 17015
United States of America
Email: info@banneroftruth.org